# ONE BIG UNION

# ONE BIG UNION
## A History of the Australian Workers Union
## 1886–1994

MARK HEARN
and
HARRY KNOWLES

CAMBRIDGE UNIVERSITY PRESS
Cambridge, New York, Melbourne, Madrid, Cape Town,
Singapore, São Paulo, Delhi, Tokyo, Mexico City

Cambridge University Press
The Edinburgh Building, Cambridge CB2 8RU, UK

Published in the United States of America by Cambridge University Press, New York

www.cambridge.org
Information on this title: www.cambridge.org/9780521558976

First published 1996
Re-issued 2011

*A catalogue record for this publication is available from the British Library*

*National Library of Australia Cataloguing in Publication Data*
Hearn, Mark, 1959–   .
One big union: a history of the Australian Workers Union
1886–1994.
Bibliography.
Includes index.
1. Australian Workers' Union – History.
2. Trade-unions – Australia – History. 3. Industrial
relations – Australia – History. 4. Strikes and lockouts –
Australia – History. I. Knowles, Harry, 1945– . II. Title.
331.880994

*Library of Congress Cataloguing in Publication Data*
Hearn, Mark, 1959–   .
One big union: a history of the Australian Workers' Union.
1886–1994 Mark Hearn and Harry Knowles.
p.   cm.
Includes bibliographical references and index.
1. Australian Workers' Union – History. 2. Trade-unions –
Australia –  History. 3. Trade-unions – Political activity –
Australia – History. 4. Strikes and lockouts – Australia – History.
I. Knowles, Harry, 1945–      . II. Title.
HD8842.A874H43    1996
331.88'0994–cc20                                                95–48996

ISBN 978-0-521-55138-0 Hardback
ISBN 978-0-521-55897-6 Paperback

# CONTENTS

# ILLUSTRATIONS

# FOREWORD

As Australia moves towards becoming a republic, this book represents a significant and timely contribution to the republican debate. Although never intended for this purpose, it can provide instructive insights for those monarchists who appear not to understand what it is that motivates those who support an Australian republic.

The history of the Australian Workers Union in many ways embodies the notion of being 'Australian'. Australian culture since European settlement has been strongly influenced by principles which are entwined with trade unionism: independence, a fair go, support of the underdog, mateship – none of these thoroughly Australian notions can be separated from Australian unionism. Many aspects of the AWU's history touch on events, issues and personalities that have fashioned the Australian soul. It is the maturation of our ethos which leads inevitably to our desire for an Australian republic.

Mark Hearn and Harry Knowles, in exposing the history of the AWU, have given us an account of the development of the Australian psyche. Such an expose of course leads to an examination of both the good and the bad constituents of that psyche. Along with the admirable qualities of Australian democracy, the development of the AWU has been dotted with some notable and regrettable traits. The White Australia Policy, consistently espoused by the great leaders of the AWU, can be considered a justifiable attempt to protect the economic livelihood of our country, but its racist, xenophobic undertones are no longer acceptable. Similarly, the grossly inadequate opportunities provided to women in the AWU have been paralleled by Australian society generally.

This book was commissioned by the Executive Council of the Australian Workers Union. It was originally intended to appear for the AWU's centenary in 1986, but, in keeping with the union's colourful history, the author commissioned to write it ended up at odds with the AWU. The development and completion of this book is in large part attributable to my predecessor (now) Senator Michael Forshaw. He was instrumental in ensuring that the project was reinvigorated by commissioning the present authors.

Mark Hearn and Harry Knowles have done a magnificent job, and the book is an outstanding tribute to them. In particular, they have answered the AWU's brief for a history that is not only comprehensive and accurate but is also readable and entertaining and should appeal to people who have neither an academic nor a professional interest in the subject.

Its timeliness cannot be overemphasised: it represents the addition of a small amount of fortifying spirit to the vat in which Australian republicanism is maturing.

Ian Cambridge
Joint National Secretary
Australian Workers Union

# ACKNOWLEDGEMENTS

The authors wish to acknowledge the kind assistance of the staff at the Noel Butlin Archives of Business and Labour, Australian National University, Canberra, particularly Ewen Maidment and Raj Jadeja; to the other institutions which provided access and assistance, including the Australian Mines and Metals Association and its Executive Director, Mr Rex Whiffin; Melbourne University Archives, the National Library of Australia and the State Libraries of New South Wales and Victoria. We would also like to thank all those who assisted in the research and preparation of the manuscript, or with advice and encouragement – particularly Dr Greg Patmore and Professor Duncan Waterson. We would also like to thank the many AWU officials and members who generously provided their time and assistance. We especially thank those who kindly consented to be interviewed by the authors. We must also acknowledge the support and assistance provided by the Australian Workers Union, and the consistent support of three general secretaries of the AWU – Errol Hodder, Mike Forshaw and Ian Cambridge. The authors would also like to thank the AWU head office staff for their assistance, particularly Mrs Wendy Pymont. Finally, this book could not have been written without the untiring help and encouragement of our families, and our special thanks go to Margaret, Elizabeth and Christopher, and Susan, Karen, Lisa and Sandra.

| | |
|---|---|
| ACSEF | Australian Coal and Shale Employees Federation |
| ACTU | Australian Council of Trade Unions |
| AFCWI | Artificial Fertilizers and Chemical Workers Union |
| AFULE | Australian Federated Union of Locomotive Enginemen |
| AIRC | Australian Industrial Relations Commission |
| ALF | Australian Labour Federation |
| ALP | Australian Labor Party |
| AMA | Amalgamated Miners Association |
| AMIEU | Amalgamated Meat Industries Employees Union |
| AMMA | Australian Mines and Metals Association |
| ARU | Australian Railways Union |
| AWA | Amalgamated Workers Association (Qld) |
| BDC | Better Deal Committee |
| BLF | Builders Labourers Federation |
| BWIU | Building Workers Industrial Union |
| CCC | Civil Construction Corps |
| CMC | Council for Membership Control |
| CPA | Communist Party of Australia |
| DLP | Democratic Labor Party |
| FEDFA | Federated Engine Drivers and Firemen's Association |
| FIA | Federated Ironworkers Association |
| FIME | Federation of Industrial and Manufacturing Employees |
| FIMEE | Federation of Industrial, Manufacturing and Engineering Employees |
| FMEA | Federated Mining Employees Association |

| GLU | General Labourers Union |
| GWLU | General Woolshed Labourers Union |
| GWU | General Workers Union (WA) |
| HEC | Hydro-Electric Commission |
| IWW | Industrial Workers of the World |
| LEL | Labor Electoral League |
| LGPA | Livestock and Grain Producers Association (NSW) |
| MIM | Mount Isa Mines Ltd |
| MLC | Member of the Legislative Council |
| MP | Member of Parliament |
| MSU | Machine Shearers Union |
| NAIWU | North Australian Industrial Workers Union |
| NFF | National Farmers Federation |
| NSW | New South Wales |
| NWC | National Wage Case |
| NZWU | New Zealand Workers Union |
| OBU | One Big Union |
| PLL | Political Labour League |
| POW | prisoner of war |
| PU | Pastoralists Union |
| PWIU | Pastoral Workers Industrial Union |
| QCE | Queensland Central Executive |
| QSU | Queensland Shearers Union |
| REAP | Rural Employees Award Plan |
| RW&GLA | Railway Workers & General Labourers Association |
| RWIB | Railway Workers Industry Branch |
| S&RWU | Shearers and Rural Workers Union |
| SA | South Australia(n) |
| SAU | Shop Assistants Union (NSW) |
| SDA | Shop, Distributive and Allied Employees Association |
| TLC | Trades and Labor Council |
| TWU | Transport Workers Union |
| UGA | United Graziers Association |
| ULU | United Labourers Union (Vic.) |
| WA | Western Australia(n) |
| WEA | Workers Education Association |
| WIUA | Workers Industrial Union of Australia |

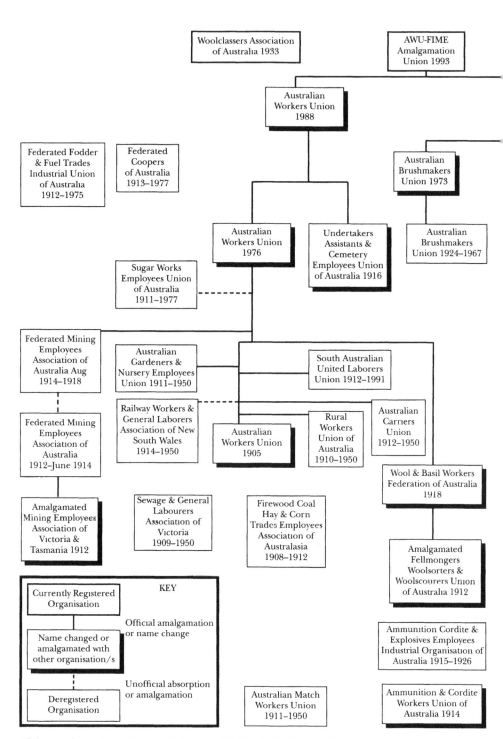

AWU amalgamations (under federal legislation), 1904 to 1993

*Note:* All dates given identify industrial organisations from year of registration under the *Conciliation and Arbitration Act 1904* (and subsequently the *Industrial Relations Act 1988*), Commonwealth of Australia. Establishment dates may differ.
*Source:* Raj Jadeja, Parties To The Award, Noel Butlin Archives Centre, Research School of Social Sciences, Australian National University 1994. p. 54

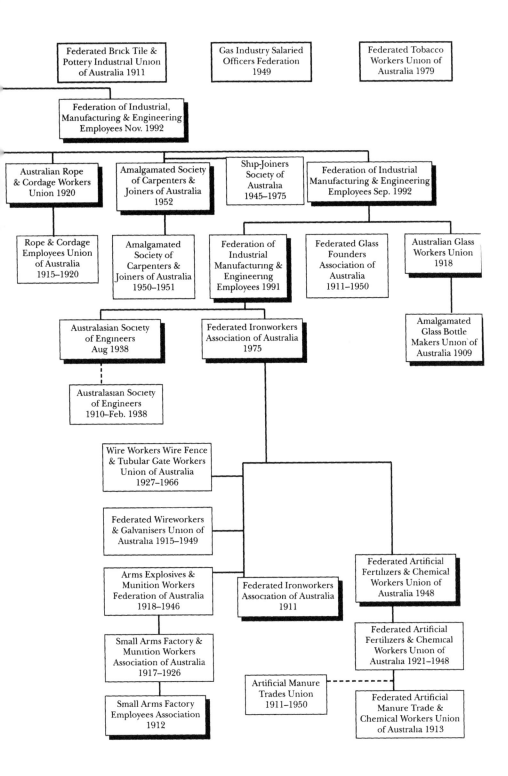

Major AWU workplaces in Australia

# W. G. Spence: the Progress of a Moderate Man

*The Ethos and Industrial Character of the*
*Australian Workers Union*

I take it that the human family is inherently good.
*William Guthrie Spence*

In June 1892 William Guthrie Spence, the president of the Amalgamated Shearers Union, addressed an Australian Socialist League meeting in Sydney on 'The Ethics of the New Unionism'. By this time the 46-year-old Spence had acquired the poise and style one readily associates with nineteenth-century civic leaders: physically benign, with an air of a dependable efficiency. Spence had the intellectual curiosity and the restless determination of the self-educated to grasp the most advanced concepts. In 1892 Spence, like many of his contemporaries, accepted an idea which threatened to smash the millennial religious certainties which had nourished his Scottish ancestors and which in many respects he still accepted, as natural to him as the love of family and his fellow man. William Guthrie Spence had embraced the relentless logic of Darwinism, and summoning his experience as a lay preacher, he dramatically invoked the principles of Charles Darwin's *On The Origin Of Species* in his plea for social harmony and justice for the working man.

'Humanity', Spence told his audience, has 'been placed at the very apex of the pyramid of created things'. Through natural selection, 'by the exercise of our superior intelligence', humankind had risen 'to control many of the forces of Nature and utilise them for our own good'. Yet this eager quest had not always yielded equal benefits for all. 'The commercial ethics of life ... develops too much of that instinct which distinguishes the savage ... Scheming, cunning, lying and dishonesty are associated with our commercial enterprise'. Great syndicates arose, crushing the smaller concerns, displacing men with machinery. 'We find

1

ourselves faced by an ever-increasing mass of men who have no work to
do although eager and willing to work.'

Even as Spence spoke, the colonies of Australia were gripped by
an unprecedented economic crisis. Banks were crashing, sucking away
the hard-earned deposits of their customers. Businessmen pilfered the
last crumbs of profit from failing companies. The finance houses of
London withheld their credit. City streets were crowded with the unemployed. A listless host of shearers and shed-hands, the unionists whom
Spence had laboured to rally, milled around the great sheep stations,
desperate for work. The pastoralists and their station managers might
have looked at the crowd scornfully, if they were of a vindictive cast of
mind. For there were few firebrand militants to trouble them now, and
the pastoralists had united to smash their recent tormentors, the
Amalgamated Shearers Union. The mighty union of shearers which
Spence and its secretary, David Temple, had struggled to build since
1886 was falling to its knees.

Spence did not despair; it was not in his nature. 'We have the power to
utterly change these conditions. We have control over the circumstances
under which we live more than any other animal, therefore we are
responsible for the conditions under which we live.' Spence believed that
through knowledge and just laws humanity could, as he said, create a
heaven on earth. People, he told his fellow socialists, were 'inherently
good. I go against that old idea of always crediting our human frailties
to original sin'. Spence declared that the 'practical ethics' of the New
Unionism offered the ideal solution to the sufferings which afflicted the
working class. Through mass combination of workers in what were
known as 'new' or general unions (as opposed to the older, traditionally
craft-based organisations formed before the 1880s), through democratic
political action, unionists would achieve political and social reform. 'A
revolution will undoubtedly be effected in our time' – although Spence
hastily added, 'When I use the word revolution – do not misunderstand
me – I mean a quiet one'.

His quiet revolution was a seamless *evolution*, which by moral force
and reasonable persuasion would exhaust the animus of its most
trenchant opponents. But this sweet reason should not be mistaken for
weakness. The Church, Spence observed, preached contentment with
life's lot: 'I do not believe in contentment. I believe in discontent'. Yet
this discontent should be channelled into the social reconciliation he
yearned for. And in this way the traditions of the past could be cherished
and renewed. For while he was disillusioned with the compromises of the
Church, Spence embraced the spirit of 'the lowly Nazarene'. *He* would
have understood the New Unionism. 'The principle underlying and
guiding it is simply the principle laid down by Him who long ago laid the

foundation of a great reform – I mean the principle of love for one's fellows'.[1]

What are we to make of W. G. Spence? Historian Ray Markey is vexed by Spence's charitable ideology; no good idea seems ever to have been turned away.

> It is difficult to take Spence seriously as a socialist. He certainly claimed to be a socialist on occasions. But he also claimed other '-isms', including nationalism, new unionism, and single taxism. Spence cut his ideological suit to complement the taste of his audience. But he was not merely opportunist about this. He seems to have sincerely believed in all these 'isms', as being essentially about the same thing: the promotion of the good of mankind.[2]

Although in *The Ethics of the New Unionism* Spence finds Darwinism a useful device for explaining his evolutionary socialism, he seems to have neatly side-stepped the unpleasant conclusion that Darwin's *Origin of Species* opened up the possibility that perhaps the Universe had managed to get along without God. Spence would later find that he could not always so easily disregard ideas or events that did not suit his purpose.

Spence wanted the working class to be integrated into colonial society, to have their aspirations accepted as no less worthy of consideration than those of other classes. He had this integrating idealism in common with two contemporary labour leaders, British trade unionist and Labour Party leader Arthur Henderson (1863–1935) and Samuel Gompers (1850–1924), the president of the American Federation of Labor. Like Spence (1846–1926), who believed that unionists 'had given a practical turn to socialism', Gompers and Henderson rejected revolutionary strategies. Justice for the working class could be won by trade union action or parliamentary representation. Raised in the Lib-Lab unionist tradition of Britain's industrial north, Henderson was 'a strong proponent of industrial conciliation and arbitration'. Gompers refused to endorse socialism, but he also rejected Spence's and Henderson's enthusiasm for democratic political action. For Gompers, American politics was a 'cesspool'. American workers could only improve their conditions through direct bargaining with employers. He was content to pursue this strategy within the prevailing capitalist system.[3]

Spence and Henderson believed society could be transformed from within, and both understood religion to be a bonding factor, and a source of rhetorical and ideological inspiration. As Ross McKibbin observes of the British experience, religion

> gave an acceptable – though utterly conventional – ethical force to working class politics. However, it also gave its practitioners a firm foothold on the status quo. Arthur Henderson, Ben Tillett's famous 'Gospel-Temperance-

Liberal election agent' is a good example. His political career was much
assisted by Wesleyanism; from it he learned his rhetoric, his ability to run
meetings and his personal and mental stability.

McKibbin (and for that matter, Tillett, the radical British unionist) might
have been describing Spence. Spence and Henderson believed in inte-
gration because they were integrated. Spence was a Creswick alderman,
a lay preacher, a respected unionist, a figure of authority in the Ballarat
district of Victoria. Henderson 'was (indirectly) a founder of Newcastle
United, a prominent figure in lawn bowls, one of the country's leading
lay methodists, as well as chief organiser of the Labour Party'.[4]

None of his colleagues in the Amalgamated Shearers Union would
have dissented from Spence's declarations in *The Ethics of the New
Unionism* (although some may have been a little embarrassed by his
fervour), and only a few in a dark moment of despair would have
doubted his confidence. They had placed their faith in the unity, if not
the love, of their fellow unionists. It was all they had.

### The Bushworkers Union

It was this simple hope which fed the desire in the late 1880s to break the
fragmented pattern of unionisation, and bind together workers in the
New Unionism, the mass organisation of workers in industries of a
common calling, so that an effective, united front could be presented to
the capitalist class. They would put an end to the employers' preference
for divide and rule. Spence had already applied this thinking to the
establishment of the Amalgamated Miners Association in 1874. In the
late 1880s, at the behest of a young and able Creswick shearer, David
Temple, he turned his attention to assisting Temple to unite disparate,
local unions of shearers, and a great body of non-unionised shearers, into
the Amalgamated Shearers Union of Australasia. Although Mr Spence
sometimes later forgot to extend due credit to David Temple for his
labours, it was Temple who did much of the organising, while Spence
fulfilled the role of respectable chairman. But Spence, as we have seen,
did more than that. He defined the moral framework of the ASU's
mission, clarifying the struggle upon which his precocious ASU colleagues had embarked. Time and again he would return to this lesson,
struggling to renew its great themes in the face of events threatening to
empty it of meaning, so many good intentions shouted uselessly into
the wind.

Good intentions had to be fed by hard work. The union which Temple
organised grew to cover several thousand shearers. The leadership group
which evolved from this organisation soon turned their attention to

A contented W. G. Spence (circled) and extended AWU family.
The *Worker* annual picnic at Mortlake in Sydney, 1912. *AWU Collection.*

signing up shed-hands and building a powerful pastoral industry union. In 1894 the General Labourers Union amalgamated with the ASU to form the Australian Workers Union. In the new century, more ambitious amalgamations would follow, as the AWU extended its coverage to metal mining, construction, the sugar industry; and not to forget the rabbit-trappers. The AWU came to cover a myriad callings which for the most part could be best understood as 'bushwork'. AWU organisation followed the bushwork trails that threaded through the Western District of Victoria into south-east South Australia, or up into the Riverina, and north towards Broken Hill; from Roma, up to Charleville, Winton, Barcaldine, Longreach, and later to the mining centre at Mount Isa. AWU members would eventually be found at work at remote and settled regions across Australia. Queensland Branch secretary Joe Bukowksi would boast that he had worked from the Gulf of Carpentaria south to Grafton in New South Wales, fencing, cane-cutting and labouring in mines like Mount Morgan.

'Bushwork' is not just a convenient tag for rural work. Many bush-workers shared a common form of remuneration – piece-work or contract arrangements – paying by performance, as opposed to weekly wages. Canecutters, miners and shearers were all familiar with these methods of payment and the pattern of work they encouraged: the harder you worked, the more you were paid. In turn, this notion of work and its rewards fed the AWU's self-awareness. They were robustly independent workers, and their industrial relations were practical and hard-headed.

It was hard to define the AWU. There was nothing quite like it in Australia or overseas. For most of its history, and certainly before the Second World War, there was no other union that rivalled its size and breadth of coverage, although other large-scale unions of rail, building and metal workers also developed. Was the AWU a 'general' union of workers? Was it an 'industrial' union? In an influential 1949 study, 'General Labour Unions in Britain, 1889–1914', British historian Eric Hobsbawm described the AWU as a 'powerful' general union like those established in England in the 1880s, enrolling workers excluded from traditional craft union membership, propelled by a 'socialist or revolutionary' inspiration. Yet he distinguished between such unions and 'industrial' unions, which he saw as militantly class-conscious, and seeking to co-ordinate all industry bargaining in a systematic way. On the other hand, in 1965 Henry Pelling stressed the New Unions' important political impact in Britain: they were 'socialistic in tendency'. Industrial action was not enough. 'Their emphasis, owing to a feeling of insecurity, on the value of legislation for the consolidation of their industrial demands made them favourable to the Socialist demand for an independent labour party in Parliament.' Australian historians Robin Gollan and Brian Fitzpatrick described a similar link between industrial organisation and politics in regard to the Australian New Unionism of the 1880s and 1890s.[5]

Historian Ray Markey dissented from these descriptions of the industrial character of the Australian New Unionism. In *The Making of the Labor Party in New South Wales* (1988) the ASU, he says, began life as an occupational union of shearers, then became an industrial union after the merger with the GLU. Yet through its rules the ASU/AWU retained a clear *craft* identity. 'It attempted to restrict entry to the highly skilled shearing 'trade' to 'competent shearers', defined by a certain level of experience. It also attempted to abolish 'barrowing', whereby learners practised shearing during "smoko" breaks.' He suggests the ASU–GLU amalgamation was largely defensive, designed to protect the shearers' agreement with the pastoralists, restraining potentially 'hothead' shedhands.[6]

Clarifying the AWU's craft or general union identity is not simply an academic obsession with technicalities. It helps to explain how the AWU retained a domineering bush ethos which strongly influenced its politics and industrial behaviour, despite the fact that over the ensuing years its pastoral industry membership declined significantly. Indeed, we would claim that this ethos, which sprang from both the imagined and actual mateship and camaraderie of the shearing sheds, has not been directly challenged until the AWU amalgamated with the Federation of Industrial, Manufacturing and Engineering Employees in 1993. This amalgamation, for the first time, brought a strong countervailing manufacturing sector membership – and ethos – to the union. In the past, the AWU leaders have been able to marginalise non-shearing influences. By first amalgamating with shed-hands the ethos of the sheds could only be reinforced. Indeed, the amalgamations that the AWU pursued in the pre-First World War period were all with unions which generally, or quite specifically, shared the same bush ethos, such as the 1907 amalgamation with the Queensland Amalgamated Workers Association, which covered a wide range of itinerant 'bushwork' jobs, including the metal-mining and sugar industries. A similar pattern was repeated with the AWU's merger with the Federated Metalliferous Miners Association in 1917; although these workers were technically miners, many had also worked in other bush jobs (most mines were located in remote or rural parts of Australia). More than a few shearers had spent time working the mining fields, and vice versa. Even as the pastoral industry membership declined gradually to 5 per cent of the overall AWU membership in the years after the Second World War, most senior AWU officials and many organisers continued to have a background in shearing.

### The Bushworker Ethos

In this book we record industrial organisation and disputes, political action, rivalries and compromises. But first come beliefs, the causes and grievances, the factors that mobilise workers to action. What did the people of the AWU believe in? What attitudes, legends and fears had they imbued from their shared working experiences, from their background as the working class of the young Australian colonies? This is the history of a trade union, but it is also the history of a set of values which transcended the industrial nature of the union. We have already considered the moral rhetoric which Spence employed to justify the union's cause. But Spence in turn was only complementing values, deeply at work in the ASU/AWU membership, which would fundamentally influence the industrial and political agenda which the labour movement would embrace in the 1890s.

Mateship was the defining creed, romanticised and sentimentalised by the faithful and their poets, the iron bond of loyalty which if broken would render the traitor an outcast, a 'scab', the lowest form of non-union life. In *The Australian Legend* (1958) Russel Ward memorably described the mythic characteristics of the traditional Australian character, as it had emerged from the adversities of convict labour in the early nineteenth century:

> According to the myth the 'typical Australian' is a practical man, rough and ready in his manners and quick to decry any appearance of affectation in others. He is a great improvisor, ever willing to have a go at anything, but willing too to be content with a task done in a way that is 'near enough' ... He is a fiercely independent person who hates officiousness and authority, especially when these qualities are embodied in military officers and policemen. Yet he is very hospitable and above all, will stick to his mates through thick and thin, even if he thinks they may be in the wrong. No ephithet in his vocabulary is more completely damning than 'scab', unless it be 'pimp' used in its peculiarly Australasian slang meaning of 'informer'. He tends to be a rolling stone, highly suspect if he should chance to gather much moss.[7]

These characteristics – the legend, as Ward called it, ingrained with historical fact – he especially attributed to the 'bushmen', the 'semi-nomadic drovers, shepherds, shearers, bullock drivers, stockmen, boundary-riders, station-hands and others of the pastoral industry'. For an ethos is about the shared identity of a community, what British political scientist Henry Drucker, in *Doctrine and Ethos in the Labour Party* (1979) calls folk memory, the 'organisational glue' which holds, in terms of his study, broad coalitions of workers – trade unions or labour parties – together. The past unifies them, 'a shared expression of exploitation, common struggle and gradually increasing power'. An ethos, a self-identity, is created out of past struggle. And as Russel Ward observed of the elements of Australian mateship, it doesn't really matter whether or not all the folk memories are 'true', or are borne in precise 'facts': as long as the memory reinforces the ethos. As Drucker explains:

> A past, in this sense, is a force making for group identity. This past defines 'us'. 'We' are those who have 'suffered under Pharaoh' ... In other words, for a people who have a past, part of what they are is their past. In this sense a past is very much alive. It lives in that group whom it identifies, and who keep alive by repeating it and by reminding each generation of children that 'we' served under Pharaoh. These repetitions serve to perpetuate the group as each generation comes to see itself as those who have served under Pharaoh ... In such a manner a past can be kept alive as long as it is believed. There is nothing about the movement of clocks which diminishes it.[8]

An ethos defies the relentless passage of time, its hard changes and myriad assaults on held values. It demands: *stay true to this. You are measured by your loyalty.* This bond extends through time not only in the AWU, but defines Australian Labor. In *Reflecting Labor*, written for the Australian Labor Party's centenary, Roger McDonald tries to hold the first year and the one hundredth year of Labor together, 'hoping to arouse in the reader an intuition of the wholeness of Labor, perceived as if at a single moment of time'. His image of stillness is the shearing shed. As an icon of Labor memory, the shearing shed is the focus of a returning spiral of traditions and connections, McDonald believes, rather than a chronological line moving away from its conditions. But returning to what? McDonald hopes that the ethos can be renewed and positively changed – 'within male unionisation is women's rights; within White Australia is land rights and anti-discrimination law'. Perhaps. The ethos, living only in us, must move forward through time. Some accept the changes, see a way of renewal. Others resist, and in them old ideals become punishments – for others, and themselves. This is the pattern of adaptation and conflict in Labor, and the AWU.[9]

For Australian pastoral workers in the late nineteenth century, Drucker's 'suffering under Pharaoh' meant the struggle with the squatters in the Great Strikes of the early 1890s. In the pages of the *Bulletin*, the Sydney and Brisbane *Workers* and elsewhere poets like Henry Lawson, Mary Gilmore and A. B. 'Banjo' Paterson celebrated the bush character and his exploits. While Spence provided reason and persuasion in defence of labour's cause, Lawson inflamed passions.

> But Freedom's on the Wallaby,
> She'll knock the tyrants silly,
> She's going to light another fire
> And boil another billy.

> We'll make the tyrants feel the sting
> Of those that they would throttle;
> They needn't say the fault is ours
> If blood should stain the wattle.

So Lawson declared in 'Freedom on the Wallaby' (1891). Some writers saw a more complicated reality in Australian bush life, as Barbara Baynton did in her stories *Bush Studies* (1902). And Henry Lawson did not always celebrate and stir. In 1890 he cast a cool eye on Andy, 'Middleton's Rouseabout', with 'the face of a country lout'.

> Type of a coming nation,
>   In the land of cattle and sheep,
> Worked on Middleton's station,
>   'Pound a week and his keep'.
>
> On Middleton's wide dominions
>   Plied the stockwhip and shears;
> Hadn't any opinions,
>   Hadn't any 'idears'.[10]

This was a male ethos, from which women and foreigners were excluded. Women were all but invisible in the AWU. Early twentieth-century amalgamations brought industries into the union which employed some women – the fruit industry, hotel and catering coverage in Queensland, industries which were peripheral to the ethos and organisation of the AWU. Historian Marilyn Lake observes: 'Challenged by the absence of women from Australian labour history, many historians responded by simply adding women – women in factories, women strikers, women's auxiliaries to trade unions, women in unemployed demonstrations – comforting images of women fighting alongside "their" men. Women were there too'. It is difficult to attempt even this degree of apparent 'tokenism' in a history of the AWU. Few women were encouraged to become active in the AWU hierarchy. Henrietta Greville was briefly an organiser for the union in New South Wales, although her pioneering work on behalf of women workers was pursued later, outside the AWU. Deirdre Swan became the first woman elected as a delegate to the AWU's Annual Convention – in 1986. Mary Gilmore wrote the Women's Page in the *Australian Worker* for many years, and she gave the men the benefit of her analysis of their habits, their failings and their treatment of women, but she was excluded from the inner circle of union leadership, probably because of this advice. Gilmore's exclusion was perhaps predominantly a matter of gender. She had also violated a more specific taboo: she had the wrong attitude on conscription during the First World War, and some of the AWU's leaders did not forgive, or forget.[11]

Asians were reviled, feared as an alternative source of cheap labour which the greedy hand of capital was plotting (so it was suspected) to employ to undermine the noble bushman. Within a few years of the formation of the ASU its rules specifically excluded Asians and Pacific Islanders from membership. As the AWU, with its tight organisation of the mass of bush unionists grew after 1894 to dominate the early colonial Labor Party, its corporate obsession with White Australia was reflected in the ideology and ethos of political Labor, as Vere Gordon Childe observed in *How Labour Governs* (1923):

> Thus the sentiment of Australian nationhood, which expressed itself in the movement towards Federation, and which was reinforced by racial prejudice against the intermingling of white and coloured races, found its natural political exponent in the Labour [*sic*] Party. Especially after Federation, national patriotism brought a large body of supporters to the Labour Party. Of course such a sentiment was in its extreme manifestations incompatible with the internationalism of the Socialist Movement, and has produced a curious reaction on Australian Socialism as expounded by the Labour Party.[12]

This 'curious reaction' found its most robust expression in the attitudes and statements of the AWU's leaders and members, and in the pages of its journals, principally the Brisbane *Worker* and the Sydney (later the Australian) *Worker*. Columnist and poet Mary Gilmore, long-serving editor (of both Queensland and national editions) Henry Boote, Brisbane *Worker* editor William Lane, and occasional contributor Henry Lawson were the intellectual and emotional prophets of the AWU bush ethos, of its heroic working-man pride and its seething racism.

The legend and the ethos have their critics. In *A New Britannia* (1970) Humphrey McQueen would have none of Ward's romanticism of the mateship myth. 'Racism', McQueen declared, 'is the most important single component in Australian nationalism'. McQueen accuses Ward of ignoring the fundamental racism of the union movement in the 1890s. William Lane, the inaugural editor of the Brisbane *Worker* and the author of the widely influential 1890 *Worker* editorial which defined socialism as 'being mates', was in McQueen's view, 'a fanatical racist'. Lane's socialism was infected with a morbid racism. By the early twentieth century, after his Paraguayan retreat from the complexities of Australia had failed, he collapsed into complete pessimism. Race war and militarism waited down that dead end: exterminate all the brutes, Kurtz in Joseph Conrad's *Heart of Darkness* (1902) finally scrawled across his uncompleted thesis. Lane's experience was a shadow of that darkness, falling across the aspirations of the labour movement. Mary Gilmore, Henry Boote and Henry Lawson stared into that same void, expressing fears widely held by Australian workers. Perhaps it was only that Australia's indigenous peoples were so scattered, relatively few in number (in relation to the encroaching white population), and because of the early federal restrictions placed on non-European immigration, that white Australia could conceal the extent of its

genocide, repression and exclusion of non-Europeans. Unlike South
Africa, as Spence unintentionally acknowledged in 1905:

> The last census found 54,441 coloured aliens in the Commonwealth, or 14.43
> per 1,000 of the population. In Queensland every seventh man was a coloured
> alien. The anti-social crowd want to bring in more on the plea of developing
> the North. They will repeat South African experience if you vote them into
> power. They prefer Lascars and Asiatics on our mail boats to white men. They
> like to own slaves, as the white worker is not submissive enough. They admit
> that the Lascar is not cheaper.[13]

### The Australian Settlement

The ASU/AWU had an ideology, or a set of deeply held values, which
powerfully defined its behaviour and influenced the broader labour
movement. Racial attitudes were one significant element. But the AWU
ethos was influential because it was itself a reflection of a broader
national ethos – what historian Ray Markey in *The Making of the Labor
Party* and political commentator Paul Kelly in *The End of Certainty* (1992)
called the Australian or National Settlement, the insular bond of White
Australia, Tariff Protection and Compulsory Arbitration forged between
the new elites: the labour movement and the liberal political ascendancy
represented by Prime Minister Alfred Deakin's Protectionists. Markey
defines this settlement as the fulfilment of AWU bush populism, the
amalgam of Spence's ethics and the aspirations – and fears – of mateship.
Thus were erected the pillars of *Protection*, and with this economic
defensiveness the cultural insularity of the AWU ethos became self-
renewing, strengthened by sympathetic union amalgamations.[14]

The 'Old Left' historians extolled the benefits of the Australian
settlement. Ward, Robin Gollan (*Radical and Working Class Politics*, 1960)
and Brian Fitzpatrick (*A Short History of the Australian Labor Movement*,
1940) drew a link between the invigoration of the labour movement in
the 1880s, its testing in the turmoil of the 1890s, and the subsequent
pioneering reforms enacted by political Labor and a co-operative
liberalism in the early twentieth century. As Fitzpatrick observed, under
the leadership of union 'giants' like Spence, the labour movement
embraced parliamentary action. Echoing Spence's rhetoric, Fitzpatrick
argued that after the industrial defeats of the early 1890s, 'Labor people
had been forced to realise that direct action alone could not worst the
capitalists and the governments, and to realise that almost no strike
tactics could succeed for years to come'. They turned to the fertile field
of political action:

> There is every reason to believe that the presence and advocacy of Labor
> members did much to bring about the introduction and enactment of a great

deal of social legislation, in the interests particularly of working people, in the last years of the old century and the first years of the new. Soon, planks of the 1891 platform could be removed, because there was no further use for them. One-man-one-vote, the general 8-hour working day, reform of mines and factories legislation, and legislation affecting the relations of employer and employee, and so on – these were achievements for which Labor in politics could take much of the credit.[15]

Despite the fact that these material gains were won for workers and their families, for 'New Left' historian Humphrey McQueen, it was all a terrible mistake, for which the AWU was significantly, if not chiefly, responsible. For McQueen, Labor's embrace of politics and compulsory arbitration were corrupting influences. Lulled by 'the siren entreaties of bourgeois culture', Labor parliamentarians betrayed the interests of their working-class supporters. In New South Wales, Labor Premier and ex-AWU organiser Holman proposed anti-union penal provisions for the arbitration system in 1911. In 1927 the McCormack (another ex-AWU official) Labor Government engaged in strike-breaking over the South Johnstone dispute. Compulsory arbitration meant '"a general lowering of the fighting spirit of the membership" because more and more unionists were merely freeloaders. Eventually compulsory arbitration became associated with compulsory unionism which sustains the corrupt empires of the AWU'. In many ways this view, handed down from Childe's *How Labour Governs*, has been the received Left-wing wisdom about Labor in politics and the AWU, repeated in Ian Turner's *Industrial Labour and Politics* (1965) and more recently in Ken Buckley and Ted Wheelwright's *No Paradise For Workers* (1988).[16]

Commenting on the politics of European (and particularly British) general unions in 1891, Eric Hobsbawm observes that 'judged by revolutionary criteria, the leaders of national unions or union federations were excessively reformist, as indeed almost all were in theory and practice'. Yet are these the appropriate criteria for judging the AWU and its leaders? None of them ever expressed an interest in revolutionary action; nor did a revolutionary impulse animate large sections of the membership. Nonetheless the AWU's pro-ALP leaders became militantly anti-communist, fearing the radical minority, barring them from membership of the union and from holding elected office. The politics of the AWU, at this crude level, are relatively well known to Australian labour historians. Less well publicised are the politics of at least some of the AWU's critics. After a scathing indictment of Laborism, Humphrey McQueen acknowledges in the last sentence of *A New Britannia* that the object of his analysis had been to promote 'the establishment of a Communist society'. This explicitly political aim would presumably have some bearing on his critique, given that from its formation in 1920, the Communist

Party of Australia competed with the Australian Labor Party for working-class popularity and support. CPA rhetoric was often couched in the language of Laborist 'treason' as it suited their political aspirations to promote this view of Laborist unionists and parliamentarians.[17]

These self-serving analyses of Labor parties and pro-Labor unions can be illustrated by Henry Drucker's assessment of Ralph Miliband's *Parliamentary Socialism* (1961), a critique of the British Labour Party. Miliband argued that British Labour has betrayed, through 'parliamentarianism', 'the true revolutionary consciousness of the working class'. In part, Drucker disputes that there was 'a revolutionary working-class consciousness to be betrayed', and we would share this scepticism about McQueen's assessment of Australian conditions. Drucker goes on to comment:

> Miliband's emphasis on Labour's parliamentarianism is also interesting because this acceptance has been accompanied by not a little suspicion in the labour movement each time Labour has been in office ... Miliband's book – and this is surely the reason for its popular success – articulates and gives academic authority to this suspicion. It is, that is to say, a successful attempt to mobilise part of the ethos of the movement against the party; or, at any rate, against its present leadership. In other words Parliamentary Socialism plays on the ethos of the movement while failing to see that, in other respects, this very ethos has been largely responsible for inspiring the actions it deplores.[18]

McQueen judges the early Labor activists by his standards and finds them wanting. Manning Clark, who wrote a foreword for *A New Britannia*, approved of this: 'Every generation writes its own history'. This form of historical relativism may conceal as much as it reveals. McQueen's analysis laid bare the racism at work in Australian Labor, but it is blind to less unpalatable motives animating the labour movement in the late nineteenth century, refusing to acknowledge the essential justice of working-class political and industrial claims, and the fact that both workers and their leaders made conscious choices about what they wanted from their unions, and the kind of colonial society they sought to create. The Australian working class was, to paraphrase E. P. Thompson, present at its own making. Their political agenda and their ethos were produced of their own experience, and their meditation upon it. We cannot reach back and thrust our motives or preferences upon them.[19]

## AWU People and Their Tradition

The stimulus for this book was a commission from the Australian Workers Union to commemorate the centenary of the formation of the ASU/AWU in 1886. Armed with that broad brief, we have endeavoured to chart the struggle to organise, and to record as much of the union's history, and the working lives of its members as was feasible in a single-volume history. It is a work which British labour historian Ross McKibbin would presumably describe as a work of labour history in the classical tradition. Rest assured that this is not an immodest claim to quality, but rather a lack of *chic*. As McKibbin observes, the 'classical' tradition 'saw the history of labour as the history of its assimilation by the liberal state and civil society', concerned with male-dominated trade unions and industrial relations practices, and the role of the political parties supported or created by the unions. Among labour historians, it is a tradition represented in the United States by John R. Commons and the Wisconsin school; in Britain, by Clegg, Fox and Thompson, and E. H. Phelps Brown. In Australia, those 'Old Left' historians, Ward, Fitzpatrick and Gollan, may be associated with that tradition.[20]

With the emergence of 'New Left' interpretations of labour history the classical tradition has seemed increasingly outmoded. Many New Left labour historians have preferred to move away from traditional union studies to focus on important questions of race, gender, class-consciousness and non-union working-class social movements and communities. We are not particularly interested in an 'us and them' approach to setting guides and rules to preferred or fashionable paths of labour history – let a hundred flowers bloom – but of the relevance of the classical tradition, we would agree with McKibbin: 'Above all, the centrality of the labour movement to the political and social history of the industrial countries in the late nineteenth and twentieth centuries, which was the ruling assumption of classical labour history, has never been successfully denied, and that alone ensures the continuing legitimacy of labour history'. McKibbin reminds us the that the 'predominantly male working class is still an historical fact, nor can it be denied out of existence; those factories, those trade unions, and those strikes still happened'. The AWU is also an historical 'fact'. It has been the subject of vilification, praise and contention, but never a full-length published history. Yet it has been perhaps the single most influential of all the Australian trade unions, dominating industrial organisation outside the capital cities, defining much of the Australian Labor Party's agenda and style, rivalling the organisation of the Australian Council of Trade Unions.[21]

Spence's *Australia's Awakening* (1909) and *The History of the AWU* (1911) are necessarily partisan accounts of the union and the era. Childe's *How Labour Governs* (1923) was a penetrating if bitter antidote. Ernest Lane's *Dawn to Dusk* (1939), Pat Mackie's *Mount Isa: The Story of a Dispute* (1989), Edgar Williams's *The Isa: Yellow, Green and Red* (1967) and Clyde Cameron's *Confessions* (1990) are all personal recollections of activists, with the strengths and weaknesses of such accounts. Turner's

*Industrial Labour and Politics* (1965), John Merritt's *The Making of the AWU* (1986) and Ray Markey's *The Making of the Labor Party in New South Wales* (1988) provide analysis of the AWU's formation and early impact and, in Merritt's case, a thorough account of the period 1886–1911. But there has been little discussion of the decades following 1920, with the exception of Robert Murray's *The Split* (1970), which examined the AWU's crucial role in the labour movement upheavals of the 1950s.[22]

This may seem reasonable cause for charting the activities of the AWU, for attempting to explain its profound impact on the labour movement and Australian society. But the classical tradition is not out of the woods yet. There remains the problem of the Great Man In History. It is certainly the case that a number of men held office in the AWU. Whether or not they were 'great', or even good, has been the matter of some dispute. Merely to describe their activities can incite accusations of 'celebratory' history— uncritically or slavishly praising the role of this or that historical actor. Raelene Frances and Bruce Scates argue that too many labour histories focus on a 'tedious recitation of factionalism and the seduction of strong personalities'. There are certainly some strong personalities in this book. Whether or not you like them is up to you. We do not 'celebrate' anybody, in the sense of glorifying their careers. We are willing to recognise the often difficult tasks men and women have assumed when they decide to organise in trade unions, to engage in political action, and for us, this recognition extends as much as possible to the rank and file as to the officials. The quality of this recognition is, again, a matter for your judgement. More significantly, understanding the factionalism of the AWU is vital to an understanding of the relationship between the AWU hierarchy and the membership, and between the AWU and the labour movement. Unsurprisingly, this factionalism is usually manifested in a relationship between 'personalities'. The labour movement cannot adequately be understood as the adjunct of an anonymous industrial or capitalist process. The labour movement is the expression of individuals motivated to political and industrial action, a motivation inherently factional and often contrary. This book is concerned with people in that movement, their values and actions, and the consequences of those actions. Within the labour movement, these activists found an expression for their identity, as they exercised choice in an historical context – forged for them, and which they helped to reshape.[23]

This book follows a conventional chronological, narrative structure. Of necessity, some chapters have a more 'political' content than others. Chapter six, for instance, examines the One Big Union issue, the impact of the 1916–17 conscription crisis and the Great Strike of 1917. Chapter seven fills in the industrial story for the period 1910–30, a period before mechanisation made a profound impact on many of the industries covered by the AWU. The chapter features a long section on the working experiences of shearers, shed and station-hands, fruit-pickers, miners and construction workers. Two chapters, ten and eleven, cover the 1950s, because of the significance and complexity of the events and issues of that decade, a key period in the AWU's history. In many ways the 1950s were the high tide of the leadership's political and industrial ambitions, as they sought to dominate the Labor Party.

### Arbitration and the Faithful

While Labor's own leaders may have contributed to the movement's mistakes and follies, the virulence of the employer reaction to labour mobilisation should not be underestimated. Pastoral employers began serious resistance to the ASU in 1890. This uncompromising hostility persisted for seventeen years, until the state compelled the pastoralists to obey the terms of a Federal Pastoral Award in 1907. For most of those seventeen years, the pastoralists would not even recognise the ASU/AWU's right to represent shearers and shed-hands, let alone to bargain on their behalf. Faced with prolonged economic depression and drought throughout the 1890s and the early twentieth century, the AWU's leaders struggled even to maintain the rudiments of organisation. By comparison, many other colonial unions, some of whom claimed several thousand members in the late 1880s, simply ceased to exist during the 1890s, only revived at the turn of the century by the intervention of pro-union state legislation. In this context, state-sanctioned arbitration was an effective method of providing wage increases and improvements for working conditions. Even as harsh a critic of the AWU as Vere Gordon Childe, who was close to these times and these conditions, could appreciate this. 'The union's adherence to arbitration, for example, may only be due to the superiority of that method for settling industrial disputes and improving conditions. Certainly the union's experience of the alternative in the nineties had not been encouraging, and the plebiscite taken in 1919 showed that a large majority of the members were in favour of the Court.'[24]

Critics have made sweeping assaults on the alleged failings of Australia's arbitration system. We have just made one in its defence. In fact the state of historiographical debate and analysis about the Australian arbitration system and its virtues is, at best, fragmentary. There are few academic studies of the history or the performance of the system, or of particular industries. One important work, Macintyre and Mitchell's *Foundations of Arbitration*, is confined to the period before 1914. There are few comparative studies of union performance. If one wishes to make

claims about the AWU's industrial performance, it would seem useful
to compare, over a reasonably broad historical period, its performance
in, for example, the construction and mining industries with that of
other unions in those same industries. Was their performance 'better'
than the AWU's? Did claims of greater militancy put more pounds/
dollars on members' tables? These studies do not exist, and in this state
of ignorance the Australian arbitration system is gradually disappearing,
returning to industrial relations conditions disturbingly similar to those
the ASU/AWU spent seventeen years trying to escape from. Yet in *The
Making of the AWU* John Merritt is convinced that the early experience of
compulsory arbitration confirmed that 'unions received from the courts
only what they had previously won in the marketplace'. Merritt broadly
notes that manufacturing unions faced a number of factors which
militated against obtaining 'good' awards (the features of a 'good' award
are not unspecified).[25]

These generalisations should be treated cautiously. Patmore has
specifically studied the effects of compulsory arbitration in the NSW
railways in the period before 1914. The NSW Railways was the largest
employer in the State (and one of the largest in Australia). Patmore finds
that compulsory arbitration weakened the railway commissioner's role in
determining wages and conditions, forcing the Railways not only to pay
award rates and conditions, but also to attempt to counter arbitration's
appeal by offering workers a range of alternative monetary and non-
monetary benefits, all measures increasing labour costs or boosting take-
home pay. It would seem that in the period before 1914 experience of
compulsory arbitration varied considerably from industry to industry.[26]

What of the AWU, and the pastoral industry? Shearers had an
economically strategic position in terms of pastoral industry production,
yet external economic factors, employer resistance and the activities of
non-unionists all combined, in the period 1890–1907, to frustrate AWU
efforts to maintain shearing rates, let alone improve them. After 1907,
arbitration provided a regular means of increasing shearing rates –
increases which pastoralists found almost impossible to force the arbitration tribunals to trim except in the most exceptional of circumstances,
for example the Great Depression of the 1930s. Experience of 'success'
in 1956 was not exactly encouraging. Having finally summoned the
intestinal fortitude to modestly cut the rate following a significant fall in
wool prices (after the benefits of the extraordinary Korean War-induced
wool boom had played out, and after repeated pastoralist applications,
since 1952, to obtain a cut in the shearing rate), the Commonwealth
Arbitration Court was forced into a humiliating backdown. There were
no further serious attempts by graziers to cut shearing rates and wages
until the 1980s, when a combination of difficult economic circumstances

for the rural sector and revived employer militancy fuelled the incapacity-to-pay claims made by the National Farmers Federation, when the NFF unsuccessfully opposed National Wage Case increases for rural awards (although their tactics did lead to long delays in the application of the NWC increases to the awards). As for unskilled workers like shed-hands and station-hands, industrial deregulation seemed to offer few benefits. Their wage rates languished in the period 1890–1907, before Higgins established a minimum basic wage of 7s a day in the Harvester judgment of 1907. Once set, minimums need to be applied, and, as Colin Forster argues in *Foundations of Arbitration*, there is no doubt that many unskilled workers had to wait, sometimes for years, for the benefits of court judgments to flow to them. Nonetheless, Harvester established the principle of a minimum wage which employers increasingly found irresistible. After 1922, the Retail Price Index was taken into account by both the New South Wales and Commonwealth arbitration tribunals when deciding on basic-wage increases – a development which P. G. Macarthy describes as 'a significant conceptual breakthrough in wage determination'.[27]

These incremental increases may have been small, and their implementation at times unsatisfactory. Yet that skilled or particularly un-skilled workers in Australia could have won more in the marketplace than what they received via these adjustments in the arbitration courts is, we think, a contentious claim. It is difficult to conceive of market-based wage determination routinely factoring in consumer price increases into basic-wage adjustments. It could be argued that arbitration wage rulings, by favouring those in the award system, penalised the less well organised outside the system. Forster notes the economic factors impinging on arbitration, the legalism of the system and its redistributional effects *within* labour, all factors contributing to wage rigidities and, perversely, to inequities which manifested with the onset of the Great Depression – relatively high wages contributed to greater unemployment. Yet it was a system designed for the benefit of the unskilled, an attempt to overcome the perceived injustices of the marketplace, and during the 1920s and after 1945, relative economic prosperity masked its contradictions: unemployment was low, employers were able to absorb higher wage costs and indexation. The ideals of the system seemed to be matched by experience. As Macarthy observed of wage indexation in 1968 (a time of prosperity), 'it was decades before other countries adopted this technique for maintaining the real value of wage-earners' incomes'. Presumably other nations wanted to make their wage-fixing systems less inequitous – inequities developed in a less regulated industrial relations system than that applying in Australia. Only New Zealand shared Australia's embrace, in the late nineteenth and early twentieth centuries, of compulsory arbitration. Commonwealth Arbitration Court president Henry Bournes Higgins believed that comparative wage justice, and the establishment of a reasonable minimum wage, could only be effectively implemented through a centralised system, a system of state intervention. For Higgins, this was a realisation based upon experience. From that same experience, the leaders of the AWU drew a similar conclusion. For much of the twentieth century, they could believe that the system was capable of repaying their faith.[28]

Some AWU members seemed to enjoy better than average wages and conditions, although this depended on a range of factors, of which union performance was only one. Shearers could earn good money; so could miners, and workers on the big civil construction projects or in the oil industry. Some of them could also access a range of allowances – shifts, safety, danger money – which boosted their pay. While these skilled and semi-skilled workers could do reasonably well, others were less well placed in the bargaining process: shed-hands, station-hands, cannery workers. In short, this experience seems broadly typical of the mixed success that most large unions found in dealing with the arbitration process. But there is no doubt that at particular historical moments, there was a widespread sentiment among workers that the arbitration system was letting them down. Such a time was during the First World War.

### Upside Down at the Bottom of the World

For his own part, William Guthrie Spence had little doubt that the arbitration system had promoted not only industrial benefits for workers, but had legitimised the role of the unions in society. In June 1915 he told a Workers Education Association conference – and the WEA was itself an expression of self-improvement that Spence would have heartily endorsed – that unions were small democracies founded on law and order, 'a training ground for that respect for orderly rule and loyalty to principle without which no nation can ever be great'. 'Today it is recognised as an institution in the community, and is considered even respectable. It no longer calls for the heroic self-sacrifice and suffering which was the lot of its active members in the past; but its work is still unaccomplished, and its mission in our social economy is not yet fulfilled.' Spence stopped short of complete self-satisfaction: something troubled him. There were too many unions in Australia; many had become too conservative, falling into old craft union habits. 'The trades union movement has hardly kept pace with the rapid economic changes.' They were preoccupied with questions of wages and hours. 'We might keep on doing this forever, but that does not touch the real work

which lies before the workers ... the overthrow of the capitalistic system.'
He wondered whether the labour movement was equipped to face this
test. In the Commonwealth Parliament, where Spence had served since
Federation in 1901, he admitted that Labor had 'entered into a new
field, and it is admittedly a difficult one'. The labour movement 'sadly
needed' more knowledge of political and economic questions – but with
an Australian thought and 'colour'. 'We don't want our minds clouded
or warped by ideas or proposals which may be justified in continental
lands, but have no practical place in Australia'. Spence could discern
problems and failings retarding the development of the labour movement, but the restless self- improver had turned his mind away from new
sources of insight and inspiration. He was already a victim of the cultural
insularity championed by the Australian settlement, and which he had
helped to shape.[29]

Within little more than a year of Spence's 1915 speech, self-sacrifice
and suffering lay waiting for the labour movement and the working class.
Spence confessed his doubts as the first Australians were tasting defeat in
a global war; within a few months, many would be swallowed by the
mayhem on the Western Front. In Australia, the war wrought changes
which Spence could not have possibly anticipated – the conscription
crisis of 1916–17, the Great Strike of 1917 – and which he struggled to
comprehend. He was not alone in that.

In 1919 Spence made his final speech to the Australian Parliament. He
was 73 years old. He was no longer a Labor representative, nor was he a
member of the AWU. In 1916 he had supported Prime Minister Billy
Hughes's determination to send conscripts to the European war. Labor
had split. The AWU, virulently opposed to conscription, had asked
Spence, in deference to his long service to the union, to resign. Yet
although Labor had changed, he had not. On 9 July 1919, Spence rose in
the House of Representatives, he said, to challenge the proposition that
'the industrial arbitration system has been a failure'. Under the arbitration system, 'Labor has been given an equal say with employers'. The
overthrow of Capitalism was now unnecessary: Capitalists can now 'do
nothing that the people refuse to allow'. Despite these apparent victories, some in the labour movement were tempted by 'direct action
advocates' preaching foreign 'economic lunacy'. The new doctrines of
the Industrial Workers of the World were 'immoral, wrong, and utterly
opposed to anything British or Australian'. Although he continued to
support 'evolutionary socialism' and government enterprises, he feared
that many workers were listening to the siren appeal of 'anarchy'.
Unions, Spence warned, must weed out the 'wild extremists'. 'No-one
but a moderate man can retain unity in an organisation of any kind'. He
had tried to be a moderate man, to welcome new ideas, to lay the

foundation of the Great Reform, the love of one's fellows. But the world had spun out of his control. Labor was divided. The war, the conscription crisis, and the Great Strike had shaken the edifice of arbitration, protection and White Australia, and the social consensus upon which it had been framed. Spence seems oblivious of the ramifications of these momentous events for the values he cherished – he makes no reference to them in the 1919 speech – and which he expected Australian unions to uphold in the face of the most severe tests. And by this time some within the movement, and within the AWU, had jettisoned the values that Spence had spent a lifetime nurturing. The certainties of the settlement were troubled and challenged, yet manifested as law, they were barely twenty years old. The society which had finally conceded the terms of the settlement was now confronted with new foreign ideas and brutally changed conditions.[30]

The AWU had been busy trying to weed out the 'wild extremists'. By 1920 it demanded its officers sign a piece of paper pledging their loyalty to the union and the leadership. Being true to your mates now apparently required a written guarantee. In the years since 1886, they had done much to create what Queensland Branch president Beecher Hay would later call 'a wonderful machine'. Surviving the bitter struggle of the 1890s, the AWU had embarked on an ambitious program of amalgamations, yielding a membership of over 100 000, predominantly in the pastoral, metal-mining, sugar and civil construction industries. Across Australia, the union administered 220 State and federal awards and agreements. Industrial strength nurtured ambition, to dominate both the Labor Party and the union movement. Former AWU officials heavily populated the Labor Party caucuses in the State and Federal Parliaments, bringing with them the common-sense laborism which had underwritten their development of the AWU. And the AWU had laid claim to that bold title, One Big Union – despite the fact that rival unions also claimed it for the great multi-industry body they were trying to organise. The AWU insisted on being defined in its own terms, doggedly true to its own image. It was all a long way from Creswick, and the urge to unite shearers in a body effective enough to resist the predatory instincts of the colonial pastoralists. And it was a difficult test of the bush ethos, and Spence's optimistic ethics, which so naturally seemed to describe a clear moral struggle between shearer and squatter.

CHAPTER 1

# The Knights of the Blade

*The Amalgamated Shearers Union, 1886–89*

In early 1886 a young Victorian shearer named David Temple refused to accept a cut in shearing rates. Pastoralists in western New South Wales had abruptly declared that shearing rates for the coming season were to be reduced from 20s per 100 sheep to 17s 6d. A shearer discharged for what the pastoralist might decree to be 'wilful bad shearing' would only get 15s per 100 for *all* sheep shorn up till the date of discharge. Shearers engaging for work with a station supporting these demands were instructed that they would 'agree to the terms specified', or do without a job. A newspaper advertisement outlining the pastoralists' decree appeared on 3 April 1886, and by early May over twenty stations in New South Wales had declared their support – bad news for both New South Wales and Victorian shearers, whose migratory work patterns took them across colonial borders, and who understandably feared that the New South Wales pastoralists' taste for rate-cutting would soon spread to the other colonies and sheds where they sought work. Above all, the pastoralists wanted to enforce their right to determine the employment contract between themselves and their shearers. It was this classic conflict between worker and employer which would define the formative years of the Amalgamated Shearers Union, and its ambitious successor, the Australian Workers Union.[1]

Temple was indignant. 'Very great dissatisfaction was expressed amongst shearers, and a general determination made to resist the reduction as unjust and uncalled for.' In 1886 David Temple was a 24-year-old with initiative and determination who hoped to improve his lot by hard work in the goldmines and shearing sheds around Creswick, in the agricultural and mining heart of the colony of Victoria, and further afield in the woolsheds of the Murrumbidgee district, the rich pastoral country which straddled the New South Wales–Victorian border. He was willing to put his own money and energies into the formation of a union of shearers, and borrowed from the pastoralists' tactics by advertising his intentions in the Ballarat newspapers. He soon found allies. In the *Australian Town and Country Journal* one unnamed shearer declared that it was time for 'ye knights of the blade' to pull together. 'I say let us unite as other working classes do and remedy our lot. You all know our troubles as well as I. A union is what is wanted.' Temple invited shearers to sign up with the new Australasian Shearers Union (as it was called before amalgamation with other shearers' unions in 1887). As he later explained, 'Steps were taken in May 1886 by your Secretary and a public meeting of shearers held in Ballarat on the 14th of June. It was then decided to form a union which would be intercolonial, and should embrace all who follow the occupation during the shearing season'. The historic June 1886 meeting in Fern's Hotel at Ballarat formally established the Australasian Shearers Union.[2]

Shearers joining the ASU had to agree to work for shearing rates no less than 20s per 100, and any shearer prematurely discharged would be paid off at this rate. This was an ambitious aim, only fitfully fulfilled by the ASU in the years 1886–90. Shearing rates around the colonies varied

The knights of the blade, at a station near Harden, New South Wales, *c.* 1886.
*Whitehurst Collection, National Library of Australia.*

greatly, determined by local agreements and conditions. In Victoria, rates could vary from 12s per 100 through to 17s 6d, and Temple soon found that the well-established pastoralists of the Western District of Victoria would resist paying 15s per 100, let alone 20s (indeed by 1887, ASU rules would officially recognise these regional distinctions in rates). Membership dues were set at 10s for shearers and 5s for shed-hands. Current rates for rations and board would also stand. Temple attended to a few other sore points. Shearers would not be required to tar the wounds on the sheep they were shearing (this was seen as a job for the tar boy, rather than a self-respecting shearer); raddling would be banned ('raddling' meant that if the boss of the board in the shearing shed marked a sheep as poorly shorn the shearer would not be paid for it. Shearers often saw this as an arbitrary practice, applied at the whim of the boss). Similar organisations of shearers developed in Wagga Wagga (NSW), Adelaide and Tasmania, but as Temple declared in June 1886, it was his ambition to unite them.[3]

### The Pastoral Industry in the 1880s

Bushworkers who could develop good shearing skills had a right to expect fair reward for the services performed in the relatively brief shearing season. Shearers apply great skill to the apparently simple aim of liberating the wool from the body of a sheep. It is exhausting work performed under pressure. Shearers compete with each other; they compete against the end of the long working day, when their tally will dictate their earnings. They compete against the boss of the board, who wants his sheep shorn cleanly, and quickly, always quickly. A good shearer could expertly shear a sheep in under three minutes. In New South Wales and Victoria the shearing season ran from June to November, in Queensland from January to March and August to October, depending on the pastoral district. Some shearers migrated from shed to shed along the length of this long shearing trail, stretching from South Australia east into Victoria, and up into New South Wales and Queensland, seeking as much shearing work as they could get. Others, perhaps most, were content with smaller orbits, focused on their local region. For those shearers able to manage a respectable tally of 80–90 sheep a day (shearing with blades or the new shearing machines, first introduced in 1888), they might earn between £4 and £6 for a six-day week. These were high rates in comparison with other bushworkers. As John Merritt notes, an even less skilled shearer in 1886, clearing £2 5s a week, would have earned twice as much as a stockman, boundary rider, shepherd, hutkeeper, sheep washer and 'generally useful man'. As for the shed-hands who swept the boards, gathered the wool, sealed the sheep's cuts with tar and supplied the shearer with his sheep, they were paid no more than 25s a week, considerably less than the skilled shearers. A figure of 7s a day is often cited as the average wage paid to unskilled Australian workers in the late nineteenth century. But as Ray Markey observes, 'it is unlikely that a high proportion of the unskilled received the union standard of seven shillings, since relatively few were unionized. In the 1890s depression, when most unskilled unions collapsed, this standard became quite mythical'. There is little doubt that this observation reflects the experience of shed-hands, on whose behalf the ASU officials only began to organise, as the General Labourers Union, in 1890, an effort soon overwhelmed by the economic crash.[4]

Wool provided bushworkers with regular if itinerant work. Pastoral life was enduring, shaped by the cycle of the seasons since at least the 1830s, and the beginnings of the great 'squatting age' of pastoral development, a way of life celebrated in song and poetry and tall tales of shearing exploits. By the 1880s wool nurtured thousands of colonial sheep stations, and an estimated shearing workforce of 56 000, of whom around 25 000 were shearers. In 1886 wool exports were valued at £12.9 million, gold at £3 million and all other Australian exports at £4.9 million. Prosperous towns developed to serve the pastoralists and their workers, and the network of large and small grain, fruit, dairy and other rural properties which grew to complement the wool industry in various colonies. From a few thousand introduced sheep in the 1790s, nearly 90 million sheep grazed across Australia in the 1880s. A vast web of rail lines spread across the colonies, often laid in reverence to the riches contained in a bale of fine wool. In the late 1880s the NSW Railways, the single biggest employer in the colony, employed 9600 workers, many of whom owed their jobs to the lucrative business provided for the Railway Commissioners by the wool industry. At Darling Harbour in Sydney, an army of rail porters and wharfies worked to unload the wool trains and load the ships bound, for the most part, for the woollen mills of England. The 1880s were the high-water mark of the long economic boom which had run from the 1860s, and to which there seemed no end, and a snowy fleece was its emblem. It was only right, in the minds of shearers like David Temple, that the working man was entitled to a fair share of this abundance. But the boom was almost exhausted, its riches diminishing as the young colonial unionists stood up to claim their share.[5]

The seeds of collapse grew quietly before the apparently sudden economic depression of the 1890s. Many pastoralists in the 1880s were burdened with mounting debts. While the total value of wool exports was high in the late 1880s, wool prices were falling. In 1873 wool commanded a price of 15d a pound in London. By 1894, in the depth of the depression, that price had fallen to 6½d a pound. As the price steadily fell in the years following the 1873 peak, the pastoralists' debt problems worsened. As Geoffrey Blainey observes, 'by the mid 1880s the annual interest owed by many individual sheep stations equalled one third or even one half of the value of the annual wool clip, and five years later the lower wool proceeds of many stations could not even meet the interest owed to the city finance houses'. Pressure to reduce costs prompted pastoralists to seek cuts in shearing rates.[6]

Shearers were not privy to the balance sheets which vexed pastoralists. They had their own problems and financial strains. Shearers' earnings might have been high in relation to other workers, but they had to deduct a range of expenses from the earnings they made during the shearing season. One shearer wrote of the pastoralists' rate cut, 'I must say I think the price is too low for a man to make even fair wages; that is, taking into consideration the time and expenses it costs a shearer looking for work of that kind, together with the high price of rations and shearing tools.' With the proposed rate cut in April 1886 NSW pastoralists had aroused a simmering discontent felt by many shearers at the difficulties they were forced to endure to stick to their calling. Shearing rates, the money you could put in your pocket when a shed cut out, was the main grievance; but there were other irritants. The standard of station accommodation for shearers was often substandard. One shearer complained that the huts were often not fit for human habitation. 'They are overcrowded, and there is nothing for the poor workers to lie on but hard boards or bark. Nearly all the men have bed ticks, but it is very seldom that a shearer can get anything to put on them, so that after his hard day's work (shearers especially, after perspiring all day), must roll on the hard boards as best they can, and rise anything but refreshed. It is very exhausting.' Shearers worked from six in the morning until six at night six days a week, with perhaps a 4 p.m. finish on Saturday. There were twenty-minute 'smokos' in the morning and the afternoon.[7]

### 'Mr. Temple's Run': Early ASU Organisation

These itinerant workers were not easily unionised. Temple relied heavily for inspiration on William Guthrie Spence, a 40-year-old Scottish immigrant, upright alderman of Creswick, union pioneer and indefatigable self-promoter. At the June 1886 meeting Spence was elected Australasian Shearers Union president and Temple was elected secretary. Spence's involvement in the ASU sprang from the initiative of Temple, who realised that Spence was a respected and well-known figure in central Victoria and possessed the credibility Temple needed to sell his fledgling union to potentially sceptical shearers. When only a little older than

Temple, Spence had founded the Amalgamated Miners Association at Bendigo in 1874, and had been involved in many industrial disputes and negotiations with mine owners and managers. As an anonymous 'member' (most likely Temple) wrote of the ASU's formation in the *Shearers' Record* (a paper the ASU financially supported) in April 1889, 'the fact of Mr. Spence being connected with it [the new union] gave the shearers confidence in the outcome'. Spence was not idle in promoting any venture with which he was associated – and his own key contribution to it. In his *History of the AWU*, published in 1911, Spence conveys the impression of the busy general dispatching his organisers to sign up members while he 'acted as treasurer and directed the work generally, as well as organising from my office' in Creswick (an office which Temple had personally funded). As an aside he notes that of the ASU's early organising activities, 'Mr. Temple took a run round the western parts of Victoria, but did not meet with much encouragement'.[8]

In mid-1886 Temple held several 'poorly attended' meetings in the Victorian towns of Colac, Winchelsea, Bambra, Coloden and Camperdown, which resulted in the grand total of sixty members and an income of £9. He spent £15 from his own pocket on the trip. He set off again in July, this time walking across the border into New South Wales. He collected just £21 15s and spent £55 of his own. He believed that Victorian shearers were 'disheartened' by previous failed attempts to form a union. Shearers were not 'inclined to brave the displeasure of the employers on slender grounds'. In New South Wales, where other shearing unions were organising, he found greater encouragement: twenty-nine out of thirty shearers joined at Nyang Station. 'The sheds were all in full swing, and he was able to lay before the men in a body his proposals ... Everywhere he was received with open arms.'[9]

Itinerant workers and smallholders were bound together by a common identity as shearers. Increasingly, Temple and the 'collectors' who offered to join him in tramping from shed to shed found that shearers were willing to sign up. This was particularly true in New South Wales, where local shearing unions sprang up in several centres. Starting out again in August 1886, Temple enrolled 1600 shearers in southern New South Wales within two months. Two collectors, James Slattery and J. A. Cooke, who according to Temple 'required no guarantee, nor did they seem to care whether they received payment or not', also organised in New South Wales, enrolling between them 2500 shearers from 186 sheds. They then proceeded to Victoria, where they continued to enrol members.[10]

By early 1887, the Australasian Shearers Union leadership had decided to amalgamate with strong shearers' unions in the Bourke and Wagga Wagga districts of New South Wales, not least because they were trying to sign up the same shearers, given the itinerant nature of the job. The old Creswick-based union became one branch of the new Amalgamated Shearers Union of Australasia, with other branches in Wagga, Bourke and Cobar (all three in New South Wales). Creswick officials dominated the new ASU, and the union was effectively run from there by Spence and Temple, possibly in deference to Spence's personal authority, and perhaps inspired by the vigour with which Temple had pursued recruitment. The new ASU claimed a total membership of 9183 shearers, 6883 in NSW and Victoria and the remainder in New Zealand, where the ambitious ASU leaders went in search of still more members; these shearers often crossed the Tasman in search of work in the much larger Australian pastoral industry. (These figures need to be treated with some caution. ASU membership figures often included unfinancial members – those who had failed to renew their membership tickets.)[11]

Organiser James Slattery had left for New Zealand in November 1886. Flushed with their successes in Australia, Temple said that the ASU leadership 'wanted to establish a thorough bond of unity and sympathy between the shearers in all the large islands and colonies that form part

The first conference of the Amalgamated Shearers Union, 1888. Spence is seated sixth from the left; Temple is seated fifth from the right. *Noel Butlin Archives, Australian National University.*

of the British Empire in this portion of the world'. In December Temple
and Cooke arrived to assist Slattery, and they soon enrolled over 2000
shearers and opened an office in the Canterbury district, with Slattery
left in charge. By April 1887 Temple claimed that even the New Zealand
sheep owners, 'who tend to treat their workers better', were sympathetic
to the union's cause. He was also hopeful of soon signing up many
Maori shearers. 'I predict a successful, prosperous and protracted career
for the ASU of Australasia.' The new union seemed to be sweeping all
before it.[12]

During 1887 the new ASU developed a comprehensive set of rules to
protect its members' interests. Essentially, the rules laid down the basis
of protecting a shearer's rates and conditions through a closed shop and
defined procedures for obtaining and performing work. Pastoralists were
instructed to obtain their shearers through the district offices of the
union, or 'send a list of names of members they wish to engage'. Members were forbidden to accept work on large stations (2000 sheep or
over) except through the union. Before work commenced, the shearers
had to elect a shed representative to deal with members' grievances. A
committee of four would be elected to assist the rep in a shed with more
than ten shearers. Members could shear as many sheep as they liked, but
they must be shorn 'in a fair and workmanlike manner'. No shearer
should tar his own sheep, unless the wound was severe. Shearers should
work a maximum forty-eight hours a week, and no more than eight hours
a day. In terms of pay and rations, rates were set at a minimum £1 per 100
in New South Wales, and 17s 6d per 100 in Victoria and South Australia,
or 15s per 100 with rations. Generally, the acceptable price for rations
should not exceed town prices, with cost of carriage and 5 per cent
added. Shearers should receive free agistment for two horses. The practice of setting 'second rates', paying a shearer less if he was discharged
before the end of the season, was outlawed. Any shearer discharged
before the end of shearing should receive full pay for all the sheep he
had shorn.[13]

### 'An Industrious Few'? The Character of the 1880s Shearer

The ASU's rules sought to control whom the pastoralist employed, how
he was selected, and under what terms he would work. Unsurprisingly,
the pastoralists were not very pleased at the prospect of their 'right' to
determine whom they should employ and the terms of their employment
– rights which many pastoralists had only recently sought to reaffirm
with the April 1886 advertisement – being defined by their employees,
sanctioned by an ambitious intercolonial union. One irate station
manager, who estimated that shearers were paid 50 per cent too much,

doubted that shearers would be able to maintain the discipline of their upstart unionism. 'Several of them work for a few weeks at shearing time only, and earn enough to keep them until the next season's shearing commences, spending their time and cheques prowling from one town to another, attending horse races, circuses, etc, or, if the opportunity offers, they are the first to rouse up a howling mob of the so-called "unemployed".' But in his criticism he distinguished between these carousing itinerant shearers and 'the industrious few, who follow shearing in season, and are otherwise employed between times. The latter class I respect and admire'. Some were employed in other bushwork, or in mining; but the best of them, in the eyes of a *Town and Country Journal* editorial, were the small selectors. 'The season over, they return to their homes, and spend the proceeds on the improvement of their farms. These are steady, reliable men, skilful shearers, and good and willing workers. They are, however, becoming scarcer and scarcer, as the progress of their own farms improves their condition and renders other employment unnecessary.' The editorial also made the point that if rates were too low, these men would probably not be attracted to shearing at all.[14]

Here was an ideal of rural employment, undoubtedly shared by pastoralists across the colonies. Historian Michael Cannon says that what the squatter demanded from his employee was someone 'as good as himself', someone who could extend his ability to subdue *his* land and reap the harvest of its abundant produce. Surely the best of these 'steady, reliable men', were those who shared the squatter's ambition to work his own land and understood the constraints that pressed upon his pastoral enterprise. But as Cannon notes of station life in the 1840s, the squatter could not always get what he wanted. The employer generally had to put up with 'the unsavoury remnants of the convict system, the chances of picking up adaptable labourers from the immigrant ships, or the wild independent ways of native-born youths'.[15]

What kind of men were these 'unsavoury remnants'? They still trod the bush tracks in the late 1880s, seeking work wherever they could find it. One of them was Thomas Smith, itinerant shearer. 'I am quite prepared to admit that we bushmen have, as a class, very many serious faults. We are reckless with our money when we have any, seldom laying by a pound for a rainy day, a large number boozing our cheques as soon as earned. We also are unsettled and wandering in habits, not staying long on one job; and we are impatient of any restraint or censorship on the part of our employers.' He conceded that between seasons a shearer could manage to get by without work – although this depends on your notion of managing, particularly when having trudged to a station, the owner refuses to provide a meal, or even supply a little flour for damper, an

experience Smith knew well: 'There are times when all these resources
fail, and the swagman finds himself face to face with a twenty or thirty
mile stage; a heavy swag and water-bag to carry, and nothing but the
remembrance of a bit of cold johnny-cake, eaten the previous evening to
sustain him on his way. All this with the heat at 109 deg. in the shade is,
to say the least, somewhat less than happiness.' Something less than
happiness drove these men to drink, bingeing to obliterate a debilitating
pattern of work and tedium. 'That life, while travelling or in work, is
such a dull affair – he has no amusements, lives in a hut without the
slightest pretensions to comfort and on the homeliest fare, and without
the civilising influence of female presence. When he gets his cheque
he has to take it to the township to get it cashed. He sees a number of
people enjoying themselves, and a few barmaids and servant girls all
smiles; and in contrast to this the thought of the track seems very
uninviting.'

Thomas Smith did not despair of his fate. In 1886 he believed he had
found one way, apart from drink, for workers to escape their subjugation
to the whims of the squatter. If only the labouring classes would pull
together, he implored, and return earnest and reliable men to represent
them in Parliament, 'then their wants would receive the attention they
deserve'. But the willingness of the ASU to participate actively in the
political process was still some years off, when circumstances had pushed
them to the realisation that industrial organisation was not enough to
defend the rights of workers.[16]

The experiences and aims of these itinerant shearers need to be
balanced against those of the small selectors who also resorted to
shearing, and who were preferred by the squatters and the editor of the
*Town and Country Journal.* Several historians estimate that humble
selectors formed a majority of the shearing workforce in the 1880s; in
part these men were probably some of those 'unsavoury remnants' who
had 'improved themselves' with the acquisition of a small parcel of land.
Their response to unionism was coloured by an ambiguous economic
status. Even as the possessors of a relatively meagre acreage, they believed
they were fulfilling a dream of self-improvement that was at least one step
removed from that of the bushworker who relied solely on the goodwill
of an employer. John Merritt says of these selectors that 'if they were not
the social equals of the pastoralists who employed them, at least they
deserved to be treated with respect. All too often pastoralists did not give
them the recognition they thought they deserved'. A 'healthy sense of
injustice' could be inflamed by high ration rates, raddling, and cuts to
shearing rates. Apparently even the 'industrious few' were prey to the
grievances which fostered unionism.[17]

### Who Rules in the Woolshed? The Shearing Seasons 1887–89

During the 1887 season shearers and pastoralists fought to assert their rights. Industrial conflicts flickered like small bushfires across New South Wales and Victoria, where the ASU concentrated its efforts. In Queensland, the fledgeling Queensland Shearers Union had begun to organise the shearers of Blackall, Winton and Longreach; the South Australian Shearers Union was also active on behalf of local shearers. Across these colonies, the industrial flames were usually extinguished by compromise. In some areas pastoralists conceded union demands, particularly over rates, and 20s per 100 was established as the going rate in many New South Wales sheds. Some pastoralists took a stand over 'second rates', as they saw their elimination as an invitation to shearers to leave stations before the shearing was finished. Where there was confrontation, shearers formed the strike camps that would become such a feature of the industrial battles of rural Australia in the 1890s. In these stand-offs, Spence believed that the ASU was often saved by the thirty-seven organisers the union put into the field in the 1887 season, organisers whose numbers had grown considerably from the handful who assisted Temple in 1886. 'Some of them had a very lively time racing from one roll-call to another', Spence wrote. 'Frequent change of horses was necessary, as one after another got knocked up. Camps had to be formed, rations supplied by the Union, and the true location of reserves and roads discovered. Maps were obtained, and in more than one place, when the squatter ordered men off his run, he was astonished to find them *set him at defiance* [*sic*] by camping within a few yards of the woolshed. They had located a road – or it may be a reserve – which he had forgotten existed.' Spence estimated that about 500 sheds 'shore union', and in most cases the ASU succeeded in increasing rates, despite pastoralist attempts to involve the press and the police on their behalf. Spence asserted that 'misrepresentation and untruthfulness were the order of the day'. Some shearers who had acted as strike leaders were charged and fined by local magistrates under colonial Masters and Servants legislation. This onerous law was essentially a convict-era instrument by which employers could control the conduct of their employees, despite the fact that the law was also theoretically designed to protect the rights of employees. Shearers, for example, could be hauled before a local magistrate by a disgruntled pastoralist for 'neglect of duty', a charge which the pastoralist and an obliging magistrate could often define as they pleased. Workers could also be summonsed for 'breach of contract', which could simply mean that they had failed to do what the employer required, even if these requirements were unreasonable. Both these charges carried sentences of three months' gaol, and often heavy fines to accompany the prison term.[18]

If the law seemed skewed in favour of the pastoralist, some shearers responded by taking the law into their own hands. ASU loyalists were often zealous in preventing non-unionists from accepting less than union demands: at one station scabs were beaten and thrown in a river. On the other hand, Spence conceded that 'many hundreds' of shearers sided with the squatters. The ASU ended the season claiming 16 000 members, and an impressive display of organisation and solidarity – certainly un-rivalled by previous fitful attempts to organise shearers. Many pastoralists must have regretted this unintended outcome of the 1886 advertisement. During the season, some of the owners had at least deferred dealing with the union by offering 20s per 100 but refusing to employ unionists. As the season ended they continued to reject the idea of negotiating directly with the union. It was a sullen silence. As W. Percy, the secretary of the ASU's Cobar Branch, observed, 'The squatters did not meet us as we desired, and there was evidently existing a tacit understanding that in the year 1888 the Union must be strangled'.[19]

In 1888 the pastoralists of the Western District of Victoria organised to meet the ASU threat by establishing the Western District Sheep Farmers Association. They soon vacillated between resistance and conciliation. One squatter said that the Western District squatters had learnt a hard lesson in the 1887 shearing season. Many non-union shearers had proved incompetent; 'the wool left on the sheep would have more than compensated them for the higher rate paid to the union men'. Another Western District pastoralist, the Honourable Thomas Dowling, set forth the principles which sustained the owners' determined opposition to ASU demands. And it was not simply a question of economics: in his eyes, men were simply not born equal. 'Some men were better fitted to perform certain labour than others, and, as hitherto, he would please himself whether he gave a man 10s or 15s or more, according to the quality of work done. He believed in rewarding good labor.' Dowling believed that it was tyrannical to be compelled to pay ASU rates, or that shearers should be the judges of their own work. He concluded: 'It all went to prove that employers should protect themselves'. Meanwhile, in Melbourne, pastoralists from New South Wales and Victoria established an intercolonial pastoralists' association in March 1888.[20]

The ASU met with the Western District pastoralists in June and July 1888, just as the shearing season commenced. The pastoralists would not pay their shearers 15s per 100, the compromise rate sought by the ASU in the Western District. They claimed that throughout the district 13s per 100 was the standard, and that was as high as they were prepared to go. Across New South Wales and Victoria the ASU prepared to resist shearing on terms dictated by the pastoralists. In the June *Shearers' Record* one correspondent warned that in the Walgett district both Llanlillo and Boorooma stations would start shearing early, 'thinking, no doubt, that as it is an early start, they will get men to turn crawlers and desert the Union for a week or two earlier shearing'. The manager at Boorooma Station also inflamed passions by declaring that he would rather employ 'chinamen and rouseabouts' than employ union shearers and adhere to union rules. Like many other stations, Llanlillo also insisted on the expensive demand that shearers forward £1 deposit when applying for a stand, to compel the applicant to turn up at shearing time. Llanlillo also charged high rates for medicines and shears.[21]

To defeat the pastoralists the union sent out agents to assist local shearers and act as strike leaders. The Creswick Branch sent out over twenty-two agents. The ASU established strike camps just beyond the gates of belligerent stations, and waited until the owners gave in. Some strikes were brief; in other cases Temple noted that some shearers sacrificed nearly the whole shearing season in refusing to accept anything less than union terms. Determination did not always require aggression. The strike at Osberene station, near Adelong in southern New South Wales, reflected the relatively mild nature of the of the ASU's 1888 campaign. The station manager, a Mr G. Hayes, called the roll on 26 November to start the shearing. Thirty union shearers stood by, refusing to shear under station agreement. An agent from the Wagga branch of the ASU, E. H. Burgess, counselled the men to be patient for a few days, perhaps weeks, 'and they would be victorious in the end'. A 'general stampede' then ensued, with the strikers jostling for the best shady spots beneath the spreading mimosa trees of their new strike camp, a couple of hundred yards from the woolshed, by a bend in the creek. While the strike lasted Hayes displayed 'great civility and gentlemanly bearing towards the men'. He said he was personally in favour of the union, but as manager had no authority from the owners to accept union terms. Also in attendance throughout the strike were Sergeant Cassim and two troopers from Adelong (Burgess complained that the squatters should have to pay for this protection themselves). Cassim never lost an opportunity to advise the men to 'keep orderly, and quiet, and you will gain the respect of your fellow men.' After a few days, and some restlessness from the bored shearers, Hayes announced that he was now authorised to accept union terms, sparking 'great joy' in the strike camp. The shearers responded generously in their efforts. 'Three or four men who were out on strike all the season got the preference of going on, a very fair style of doing things ... the shearing went on splendidly, and the manager said he was well satisfied with the men on the board.'[22]

In other sheds, scabs undermined solidarity. An ASU agent in the
Murrumbidgee said that fourteen scabs, calling themselves 'Tubbul
unionists' (Tubbul was a town near Young in New South Wales) had
accepted station terms to shear at Benerambah. The agent noted with
disgust that these 'poor, misguided fools' had accepted the terms 'a
month before they left home'. They were organised by their 'self-styled'
secretary, who took 5s each from them and guaranteed to find them a
shed – 'which he does by writing to non-union squatters, and signing
their agreements'.[23]

There was little tolerance of scabs among ASU shearers, leading to a
serious disturbance at Brookong Station in the Wagga district of New
South Wales. Confrontation erupted on 15 August when 200 unionists
camped near the woolshed attacked non-union shearers, resulting in
some minor injuries and the 'kidnap' of several scabs to the strike camp.
The incident prompted a short-lived wave of panic in nearby Wagga, and
William Halliday, the owner of Brookong Station, called for forty
revolvers and 4000 rounds of ammunition, a request described in the
Shearers' Record as 'the most sensational thing ever heard of outside a
sixpenny novel'. The strikers dispersed when police arrived and read the
Riot Act. Nevertheless the heavy hand of the law was soon felt by the
Brookong strike leaders, who were sentenced to three years' hard labour.
Local ASU Branch secretary Walter Head described them as 'martyrs',
and some sections of the local press also protested at the severity of the
sentences. Head hoped for the day when 'Australians will decide to have
their laws made and administered by other than those whose class
interests are opposed to all progressive legislation'. But the ASU was only
beginning to learn that colonial law and its enforcement were weapons
the pastoralists were well placed to exploit to their advantage.[24]

Some pastoralists may have believed they had also found an ally in new
technology. In October 1888 a dispatch from a Bourke district correspondent noted that Dunlop Station was equipping its woolshed with the
new Wolseley shearing machine, 'to show determination to oppose the
Union'. In the context of so much industrial turmoil, shearers were
naturally fearful of a machine which, it was claimed, could shear far more
cleanly and quickly than a shearer with blades. During 1887, when
Frederick Wolseley first demonstrated his machine to the public, the
Town and Country Journal sang the machine's praises throughout
successive editions. 'It is claimed for the invention that it works faster
than hand labour, leaves no second cut, does not injure the skin in the
slightest degree, and can be so regulated that the fleece can be removed
of any length desired.' Driven by an 8-horsepower steam-engine, the
machine could drive 100 shears, with a shearer working each arm. At its
first demonstration in the Goldsbrough Mort woolstores in Melbourne a

sheep was shorn in four and a half minutes, a little slow when compared with a 'gun' shearer who could shear a sheep in under three minutes, but nevertheless a clear indication that with practice, shearing would generally become faster with the new technology. But to achieve that result a shearer was still required to work the machine, although as the *Town and Country Journal* noted, 'manual labour in connection with sheep shearing will no doubt be greatly reduced. An average of 120 sheep per day for 10 hours would seem easily attainable; and the clip will be more regular.' Shearers reacted ambiguously, as a Bourke Branch correspondent noted in October 1888. 'Some of the shearers approve of them, while the majority of the men say they are not to be depended upon, there being too many stoppages through breakages.' Nevertheless the shearers at Dunlop Station had extracted some advantage from being compelled to use the machines. In return for using them they obtained a commitment from the station manager for adherence to the ASU agreement and free combs and cutters.[25]

During the 1888 and 1889 shearing seasons the ASU continued to win more sheds, and increasingly pastoralists succumbed to union terms. In February 1889 Temple believed that the ASU was 'on the eve of a complete victory'. At meetings in Wagga, Forbes and Port Augusta (South Australia) the pastoralists agreed to the ASU's terms. But complete victory proved elusive for the ASU. A Quirindi shearer warned in June, just as the season was about to get under way, that local owners planned to thwart the union by offering £1 per 100. 'They will prevent a good many men from joining the Union and entrap them into signing the station rules.' In July an editorial in the *Record* noted that in Victoria, and particularly in the Western District, the owners remained 'militant', obstinately refusing to pay union rates. The Victorians resisted ASU demands for 14s 6d (trimmed again to encourage compromise), agreeing only to 14s per 100. According to the *Shearers' Record*, the Victorian pastoralists 'prefer fighting rather than make the concession of less than half a farthing per fleece'.[26]

### Building Co-operation? Amalgamation Plans and the London Dock Strike Appeal

ASU Organiser Arthur Rae was not deluded by the union's apparent success. 'Do not let yourselves imagine', he advised his fellow shearers in July 1889, 'that because we have done so well in the past that we are going to have things all our own way in the future'. Rae believed that the ASU could not stand alone against determined employers. He had little doubt that many pastoralists 'would spend a good sum of money even now to crush us, and if they liked to combine their funds they might yet be able to do it'. He wanted the ASU to affiliate with the Melbourne Trades and Labour Council, to begin the process of building labour co-operation across the colonies, and throughout the world. 'That is my idea of the ultimate aim of trades unionism.' Despite his concern for the ASU he remained an idealist, even if his dreams of a united world of labour did not extend to the Asian labour so feared by Australian workers in the late nineteenth century. 'It is a grand country, but you might as well hand it over to the chows as to let the selfish squatters and their friends and hangers-on have it all their own way. So let us hang out for a fair thing, while there's a shot in the locker.' A small, intense man with a walrus moustache, shearer Arthur Rae joined the ASU in 1886 in his native New Zealand. In 1889, aged 29, he arrived in Australia and immediately took up organising duties in New South Wales and Victoria. Rae certainly did not lack pluck. During the 1889 season he had tried to coax non-unionists at a Victorian woolshed away from their loyalty to the local owner by signing on as a 'shed rules' shearer and, once in the shed, agitating among them to join the ASU. Rae 'left in a hurry' when an unimpressed shearer told the manager of Rae's activities. The riled manager promptly summonsed Rae under the Masters and Servants Act for leaving his position before the shearing was finished, that is, for 'breach of contract'. Over the next few months Rae encountered no less than four officers attempting to serve the summons. In the ASU office in Creswick Rae told one frustrated constable that he knew the wanted individual intimately – he had just left on a long sea trip. In another town Rae assisted an officer to keep an eye out for him – until a 'pressing engagement' called Rae away. The summons was never served.[27]

By the time of the ASU's fourth annual conference in February 1890 the union claimed 19 776 members across New South Wales, Victoria and South Australia, with the South Australian Shearers Union having merged with the ASU in 1889, and where the union enjoyed the co-operation of 'liberal' sheep owners and a high rate of unionisation. In these three colonies the ASU estimated that there were 2392 'union' sheds, with only 400 remaining outside the fold. The report also surveyed the possibility of amalgamation with the recently established Queensland Shearers Union, and the creation of a Tasmanian branch.[28]

Spence was a keen advocate of an amalgamation between the ASU and the QSU. But the 3400-member QSU was fearful of being swamped by the larger organisation, with the ASU already encroaching on QSU territory by organising shearers in southern Queensland. The QSU's leaders were also concerned at what they saw as the ASU's weak attitude to the employment of Asian – mainly Chinese – labour (although the QSU's leaders need not have worried; reflecting widespread working-class fears of Asian and Islander labour taking European jobs and undercutting wages, the ASU specifically banned Chinese and South Sea Islanders from membership in its 1890 rules). Some of this tension was reflected at the February ASU conference. Fanning, a QSU official, attended the conference as an observer, and found one L. A. Garry in attendance, who rose to outline the unhappiness of 600 Queensland shearers with QSU working rules. Despite Fanning's protests Garry said that the QSU compelled members to deposit their tickets with the owner, preventing them from engaging another stand before the previous shed had cut out. The QSU executive also nominated approved members for stands, 'whether the employer or shearer liked it or not'. Garry said that the discontented shearers had met at Augathella in Queensland on 28 January and now sought 'relief' from the ASU. Fanning responded that Garry really only represented thirty or forty malcontents who wanted to avoid paying fines for breaking QSU rules. For its part the conference did not specifically support Garry's complaints, but on a motion moved by Spence diplomatically urged shearers to work under their existing rules. The motion asserted that the best interests of all shearers would be served by a QSU–ASU amalgamation, but Fanning departed the conference with a poor opinion of the ASU, and during 1890 successfully urged QSU members to oppose amalgamation.[29]

By February 1890 the ASU leader's had the right to feel that they done remarkably well in a relatively short time, and their optimism extended to generosity towards other workers in need. In 1889 ASU members subscribed a total of £828 7s 4d to assist striking London dock labourers. Australians of all classes, but mainly workers, subscribed the extraordinary sum of £30 000 to the strike fund. It was part of a response Robin Gollan has described as a flowering of 'successful unionism and social idealism'. The 'new unionism' movement of the late 1880s had produced mass unions in most major industries in both England and the Australian colonies, and for David Temple subscription to the dock strike fund represented an irresistible opportunity to confirm that 'successful unionism' had entrenched itself as a powerful force in the colonies, able to mobilise its members to defeat the old order of the bosses with their united action. As 'social idealism', subscription to the fund – which Temple described as that 'distant but pitiful appeal' – was also the high-water mark of the precocious Australian class-consciousness which had developed since 1886, an attempt to liberate working-class spirit from the culture of the penal colony, cringing in the shadow of the overseer. Temple relished the opportunity to imply that the colonial boy was as good, if not better, than those 'poor down-trodden toilers in the old country', and £30 000 was the tangible proof of a force to be reckoned with. 'Australia will be known and respected by hundreds of thousands of people in the Old Land who previously had scarcely heard of us.' He concluded: 'This is a great deal to be proud of, and if Australians were willing to do so much for their fellow workmen so many thousand miles away, how much more will be expected of them here?' Those expectations were about to be put to the test.[30]

CHAPTER 2

# Looking for Justice

### The Maritime and Pastoral Strikes, 1890–91

The working man must take his proper place in the nation.
*W. G. Spence*[1]

Should the Shearers' Union be affiliated with the Seamans' and
Lumpers' Union, and a dispute arose with the Sheepowners, and the
seamen and lumpers refused to ship non-union wool, such an
enormous pressure would be brought to bear upon the wool-growers
as would compel them to satisfy demands based upon justice and
equity. By such a combination the Unions would have it in their
power to insist upon British fair-play, which is all we ask.
*David Temple*[2]

The long and debilitating industrial war that raged between the bush
unions and the pastoralists throughout the 1890s began at Jondaryan
Station, in the prosperous Darling Downs of southern Queensland, in
May 1890. The station manager refused to use union labour in the
1890 shearing season. His decision was backed by the Darling Downs
Pastoralists Association, alarmed by the 1889 affiliation of the
Queensland bush unions – the QSU and the Queensland Labourers
Union (which organised shed-hands and other bushworkers) – to the
Australasian Labour Federation. The bush unions saw this step as necessary to fulfil the same strategy that Spence and Temple recognised as
crucial in the southern States: the extension of industrial resistance in
the woolsheds to the carriers, the wharf labourers, the seamen, to all who
could deny the pastoralists the opportunity to defeat the unions on
another battlefront. To this end the ASU had also affiliated with trades
and labour councils in Victoria and New South Wales. In response, the
pastoralists also began to organise on a colonial and intercolonial basis.[3]

The issue which united the pastoralists was freedom of contract, their
right to employ whoever they chose on conditions determined by them.
Jondaryan was a premature assertion of this privilege. Union labour
having been successfully banned on the station, the wool was transported
to the Brisbane wharves, where the ALF and its secretary Albert
Hinchcliffe were determined it would stay. Hinchcliffe and the ALF's
negotiating committee bluffed the owners of the ship *Jumna* and city-
based businesses that a general strike co-ordinated by the ALF would stop

Queensland commerce in its tracks, and, crucially, would spread to the
other States through the support of unions like the ASU; this was
seemingly confirmed by Spence's joining the ALF's negotiating team
midway through the dispute. With the maritime unions already united in
refusing to handle Jondaryan wool, all the pastoralists had to do to avoid
complete industrial chaos, Hinchcliffe assured a 12 May conference of
the shipowners and squatters, was to concede a closed shop for union
members. The employers caved in. The Darling Downs Pastoralists
Association conceded the closed shop to the QSU.[4]

The ASU expected that Hinchcliffe's bluff could be successfully repeated in the southern States. In May 1890 Temple reported that the
Creswick Branch had affiliated with the Melbourne Trades and Labour
Council, hoping that this would prevent non-union wool from leaving
Melbourne wharves. 'What is a difficult task to a single union becomes
light work to federated labour, and before such a mighty combination of
forces, the unreasonable opposition of our enemies must go down.' So
confident they seemed of the irresistible coalition they were building that
in June the ASU could view 'with satisfaction' the formation of the
Victorian Pastoralists Association. There was apparently 'ample evidence'
that these leading employers were on the brink of conceding the ASU's
reasonable claims. This blossoming affection soon froze. By July the
*Shearers' Record* was ruefully commenting: 'There has been all through a
strong effort made by a number of the most wealthy squatters to organise
their class for the express purpose of destroying the ASU'.[5]

The campaign of destroying the ASU's illusions began soon after
Jondaryan. On 28 June 1890 several major pastoralists from the Hunter
Valley and New England – centres of resistance to the ASU – placed an
advertisement in the *Maitland Mercury* and the *Australian Town and
Country Journal* seeking the names of shearers willing to shear for 20s per
100 under station rules. Simultaneously rumours spread of a campaign
by squatters to raise a £50 000 fighting fund to defeat the ASU in the 1890
shearing season. In July the *Shearers' Record* reported the collusion of
eastern New South Wales pastoralists and shipping firms to carry wool
with non-union men. The Australian Agricultural Company was said to
be a major organiser of this activity. 'It is pure self defence, then, that the
ASU decided upon blocking the wool shorn by non-unionists.' On 3 July
1890 the ASU's Executive Council unanimously resolved to urge other
unions to refuse to handle 'black' wool, and to 'draw a cordon of
unionism around Australia' to prevent its export. This famous appeal
declared that Australian unionism, which 'has not advanced as it might
have done', had now to embrace a federal spirit and rally behind the
struggles of individual unions. The manifesto grimly observed that if
the ASU was defeated unions in other areas would be attacked by

emboldened employers. Spence, Temple and Slattery travelled to Melbourne to lobby the Trades Hall Council, Wharf Labourers Society, Stevedores Union and the Seamen's Union to resist the carriage of non-union wool. The Amalgamated Miners Association was asked to stop the supply of coal.[6]

### The Maritime Strike

During July and August 1890, as the union prepared to thwart the pastoralists in the field, Spence was engaging in some carefully worded correspondence with the pastoralists' associations in an effort to negotiate a resolution to the 'freedom of contract' dispute. The fledgeling NSW Pastoralists Association, formed on 9 July 1890, wrote to Spence on 14 July advising of its formation and making it clear that any negotiations entered into with the ASU would only be conducted on terms suitable to the Association. Its pro-tem secretary, J. W. Ferguson, told Spence that New South Wales pastoralists were committed to agreements entered into with non-union shearers for the 1890 season. In any event pastoralists required 'the undisputed right to shear under their own agreement and rules'. But Ferguson reassured Spence that if only the ASU recognised the pastoralists' right to do as they pleased, the pastoralists would tolerate their non-union shearers joining the ASU after the 1890 season – provided that those shearers were not compelled to pay ASU fines. Ferguson added that the association would confer with the ASU, but only after the 1890 season. Spence responded that ASU members could not shear with non-unionists; the onus lay with the pastoralists. 'Your members have only to declare their intention of accepting the Union, and the shearers wishing to do so can withdraw from the position of considering themselves as bound to shear under station rules.'[7]

Far from the shearing sheds, tensions on the waterfront drew the simmering pastoral dispute into a wider conflict. In early August the Sydney wharf labourers announced that they would break an agreement with the Steamship Owners Association by refusing to handle non-union wool. The owners responded that they had 'no alternative' but to seek non-union labour to handle the wool. Simultaneously the Marine Officers Association, frustrated with the steamship owners' refusal to negotiate wage claims, announced its affiliation with the Melbourne Trades Hall Council. The Marine Officers saw affiliation as a means of uniting other unions behind their struggle. But the steamship owners were no more willing to accept this combination of workers than the pastoralists. They continued to reject negotiation and by 20 August marine officers, seamen and wharf labourers in Melbourne, Sydney, Adelaide and Brisbane had walked off the job. *The Town and Country*

*Journal* estimated that 5000 men were on strike in the biggest industrial dispute ever to occur in the colonies.[8]

The strike quickly exposed the weaknesses of the young union movement. In all major ports there were plenty of unemployed workers and other strike breakers willing to handle cargoes and man ships. In Brisbane loyal clerks worked the wharves and upright public servants paraded as special constables. In Sydney large numbers of special constables were sworn in to arrest 'disruptive' strikers. Angry unionists might try to confront pastoralists driving wagons laden with wool bales making for the wharves, but they could only stand helplessly by as the wool was loaded on to the ships and the ships sailed away. Against them were arrayed the scabs, the police, the military, Parliament, the conservative press and the combined employers. It was into this gathering disaster that the ASU stepped in late September.[9]

The ASU had been involved in the strike's organisation through Spence since 11 August, when Spence had organised the Labour Defence Committee in Sydney to, as he put it, 'control matters'. Spence was also a delegate to an intercolonial union conference attempting to co-ordinate union activities. As the strike floundered on the wharves pressure grew on the ASU to draw its vast army of organised workers into the dispute, to take direct action against the pastoralists. On 24 September the ASU members were instructed to strike, although the Scone district, Victoria and South Australia were exempted from the call-out (the ASU leaders simply believed that union loyalty in those areas was too brittle to be tested). Nevertheless Spence later wrote of the New South Wales members who obeyed the strike call, 'to the astonishment of the public, 16 500 men stopped work at once without a question as to the why and wherefore except that it was necessary in the interests of Unionism. It was one of the finest examples of loyalty the world has ever seen'.[10]

In the eyes of the pastoralists, arrogant union leaders had 'completely lost their heads'. The pastoralist leadership conferred with 'commercial, shipping and mining' interests in Sydney in September and resolved to defend freedom of contract. Many pastoralists agreed with the view of the pastoralists' union leadership that the walk-out by the shearers in mid-season was a 'wanton and discreditable breach of agreement'. In the Albury district, some shearers were unwilling to break their commitment to shear. At Grenfell, shearers refused to obey the strike-call. The *Town and Country Journal* claimed that 'all our country correspondents' spoke of shearers regretting the call-out. Many remained loyal to the union, but 'were entirely opposed to the extreme measures taken, and at least desired to finish the contracts on which they had entered'. As far as the colonial pastoralists' unions were concerned, the shearers' union agreement 'could never again be universally accepted'. They met in Sydney in late 1890 to frame their own agreement for 1891. The ASU had handed them an advantage to be played home the following year.[11]

In the bush many striking shearers suffered for the cause. Magistrates were now added to the ranks of employer allies, punishing the striking shearers with harsh fines under the Masters and Servants Act for breaching their shearing agreements. In the Deniliquin district of New South Wales sixty men were fined the heavy sum of £10 (at least two weeks' wages for a good shearer) each and their wages were forfeited (including, of course, sums for work completed before the strike). In the Wagga district alone there were 350 cases of wages forfeited, totalling £3500 in lost earnings. Spence calculated that in six districts across New South Wales there were 1377 cases involving £15 147 in lost wages. Prominent among the sufferers was that redoubtable organiser Arthur Rae. For his part in calling on shearers to strike – and breaking their station agreements – Rae was summonsed for sixty-one offences under the Masters and Servants Act. He was found guilty and fined £320. Unable to pay this exorbitant amount, he faced two and a half years in jail. He was released after a month's servitude following a public outcry.[12]

The Great Strike of 1890 ended in defeat for the unions on 5 November, but the ASU membership had already been back at work for a month, returning on 2 October. Spence, who had always been opposed to the ASU participating in the strike, had taken control of the shearers' section of the strike after the intercolonial conference had found that the ASU had 'bitten off more than it could chew'. Spence at once 'ordered the men back to work'. He said he did so only after being promised negotiations by the pastoralists, but the pastoralists subsequently reneged on this promise.[13]

Spence's objection to the strike had been based on his fears of a squatters' backlash through the police courts. He was undoubtedly also mindful of the backlash which would be generated against the union from shearers receiving fines and forfeiting wages. A shearer named White spoke for more than a few members when he described the strike as 'a big bungle' and completely counterproductive. 'It inflicted a great loss on the union shearing squatters, and has roused their hatred against us and the union.' For his own part, White said he had lost his pay of £11 10s, and was forced to pay a £10 fine for striking. He had no money to take back to his family in Melbourne and now the union wanted him to pay a £1 levy for 'striking marine officers'. Spence later claimed that the union made good all fines and forfeited members' wages at a cost of £9000 (a figure at variance with the previously cited £15 147, which was for fines and lost wages for just six districts of New South Wales), and used the levy to generate approximately £11 000 which was sent to assist those maritime workers 'locked out on the coast' ('locked out' meaning that they had lost their jobs to scabs). It should also be stressed that in many cases pastoralists withdrew summonses and threats to forfeit wages when the men returned on 2 October.[14]

Despite the strike, the ASU leadership claimed that the 1890 shearing season had been a success. In most areas the sheds were overwhelmingly union; in his 1891 report Temple claimed that 3100 sheds had worked union in ASU areas and only 281 had not. Many members obeyed the strike-call. The Bourke Branch reported that 'at no place where the news reached did carriers, labourers or shearers work', although the report confirmed the view expressed in the *Town and Country Journal* about the local owners: 'some of the squatters hardly gave the men time to put their coats on before they were in Bourke for summonses'. The Adelaide and Creswick branches, which did not participate in the strike, reported successful seasons, although Adelaide noted that some farmers and farm-hands had gone to work the wharves.[15]

Edmund Mitchell, secretary of the Pastoralists Union of Victoria, claimed that 'scores' of sheds had worked non-union in the 1890 season. In his rebuttal of ASU claims to a virtual monopoly of Victorian sheds, published in the Melbourne *Argus* in October, he said that Spence and Temple

> ingeniously contrive to make a great display in their list of Union sheds by counting as such stations where the men are union no doubt, but where the old station or verbal agreement is in force, the sheep owner refusing to recognise the Shearer's Union under any shape or form, and simply telling the men they can be union or non-union for all he cares. I am within the mark when I say that at least 50% of the sheds on Mr. Spence's loudly-heralded 'list of victories' in Victoria are claimed by him on this absurd and misleading basis.

Even if Mitchell's objectivity may be doubted, his letter probably reflects the subtleties of the situation: that some unionists might shear at non-union sheds, and that some unionists, for the sake of work, might agree to shear for a lower rate, or lesser conditions, than those acceptable to union rules.[16]

For Spence there were several lessons to be drawn from the strike: the unionisation of all workers and the enrolment of those united workers on to the colonial electoral rolls. At the same time that the ASU notified the strike's collapse it announced a drive to enrol ASU members to vote for working-class candidates in the 1892 Victorian elections. Spence said working men had to 'root out class representatives from Parliament'. But unions had also to redouble their efforts. Unions, Spence wrote, 'lacked that federation which not only ensures united action when necessary, but checks hasty action which often leads to serious trouble'. Past successes had made unions over-confident. They would continue to be outflanked so long as non-unionists could take their jobs during strikes.[17]

Spence subsequently told the Royal Commission into the 1890 strike that the ASU was willing to consider referring disputes to a board of conciliation. 'He was sure that at the present day the trades unionists preferred trusting to the justice of their case rather than to their strength.' He added that both unionists and squatters should retain the right to 'resist judgements of the board'. In the wake of the debilitating industrial difficulties the ASU previously faced each year with the pastoralists – and the even more determined resistance looming in the 1891 season – the intervention of an independent board no doubt held appeal. But the seductive protection of arbitration was more than a decade away.[18]

One way of overcoming poor unionisation and lack of unified support for campaigns was to unionise those who worked beside the shearers in the woolsheds and on the stations. In July 1890 the ASU's Executive Council decided to settle the 'rouseabout question' by forming a General Woolshed Labourers Union. In September the ASU published a prospectus for the GWLU, stating that GWLU working rules and fees would be decided at an inaugural GWLU conference in Adelaide in February 1891. The GWLU could also decide then if they favoured affiliation with the ASU. In November the union's name was shortened to the General Labourers Union, reflecting the ASU's desire to sign up as many bushworkers as possible – boundary riders, bullock drivers and general farm labourers, for example, as well as shed-hands.[19]

By the time of the February GLU conference – held immediately before the ASU's own gathering – the ASU's agents had enrolled 5150 members on behalf of the GLU. Spence, who was elected GLU secretary by the conference, felt that was only the beginning. His eyes must have sparkled at the prospect before him of a union which could dwarf even the ASU in membership. He told the delegates that there were an estimated 22 100 station-hands and 80 000 farm-hands in New South Wales alone. He believed it would be possible to enrol 60 000 GLU members in three years. For his part, Temple saw somewhat more subtle benefits for both unionism and the labourers themselves. The GLU would destroy scabbery, 'for it is from the hordes of the unorganised, helpless, unskilled labourers that the employers are enabled, in a way, to carry on during strikes'. The labourers were victims of their disorganisation. 'There are thousands of able-bodied men working 10 to 14 hours per day at an average wage of from 12s to 20s per week.' Labourers had to realise that in working more than eight hours a day, they were denying fellow labourers work. The 1890 strike had taught David Temple a hard lesson. Having been spurned in the appeal to 'British fair play' that Temple had said in 1889 was all he sought from the pastoralists, he told the GLU delegates in 1891 that the union of Capital with Labour 'is the union of the octopus with its prey'. The salvation of the labourers rested with the labourers themselves. Those who wished to be free must strike their own blows, and not beg 'leave to toil' from the capitalist.[20]

### 'A Species of Military Terrorism': Queensland, 1891

While the GLU and ASU officials pondered co-operation, to the north the practical obliteration of the Queensland bush unions was ruthlessly unfolding. In December 1890 meetings of pastoralists in Sydney and Melbourne decided to capitalise on the advantages gained in the maritime strike by drawing up a new shearing agreement, prefaced by their own definition of freedom of contract:

> That an employer is to be free to employ whom he pleases, and an employee is to be free to engage, or to refuse to engage, to work as he pleases.

This confrontation of union aims to shut non-unionists out of the pastoral industry was designated to begin in Queensland, when the shearing season commenced in January 1891. A correspondent from the *Town and Country Journal* reported in November that the Queensland Pastoral Employers Association held a private conference, which discussed 'the federation of capital'; the association was awaiting communications from Melbourne. One 'prominent pastoralist' told the correspondent that 'his union was formulating a plan which he believed would forever put an end to dissentions with the workers, that is with the bona fide labourer'.[21]

Shearers at the Logan Downs Station in Central Queensland were offered the pastoralists' 'agreement' on 6 January. They refused to accept it and established a strike camp at Clermont. The unionists said that the agreement made the squatter 'judge and jury' of every worker in their employ, with the power to legally steal the hard earnings of any man who broke the agreement. Wages could be forfeited without appeal to law; shed-hands and labourers must submit to 'wholesale' wage cuts of between 15 and 33 per cent; the principle of the eight-hour day was ignored; shearers were compelled to pay for combs and cutters. The bush unions were determined to fight for their rights, but there was a note of concern in the *Worker*'s call to battle. 'The defeat of the maritime bodies has for the time being robbed the bush workers of allies able to stand in the breach and retrieve on the coast any misfortunes which might happen in the interior.' For their part the pastoralists also claimed that an instinct for self-preservation drove them. Unions wanted to establish a 'ring' to dictate the terms of employment to the pastoralist.

They rejected the claim that there was any 'real' dispute over wages and conditions: 'The stand made on both sides is simply and solely freedom of contract'. They were making a stand, they said, for liberty.[22]

William Lane had a different idea of whose liberties were threatened. Lane, an intense and self-educated radical journalist who had become editor of the *Worker* in Brisbane when it was established as the journal of the ALF in March 1890, editorialised under the pseudonym 'John Miller'. For him, freedom of contract 'simply assists frenzied profit mongers in weeding out unionists'. In the hands of the squatter, freedom of contract was a perpetuation of wage slavery. 'No man is free excepting the man who has the power to work without asking leave of another; no man but the citizen of the community which insures work to its citizens as a right.' Lane believed the new unionism, the organisation of the mass of workers typified by the bush unions, would lead to a 'social revolution', although his definition of this was not as rabidly irresponsible as the pastoralists claimed. He wanted a 'peaceful, orderly, constitutional revolution of the intelligent majority'. The strike was *not* a fulfilment of these aims. Lane saw 'the fruits of a generation of patience' risked in the passionate anger released by the strike. He was right.[23]

Within a month the employer mobilisation against the strikers began in earnest. Strike-breakers were brought in to commence shearing operations; police and military forces moved into the district and the government issued a proclamation ordering the strikers to lay down their weapons and disperse from the camps which had spread across central Queensland. On 23 March the strike was officially extended across the colony with a call-out of the QSU, QLU and Central Queensland Carriers Union membership. The government responded by arresting the Barcaldine strike committee, charging them with conspiracy.[24]

The March 1891 edition of *Pastoralists' Review*, the new journal of the combined colonial pastoralist unions, praised the Queensland Government's 'yeoman service' in protecting the free labourers who were taking the strikers' jobs: 'So far so good'. The pastoralists' growing confidence in their ability to resist the strikers was reflected at a meeting of the Queensland Pastoralists Association in mid-March, which decided to advertise for shearers and rouseabouts to work under station agreement. The association said that owners wanted to employ Queenslanders, but if the unionists held out then more free labourers would be brought in. The advertisement added that those recruits would have to be given a guarantee of 'extended employment'. 'So that there will be no employment available for the unionists should they subsequently desire to go to work.'[25]

As the strike progressed the arrests continued, as did government over-reaction with a continued build-up of troops. As a response to 'outbreaks of lawlessness' – burning down of woolsheds, attempted derailment of trains – 1000 troops under the command of Colonel French, Commandant of the Queensland Defence Force, were concentrated around Barcaldine. Colonel French also brought with him cannons and gatling guns. Without a glimpse of irony the *Pastoralists' Review* claimed that this display of military might was necessary because of the criminal acts of conspiracy and intimidation perpetrated by the strikers![26]

The unionists treated these claims with contempt. Throughout the strike the *Worker* reported 'the latest horrors from our own horrified correspondent', 'Jerry Grumble'. Writing from Clermont, 'Grumble' offered such ironic observations as 'On Monday, 120 mounted unionists passed Wolfgang [Station] and gave the blacklegs a great fright. They flew to arms, and in the confusion they overturned an overgrown tar-boy, and would have committed great havoc among themselves generally if the bell had not rung for smoke-ho'. Another correspondent rejected this 'twaddle about lawlessness'. 'There is amazingly little disorder or drunkenness in towns filled with unionists and void of police and military ... most of the grass fires are from the squatters burning off themselves; and in three months only three sheds have been burnt, with no evidence that any one was started by unionists ... so hard up is the capitalistic press for sensations that it has had to descend to personal comment upon the appearance of the bushmen.'[27]

With the strikers half-starved and dispirited, with union strike funds exhausted and many key union personnel in jail (QSU secretary William Kewley was arrested in May at the QSU's Blackall office, and union money and papers confiscated), the strike was officially called off on 15 June. The ALF had written to the Premier, Sir Samuel Griffith, seeking a conference with employers, but Griffith felt that his efforts to bring the parties together 'have been altogether neutralised by the policy of violence and intimidation pursued by the unionists'. The pastoralists were hardly magnanimous in victory. 'Work will be given where it remains to the better sort of the strikers.' 'The poorest citizen', they trumpeted, 'can henceforth obtain work without asking the permission of a union'. This refrain would soon echo below the Queensland border.[28]

The strike leaders were punished by the state on behalf of the squatters. Fourteen unionists were charged with conspiracy under a statute which was no longer enforced in England. Two were found not guilty and the rest were sentenced by Judge Harding to three years' hard labour in Rockhampton Gaol.[29]

William Lane travelled to Rockhampton for the trial. He sardonically observed that the Crown did not require a prosecutor for Judge Harding assumed that role for himself. To his eyes, the roughly dressed prisoners,

Mythology in the making. Scenes from the Queensland Shearers' Strike, 1891. *Illustrated Australian News*, 1/4/1891, *National Library of Australia.*

with their broad, browned hands and spirit of bush freedom, seemed out of place in the cold precision of the courtroom.

> The judge and the police, the lawyers and the squatters, are all so sleek and so prim; the walls are so white and the ceiling so carefully painted and the whole surroundings so utterly philistine that the bushman has no more show here than has a butterfly in a sixpenny restaurant. So he looks rough and uncouth – and the squatter looks as though the building was made for him ... Now, do you see the connection and how it is that Judge Harding can be grossly prejudiced without being wilfully or consciously unfair?

With seamless ease the state had mobilised on behalf of property to defeat the strikers, untroubled by any doubt that justice might equally uphold the interests of workers and the prisoners in the dock, penned, as Lane described, in the cauldron of 'class-jealousy, class-hatred, class-prejudice'. For Lane, Australian society was on trial in Rockhampton, 'tried here as it is being tried wherever the opposing elements of society are brought face to face, wherever the upspringing of Humanity finds an advocate or meets a foe'.[30]

If the nature of society is vividly revealed in its crises, then the pro-squatter governments of colonial Australia in 1891 displayed a dis-position for a tenacious defence of property, a fear of disorder and dispossession from the fragile kingdoms the pastoralist had wrung from the land and the native population. Pastoralists were, in their own eyes, 'men who, by superior intelligence, enterprise, and business aptitude have built up for themselves pastoral properties, which really mean the savings of a lifetime'. They were 'the real builders of the national wealth and prosperity of these colonies'. To all these riches the unionists were apparently blind. The *Pastoralists' Review* concluded that men who preached doctrines of burning grass and giving up woolsheds to the flames would kill the goose that laid the golden eggs.[31]

But who fed from the fat of the land? Not the worker. The manifesto of the Barcaldine Strike Committee ruefully declared that 'disenfranchised though we are, we are the men whose labour mainly upholds Queens-land. It is our toil that brings rich dividends to banks and fat incomes to squatters, and profitable trade to great cities'. They were aware of the value of their labour, the dignity of their work; they had organised, and persisted in the face of tremendous hostility – which the *Shearers' Record* described as 'a species of military terrorism' – and now they chewed on the crust of their defeat.

> And now that we have made the land
>   A garden full of promise,
> Old greed must crook his dirty hand
>   And Come to take it from us.

In 1891 Henry Lawson sang the sea-change of the Australian working man's self-awareness. Industrial battle bred a legend of struggle and sacrifice. In 'Freedom on the Wallaby', first published in the *Brisbane Worker* in May 1891, a yearning for a measure of freedom was changed in the crucible of vindictive rejection to something new, unleashed in the language of revolution, but more expressive of a determination not to be denied acceptance by society as equal citizens.

> But Freedom's on the Wallaby,
>     She'll knock the tyrants silly,
> She's going to light another fire
>     And boil another billy.
> We'll make the tyrants feel the sting
>     Of those that they would throttle;
> They needn't say the fault is ours
>     If blood should stain the wattle.

But the strike and direct action had failed their ambitions. The bush workers would soon be encouraged to believe that through the colonial parliaments, a new path had opened up for workers to take their place in the nation.[32]

## 'Compromised Matters': the ASU in 1891

Following the defeat of the Queensland unions, the ASU faced the same choice between confrontation, or capitulation to the pastoralists' demand for freedom of contract. The ASU decided on a cautious strategy. At the February 1891 ASU conference Temple moved to pre-empt any hot-headed strike demand with a resolution declaring that a ballot must be held, and 'the full position explained', before any general strike could be called. Even in an 'extreme emergency' a two-thirds majority of Executive Council members had to approve the decision to call a general strike. In June, as the season was due to commence, the various branches requested members to postpone leaving for the shearing sheds until the last moment, and await ASU attempts to negotiate a settlement with the pastoralists' unions. On 6 July Temple wrote to the Federal Pastoralists Council seeking a conference. In the letter he recognised freedom of contract as a sticking point, claiming that the ASU couldn't understand what the pastoralists meant by the term. 'In the opinion of my Council there is no such thing as absolute freedom of any kind either in a civilised or uncivilised community.' For its part, the inaugural meeting of the Pastoralists' Federal Council in March 1891 had decided that freedom of contract would be the prerequisite of any conference with the unions.[33]

Some ASU officials could see the writing on the wall. James Toomey, the secretary of the ASU's Young Branch, wrote to Whiteley King, the secretary of the Pastoralists' Federal Council, on 13 July and asked: 'in the event of the ASU conceding freedom of contract, will the Pastoralists' Union guarantee to enter into an open conference, without the ASU formulating any specific questions previous to conference?' King insisted on written confirmation that a prerequisite of any conference would be a concession by the ASU of freedom of contract. On 22 July Toomey conceded: 'Members of this union may work with non-members this season'. Toomey seemed to speak on behalf of the entire union. This was confirmed on 24 July, when King offered a conference between the NSW Branch of the Pastoralists Union and the ASU's Young Branch, only to receive a request from Toomey for three executive officers of the union to negotiate an agreement for the entire colony. King left this to Toomey to arrange. On 30 July Temple recognised that the ASU would confer with the Pastoralists Union 'on lines agreed by Toomey'.[34]

Toomey was quickly made a scapegoat by Spence and Temple over the concession of freedom of contract. At the ASU's February 1892 conference Temple attacked Toomey for undermining his own attempts to tacitly ignore the freedom of contract issue in negotiations with the pastoralists. Spence repeated this line in his *History of the AWU* – and in doing so implicitly recognised that the ASU's position was untenable. Toomey, he said, 'precipitated matters, and we had no choice but to agree, as his action *showed our weakness* [our emphasis] and did not tally with the bold front put on by the General Secretary and myself'. Yet Spence had already told ASU members in September 1891 that after the defeat of the Queensland bush unions, 'how could New South Wales shearers expect to win? It was considered to be bad policy to advise a strike'. The ASU had decided to seek the best settlement possible, and were 'determined to secure a conference even if they compromised matters'. Hence Toomey's actions reflected the prevailing views of the ASU leadership.[35]

At the conference held between the pastoralists and the ASU in August 1891 the pastoralists made it clear that there would be no agreement without a concession of freedom of contract. One of them, Elder, said that 'we deem it of the very first importance that the definition of freedom of contract should go forth to the Australasian world'. It was their intention that it go forth as a preamble to any new agreement between them and the ASU. Spence argued that such a preamble would create 'ill feeling' among shearers. Nevertheless the pastoralists relentlessly pursued the ASU representatives, Abbott gleefully noting that the pastoralists had never before been able to obtain a definition of freedom of contract from a labour union. Toomey pleaded that 'the agreement as signed represents a definition'. Spence irritably interjected: 'you have had it all your own way'. Abbott gloated. 'We look upon that definition as our charter of freedom, and ... the charter of freedom of the men who have refused to put themselves under the tyranny of any union.' Eventually this form of words was contained in the preamble: 'That employers shall be free to employ and shearers shall be free to accept employment, whether belonging to shearers' or to other Unions, or not, without favour, molestation, or intimidation on either side'.[36]

Spence tried to make the best of the new agreement. The ASU published a full transcript of the conference, and in the introduction Spence referred to the benefits gained for ASU members. 'The recognition of the eight-hours principle, and the supply of one comb and four cutters for every 1500 sheep shorn, are important concessions in the working rules; whilst recognition of the ASU is important in principle.' He still insisted that recognising that ASU shearers could work with non-union shearers was somehow not the same as conceding the forbidden words 'freedom of contract'. 'We can honestly say that we have not accepted it. We were not even asked to accept it.' The pastoralists believed that they had obtained a full concession from the ASU, as the *Shearers' Record* ruefully complained in September 1891. The ASU had not seen the conference in terms of victors and vanquished; two honourable parties had reached an agreement. Now the pastoralists were crowing, yet they had conceded union pay rates and 'the whole of the unionists' demands'. It is true that the pastoralists had conceded many union terms on wages and conditions, particularly on the payment of the 20s per 100 shearing rate, although shearing rates had not been at issue during the Queensland strike. In Queensland and New South Wales, pastoralists generally conceded 20s per 100; this rate had even found general support from Victorian pastoralists. Queensland shed-hands and bushworkers suffered wage cuts as a result of the unsuccessful strike, but the pastoralists had also won a more decisive victory. Across the colonies, they could employ non-unionists as they pleased (although Abbott said that there would be no discrimination against unionists). The implications of that concession for the Australian bush unions would soon become clear.[37]

### The Infant Child of the Great Strike: Political Organisation, 1891

In November 1890 Spence declared that the failed maritime strike 'should stir every member of the ASU to a sense of the importance of securing a place on the electoral lists'. The *Shearers' Record* published manifestos exhorting shearers and labourers to register for the vote. The ASU's leaders welcomed the campaign by the colonial trades and labour councils to build a political organisation, a process which had been developing throughout the 1880s and was given renewed impetus by industrial defeat. In October 1890 the Sydney TLC adopted a political platform and in November resolved to establish Labor Electoral Leagues across the colony, to provide material support for working-class candidates for the NSW Parliament. At the February 1891 conference Temple moved that the ASU adopt a political platform and take steps to assist in mustering 'the labor vote'. Temple said the 'political leagues' would embrace all workers who favoured 'progressive democratic legislation', a condition he did not define. The platform was left to an ASU committee to determine.[38]

From the start the ASU's leaders wanted to build a broadly popular political party, rather than one based in some notion of 'class', a term they seemed to identify with their enemies. Working men, according to Spence, had to root out 'the class representatives from the colonial parliaments'. As well as wage earners, Temple sought the support of small employers and selectors, 'whose interests are more in touch with the workers than with the squatters and other big capitalists'. He suggested that opposition to monopolies, particularly land monopolies, would unite these disparate elements. He supported the single-tax solution advocated by English political thinker Henry George, who suggested with beguiling simplicity that a tax on land values could effectively replace all other taxation – music to the ears of the pastoralists' enemies, but nevertheless a solution at odds with the real complexities of colonial capitalism.[39]

The first test of this enthusiasm for politics came with the 1891 New South Wales elections. In 1891 thirty-five Labor candidates (most official, but some 'independent Labor') were elected to the 141-member NSW Parliament for various metropolitan and rural electorates. Among several ASU members who stood for election, Arthur Rae was successful in the seat of Wagga (although he was subsequently defeated in 1894). The Labour Electoral League now held the balance of power in Parliament, and had redefined the political identity of the colony. As the *Shearers' Record* proclaimed, 'the working classes have become a factor in the state'. What was it that had produced a result far beyond the expectations of Temple, and others in the colonial labour movement? An ASU rep from Deniliquin had few doubts. Local shearers, he said before the vote, were keenly following the forthcoming elections, and closely questioned their prospective candidates. Will he support one man one vote? Will he support measures to place employer and employee 'on a more substantial footing?' The rep concluded, 'the unusual interest manifested by the workers in politics is the infant child of the late great strike. Let us hope this child may grow to a powerful giant, who will make his strength felt across Australia'.[40]

The worst nightmares of the *Pastoralists' Review* were seemingly ful-filled. From the first edition in March 1891 the *Review* accused Australian labour leaders of plotting to capture Parliament. United pastoralists might succeed in defeating the bush unions, but it would be no easy task to 'check the advance of socialism through legislative channels'. The 'forces of order' must organise 'a powerful country party' to defeat the union leaders' plans to overthrow the 'landmarks' of society and rob property owners. In June, the *Review*'s celebration of their victory over the Queensland strikers was again tempered by the belief that the defeat of the new unionism in open conflict would be revenged at the polls by socialism. But the *Review* was confident that this revenge 'can be averted by timely organisation on the part of the steadier classes'.[41]

Arthur Rae and Walter Head, the leaders of the ASU's Wagga Branch, were willing to fulfil the prophecy of the *Pastoralists' Review*. In October 1891, in an editorial in the first edition of the *Hummer*, the Wagga Branch's newspaper, they declared that 'we have taken the advice given us during the Big Strike by the metropolitan papers, namely: to act constitutionally by redressing our wrongs at the ballot box. We haven't done half enough in that line yet, though'. The *Hummer* was expressive of a new self-confidence among many workers, a realisation of what they were worth – and their determination to share society's prosperity. 'We start out with the assertion that every man, or woman either, is entitled to the whole produce of his or her labour; and from a literary point of view we are prepared to sweep the floor with anyone who denies it.' In late 1891 the labour movement seemed poised to claim through Parliament a just recognition of that assertion. But their political success would be undermined by the legacy of the industrial defeats of 1890 and 1891, and the economic depression which in late 1891 was beginning to grip colonial Australia.[42]

# CHAPTER 3

# The Hustle for Jobs

*Economic Crisis and the 1894 Pastoral Strikes, 1892–94*

By 1892 the ASU's leaders had experienced six years of struggle to establish the union as the united representative of southern Australia's shearers, and to link the whole pastoral workforce to the increasingly successful shearers' union. Yet the bush unions in Queensland resisted the ASU's urgings to amalgamate, and organising the General Labourers Union, and merging it with the ASU, had also proved more complex than Spence and Temple might have imagined in the first flush of enthusiasm. With each shearing season opposition to the ASU had grown more determined and sophisticated. Throughout the crises of 1890 and 1891 the ASU leadership had remained remarkably united despite the pressures on them. But by the union's sixth conference in Melbourne in February 1892 it was clear that unity was breaking down. There were rivalries between individuals and between the branches, and doubts about the direction of the union. An organisation which now claimed 20 000 members, with eleven branches across New South Wales, Victoria and South Australia, and which had endured repeated challenges to both its ambitions and its very existence, was beginning to show the strain.

In their opening speeches to the conference both Spence and Temple acknowledged the tensions created by the acceptance of freedom of contract. Spence recognised that the members 'had to work under new conditions – conditions which are undoubtedly trying to members'. He also noted that several officials, including Temple, had been challenged in recent elections, although all had been overwhelmingly re-elected.

Temple said that while 1891 had been a 'critical and trying time for all of us', the members had generally adopted the new agreement.[1]

It was the assertiveness of the Wagga Branch which drew resentments and rivalries to the surface. James McInerney, the Goulburn Branch secretary and no friend of the neighbouring Wagga leadership, asked Wagga secretary Walter Head who had authorised the branch to spend money on a newspaper, the *Hummer*, established by the Wagga Branch in October 1891 and which provided robust and unwelcome competition to the *Shearers' Record*, the privately run journal which the ASU had adopted as its official mouthpiece. Head and Rae claimed that the Branch had authority under its general control of its own funds, but most of the other delegates were unconvinced. Temple said that branches did not have full control of their funds, and that 'all over working expenses had to be sent to the general fund'. J. A. Cook from Adelaide moved that the Wagga leaders should refund the ASU the money expended on the *Hummer*. There was a bitter exchange between Rae and Alexander Poynton from Port Augusta. Rae said the conference could carry the motion fifty times – he didn't care; Poynton retorted: 'You, in your greatness consider that any man whose name contains more than three letters knows nothing'. Poynton added that 'if the Wagga Branch is right there is no limit to the expenditure a branch might enter upon'.[2]

The *Hummer* argument rages for several pages of the conference report, interspersed by several other acrimonious debates. Bourke Branch, which had been the only other branch to support Wagga in the *Hummer* debate, moved that no branch secretary should hold the position of general secretary. Temple took this as a direct attack on himself, as he was also Creswick Branch secretary. Rae supported the Bourke motion, which was lost, although as with many debates at the 1892 conference, not before a division had been called. Bourke Branch then heaped more fuel on the fire with a resolution that no branch secretary should be an executive councillor or delegate to conference. Bourke branch delegate Donald Macdonell argued that a branch secretary should devote his whole attention to the duties of his office. Arthur Rae was blunt. 'Secretaries attending conference in a body legislated unconsciously to their own advantage.' Poynton again leapt to the defence: 'either secretaries were to be trusted or they were not'. The minutes record that Rae was repeatedly called to order for using 'personal remarks'. Eventually another division saw the motion overwhelmingly defeated.[3]

Debate on the *Hummer* expenditure resumed on the sixth day of the conference, and almost led to an outright split. Delegate Williams from Scone moved, after much heated debate and challenges to the chairman (who in this case was Charles Poynton, Spence having left to attend the

Amalgamated Miners Association conference in Victoria) that no branch
funds be expended for either parliamentary or journalistic purposes
without consent of two-thirds of branch members; and the sum
expended was not to exceed 1s per financial member per annum. When
this was carried 16:6 Macdonell promptly moved that the names of the
dissenters be recorded to recognise their protest that Williams's motion
was 'unconstitutional'. After this was carried Rae read a long statement
on behalf of both Bourke and Wagga branches, declaring that they were
withdrawing from the conference until the branches' rights were recognised (Bourke had also been swept into the criticism of unauthorised
expenditure over money used in parliamentary elections). The implications of this soon became apparent when both branches' representatives
remained at the conference, but refused to vote. Cook remarked: 'This
looks as if the Wagga and Bourke representatives want to have a burst. It
is not the first time they have threatened'. Much abuse was directed at
the dissidents, particularly Rae, and the conference degenerated completely. A motion criticising Wagga and Bourke branches for unauthorised expenditure was rescinded; separate motions criticising them were
successful, despite a suggestion from Williams, after the rescission
motion had been passed, that the matter be left to rest. In exasperation,
chairman Poynton remarked at one stage, 'Things have greatly changed
since the President left'. McInerney wondered what the ASU's enemies
would make of it all. Hostilities only ceased with the adjournment at
5.45 p.m. The final entry for that debilitating day reads: 'Mr Burgess
said a city photographer desired to take the members, but delegates
did not seem to be in a humor to entertain the matter'. And so they
adjourned.[4]

Tension within the ASU was not confined to the leadership. Some
members were unhappy with the 1891 agreement with the pastoralists.
Members at Broken Hill 'bitterly protested against the terms of the
settlement'. The ASU's Broken Hill office, which was only opened in
early 1892, had to be almost immediately closed again because of the
support of its official, H. McDonald, for the settlement with the owners.
Other shearers were opposed to the ASU–GLU amalgamation. The 1892
ASU conference had established a committee to prepare 'a simple and
practicable scheme' for an amalgamation to create the Australian
Workers Union, a union broad enough, in Spence's description, 'to
embrace all labour, close enough to bind the whole continent in one,
and free enough to leave to the various sections full and complete liberty
in the control of their own local affairs'. In May 1892 the *Shearers' Record*
reported that ASU members in Creswick disapproved of the ASU–GLU
amalgamation. 'It is certain that they will unanimously vote against it.' In
November, after the proposal had been defeated (much to the surprise

and disappointment of the ASU leaders), the Record said Creswick ASU and GLU members had voted No because they didn't understand the question. The shearers had also feared that they might be drawn into the labourers' strikes.[5]

An amalgamation of the Queensland shearers' and labourers' unions was completed in October 1892. In contrast to the more centralised structure of the ASU, the new Amalgamated Workers Union of Queensland was a loose federation of three district branches, Charleville, Longreach and Hughenden, designed to retain 'local self government'. Each district had its own working rules and elected its own officers. There would be no general officers of the AWUQ; nor would any general funds be held by the union at large. The AWUQ's annual conference would only be consultative: all resolutions affecting the working of the union would be referred to plebiscites of members.[6]

### The Economic Crisis

Whereas industrial conflict over disputed pay rates set the tone for the 1890 and 1891 shearing seasons, shearing in 1892 was defined by elemental economic forces. Since 1890 a financial crisis had been developing in London. The ready flow of English credit which had subsidised the rapid economic growth of the colonies in the 1880s now shrivelled, and with it the pretensions of the local capitalists. Unemployment had been rising in the Australian cities during 1891, and in 1892 the plaintive presence of the unemployed began to be felt in force on the wallaby, as they tramped across the colonies in search of work.[7]

They fled the cities to the sound of crashing banks and finance houses. In July 1892, just as the shearing season was getting under way in the southern colonies, the provisional liquidator of Melbourne's Mercantile Bank acidly observed that the local managers seemed to regard the bank's London directors as 'a conduit pipe, converging the money of English depositors'. He was at a loss to explain how the local managers had spent the bank's money. In the same month the Victoria Mutual Building and Investment Society stopped payment. The directors were unable to pay a dividend; depositors had made a run on funds, despite desperate pleas from the directors that the society had been economically run, and had never 'trafficked in real estate'. But in Victoria, and in the other colonies where similar tales of collapse and fraud were revealed, it was clear that confidence had vanished down the same dry hole as British credit.[8]

For every stand there seemed a hundred willing shearers, and another growing army grasped after any station work going. In the sheds around Albury and Hay hundreds of men were unsuccessful in obtaining work.

A correspondent for the *Town and Country Journal* recorded, 'it is painful to see so many men as have been in search of work this season walking about idle'. Around Condobolin there were many more shearers and labourers than were needed. Their numbers had been swelled by hopefuls from Sydney and Melbourne. Even the weather tormented the unlucky: drought gripped western New South Wales. Around Bourke, Balranald and Louth, 'many pastoralists will not be able to shear until very late, if at all'. The western paddocks were bare of grass. 'Most stations can't shear until grass grows grows sufficiently to enable the sheep to be brought in from the back of the runs.' For some, the struggle proved too much. In September a boundary rider on the 'arid and waterless plains' west of Wilcannia found the body of a shearer named Johnston. He had been dead six months. In a letter to his wife found on his clothing he explained that he had been walking from a station 'many miles distant', on his way to Broken Hill, thence Adelaide, in the search for work. He had evidently wandered from the track and died of thirst. His remains, including boots and clothing, weighed just 30 pounds. The note to his wife in Melbourne explained that on his return he 'intended to reform', and not keep late hours any more.[9]

From Queensland a Barcaldine correspondent offered this description of shearing in 1892:

> From stations where shearing is commencing the same information comes that the unemployed are crowding about hoping to get work, and those who cannot be taken on go away bitterly disappointed at their non-success. Those who are fortunate enough to be engaged buckle to work like tigers. They are scarcely settled on the job ere the inevitable delegate comes round with his little book of tickets for levy and subscription, and carries away with him a decent cheque for the union. As a rule, both old unionists and free labourers pay the subscription, the latter because it is the easiest way to avoid unpleasantness while in the company of their fellow workmen.[10]

In this unflattering description an enduring dilemma of unionism is succinctly expressed. Faced with the realities of industrial defeat in 1890 and 1891, and now a gathering economic crisis, the ASU was reduced to urging caution on its harried members, as they also continued to urge their support, financial and moral, for a cause struggling in the face of enervating resistance. Even the combative Wagga Branch advised labourers that it would be futile to pursue wage increases in 1892. The cities and towns were crowded with unemployed, willing to take work for whatever wage offered. Labourers should seek the best wages possible without risking a strike. They had to persuade the non-unionist to close ranks with them.[11]

The ASU was also reduced to protest at the apparent success of the pastoralists' exploitation of office engagement. Under this system, the colonial Pastoralists' Union offices secured sheds for shearers provided they forwarded a £1 deposit. The PUNSW also sought to obtain work for unemployed workers registered with the NSW Government's labour bureau. Despite PU assurances that they did not discriminate between unionists and non-unionists, the ASU remained deeply hostile to pastoralist control of the labour market (although in the interests of income the Wagga Branch did tolerate PU advertisements for office engagement in several editions of the *Hummer*). One ASU supporter from Bourke wrote that the pastoralists were using this system to create a boycott of 'western bushmen'. 'Shearers who have been living and working for years in the district are walking the country in a fruitless search for work, their places filled with men from New Zealand, Victoria and distant parts of the colony.' Whiteley King, the secretary of the PUNSW, dismissed the ASU's criticisms. He claimed that the PU had always preferred to engage local men, unionists or non-unionists. He said figures from the Labor Bureau showed that of 5000 shearers engaged, only 600 came from other colonies, and only 89 from New Zealand. He also said that Temple had agreed to office engagement as part of the 1891 agreement, a claim hotly denied by the ASU secretary. King smugly concluded, 'the secretaries and agents of the ASU are completely staggered at the success which has attended the operations of the Pastoralists' Union'. The best the ASU could manage in 1892 was the provision for discounted rail passes for Victorian members travelling from Melbourne to the shearing sheds – an advantage quickly spread to non-unionists by the Victorian rail commissioners after the angry intervention of the Victorian PU.[12]

Both the ASU and the QSU continued to look to the colonial parliaments to provide solutions for their industrial troubles. In 1892 the ASU hoped the imminent Victorian parliamentary elections would render strikes 'a thing of the past'. The union wanted the establishment of a Department of Labour, and arbitration boards 'where all disputes between employers and employees could be referred to for settlement'. In December 1891 the QSU's annual general meeting declared, in successive resolutions, that compulsory arbitration should be enacted by Parliament to prevent strikes and lock-outs, and that the Queensland Parliament should support one vote one value, 'so that the disenfranchised population may help to make the laws by which they are governed'.[13]

In New South Wales, at least, where labor representatives had been elected in mid-1891, some headway seemed to be made. In July 1892 the Dibbs Government legislated to create conciliation and arbitration boards. Unions and employers would have representatives on eight boards covering various industries – except the pastoral industry,

conspicuous by its absence. Whereas Premier George Gibbs told Parliament that 'the trades unions in the colonies embraced the most
intelligent artisans, and it was a great mistake on the part of capitalists to
distrust them', the pastoralists described unionism as 'a despotism of the
most shameful order'. Each edition of the *Pastoralists' Review* worked
obsessively to expose ASU leaders as scheming revolutionaries, stealing
and squandering their members' money. 'Money hunting is ever the
foremost principle with the new unionism', the *Review* declared, hoping
that a relentless exposure of these 'facts' would hasten the disintegration
of the meddlesome bush unions.[14]

### Masters and Mates: the Clash of Values

Beneath the industrial struggle which divided the pastoralists and the
AWU lurked a deeper division between the ideals of individual action
and self-improvement on one hand, and the bonds of brotherhood and
mateship on the other, bonds which nurtured unionism and which
offended the pastoralists' sense of manly independence: as they saw it,
the unionist simply did not understand his proper place in the social
structure. When James Toomey suggested that unions should support
commercial co-operative ventures, the *Review* scoffed, 'union leaders are
absolutely incompetent to conduct a co-operative business, or else they
would long ago have been employers themselves'. This, the *Review* said,
was the bedrock of the pastoralists' rejection of arbitration: 'The new
unionism is fighting against human nature'. As Western District squatter
Thomas Dowling had observed in 1888, some were born to lead, others
to follow. A man who had struggled to place his stamp on the blind
hostile bush, who had withstood the vagaries of weather and trade, could
manage his business better than other people could manage it for him.
New South Wales pastoralists refused even to attend a lecture for business
leaders in Sydney by Dr Garran, who had been appointed by the Dibbs
Government to head the new Council of Conciliation and Arbitration.
The *Review* was certain that Garran was able and well-meaning, but the
struggle between unions and employers into which he would intervene
was 'one of whether the employer shall be allowed to manage his own
business'. They felt no compulsion to surrender their prerogative.[15]

   For William Lane, the dogged triumphs and fears of the individual in
business held no appeal. Socialism was being mates. 'The new unionism
is as wide as the community and is avowedly based upon the grand ideal
that we are all mates if we are workers – no matter what trade or occupation.' Lane did not believe, however, that state socialism could ultimately
be legislated. Lane favoured what he described as an 'anarchistic
evolution of voluntary co-operation'.

A champion of mateship. William Lane, the inaugural editor of the Brisbane *Worker*. *AWU Collection.*

Legislation will bring about some form or other of state control of industry which will remove the pressure that now makes us hustle one another for a job; and that as we become accustomed to being mates, and our children are born and bred into the same atmosphere, all need for legislation or for state force of any kind will pass away, and we shall evolve a truly socialistic method of co-operation which we shall uphold without law because we shall all love being mates and all hate the very notion of competing with each other as we do now.

Lane wanted to elevate mateship into something grander than the simple loyalty of one bushworker for another, and building a life without law became Lane's driving imperative. But when in early 1893 he sailed with his New Australia movement to build a co-operative socialist settlement

in Paraguay he made such laws to regulate human behaviour that his
supporters revolted. Lane turned his back on Australia, he said, because
he could see no future for building socialism in a land of repres-
sive capitalism, tormented by an economic crisis. Australian workers
apparently had to flee their adopted land to be reborn as true mates.
Some of the mates he left behind, including William Spence and Arthur
Rae, stood in a steam launch and watched as the *Royal Tar* slipped
through Sydney Heads on 16 July 1893, bearing 220 nascent socialists
towards their new home. Spence and the members of the ASU were left
to face unemployment and renewed confrontation with the squatter.[16]

Not everyone was a mate. William Lane's mateship was the cocoon of
a closed Anglo-Celtic world, 'the sentimental syrup of the man's world',
as Manning Clark observed, 'the mythology of a tribe who loved men of
their own kind, while entertaining the most savage hatreds against all
strangers, all newcomers, all coloured peoples, Aborigines, natives of the
islands of the Pacific, Englishmen, Jews – members of any group which
was deemed to constitute a threat to their way of life'. Many newspapers
and union journals reflected an obsession with a fear of Asian labour,
summoned by the agents of business, stealing the jobs of Australian
workers – the great and imminent conspiracy of race and capital, to be
unleashed at any time on honest Australian workers. Few union leaders
seemed to have paused to reflect that the local capitalists were probably
no less racist than their employees. Time and again the minutes of
the QSU reiterate their hostility to what they called 'Chinese' labour,
although all non-European – or indeed non-Anglo-Celtic – peoples were
reviled. The 1891 annual general meeting insisted that no member work
with 'Chinese' labour in any capacity; in fact they were requested not to
deal with 'Chinese' at all and to 'patronise white gardeners'. Perceived
softness over the race issue contributed to QSU wariness of affiliation
with the ASU, but the ASU claimed to be every bit as hostile to the
Chinese as their Queensland compatriots. A *Hummer* correspondent
claimed that Afghan camel drivers in the Bourke district stole the jobs of
white carriers and did nothing to support the town: 'It is about time the
afghan, the camel, and the chow were given notice to quit'.[17]

The ASU's 1890 rules banned 'Chinese and South Sea Islanders', and
the AWU's first rules in 1894 extended the ban to 'Kanakas, Japanese and
Afghans'. During the 1890s the ASU/AWU were fervent champions of a
restrictive immigration policy, using their considerable influence in the
Labor Party to ensure that a commitment to a 'White Australia' was a
prominent plank in the party's platform. Aborigines, recognised as
'natives of the colonies', were admitted to membership on payment of a
slightly discounted fee (nor were they required to pay the entrance fee)
following a decision of the union's 1891 conference. The AWU believed

Aborigines were distinguished from other non-white races by their prior settlement of the land. While figures are not available, it is unlikely that many Aboriginal bushworkers were qualified as shearers, although a greater number presumably worked as shed and station-hands. One Aboriginal shearer, William Ferguson, rose through the ranks to serve for several years in the late 1890s as an AWU organiser in the Riverina. Ferguson followed a well-trodden AWU path to activism in the affairs of the Labor Party, but his pioneering efforts in the 1930s and 1940s to win citizens' rights for indigenous people led not to parliamentary privileges but to frustration and disillusionment.[18]

Even New Zealand shearers did not escape criticism as poachers of ASU and QSU members' jobs, although racist slurs were not thrown across the Tasman. In February 1892 Temple said that there was an urgent need to organise New Zealand shearers. 'In connection with the recent struggle in Queensland, a great part of the so-called free labor employed was procured in New Zealand, and while the shearing labor remains unorganised, it is a standing menace to the ASU.' As noted earlier, PUNSW secretary Whiteley King rejected claims that the pastoralists were trying to shut unionists out of shearing jobs by importing labour from New Zealand or other colonies. Nevertheless, on a trip to New Zealand in late 1891 Whiteley King told a reporter that as far as New Zealand shearers were concerned, 'on all sides the New South Wales squatters are full of their praises, and many of them have agreed to take full boards of New Zealanders next season'. He effusively praised New Zealand shearers as 'thrifty and industrious', and claimed that 'I believe it is quite true that one party of seventy shearers brought back £6000 between them from Queensland'.[19]

His remarks had the desired effect. On one hand, he encouraged New Zealand shearers to believe that for them Australian sheep were fleeced with gold. He also successfully antagonised New Zealand opinion against the Australian unionists, with the *New Zealand Times* editorialising that the Australian unions resorted to 'lynching, lies and legislation' to stop New Zealand shearers make a fair wage in Australia. The New South Wales Labor parliamentarians tried to pass an aliens bill, aimed at buttressing Labor's hope of maintaining a White Australia, but also preventing New Zealand shearers from working in Australia. In 1893 the NSW Parliament passed the Chinese Restriction Act, and three years later extended its terms to cover all Asians. New Zealanders, however, were still tolerated. The editorial concluded, that 'solidarity between the labour parties of New Zealand and Australia is undesirable, and, from the superiority of New Zealanders, impossible'. But the NZ Amalgamated Shearers and Labourers Union made efforts during the 1890s to prevent New Zealand 'blacklegs' from crossing the Tasman, even to the extent of sending union delegates on ships carrying the non-unionists, urging them to join the ASU.[20]

Unemployment and the financial situation both worsened in 1893. In May the imminent shearing season was preceded by a five-day bank holiday in Victoria, a desperate measure prompted by continued depositors' runs on failing Victorian banks. In April the England, Scotland and Australian Chartered Bank suspended payment after £2 million had been withdrawn – £200 000 in the last few days before suspension. The Savings Bank of NSW, described as 'one of the safest banks in the world', was also rushed by depositors in April: that it should be rushed 'shows the extent to which people lose their heads in a financial crisis'. They also lost their jobs. The NSW Labour Bureau reported that in March 1893 the number of men seeking work through the bureau's Sydney office ranged from 400 to 600 a day.[21]

How this severe unemployment constrained the industrial militancy of shearers and shed-hands can be seen at Burrawong Station in New South Wales in 1893. When the roll was called for the start of work the shed-hands struck for weekly wages, refusing to work under daily rates. However a *Pastoralists' Review* correspondent, who witnessed this defiance, said that 500–600 job seekers had also turned up for the roll-call, and by next morning only about forty of the shed-hands held out for weekly wages. 'Fresh men were sent for to take their places.' To counter this, the shearers at the station offered to keep the strikers in rations, and as the *Review* correspondent observed, 'this generous offer really ended in their feeding the whole crowd assembled, in addition to the numbers who daily rolled up on hearing the glad tidings, that a strike was on, and a camp to be formed'. He also noted that the shearers 'manfully stood this abuse of their generosity for three days', but then sent the police in to shift the crowd, including, presumably, the strikers. As our witness wryly concluded, the shearers' 'professions about the dignity of unionism and the brotherhood of labour were taken too literally'. But also bearing down on the shearers was the spectre of impoverishment, and the grim prospects of finding another stand. When Burrawong cut out they too would be part of the desperate crowd.[22]

This *Review* correspondent had an idyllic season, observing at leisure the workings of the mighty Burrawong Station, 'the best wool shed in Australia and, that means, probably the world'. Up to 6000 sheep could be shorn in a day. The shed was nearly 300 feet long, fitted with eighty-eight Burgon & Ball shearing machines. There were two shearing floors at either end of the building; the wool room ran down the centre, through which also ran a tramway, which picked up the fleeces and carried them to the sorting tables. Two steam presses baled the fleece. Yet despite the perfection of the shed, and that 'nothing is spared to

Shearing at Burrawong Station, *c.* 1895. *National Library of Australia.*

make shearing there a success for both employers and men', labour
troubles, such as the shedhands' abortive strike, still occurred. Such
ingratitude was rarely seen in the 'late' sheds in the back country. He
travelled in the same season to the hills and tablelands of central New
South Wales, where the men he saw clamouring for their rights at the
bigger sheds on the plains apparently dropped such militancy as they
worked these last sheds. 'It doesn't do in the hills. In these late sheds
everyone has something more serious to think of, viz., how to keep a
stand when you have it.' Here shearing seemed ageless, plied in the same
fashion since sheep were first sent to feed from the pastures culled from
the forest and the indigenous people expelled. Here architecture was
'good old early colonial style' slabs and shingle; there was one open-air
catching pen for fifteen shearers, and no wool press. The shed was an
empty shell in which shearers crowded and went to work with blades. In
the early 1890s blade shearing still competed strongly with machine
shearing, even at some of the biggest stations. Of twenty-eight large
stations surveyed in August 1892 by the *Pastoralists' Review*, sixteen shore

with blades and twelve had machines. Kilfera Station shore between 100 000 and 120 000 sheep during the season with sixty blade shearers.[23]

### Defying the Times: the Birth of the Australian Workers Union

In 1894 Spence and the ASU leadership trod persistently towards amalgamation at the February 1894 conferences of both unions, despite the grim economic circumstances and the fact that Temple's secretary's report for 1893 acknowledged that an amalgamation vote taken during the 1893 season – the second occasion upon which members had been asked to vote – had produced a result even less favourable than that of the 1892 ballot. Nevertheless he concluded that 'there seems to be an increasing feeling of regret that the proposal has been defeated'. Perhaps it was this optimistic assessment which led New South Wales delegate Donald Macdonell to propose to the conference 'that in view of an aggregate number of votes in NSW having been cast in favor of amalgamation, NSW be permitted to carry it into effect'. In Macdonell's view, 'the laborers had been loyal to the shearers in the past, and it was now the turn of the shearers to come out of their conservatism and take a decided step toward the unification of Labor'. Several delegates, however, clung to their conservative instincts. Some, like Toomey, feared the effects of the united union attempting to enforce high wage rates 'in the face of the enormous crowds of unemployed which now swarmed right through the colonies'. Williams doubted that the conference had the authority to impose amalgamation for New South Wales alone, when the required two-thirds majority of both unions had not decided in favour of merging. But the urge to build a bigger union had grown too strong to be denied. Macdonell's motion was passed 15:8, well short of the unanimity which Spence hoped would greet the creation of the Australian Workers Union. The prosperity which had fed enthusiastic unionisation in 1886 had been subdued by the debilitating economics of the 1890s. The GLU's 1894 conference followed hard on the heels of the ASU conference, and with its proceedings dominated by ASU officials and amalgamation advocates (Rae was GLU president and Spence was secretary) the GLU quickly voted in favour of amalgamation with the ASU.[24]

There were other important changes at the 1894 ASU conference, changes which revealed the growing sophistication of the emerging AWU and a shift in power within the union's leadership. By then the union had dispensed with the services of the privately run *Shearers' Record*, and had supported instead the Sydney-based *Worker*, an offshoot of the Brisbane *Worker*, edited by William Lane before his departure for Paraguay. The Sydney *Worker* absorbed the Wagga Branch's *Hummer* in September 1892.

A weekly publication funded and controlled by the AWU, the Sydney *Worker* was seen as a step towards the creation of a national daily labour newspaper. Spence also believed that the new *Worker* was a powerful educative tool in the hands of the union, enabling members better to grasp 'social and political questions'. But not everyone was impressed by its messages. When the conference convened for the fourth day secretary David Temple and Creswick Branch delegate Lawless cast some 'insinuations' on the integrity of the *Worker*'s reporter at the conference, apparently complaining about his reporting of conference events (although the minutes do not record the nature of the alleged grievance). The conference resolved to express its confidence in the *Worker* reporter's integrity; Temple evidently took this to indicate that this meant that the delegates were now casting insinuations upon his honesty. He resigned as secretary and immediately left the conference. Spence was elected to act in his place.[25]

Temple had been drifting away from the other officials for some time. Historian John Merritt observes that Temple's secretaryship lacked 'enthusiasm and vigour' by 1894, and he was particularly alienated from the New South Wales delegates, who 'believed the Victorian branches should have done more to curb the PUV's recruiting of "free labourers" and to promote a Victorian labor party. Most of them thought that the union's headquarters should be in their colony'. Clyde Cameron is less sympathetic to the New South Wales officials, whom he sees as undermining Temple over a long period. Cameron presents Spence and Macdonell as manoeuvring to oust Temple before 1894, via a resolution at the 1893 ASU conference preventing branch secretaries from holding the office of general secretary. Indeed Temple had indicated on the first day of the 1894 conference that he was now merely acting as pro-tem general secretary, following the 1893 resolution. But he had resigned and walked out before the conference had made a more definite arrangement about the general secretary's position, and his own temporary status. Cameron adds that Spence's and Macdonell's hostility grew from overweening personal ambition and because of their insistence on amalgamation of the ASU and GLU.[26]

There is little doubt that Donald Macdonell was impatient for action at the 1894 conference, action which perhaps would serve both his own and his members' interests. Trade union leadership tends to attract ambitious, self-assured individuals. Such a man was Donald Macdonell. A physically imposing shearer and a founding member of the ASU, the 31-year-old Macdonell was elected secretary of the ASU's Bourke Branch in 1893. He had won the respect of local members through his spirited defence of shearers, in the courtroom and in the field, in the 1891 strike. By 1894 he was making his presence felt in the forums of the ASU. At the

1894 conference Macdonell was prominent in the major debates. It was Macdonell who urged the relocation of the ASU general office to Sydney (the motion was narrowly defeated), and who led the debate on NSW ASU–GLU amalgamation. It was also Macdonell who increased the temperature of the debate over the *Worker*'s coverage of the conference by suggesting that Temple and Lawless should withdraw their insinuations about the reporter and apologise to him. Once the conference expressed its confidence in the reporter, Macdonell's 'suggestion' must have hung over Temple as an added humiliation, a spotlight on his isolation. He chose to leave. Macdonell emerged as a voice of the future, having defeated the old champion. When Spence was unanimously chosen as the new secretary, there were tributes and light-hearted regrets at his retirement from his 'perpetual presidency'. There were no tributes for David Temple. From the moment he walked out he was relegated to an historical obscurity which has only been rectified in recent years by Merritt and Cameron.[27]

Industrially, the new AWU leadership united over their response to the continuing challenge posed by the pastoralists. Macdonell's resolution that no shearer should engage a stand through the Pastoralists Union office was carried unanimously, although some were uncertain the shearers would rally to a fight with the pastoralists. During the debate on the motion Macdonell made it clear that the union not only rejected office engagement, but also the PU's new tactic of recommending stations to provide references for 'approved' shearers. Arthur Rae wanted to 'take a stand'; McInerney urged caution: 'A number of men carried the reference in one pocket and their Union ticket in the other'. But attitudes were hardening. Bourke delegate Langwell said there was certain to be a fight, and it was better to go down fighting than let the pastoralists 'victimise men in such a wholesale manner'. Later in the conference, the delegates considered their response to the persistent predictions that the PU would break their 1891 agreement with the AWU and cut the shearing rate for the 1894 season. Smith from Wagga and Cook from Adelaide suggested that in the event of a cut being announced, they should pursue the cautious tactic of calling on shearers to 'stay at home'. Macdonell was almost contemptuous in response. 'Seventy-five per cent of the shearers had no home, never had one, nor any chance of making one ... once we had a fight it was as well to put a little devil in it. He would not advocate violence, never did, but, like the Queenslander, "he never let a sheep bite him yet, and wasn't going to."' The motion was defeated, although no alternative strategy was discussed. Without a clear course of action decided, the fledgeling Australian Workers Union, a union which now defied its problems and divisions with a national name and national ambitions, faced 1894 expecting a fight.[28]

## The Lick in the Lug: the 1894 Strike

Across the colonies, the plunge into conflict accelerated in early 1894. In March J. A. Cook advised the AWU's Executive Council that the Adelaide Branch had been notified by James Stirling, the secretary of PUSA, that the 1891 shearing agreement was inoperative. The generally accepted rate of 20s per 100 was cut to 18s per 100 for hand shearing and 16s 8d for machine shearing. From Coonamble in New South Wales Charlie Poynton reported that after bickering among themselves, the local pastoralists had decided to pay 20s per 100 in the early districts but only 18s in the late places. 'All the sheds in the Riverina district will come under the new idea … Twenty members of the PU threatened to leave that body unless their request was granted re reduction.' In Queensland, pastoralists ominously stalled in responding to an AWUQ request to negotiate over grievances. In June the UPAQ decided not to meet with the AWUQ after consulting with the Pastoralists' Federal Council. By then the federal councillors had made up their minds. At a meeting in April they drew up a new agreement, to 'equalise rates' between machine and hand shearers. Whiteley King insisted that across most of New South Wales, no rate cut would occur, but he confirmed Poynton's report of cuts in the Riverina, where pastoralists were 'not accustomed to pay more than these rates [18s per 100] until the formation of the pastoralists union'.[29]

It was clear that the pastoralists were also weary of dealing with the AWU. In a circular letter to PU members in January 1893 Whiteley King emphasised that disputes over shearing 'allegedly' wet sheep, working on Saturday afternoons, the position of the shearers' cook – it was these tedious disputes with the AWU which would prompt 'alterations' to the 1891 agreement. Hence in April the Federal Council added a new clause 8 to their preferred shearing agreement: now the pastoralist would 'decide all questions arising under this agreement or the rules endorsed hereon'. There would be no interminable consultation with shed reps and organisers. The ancient privilege of the master to order the working life of his servant was reasserted.[30]

There is little doubt that what the AWU really wanted was a main-tenance of the status quo. It was the AWU and the AWUQ which lobbied for negotiation; it was the pastoralists' unions which spurned these overtures. In April the ASU's Executive Council still hoped to revive the 1891 agreement. The council unanimously resolved to maintain the agreement, but to resist the rate cuts and clause 8. Spence wrote to Whiteley King, expressing the AWU's surprise at the creation of a new agreement without consultation; the AWU had faithfully adhered to the 1891 agreement. But like the mood of the February 1894 conference, the executive councillors seemed resigned to strife. In the *Worker* report of their meeting members were assured that 'complete arrangements were made for meeting all emergencies as they arise, and the utmost unanimity prevailed. Members will understand the significance of this telegram'.[31]

Even William Spence seemed to believe by May 1894, as the shearing season approached, that 'moral 'suasion was all humbug'. Invoking the spirit of Eureka, he told *Worker* readers that it was time to give capitalism a 'lick in the lug'. Despite his long-standing aversion to involving the old ASU in strikes, and his hope that one day arbitration would defeat the treachery of the squatter, Spence now acknowledged that 'those who condemn strikes are generally strong upholders of things as they are ... you can only make capitalism think of or look at you at all by hitting it in the pocket'. Soon the attention of the pastoralist, and the state, would be firmly concentrated on the bushworkers who once again challenged their privileges and rules.[32]

By July the *Pastoralists' Review* claimed that in New South Wales shearing was in full swing in the early districts. Shearers were accepting the new agreement without demur. 'Large numbers of shearers are arriving by every steamer from New Zealand, and hundreds of both shearers and shed hands continue to make application for work at the Pastoralists' Union office.' But strikes broke out around Young, Moree and Bourke. Other stations indicated that they intended to shear under the 1891 agreement. In Sydney Walter Head met every boat from New Zealand and interviewed the shearers; Whiteley King was said to be 'furious'. One shearer from Scone said the blacklegs could be readily identified as selectors, 'who are upholding the traditions of their cult: while the men who have nothing but their labour are holding out manfully'. A report from New Zealand added that most shearers from the North Island were farmers and their sons from Palmerston North.[33]

The 1894 strike was characterised by greater violence, and more bitter feeling between shearer and squatter, than the 1891 strike. This was particularly evident in Queensland, where a mood of angry militancy prevailed among bushworkers. The AWUQ, particularly Longreach Branch secretary William Kewley, favoured a more aggressive stance than that which Albert Hinchcliffe and the ALF wanted to pursue; Hinchcliffe was more at home with the spirit of negotiation and caution favoured by Spence. In June the AWUQ leapt to the defence of shed-hands, demanding that their wages be returned to 30s a week. The refusal of the pastoralists to oblige was succinctly expressed by William Allan, president of the UPAQ. He said that profit margins had been eroded by falling wool prices, increased shearing rates and high transport costs. 'Labour may be said to get the only certain dividend from stations now.' If the labour leaders decided to strike then the pastoralists would have to defend their position.[34]

In Queensland and New South Wales, any lingering chance of negotiation went up in flames. In July Ayrshire Downs woolshed near Winton was burnt to the ground. The *Town and Country Journal* reported that 'it is said that a number of shearers impeded the efforts to save the shed'. At Kallaa Station near Bourke, several police were sleeping in a hut (they had been sent to guard the woolshed) when fifty or sixty strikers began to stone their rickety shelter. They fired several shots and the crowd dispersed. When they emerged from the hut they found the woolshed on fire, but the flames did little damage. In September the most notorious incident of the strike occurred when the steamer *Rodney* was burnt to the waterline on the Darling River near Bourke. The steamer had been bearing non-unionists to Bourke district woolsheds.[35]

In September the NSW and Queensland Governments intervened to aid the pastoralists. On 30 August the NSW Government proclaimed that it would vigorously prosecute anyone intimidating or interfering with 'persons engaged in the lawful pursuit of their occupations'. Those involved in 'incendiarism' and riot would also be pursued. New South Wales Premier Sir George Reid said that his government had but one object: 'the protection of every human being in this country from outrage either in person or property'. However, 'as a private citizen he regretted that the pastoralists had not conferred with the shearers'. His regret neatly side-stepped the effect of his government's actions; by defending the pastoralists' woolsheds he was stiffening their ability to resist the strikers and defeat their aims. The shearer had no property to protect. As the *Worker*'s Scone correspondent observed, the working shearer had nothing but his labour, the price of which had been arbitrarily discounted by the pastoralist. In Queensland, a government of pastoralists, led by wealthy squatter Hugh Nelson, was more emphatic in its intimidation of the strikers. In September the Queensland Parliament passed the Peace Preservation Act, despite the furious objections of Labor parliamentarians. In order to preserve the peace the Act withdrew the right of an accused to refuse to answer questions. They could be imprisoned at the discretion of the Governor – effectively the government – and they had no right to trial by jury. But before the Act could come into force the strike had collapsed.[36]

After three months of struggle AWUQ Longreach secretary William Kewley announced that the union's finances were 'extremely harassed'. The union was in debt; it cost £500 a week to maintain the strike camps. And most significantly, 'we have not gained one shed belonging to the Pastoralists' Association'. The union's committee called off the strike on 10 September. In the southern States the results were inconclusive, and

the strike lingered until November. Both sides claimed success. In
February 1895 Spence told the AWU's annual conference that 'we can
unhesitatingly claim the victory ... we can claim 75 per cent of the sheds
to have shorn under our terms, and with Union men. Practically, the PU
acknowledged itself beaten by its confessed inability to supply men'. In
November the *Pastoralists' Review* adopted a tone of confidence, but
could only really claim that those who wanted to shear under the 1894
agreement 'had no difficulty in doing so'. But in December a New South
Wales correspondent conceded that 'no one can claim to have gained
anything. There have been losses on both sides'. The pastoralists could
only really claim that 'they have established the new shearing agreement
for future use, and have thus obtained better control of the management
of their business'. On the other hand, the pastoralists were pleased with
their clear victory in Queensland, and their success in Victoria and South
Australia. But in New South Wales many pastoralists did not cut their
rates. As the *Pastoralists' Review* itself predicted in May 1894, there were
owners prepared to resign from the PUNSW rather than enforce the
cut in rates.[37]

More tellingly than official claim and counter-claim, 'Waltzing Matilda'
clarifies the defeat inflicted upon the bush unions in 1894. Banjo
Paterson's 1895 poem represents a fundamental shift in the romantic
rhetoric of the bushworker ethos. In 1890 Lawson's 'Freedom On The
Wallaby' captured the spirit of the fight with a call for mass resistance,
brotherhood and common struggle against Old Greed, crooking his
dirty hand. 'Waltzing Matilda' reputedly records the final act of defiance
of a bushworker named Hoffmeister, who along with a group of fellow
1894 strikers had burned down the woolshed at Dagworth Station (near
Winton in central Queensland) before the final confrontation played out
in the poem. In 'Waltzing Matilda' the common struggle of 1890
becomes the desperate gesture of a solitary swagman, whose solution to
escaping the pursuing agents of Old Greed, the dutiful troopers, is to
throw himself in a billabong. Like burning down a woolshed in the dark,
or as a mob roughing up scabs, 'Waltzing Matilda' represents a frustrated
lashing out by the bushworker, a gesture which defies the conditions he
endures but cannot change. Its appeal soon greatly increased as a
popular song, 'Waltzing Matilda' is rich with a sense of sacrifice in an
unmistakably Australian idiom, a stoic voice resigned to defeat. The great
pastoral strikes had failed to change the system. The system now failed to
provide work. The swaggie was left to his own meagre resources.[38]

The pastoralists' unions continued to recoil at one potential solution
to this harsh social alienation, a solution which continued to hover like a
phantom offstage, despite all their efforts to repel it before it manifested
in full splendour. During the strike the *Pastoralists' Review* rejected calls

being made in some States for industrial disputes to be settled by compulsory arbitration. Although the pastoralists' unions looked to the NSW Government for assistance against the strikers, this pressing need did not prevent a firm response to the New South Wales Governor's lament, as he opened the Parliament following the July 1894 elections, that the 1892 Trades Disputes Conciliation and Arbitration Act had failed. The Governor said that an amending bill would provide for compulsory investigation of disputes on application of either employer or employees. The *Review* made it clear that the PUNSW would never be an applicant. The pastoralists had 'no dispute with the men who worked under the new agreement'. The article reminded the legislators that the strikes of 1890–91 and 1894 were 'brought about by the refusal of men to accept terms which other men were willing to accept, and did accept. There can be no dispute with workmen who refuse to work, and no board of arbitration can compel men to work if they do not wish to work'. Whatever the outcome of the 1894 strike, the pastoralists' unions still believed that their best chance of defeating the AWU remained in the woolshed, where they hoped one day to decisively shut the door on all those who resisted their authority.[39]

CHAPTER 4

# Driving in the Iron Heel
## *The Struggle for Survival, 1895–1901*

In February 1895 the leaders of the working class met in Sydney to pressure the NSW Government to address the unemployment crisis gripping the colony. The unions, the LEL and the ALF, the Socialist League, the Active Service Brigade and 'J. Tennant, Unemployed', demanded more public works, village settlements and 'some better system of gold fossicking'. Their demands were disjointed and desperate. They saw suffering every day before their eyes; they saw many unemployed, but they had few firm indications of the depth of the crisis, its causes, and the precise numbers thrown out of work. Their knowledge was poor because in Australia in the 1890s, when men and women lost their jobs, when they tramped the bush roads in an anonymous trek from one shearing station to another and when their children went hungry, they fell into an abyss where few inquisitive bureaucrats followed. So when the representatives of New South Wales labour met that summer's night their first priority was to ask the secretary of the LEL to prepare a statistical return on 'the actual state of industrial conditions', from information provided by the various unions, the only public organisations with a close relationship with the working class and an awareness of their problems. Yet Mr Moses, the LEL secretary, might have replied that first he would attempt to find unions which were still effectively functioning. Because the wave of unions thrown up by the prosperity of the 1880s was disappearing with their members' jobs.[1]

In 1895 the registrar of Victorian trade unions reported that in 1890, just as the sun was setting on the inflated real estate of Marvellous

Melbourne, there were seven registered unions with a combined membership of 49 613 and with £38 650 in funds. In 1894 there were still seven registered unions, but their membership had plummeted to 6930 and their funds were now a meagre £247. In New South Wales the situation was just as grim, with the Sydney Trades and Labor Council disintegrating in 1894. Reorganised as the Sydney District Committee of the ALF, it represented no more than a few hundred unionists. It is estimated that in 1895 there were 26 000 unemployed in Sydney alone, and at least 25 per cent of workers in the various colonies were without jobs.[2]

Yet in his secretary's report to the February 1895 conference, Spence was characteristically optimistic. Despite high costs produced by the 1894 strike, the accounts showed a credit balance. Labor was advancing politically in the various colonies, and the colonial labour councils were edging closer to effective federation. 'Generally, Labor is coming to the front as it has never done before, and if activity and earnestness is maintained, and organisation extended, we will soon reach the turning-point, and need have no fear of either the banks or the Pastoralists Unions.' The conference was unwilling to be weighed down by the failing economy. The delegates dealt brusquely with the question of closing branches, delaying a decision until the next conference. They resolved unanimously to defend the 1891 shearing agreement, and decided that any shearer who accepted a pastoralist's reference would be fined at least £1 and up to £5. Only Toomey urged caution: 'A large number of men had suffered during the past year'. But another season of confrontation seemed imminent, and the pastoralists angrily rejected the call for a conference between the two organisations. Whiteley King told Spence that given the AWU's apparent determination to repeat the 'outrages' of last year, he was instructed to decline any further communication with the union. The *Pastoralists' Review* commented that a conference would merely play to the vanity of the AWU's leaders. 'What there is to confer about is the question which is puzzling everybody.'[3]

### 'Fighting Methods'? the Struggle to Survive, 1895–98

While the AWU leaders remained determined to build a more powerful union, the pillars of the structure were crumbling. Members who found it difficult to get a stand in the 1894 season would find only more frustration in 1895, and unemployed shearers and shed-hands did not renew their AWU membership tickets. The strain began to tell; some officials seemed to be growing weary of fair-weather or, as the *Worker* described them, 'ten bob a year' unionists, the type who 'says the *Worker* is no good and never reads it' and 'thinks every official is paid too much, but expects to be paid for everything he does'. One

AWU organiser claimed that the AWU was bringing about its own ruin by signing members who only joined to secure a shed. 'Such creatures only join from necessity, and not from principle. They are scabby sheep, and throughout their whole lives they scatter disease broadcast.'[4]

The potential for membership unrest was exacerbated by the manifesto issued by the AWU's Executive Council on 4 May, outlining the union's policy for the imminent shearing season. The confidence of February was gone. Members were now told that after two years of attempting to force the pastoralists to return to the 1891 agreement, the AWU had also decided to abandon it. The AWU required 'breathing time' to accumulate funds – in short, the union could not afford a strike. Union rules relating to working agreements were suspended for the season. Local branches were empowered to make 'local agreements'; members were told, somewhat hopefully, to secure the 'best available' agreement. They were to hold out for shearing rates of 20s per 100, although it was plain that the AWU would not attempt strike action to defend this demand. The manifesto explained that a change in 'fighting methods' was 'neither a give-in nor a back-down, but simply a pause preparatory to the adoption of more effective means for gaining our objects'. These 'more effective means' were not defined. The members were also asked to remain loyal to the organisation and sign up as many new members as possible.[5]

Now the members who had invested more in the union than the price of a ticket began to have their say about the running of the AWU. In the *Worker* a shearer named Williams claimed to speak for 'every member I have met since the manifesto was issued' when he lashed out at the executive's 'back down'. Without consultation with the members, the Executive had betrayed the trust of all those who had 'fought an uphill battle since '86'. He said that 1894 had been a bitter year for many members and their families; they would feel its effects for years to come. Yet they had won 75 per cent of the sheds, and this year, with the grass scarce and the wool price low, a disorganised PU was vulnerable to another onslaught. 'Yet in the face of this we are *ordered* to knuckle down and eat humble bread by accepting the cast-iron agreement the PU will offer us.' He scorned the executive's belief that increased membership and more funds would win battles. 'By insulting the manhood of our best members in the manner they have done, they do more harm than the enrolment of ten times that number of weak-kneed individuals can ever make good.' He also predicted that the manifesto would encourage the pastoralists to cut rates. 'It is generally anticipated that wages have struck bedrock, but don't let us be deceived. We have a long way to go before that is reached.' The AWU's leaders did not appreciate this advice.

In June president Arthur Rae responded in the *Worker* to 'numerous criticisms' from members (the *Worker* had previously acknowledged that it lacked the room to reprint all the criticisms of the manifesto which it had received from members): 'As some members will persist in pub-lishing the mistaken opinion that they know more than all their selected representatives combined, it is just as well to show them where they are wrong'. He said that the AWU could not afford to repeat the 1894 strike expenditure (estimated at between £12 000 and £13 000), and that con-centrating disputes to the question of price would prevent a cut in the rate, 'and if they can't cut the prices down, we may be sure they won't trouble for very long about the agreement question'. He claimed that the PU was trying to exhaust the AWU with 'a big, ruinous strike' every two or three years.[6]

In June the *Pastoralists' Review* confessed to 'a feeling of relief, almost equal to the relief felt at the break up of the drought, has been experi-enced at the shearers' decision to abandon the suicidal policy which guided them last season'. During the 1895 season the pastoralists seemed little troubled by disputes over price. Through office engagement the PUNSW and the PUVIC experienced few difficulties in placing an abundant supply of shearers in sheds adhering to the pastoralists' 1894 agreement. Each shearer and shed-hand paid his £1 deposit and pro-duced a reference. In New South Wales the men were reported to be 'quiet and anxious for work', although few found a second shed. Six thousand shearers applied for work through the PUVIC office; stands could be found for only 1227. In South Australia, the AWU failed to challenge the PU's rate of 18s per 100; there was little trouble in Queens-land: an irritating late strike in October by shed-hands in the Winton district, striking to increase their wages from 24s to 30s per week. This had been 'refused in every case'. Willing workers had been sent for. There were 'a large number of men seeking work'. In the Young district of New South Wales, the police were being called in to disperse an army of 'chronic unemployed' who swarmed around the shearing sheds, 'practically eating the working shearers out of tucker'. The local shearers were re-enrolling in the AWU, but not the shed-hands. 'The system of amalgamation is not working satisfactorily in their opinion.' They received little attention from AWU officials, and 'intercolonial men' were taking their jobs. Other correspondents reported a similar reluctance by shearers and shed-hands to re-enrol. At Nulty Station near Bourke, a resolution from the shearers turned this frustration against the AWU leadership. They expressed their 'entire disapproval' of the number of paid officials and agents throughout the colonies; to conserve funds all branches should be abolished, and one office established in all Aus-tralian capitals. They wanted all AWU members to vote on the proposal, but the February 1896 conference would again postpone the closure of AWU branches.[7]

From Creswick, a branch secretary who had tramped the colonies to draw shearers to the cause of unionism now attempted to rouse them once more. In August 1895 David Temple appealed to members to re-enrol and encourage their fellow workers to do the same. He recognised that capitalism mercilessly cut wages again and again, breaking up their unity: 'the iron heel is driven in deeper and deeper'. But this was no excuse to be 'chicken-hearted' and lose confidence. He assured the dispirited members that with the clearing away of the depression, 'we will rise like a giant refreshed, stronger and more powerful than before.' But the century would close before the AWU's membership and industrial campaigning began significantly to revive.[8]

The membership's response to this crisis was probably as contradictory as any policy developed by the leadership. In 1895 the AWU had asked the members to vote on six referendum questions. A clear majority rejected amalgamation with the AWUQ, largely because of that union's demand that AWU membership fees rise in line with Queensland fees – up to £1 per member, not an attractive proposal to a depression-stricken bushworker. Members also rejected co-operative land settle-ments (which were to be funded by part of the proposed membership increase), to hold branch secretary's fees at £175, and to retain James Medway Day as the editor of the *Worker*. In terms of policy for the 1896 shearing season, the leaders asked the members two ambivalent questions and received two ambivalent answers. Members said Yes (narrowly), they would work under the same agreement in 1896 as that outlined in the 1895 manifesto; and they also said Yes, by a much larger majority (2845 Yes and 1649 No), to the proposition that the AWU should frame its own agreement for the season if the pastoralists refused to confer. Well, the pastoralists refused, and the union set its own 'agree-ment': the AWU's 1896 manifesto to members repeated the terms of the 1895 edict. The 1896 manifesto noted these ambiguous results, telling members 'you have carried contradictory proposals, one of them in favor of fighting for a new agreement on union lines, and the other in favour of pursuing the course that was followed last year'. But the members could hardly be blamed for reflecting the ambiguous feelings of the leadership, struggling to maintain some vestige of industrial assertiveness despite all indications that such a stand was beyond the union's resources. Spence's secretary's report blamed fair-weather unionists for the AWU's troubles, claiming that the fall in membership was due to men 'utterly devoid of union principle', who squandered their ten bob renewal fee in the pub. There must have been a lot of hard drinking done by irresponsible bushworkers in 1896, because estimates from the

AWU branches and other sources suggest that the AWU's membership fell from 17 000 in early 1895 to around 7000 by the end of the year, a sharp decline which would continue for the rest of the decade.[9]

With each year the pastoralists felt more certain that while the AWU might remain as a nuisance, the union could no longer win the battle in the woolsheds. In March 1896 the *Pastoralists' Review* gloated over the collapse of the the AWU, the 'engine of mischief and an organ of misrule. The AWU will never again be the power it was during the period 1891–94, but it still wants watching'. The *Review* contentedly reported that the sheep of New South Wales had been shorn 'peacefully and well' in 1896, a satisfaction shared by pastoralists in Victoria, South Australia and Queensland. A *Review* correspondent from the Maranoa district (around Roma) in Queensland also noted another phenomenon: the disappearance of the travelling shearer. The strikes had 'put paid to them'. Now young locals, the sons of resident farmers and shearers, had been trained and promised stands well before the shearing began. 'The professional shearer (and card player) has little chance of following the sheds ... he can be done without.' Consequently, he wrote, little was heard these days of the shearers' union, with its organiser and its levies. The world would indeed have been comfortably reordered but for problems of wool prices and weather, troubles which plagued the pastoralists in 1897 and 1898. Drought, which had been steadily tightening its grip across the colonies since the early 1890s, rendered the 1897 season disastrous. Sheep flocks were decimated as the drought persisted, season after season, until 1903. In 1894 there were 57 million sheep in New South Wales; by 1903 there were only 26.6 million. The other colonies experienced a similar collapse in numbers throughout the last years of the nineteenth century. In New South Wales in 1897 the wool clip was also light in weight and poor in quality. In Queensland there were foreclosures of pastoral properties. As a result, there were no labour troubles worth reporting in 1897 or 1898. A surplus of willing labour to shear the much-reduced sheep stocks remained a blessing for the hard-pressed squatter, and allowed a welcome flexibility in the rates set by the pastoralists' unions, which around the colonies was generally 17–18s per 100. In New South Wales, rate setting had been decentralised to district committees, with many pastoralists determined to reduce pastoral labour payments as much as possible.[10]

In these trying circumstances AWU organisers had to be resourceful. In the Central Branch (based at Orange in New South Wales), Ted Grayndler did whatever he could to enrol members. Apparently he was 'a very fair singer and he often finds it stands him in good stead when he strikes a shed for making himself agreeable among the chaps'. But sometimes a song was not enough. In November 1898 Grayndler visited

the Mountain View Station near Wellington, where the boss would pay
no more than 17s 6d. Grayndler reported, 'the boss had six of them
squared, and they stood like criminals in the dock. It was impossible to
get them to ask for £1. When asked if the terms suited, they simply hung
their heads and said nothing. "Silence gives consent". The boss was quite
satisfied with their attitude'. But a week later he reported that shearers at
Boomey Station successfully held out for £1, although at a 'price' – the
boss had spitefully refused to take on the men who had been 'conspicuous in asserting their rights'. Nonetheless, Grayndler felt that 1898
had been a successful year for the Central Branch. He had enrolled over
500 members and brought in £200.[11]

By 1898 the AWU's operations were under severe financial pressure.
The general secretary's position had been made honorary by the 1898
conference, and the union's head office in Sydney closed. The Eastern
Branch in New South Wales was also closed. This branch had only
been created a year before: in February 1897 the decline in membership
and finances finally forced the AWU conference to close the Moree,
Goulburn, Young and Sydney branches. The four remaining NSW
branches were reorganised as the Eastern (based at Scone), Western
(Bourke), Central (with the office moved from Coonamble to Orange)
and Southern (Wagga). During 1896 the Casterton branch in Victoria
had also closed, its territory divided between the Creswick and Adelaide
branches. The AWU in Victoria and South Australia now only consisted
of a single branch in each colony. Branch secretaries' salaries were also
reduced by £19, and, in the most dramatic – and public – indication of
the union's troubles, the *Worker* was closed until the shearing season.
Some felt that the *Worker* could be entirely done away with. Organiser
William Holman (the future NSW Premier) told the conference that 'the
*Worker* has done no good and great harm; had not made a single convert,
and the money spent on it might have been as well thrown in the sea'.
Few other delegates were as hostile, with Temple strongly arguing that
the *Worker* was 'a powerful organising agent', although a consensus grew
that Medway Day should be dispensed with as editor – at one time or
another he seems to have editorially trodden on the toes of many of his
several bosses. After a typically protracted debate Medway Day was
removed and the *Worker* temporarily closed. Responsibility for reviving
the paper was passed to the Bourke Branch, the only branch financially
strong enough to sustain it.[12]

### City versus Bush: Organising Political Labor

To alleviate its chronic problems the AWU looked towards political
organisation in the late 1890s, although political Labor in New South

Wales and the other colonies had failed to build upon the initial success of 1891. The Labor Electoral League's 1893 conference had exposed a fundamental breach between the parliamentarians and the rank and file over 'the pledge', which required the politicians to adhere to the direction of the Caucus and the party platform. Several of the Labor representatives rejected this control, and the split between the factions led to a collapse in the Labor vote at the 1894 New South Wales elections, retaining only thirteen representatives in the new Parliament, a heavy fall from the thirty-five of 1891. Labor's poor parliamentary representation in New South Wales after 1894 was also reflected in the other colonies. In Victoria, the reality of Labor politicians in Parliament destroyed the hopes of many who voted for them. The depression also played a cruel hand in this. 'Radical', a *Worker* correspondent bitterly disillusioned with Labor politicians, wrote in the autumn of 1896 that the depression was intensifying every week, with great distress among the working class of Melbourne. 'This winter will bring us face to face with the most aggravated type of poverty ever witnessed in this so-called "workingman's paradise".' He claimed that William Trenwith, the nominal leader of Labor in the Victorian Parliament, had done nothing to alleviate the distress. Trenwith preferred to work with the Parliament's Liberal administrations, an association many Laborites saw as betrayal.[13]

The AWU was also frustrated with the slow progress of political Labor, and the union was critical of the centralising, city mentality of the LEL. In the bush the AWU backed political organisation through the Australian Labor Federation, an arrangement which essentially reflected the divergence between the AWU and the LEL. These differences were buried in 1895 with the merger of the LEL and the ALF to form the Political Labor League, with Spence and Rae sitting on the new PLL executive, and with Rae also acting as an honorary PLL organiser in the bush. The *Worker* welcomed the reunification of Labor, and appealed to 'every farmer, artisan and other worker' to support the return of Labor candidates at the 1895 elections, at which Labor was only able to secure 19 of the 125 available seats, although it did retain the balance of power, and the ability to influence the legislative program of the free-trade government of George Reid. The PLL pressed Reid on income and land-tax reform, coalmining regulations, workshops and factories legislation and old age pensions, but there was little attention to the immediate concerns of the AWU: compulsory arbitration and the often appalling accommodation shearers and shed-hands had to suffer.[14]

The *Worker* believed that the continuing struggle between the squatter and the shearer necessitated that arbitration legislation be introduced 'at the earliest possible date'. The unions lobbied the Reid administration for compulsory arbitration reform in 1898, with a deputation to Labor

Minister Garrard arguing that Dibbs's 1892 voluntary legislation, the
Trades Disputes Conciliation and Arbitration Act, failed to prevent industrial disputes. Garrard promised to consult Cabinet. But the *Worker*
ruefully noted that even if the Reid Government did introduce legislation, the conservative Legislative Council would block the bill. Efforts
to press for a shearers' accommodation act to set reasonable minimum
standards of accommodation encountered the same frustration and
delays. In February 1899 the entire nine-member AWU conference delegation, together with several Labor MPs, met with NSW Labour Minister
Hogue, who expressed surprise at the AWU's tales of disgraceful conditions of shearers and station-hands. He promised to raise the matter
with his Cabinet colleagues, but it would be another two years before
legislation passed through the NSW Parliament.[15]

Society denied the AWU legitimacy, as Arthur Rae ruefully observed in
November 1895. He explained to members that although the AWU could
theoretically register under the NSW Trade Union Act, it would be
entirely counterproductive for the union to do so. Under the terms of
the Act, registration would prohibit the ownership of a newspaper and
the participation in political action and co-operative enterprises. As Rae
observed, what members could do as individual citizens they were prohibited from doing collectively as unionists. Hence 'we are more or less
at the mercy of the dishonest and outside the pale of the law, which
refuses to allow us the only means of entering its sacred portals'. Rae
emphasised that despite the fact that the constitution of the AWU was
framed 'for the express purpose of getting away from the barbarous old
system of strikes', and that the union was only too willing to renounce
confrontation and direct action, society's rules were stacked against it.[16]

The AWU's political agenda was also motivated by an ideal of inte-
gration with society, drawing a coalition of 'farmers, artisans and other
workers' to demand recognition of their needs. This urge for acceptance
deeply coloured AWU attitudes to socialism. The PLL platform of 1895
contained a series of piecemeal reforms, with no mention of nationalised
industries or public ownership. There were few in the labour movement
who seriously attempted to define the characteristics of an Australian
socialism. In August 1895 Medway Day, who was an unsuccessful PLL
candidate at the 1895 elections, told *Worker* readers that he rarely
described himself as a socialist, 'because twenty different people would
attach twenty different meanings to the word'. He thought it 'an
indulgent hope' to define socialism as 'the nationalisation of all facets of
life'. He defined socialism as 'a natural, scientific plan for life', whatever
that was – he didn't say. Donald Macdonell, on the other hand, had
firm views of what the electorate would not tolerate. In 1897 he argued
that Labor had to concentrate on improving the immediate, material

condition of the working class; it had no business pursuing the vague hope of some future millennium.[17]

In pursuit of practical political achievement AWU officials began to move into the colonial parliaments. At the 1898 New South Wales elections Spence won the country seat of Cobar, where many bush-workers and goldminers had a vote. Holman, who had acted as an AWU organiser, was elected for Grenfell. In order to enhance its influence in PLL activities, in 1899 the AWU was the first union to gain direct representation at PLL conferences, soon to be followed by many others. Ties with the AWU had also been boosted in 1898 when new *Worker* editor Hector Lamond, a former bush journalist and unsuccessful Labor candidate, became PLL organising secretary. In 1900 the AWU formally began organising on behalf of the PLL in country areas, recognising the crucial role of the AWU organisers in getting out the Labor vote at a time when voting was voluntary, and ensuring that AWU members turned up at PLL branch meetings to keep the local party structure alive. Hard work bred high expectations, and the AWU resolved at the 1901 conference that unless the party did more propaganda work during the parliamentary recess the AWU would not support the PLL at the next election. The conference delegates were unanimous in their condemnation of the 'lame excuses' Labor Members of Parliament made about their inability to visit country electorates. In other States, Labor's fortunes were equally mixed. There was success in Queensland in 1899, where Labor was briefly (for six days) able to form the world's first Labor government. Political success was elusive in Victoria, however, with a series of splits and divisions among laborites throughout the 1890s.[18]

### Recovery and Recrimination: the AWU, 1900–1

As the nineteenth century drew to a close, the AWU was willing to renew the industrial fight, as economic conditions seemed slowly to improve. In January 1900 the AWU conference 'decided to make a stand for union rates'. The manifesto issued by the union said that while no general strike was intended, 'the policy is to be a shed to shed fight in the low priced sheds'. Wool prices were up, labour was increasingly scarce; 'we can never expect a better opportunity'. Although the pastoralists were offering 20s per 100, they were still 'left-handedly' attempting to keep down wages in the eastern New South Wales districts, where the AWU was perceived to be weak. The union was even determined to defy the drought. 'Pastoralists who have suffered most from the drought still pay the Union rates. Only those who have suffered least and gained most have cut wages.' The AWU was flexible about the form of agreement between shearer and squatter; members could engage through the PU offices and use references. The union remained opposed to shearing contractors and the purchase by shearers of shearing machines, a practice which the pastoralists' unions were encouraging in an effort to offload the cost of the machines to the shearer. For shed-hands, the AWU insisted on 25s a week and rations as the uniform rate, or where daily rates were paid, no less than 7s a day. John Meehan from Bourke Branch expressed the renewed determination of the AWU conference: 'The repeated state-ment that they must not do this or that for fear of offending the watery gentlemen who were shearing under Union rates and in every way doing what they could to break down the organisation we were supposed to maintain was disgusting our best members and driving them from our ranks. He was strongly of the opinion that they should make a stand for principles and abandon mere expediency, which had been their curse and weakness for years past'. Nonetheless Donald Macdonell, the new AWU general secretary, wanted the AWU conference to tolerate a little practical expediency. Macdonell moved that the conference rescind a resolution which forbade the issuing of tickets to those shearing for less than 20s per 100. He argued that 'it was unwise to do anything to cripple their resources at such a juncture'. Meehan impatiently attacked Macdonell's arguments as 'an old rehash' for justifying accepting the dues of any 'cronk who paid a few shillings'. The conference rejected Macdonell's recission motion.[19]

Another old dispute distracted the AWU conference from the business of rebuilding the union. Tensions between Creswick Branch secretary David Temple and several AWU officials resurfaced over allegations of financial irregularity. On 8 February Temple arrived at the conference and resigned, perhaps intending to pre-empt further inquiry into the affairs of the Creswick Branch. Nevertheless Lundie and Macdonell were instructed to 'inquire into the general management of the Branch and as to the best place in which the Branch Office should be situate'. Their subsequent report could find 'nothing favourable' about the way Temple had kept the branch's accounts: 'Moneys have been received and paid without going through any bank'. Bank accounts had been carelessly kept; neither Temple nor the branch auditors had satisfactorily main-tained the branch's finances. Ticket ledgers and butts from various years were 'promiscuously' mixed together; no ticket book, nor telegram book, nor a members' roll, had been kept. Temple had claimed that he had placed all pre-1893 records in an outhouse, where they had been des-troyed by rain. 'We can only say that he failed to produce any remnants of the books in support of his statement.' Of charges of neglect of duty by Temple, Macdonell and Lundie observed: 'In regard to the charges of neglect of duty, it is clear that for a considerable time past Mr. Temple has failed to give his undivided attention to the work of the Union. He has lived in Melbourne for a considerable portion of last year, being at one place in Fitzroy for fully two months, and this without the authority of any Committee or General Meeting'. Macdonell and Lundie made no specific recommendations concerning Temple, but they did recommend that the union adopt tighter audit procedures and familiarise auditors with union rules and the responsibilities of branch secretaries, instructing them to advise the general president or branch chairman should they discover irregularities. They concluded by regretting their inability to provide a more favourable report, 'in view of the good work done by Mr Temple in the earlier history of the Union'.[20]

Clyde Cameron has written in defence of David Temple, claiming that Spence and Macdonell were manoeuvring Temple out of the Creswick secretary's position to instal a Spence yes-man, Edward Grayndler. But Cameron offers no evidence to rebut the findings of Macdonell and Lundie's report. It may be true that Temple became increasingly despondent during the late 1890s, estranged from the other AWU officials; and William Spence is always centre-stage in *The History of the AWU* and *Australia's Awakening*, his own accounts of the early years of the union. Nevertheless it seems that by 1900 Temple's effective control of Creswick Branch affairs had lapsed (Macdonell and Lundie did not suggest that Temple misused branch funds for personal gain). As for Grayndler, he had established a reputation as an able Central Branch organiser, and as John Merritt notes, as the new secretary of Creswick Branch (soon to be renamed the Victoria-Riverina Branch), 'he was bursting with ideas for future action', and was instrumental in increasing branch membership by 100 per cent. He also moved the Creswick Branch office closer to the Riverina area, in order to better administer the branch. If Spence and Macdonell had been determined to remove Temple, it can only be said that Temple seems to have played into their hands.[21]

That finances were hard pressed is reflected in the conference's decision to close the Southern (Wagga) Branch, dividing its territory between the Central and Bourke branches. Eastern (Scone) Branch had been closed in 1898; there were now only two New South Wales branches. And a plan to boost the appeal of the *Worker* stalled when the new editor appointed by the Bourke Branch (which still controlled the *Worker*), William Lane, stayed only a few months in the job. Dispirited by the failure of New Australia, Lane was drifting away from the labour movement. After quitting the Worker he became a leader writer, then later editor, of the conservative *New Zealand Herald*, embracing militarism and attacking union militancy.[22]

In 1900 the Boer War (1899–1902) fed a colonial passion for militarism. The *Pastoralists' Review*, while disturbed at the trend in the labour

market, ironically supported a call for erecting a statue of Boer President
Kruger, 'for his services in consolidating the British Empire'. The *Review*
even reprinted Henry Lawson's 'The Bushmen's Brigade':

> We struck for our rights (and for extra, perhaps),
> But the boss is a private along with the chaps,
> And we're done for the time with all trouble and trade –
> All tickets alike in the Bushmen's brigade!

Like Lane, Lawson believed war would unify and smooth over the
differences between master and servant. No doubt many pastoralists also
hoped that war might finally succeed in undermining the appeal of
troublesome trade unions.[23]

The AWU expressed only muted opposition to bushworkers fighting
on the Empire's behalf in South Africa. The prospect of federation was
another matter, however. The AWU was concerned that the working man
would not benefit from the creation of the Australian nation. The only
aim of some federationists, the *Worker* asserted, was to remove colonial
obstacles to the exploitation of workers. Editor Hector Lamond was even
driven towards republicanism. He doubted that nationhood, under the
umbrella of the British Empire, would sufficiently safeguard White Australia. The coloured hawker 'is now as familiar in Central Australia as
the out of work, whose numerical increase keeps pace with his own'. He
had little faith in British action to stem the Asian tide, although he didn't
want Australian nationhood for its own sake, but unfettered action in the
interests of 'our own people'. His own people would soon be reassured
by the Immigration Restriction Act, a law designed to uphold a White
Australia and to exclude migrants from the Asia–Pacific region. The
Act was passed in 1901, in the first session of the new Commonwealth Parliament.[24]

During the 1900 and 1901 shearing seasons the AWU had made headway in its struggle with the pastoralists, with the union claiming that 5000
new members had rallied to its cause in 1900, and 'hundreds of sheds'
had been won. The NSW Pastoralists Union played down the industrial
difficulties, claiming success in replacing strikers, but nonetheless
reminded owners that this only reinforced the need for PU membership,
'which may have been lost sight of by some during recent years'. It was
an oblique confession of their inability to stem the AWU's revival, which
in 1901 was marked by even greater confidence. The 1901 manifesto
declared that unionism was making 'giant strides' along the road to
recovery: 'forty-six Labor bodies have been reorganised within the past
eight months'. In New South Wales, the PU had conceded 20s per 100;
and little strong resistance was expected in Victoria and South Australia.
Such was the union's confidence that the manifesto forbade members to

AWU expectations of the new Australian Commonwealth. In this November 1901 cartoon from the Brisbane *Worker*, the bright moon of White Australia rises despite the howls of pro-'coloured slave labour' business. *AWU Collection.*

engage through the PU offices, although the use of references was still tolerated. Members who broke any of the manifesto's conditions would be fined £2. However, as the debate at the 1901 conference about conferring with the PU indicated, the AWU still had hurdles to jump. Grayndler noted that the Victorian Branch would be quite unable to win wage rises for shed-hands through industrial action; the labourers were

simply too 'disorganised'. This lack of results on behalf of shed-hands
contributed to recurring calls for the dissolution of the AWU and its
replacement by separate unions for shearers and shed-hands. Such a
resolution was debated at the 1901 conference, which rejected the
proposal, and instructed Macdonell and Rae to draft 'ten good reasons
for amalgamation'; these were published with the conference report.[25]

Conference also decided to be practical about freedom of contract.
The 1901 manifesto, although more aggressive than that of 1900,
studiously avoided mention of freedom of contract. As Macdonell noted,
starting another fight about working in the same shed as non-unionists
was not the essential issue. The AWU, buoyed by its success in the field in
1900, now sought revival through a renewed effort to achieve gains
in wages and conditions. The freedom of contract crisis of 1891, Macdonell observed, had not delivered the death blow to the AWU. 'The
squatters had not gained, nor our members lost, to the extent that either
side had anticipated by the adoption of that principle, and if the PU
consented to meet us and conceded all other important points we well
might allow freedom of contract to stand as it is for another year.'[26]

Macdonell's tolerance of freedom of contract, verging on complacency, was born in the knowledge that the AWU had, despite all the
hopes of the pastoralists, survived the rigours of the 1890s, a disastrous
decade for many working Australians and their families. But to consolidate an AWU revival, and to extend industrial gains to the restive
labourers, would require more than survival, and guerrilla warfare in the
woolsheds. They would seek justice through compulsory arbitration,
which the AWU believed would relegate 'the strikes and struggles and
bitterness of the past to the limbo of forgotten things'. New South Wales
arbitration legislation was now only delayed by the last intransigence of
the Parliament's Legislative Councillors, many of whom could remember
a time when workers were more likely to produce a ticket of leave than a
union ticket. Australia had changed.[27]

One Australian who wanted change, and who wanted to consign strikes
to the limbo of forgotten things, was Henry Bournes Higgins. In June
1900 Higgins was invited by Edward Grayndler to open the new Victoria-
Riverina Branch office at St Arnaud, in western Victoria. A lawyer
and a liberal-minded politician in the Victorian Parliament, Higgins
increasingly supported the role of the state in economic and social
reform. A thoughtful, strong-willed individual, Higgins would become
the pioneering president of the Commonwealth Arbitration Court in
1907. But even in June 1900 it was evident that he had been pondering
the vexatious relationship between worker and master for some time.
He told the members and guests at the opening that the difficulties
between employer and employee should be settled by conciliation and

arbitration. He had faith in unionists; 'he knew that members had carefully weighed everything before they complained'. Conversely, employers were frequently wrong in claiming the 'privilege' of freedom of contract. The reply of the worker, Higgins explained to his audience, was 'very emphatic – simply because there could be no contract if only one man made it'. Having justified the resistance of the unionist to the self-serving dictates of the employer, Higgins defined comparative wage justice, and the principles he would implement seven years later:

> If the condition of the shoemaker was lowered, so then was that of the shearer, or that of any other occupation ... there were three problems in every industry – first, what was to be produced; second, by what means; and third, the conditions under which the human agents were to be employed.

Higgins clarified the ideals of the AWU, channelling them towards the reconciliation of arbitration, which the leaders of the AWU hoped would liberate their members from the punishing conflict and exploitation workers knew as their lot in life, and which through unionism they struggled to cast aside. Edward Grayndler, who would preside as AWU general secretary for most of the years Higgins served as president of the Arbitration Court, could not have known, that day in 1900, that Higgins would be the most powerful intellectual force in shaping Australian arbitration, the structure upon which the AWU would be built into the largest and most powerful union in Australia.[28]

CHAPTER 5

# The Giant Refreshed

*Awards and Amalgamations, 1902–14*

In January 1902 the AWU's leaders, gathered in Sydney for the union's sixteenth annual conference, were congratulated by Donald Macdonell on their splendid success in rebuilding the AWU. Within the space of a single year, membership had risen, he estimated, from 12 600 to 20 522; even the Bourke and Adelaide Branch districts claimed membership increases of 3000, despite the South Australian pastoral leases turning to dust and the Lachlan River drying out, grim consequences of a devastating drought which had persisted since 1895. AWU finances were also restored, with nearly £8000 in the bank. For Macdonell these triumphs were born in the 1901 conference decision to 'discard the iniquitous PU agreement and frame and fight for one of our own'. During the 1901 season he estimated that 90 per cent of the shearing sheds had 'accepted our policy'. The AWU, Macdonell asserted, had called the Pastoralists Union's bluff. There is no doubt that the AWU's position had markedly improved since the grim period 1895–99, but Macdonell's enthusiasm needs to be treated a little cautiously, particularly concerning membership estimates. In 1905, for example, Macdonell would also then claim that the AWU's membership had increased, from 12 000 in 1904 to 20 000, after the merger with the Amalgamated Workers Union of Queensland, which covered the Queensland pastoral industry. Membership numbers undoubtedly continued to seesaw in the period 1902–5, given the drought and varying pastoral conditions around the States. But it is unlikely that membership routinely dropped to 12 000, then suddenly soared to 20 000, without the intervention of some extraordinary fillip such as an amalgamation. It is most likely that AWU membership in the period from 1902 to the AWUQ amalgamation settled somewhere between 12 000 and 14 000.[1]

### Down by the Law: the MSU Challenge and the 1902 Strike

Macdonell believed that the future of the AWU was secured with the union's registration, on 14 February 1902, under the NSW Industrial Arbitration Act. The Act, he told the delegates, 'is one that should make for the industrial peace of the community, and since under its provisions the Court will have power, other things being equal, to give preference to Unionists, it should make strongly for the advancement of organisation'. Other things are rarely equal. On 28 February 1902 the Machine Shearers and Shed Employees Union (MSU) was also registered under the NSW Industrial Arbitration Act.[2]

According to secretary John Leahy, the MSU was formed to allow shearers and shed-hands to escape the tyranny of industrial struggle and political entanglement, to 'improve relations between employers and employees, and to settle disputes by means of conciliation and arbitration'. The strike was the divisive and futile tactic of the AWU, and MSU members were 'disgusted' with its industrial methods, its political ties, its high fees and highly paid officials. But the advent of compulsory arbitration 'bade fair to wipe off the old order of things and compel us to join an army of men who had simply been ruled by their leaders'. The PUNSW quickly negotiated a shearing agreement with the MSU in late April 1902, an agreement shrewdly designed to undercut the AWU's appeal by guaranteeing a shearing rate of £1 per 100. Freedom of contract was the first provision of the agreement.[3]

Macdonell was furious at the registration of the MSU. 'Obviously, if the Act permits the registration of two unions for every trade or calling, one genuine and the other bogus, the first representing the men and the latter the employers, then that is not the Act that the people of this state asked for or expect.' The *Worker* knew why the Pastoralists Union was keen to negotiate with the MSU: 'to discredit the claims for higher rates and better conditions made by the AWU by citing to the Arbitration Court the satisfaction of the Bogus Unionists with the rates paid and by producing figures to prove what high wages are earned by its members'. The AWU unsuccessfully attempted to deregister the MSU, which was able to survive through legal technicalities – a process much encouraged by the court, according to Macdonell. 'Mr. Justice Cohen has made the Court as petty as a Police Court. For equity and good conscience he has substituted technicality and precedent.' The AWU had feared the Arbitration Court would become another feasting house for lawyers. The

1902 conference unanimously urged the Labor Party to amend the legislation to prohibit lawyers appearing in the court, but to no avail. A year later, Macdonell was ruefully claiming that Justice Cohen 'quoted more legal authorities in the one judgement upon our application than the New Zealand Court has quoted in the whole eight years of its existence'.[4]

The January 1902 AWU conference set the union's demands for shearing rates at 25s per 100 for New South Wales, and 18s found and 20s unfound for Victoria and South Australia. Shed labourers' rates were 30s (New South Wales) and 25s (Victoria and South Australia). However, the PUNSW said that there would be no agreement unless the AWU accepted the terms of the MSU–PUNSW deal. Cohen's decision upholding the MSU's registration came down on 23 June, on the verge of the New South Wales shearing season. This left the AWU facing the alternative of a belated application for an increase in rates before the NSW Arbitration Court – from which it had just been spurned – or encouraging its members to fight in the field for their claims. On 9 August, the *Worker* published a revised manifesto urging New South Wales members to seek justice in the woolsheds and strike, if need be, for 22s 6d per 100 – down from the original demand of 25s per 100. Labourers were still urged to demand 30s a week.[5]

Around Hay and Gilgandra shearing was soon disrupted by strike camps. The most intense struggle of the dispute centred on Coonamble in northern New South Wales, where five strike camps were formed, and aggressive pickets patrolled the pastoral stations and incoming trains. On 23 August a body of AWU members prevented sixty strike-breakers from proceeding to Warrana station, escorting them to the strike camp. There was some indication that the strikers were less than gentle with the would-be scabs, but police visited the camp and could not find anyone unwilling to be there.[6]

'Banjo' Paterson visited Coonamble as a newspaper correspondent. He believed that only the most courageous would defy an invitation to visit the strike camp, which he described as a collection of sheds, tents and humpies in which 200 bored strikers waited for victory – or defeat. 'A dog fight started, and was naturally followed by a man fight. Life in camp is all idleness, except when an occasional picket on telegraph duty brings any news of movement. That brings the shearers up and attracts crowds of men on foot and on bicycles.' At Wingalee station, also near Coonamble, sixty masked men surrounded a hut containing twenty scabs and called on them to come out. A police constable emerged from the shed and fired into the air. As Paterson reported, 'then the mob ran in all directions. One man tried to rally them, and said, "Come back, you cowards; what did you come here for?"

A hurried flight ensued ... one man fell over a wire fence and said, "Oh, my poor mother".[7]

Whatever the comic aspects of some of the strikers' efforts, the consequences of the 'kidnapping' of the Warrana strike-breakers were serious for the AWU. Station owner William Keogh sought an injunction restraining the pickets and damages from the union (his solicitor was Alfred De Lissa, who was also the MSU's solicitor). The court was told that most of the kidnapped shearers were MSU members. An injunction was granted by the court; but on 5 September Keogh made a further application to sequester the AWU's funds because of their alleged flouting of the injunction – MSU members gave evidence of continued harassment. Simultaneously, reports emerged of AWU members deserting the strike camps, even around Coonamble. The *Worker* reported on 13 September that the strike was being called off. AWU creditors were panicking about the threat to AWU finances posed by the court action. 'Had our funds lasted another fortnight, we could have won fully eighty percent of the remaining sheds.' But there seemed little enthusiasm among members for such a protracted dispute.[8]

The *Pastoralists' Review* celebrated the AWU's 'blunder'. The timing was disastrous, coming during a prolonged drought which forced shearing to start late in many areas; and although the AWU appeared to believe that the strike would boost its claims before the Arbitration Court, the *Review* asserted that with the strike's abject failure, 'the Pastoralists' Unions will go into the court with their previously strong case still further strengthened by the events of the present season'. NSW Attorney-General Wise hoped that the differences between the parties could be resolved by arbitration before the 1903 season, 'but it is right to say that the unwillingness to face the Court has not proceeded from the employers'. Macdonell claimed that Wise had deceived the union. The Arbitration Act, despite assurances from Wise, failed to protect legitimate unions. The AWU found itself in a tangle of expensive litigation, sued by Keogh and another disgruntled owner, as the union continued with legal efforts to deregister the troublesome MSU. Macdonell was angry that two judgments against British unions, *Taff Vale* and *Quinn v. Leatham*, permitted litigants to sue the AWU for damages, and hold the union responsible for its members' actions. He believed the law struck at the root of trade unionism: 'Any unionists adopting the most peaceful means in persuading a blackleg of the error of his ways may now render his union liable for damages. No-one, according to the present Judge-made law, can come between the employer and his servant'. In short, the AWU found itself in precisely the same position it faced in the wake of the industrial defeats of the 1890s, when it hoped the law, through arbitration, could step between the warring parties and

administer justice. In New South Wales justice did not favour the trade
unionist.[9]

The separate legal issues before the AWU fed on each other. In July
1903 the registrar of the NSW Arbitration Court considered another
AWU application to deregister the MSU. The registrar said that Keogh's
case (which had been decided in his favour, with damages of £872
awarded against the union) made it clear that the AWU embraced an
aggressive militancy. If he deregistered the MSU its members 'would
either have to forego the advantages of industrial unionism, and thus
probably be outside the pale of employment, or they would be compelled
to join the applicant union. It is necessary, then, to enquire into the
character of that union.' Concluding that the AWU reiterated its commitment to militancy at the January 1903 conference, he rejected the
union's application.[10]

Macdonell again looked to Parliament to overcome the difficulties
facing the AWU. With Federation in 1901, the AWU's political influence
extended into the first Commonwealth Parliament, with Spence elected
as the Member for Darling. By September 1903, with Labor emerging as
the third national political force between Barton's Protectionists and
Reid's Free Traders, Macdonell told *Worker* readers that the AWU could
soon expect federal conciliation and arbitration legislation, capable of
making awards for all States. 'We would be in an infinitely better position
going before it, seeing that the incubus of a bogus union would not be
upon our backs.' The hope of federal legislation encouraged a cautious
industrial strategy, already fuelled by the failure of 1902. 'It would be
little short of suicidal now that we should do anything calculated to
endanger our chances of getting before it [a federal arbitration court],
and upon the fairest conditions.'[11]

With Spence's elevation to the Federal Parliament, Macdonell was
elected to fill his vacancy for the seat of Cobar in the NSW Parliament.
He was not about to waste the opportunity to pursue the MSU. In September 1903 he successfully moved for the establishment of a select
committee into the organisation and bona fides of the MSU. When
Leahy refused to give evidence, Macdonell pressed, again successfully, for
a royal commission, which could compel witnesses to appear. Leahy,
along with other MSU officials, a shearing contractor and others associated with the MSU, again refused to appear and were fined by a Sydney
magistrate. In June 1904, however, the NSW Supreme Court declared the
Royal Commission illegal ('an unjustifiable attempt to invade private
interests') and awarded costs against the AWU. The High Court of
Australia subsequently overturned this decision, and upheld the
magistrate's decision to fine Leahy and the others £1 each. The MSU,
apparently never short of funds to fight expensive legal actions, took the

case to the Privy Council in London. (According to the MSU's balance sheets, 57 per cent of its income was provided by employers through direct contributions and anonymous donations, of which the only credible source could be employers or shearing contractors. The MSU's own auditor criticised the fact that these contributions had not passed through the union's bank account.) However, by January 1906 Macdonell was finally able to report that the MSU's appeal had been lost, and the Royal Commission's finding that the MSU was indeed 'bogus' – based particularly on testimony which showed that shearing contractors had paid for MSU advertising – was allowed to stand untarnished by another legal veto.[12]

The AWU was registered under the Commonwealth Conciliation and Arbitration Act on 16 May 1905, after the Reid Government finally passed the Act after prolonged debate in the Parliament. Macdonell was impatient to prepare a case for a federal pastoral industry award, but his efforts were first drawn to eliminating the MSU. The AWU, armed with the NSW Royal Commission's findings, launched proceedings to deregister the MSU, which had also recently registered under the Federal Act. Faced with this renewed attack, the MSU abandoned its attempt to become a federal union. The MSU went into permanent decline after 1905, and by 1907 its membership dwindled to a few hundred members (the AWU estimated that the MSU never had more than 1200 members). Macdonell observed that Leahy had become 'a sort of shearing contractor' being pursued in court over an unpaid wages claim.[13]

The AWU's leaders continued to pursue ambitious growth in the period 1904–5, and it seemed the state was finally moving to nurture this growth. Deakin's 'New Protection' incorporated the essential edicts of the 'Australian Settlement', which confirmed that the concerns of the AWU and its members, and the working class, would be recognised by the young Commonwealth. *The Immigration Restriction Act 1901*, introduced by the Barton Government in the first session of the new Commonwealth Parliament declared, like the feisty, intemperate *Bulletin*, that Australia was for the white man. Intending immigrants would be excluded if they failed a dictation test in a European language. Workers need not fear the contest of cheap 'coloured labour' in Australian workplaces. *The Excise Tariff (Agriculture Machinery) Act 1906* laid the foundation of tariff pro-tection and provided Higgins with a stage for the promulgation of a 'living wage' – the Harvester decision of 1907, which established the principle of a minimum wage. The Harvester decision paved the way for the apparent fulfilment of economic justice for the white working man, a decision to be refined and entrenched through the arbitration machinery created by the *Commonwealth Conciliation and Arbitration Act*

*1904*. The fulfilment of these aspirations did not simply confer general benefits on the AWU and the membership. It provided a state-supported context in which the AWU could expand its industrial coverage, a sympathetic environment which the AWU would fully exploit through a series of amalgamations in the period before 1920. The first of these amalgamations occurred in 1904, when the AWU conference revived the long-frustrated aim of amalgamating the Queensland Amalgamated Workers Union with the southern AWU.

Macdonell, fearing an old resistance to amalgamation from members, promised that branches would still elect their own officers and control their own funds. He said their common aim was to win fair pay rates for bushworkers across Australia. 'Why should we stand apart, perpetuating jealousies, bickering over exchange tickets, affording opportunities for loafers on the union to escape payment of contributions?' The united organisation would remain the Australian Workers Union, a union which by its power and influence 'would justify its claim to that distinctive title'. By early 1905 the amalgamation had been approved by membership vote, with 7663 members voting Yes and only 823 opposing (traditionally, union referendums and amalgamation ballots attract a low voter turn-out, perhaps through a combination of apathy, poor publicity and, in the early twentieth century, difficulties of communication in non-urban areas). Members of the three AWUQ branches – Longreach, Charleville and Hughenden – voted in support of the amalgamation, although Hughenden expressed some concern over the AWU's commitment to the federal arbitration system, particularly the Act's lack of preference for unionists. Concern over the possibility of MSU federal registration, however, convinced the doubting Queenslanders of the need for completing the amalgamation and pursuing federal registration for the AWU. In Macdonell's estimation, the amalgamation helped to boost AWU membership from a low 12 000 in early 1904 to nearly 20 000 by 1905, by far the largest single union in the country.[14]

In the early twentieth century, most Australian unions remained relatively small State-registered organisations, still struggling to cast off the crippling setbacks of the 1890s. In the various State rail systems, railway unions, preoccupied with unionising the workforce in their States, did not amalgamate until the 1920s. Unions in non-rail transport or the waterfront tended to remain fragmented around their particular locality; other unionists in manufacturing and building still preferred the affiliation of their craft, rather than embracing an identity based around an industry – that too would come after the First World War, galvanised for many unionists by the traumatic experience of the 1917 strike. In non-urban industries, the AWU had virtually an organising monopoly, and in the period 1904–18 membership growth accelerated.[15]

## The *Worker* Grows

The reinvigorated bush union came to town to parade. In Sydney, the visible power of the AWU rose as the new *Worker* building at 129 Bathurst Street. Completed in July 1905 at a cost of £3885 8s 4d, the three-storey building 'has a northerly aspect, and it is splendidly lighted. It, and the Trades Hall, are the only buildings in the city built entirely by trades unionists working under the day-labor system'. The façade featured the Australian coat of arms in relief and the inscription 'Advance Australia'. Complete with electric lighting, the building also served as the AWU's head office. The ground floor featured 'the American innovation' of placing the printing machines in public view. Indeed, the printing machinery was a substantial investment; in 1901 the union had purchased a linotype machine and a Cox Duplex printer, capable of printing and folding 6000 copies an hour. Another linotype machine was purchased in 1904, and the gilded stone lettering on the building's façade also let the world know that publishing, general printing and engraving services were available to help pay for it all.[16]

From time to time the AWU's leaders – and no doubt some members – expressed doubts about the return on the ambitious investment made in the weekly *Worker*. The 1902 conference hotly debated the paper's future. Macdonell noted the expensive equipment purchases in his secretary's report, and commented that 'until we are in a position to undertake the responsibilities of the much-needed Labor daily, our aim must be to so improve the weekly that it can fairly claim to fitly represent the cause of Labor'. Macdonell was hopeful that other unions would join in a scheme to help pay for the *Worker*. He did not add that successive AWU leaders had hoped for years for the imminent publication of a Labor daily, and that other unions might contribute to *Worker* costs. As it was, the 1902 conference felt that the union lacked sufficient control of the *Worker*, and decided that the AWU president and general secretary should henceforth sit on the *Worker* Board of Control. Delegate Carter from Bourke Branch also moved that the *Worker* be placed under new management. In his view, Hector Lamond, the current manager, presided over a 'wasteful and extravagant' operation. Adelaide Branch secretary Frank Lundie also felt that it was time for a change. Grayndler and Macdonell defended the current management, and pointed to much boosted circulation (approximately 10 000 members were receiving the *Worker* by direct mail in 1905. Members only received it upon payment of the *Worker* levy, introduced in 1897 to guarantee continued publication). In self-defence, Lamond pointed to the *Worker*'s growth over the years: 'jobbing work', advertising and sales had all increased dramatically since 1896, when he had been appointed. Lamond also

noted that principled unionism and touting for advertising were not
always happy companions, referring to 'the general prejudice of the
commercial classes against unionism'. His job was saved by 11 votes to 5.
The conference then turned to George Black, the ex-Labor Member of
the NSW Parliament who served as *Worker* editor 1900–4. Lundie wanted
a plebisicite of members to see if Black still met with their approval; he
was irritated that some Adelaide Branch Organisers' reports 'appeared
too late to have the effect intended'. White felt that Black was inclined to
disparage the poor grammar of rank-and-file contributors, and failed
to give sufficient prominence to AWU policy. Black also survived, with the
majority agreeing with Macdonell that the *Worker* Board of Control,
rather than the members, was the best judge of the editor's performance.
At subsequent conferences several delegates, particularly Lundie,
continued to closely scrutinise the *Worker* balance sheet and to question
Lamond's performance. However the *Worker* did continue to perform
strongly in the early 1900s, not least because it did so much more than
record AWU affairs. As Women's Page editor Mary Gilmore observed of
vice-regal approval (apparently an impressive benchmark for her) of the
pre-First World War *Worker*:

> The Worker was a power then: Lord Carmichael, when Governor of Victoria
> told me in 1910 or 1911 that he based all his political reports to the British
> Government on the *Worker*, as it was the fairest of all the papers; he said his
> orders were to get it as soon as it came out, and he read every word I wrote.

By 1914 Hector Lamond was contemplating increasing the print-run
from 80 000 to 120 000 copies. The *Worker*'s popular editorial features
were greatly enhanced by the fine black-and-white art of Claude Marquet
and Will Donald, who began contributing in the early 1900s and
continued on for many years. And during the same period Mary Gilmore
and Norman Lilley made an outstanding contribution to Australian
journalism in the pages of the *Worker*.[17]

Along with other poets such as her friend Henry Lawson, Mary
Gilmore had an association with the *Worker* stretching back into the
1890s, but her pioneering contribution to the paper was made between
1908 and 1931, when she edited the *Worker*'s Women's Page. Through
this page she exposed a neglected dimension of working-class life in
Australia, the pressures and strains placed upon women and family life
by the struggle for wage justice and decent living and working conditions. She offered all kinds of practical advice for wives and mothers
on limited budgets, the kind of column the AWU probably expected of
her. But from the outset she asserted her right to range widely in subject
matter, to describe woman as 'the fulfiller of her all-round destiny ...
because woman, as a politician, is only in her infancy, for, after all, politics

Mary Gilmore, editor of the *Worker* Women's Page between 1908 and 1931. *Moir Portraits, State Library of Victoria.*

and a knowledge of industrialism are but a part of that life which is so good to be truly lived, and which woman can never wholly leave and be woman, whatever man may do'.[18]

What man did sometimes filled Mary Gilmore with despair. In the Women's Page she explored the less flattering expressions of the mateship so beloved by the almost exclusively male AWU. 'Man takes his drink and comes home', she wrote in January 1909. 'If the home is cheerless, he jingles his coins in his pocket, goes out and drinks again. What matter to him the mental, moral and physical enfeeblement of the

child his wife bears to him … is it any wonder women send their children
to Bands of Hope, and join Women's Temperance Unions?' She also
antagonised male readers (and alarmed Hector Lamond) in 1908 by
railing against the evils of gambling, another predominantly male activity
which often left families without a living income. In 1915 she cam-
paigned for better maternity care; in 1919, with devastating simplicity,
she published a number of letters from women under the heading 'tired
mothers', which recounted the often desperate experiences of mothers
trying to care for young children on threadbare incomes. Several
described how their children had died in infancy.[19]

These contributions challenged male and AWU attitudes. Other contributions reflected the prevailing social ethos. In 1908 she castigated
several conservative newspapers for supporting the reintroduction of
Kanaka labour in the North Queensland sugar fields. Gilmore may have
believed that women were the equal – if not the intellectual superior – of
men, but she was certain that there could be no equality between the
races. She attacked the Women's National League for their apparent
support of the newspaper campaign. 'There is a screw loose somewhere,
when women are willing, either directly or indirectly, to mix with color.'
Along with other contemporary white supremacists, she shared a vision
of apocalyptic despair at the dilution of the White Australia policy: 'once
we let that break down, and the white man's civilisation will pass from the
black as the white light of day passes from the sky – to be followed by
blackness and night'.[20]

A few pages further on from Gilmore's column, literary editor
Norman Lilley reported the world of Australian and international letters
on 'Page Twenty-Seven' (later, when the *Worker* was slightly abbreviated,
'Page Twenty-One'). He published a wide range of verse and short
stories, reviews of Australian poets like Bernard O'Dowd and Hugh
McCrae, and notes about the comings and goings of Australian writers.
In 1908 he reported that Miles Franklin had taken a secretarial position
with a Chicago 'philanthropist': 'Nothing of the same charm has yet
followed "My Brilliant Career", but during the last few years the young
writer has sought varied experiences from which her literary gift may yet
evolve something big'. Lilley also noted the return to Australia of Barbara
Baynton, whose 'powerful' *Bush Studies* provided such an honest and
eloquent account of Australian bush life – although such writing was not
to everyone's taste. In a series of articles, 'Australian Writers and the
Bush', Lilley robustly defended Australian authors against the charge of
'morbid pessimism' and other failings. Leading this charge was the
*Sydney Morning Herald*, which Lilley suggested was 'animated by a desire
to destroy the native product in the interests of those foreign
importations from which newspapers draw so much of their revenue'.

Lilley especially took issue with critics of Henry Lawson, whom the *Herald* presumably had in mind when it referred to Australian bush writers who knew intimately 'every brick in George Street', but little of outback realities: 'There is no writer in the world, unless it be Maxim Gorky, who can so truthfully describe the features of a country the heart feels as Henry Lawson does in "The Drover's Wife, "The Bush Undertaker", or "Peter McLaughlin". The simplicity of perfect truth has a beauty and sublimity'.[21]

The AWU wanted to control a high-quality publishing empire, and had long hoped that other unions would contribute funding to both the *Worker* and the ambitious plan to establish a daily labour newspaper. To that end the 1909 convention voted to establish a company whose shareholders would consist of the AWU 'and approved unions'. Labor Papers Ltd was established in 1910, and a special levy of members struck to finance the venture. It was just as well: the financial support of other unions proved lukewarm. The funds accrued did however pay for Macdonell House, an imposing eight-storey building constructed at 321 Pitt Street, Sydney, at a cost of £106 000, which was, according to the union, 'replete with every modern convenience and easily the best newspaper office of its time in Australia'. The purchase and installation of the new printing machinery cost a further £38 000. Macdonell House, which also served as AWU headquarters and *Worker* offices, was officially opened in 1914, but the onset of war put aside any question of using this elaborate infrastructure to produce a daily newspaper. It was the first in a long series of frustrations for Labor Papers Ltd.[22]

The Brisbane *Worker* shared the editorial concerns of its Sydney sister during the pre-war years. Before moving to the Sydney *Worker* (the Sydney *Worker* became the *Australian Worker* in 1913; the Queensland paper was always simply referred to as the *Worker*), pioneer labour journalist Henry Boote edited the Brisbane *Worker* from 1902 to 1911. In his hands the *Worker* was 'the vehicle of a strong Australian Sentiment', a staunch defender of a White Australia, opposed to militarism, impatient for Labor to win office and pursue its reform agenda. Boote was an advocate of a practical socialism: 'the policy of Labour-Socialism ... is to get more and still more until Justice is satisfied'. Founded in 1890, the Brisbane *Worker* had featured other strongly socialist editors such as William Lane and William Guy Higgs. The paper also reflected a working-class literary interest, publishing poems by Lawson, Mary Gilmore, and Julian Stuart, one of the twelve Shearers Union members jailed for conspiracy after the 1891 strike. Jim Case emerged as the leading black-and-white artist of the *Brisbane Worker,* and during the war years relished the opportunity to lampoon the well-creased and risible features of Prime Minister Billy Hughes during the bitter conscription referendum debates. Despite the *Worker*'s popularity with Queensland readers (about 30 000 by 1912) and financial success (from both the sale of advertising space and 'jobbing' printing work), the participation of unions other than the AWU in the management of the *Worker* was fitful, coloured by personal and factional rivalries. Its management was increasingly dominated by the AWU, and in time Dunstan House, a Brisbane landmark and the headquarters of the AWU, would also serve as the *Worker* offices, a symbol, like Macdonell House in Sydney, of the AWU's power and wealth.[23]

### The Pastoral Industry Award, 1907

The hearing of the AWU's pastoral claims finally opened before Justice O'Connor on 10 June 1907, after the Pastoralists' Federal Council had reluctantly succumbed to the reality of the new Commonwealth Conciliation and Arbitration Act. The AWU's claims were a list of frustrated ambitions, reflecting not only a demand for improved wages but also an insistence on recognition as the legitimate representative of the industry's workers. The AWU sought an increase in shearing rates from 22s per 100 to 25s per 100 for most States (for part of Victoria and south-east Australia the union was willing to accept 22s 6d), with double rates for rams and stags. Thirty shillings a week was claimed for shed-hands. Shearers should be paid for lost time, at the rate of average earnings, from wet weather or any other cause; all shearing was to cease promptly at midday on Saturday. AWU members should be preferred for employment; AWU reps should have unfettered access to shearers' huts; and, most galling of all for the pastoralist who rejected AWU interference in the shearing shed, the pastoralist was called upon 'to accept AWU membership tickets as a guarantee for the fulfilment of their agreements by the men'. Unsurprisingly the pastoralists claimed that shearers earned more nowadays through machine shearing, that 20s per 100 was an adequate rate for shearers (17s 6d in the excluded areas of Victoria and South Australia), and that shed-hands should only receive 25s, except in Queensland, where 30s was conceded. The pastoralists also sought the maintenance of freedom of contract and resisted preference for AWU members on the grounds that the union used members' funds for political purposes. Indeed, the claims outraged the *Pastoralists' Review*. 'They took no hand in the struggle of the man who provided their means of livelihood except to make the struggle more difficult and bitter.' The *Review* seemed ignorant of the possibility that the shearer might also damn the intractable pastoralist with the same words.[24]

The 1907 hearings provided a compelling picture of the life of the travelling bushworker. From the outset, the AWU emphasised the itinerant nature of the shearer's calling, the long distances travelled between sheds, and the need to work as many sheds as possible to earn a decent living. Many shearers and shed-hands resorted to pushbikes to avoid costly train travel. In 1899 shed-hand Arthur Lamb told the court that he had travelled between 400 and 500 miles looking for work; in 1905 he got seven weeks' work at one station – and nothing else. He walked along the rail line looking for work and eventually arrived back in Sydney where he 'did a little dealing' – selling vegetables from a cart. Often only paid on a daily basis, if wet weather disrupted the shearing he would get nothing at all.[25]

It was nothing to travel enormous distances in search of work. In the early 1900s shed-hand Syd Fernandez worked the harsh country around Broken Hill. In 1906 he walked 285 miles to work two sheds. In 1907 he hoisted his swag over his shoulder again and walked 390 miles, *then* walked south to the Mildura region – another area where he regularly found work – and, when sheds cut out down there, tramped back to Broken Hill. In total, he estimated that he walked 980 miles in 1907–8. His little frayed diary is a tribute to the stamina of a pair of legs – he didn't get a pushbike until 1910.[26]

In terms of the shearing process, Macdonell insisted in his evidence that in recent years there had been 'a tremendous increase in the wool carrying capacity of the sheep': they now carried 2–4 pounds more. This in his view made the sheep 'infinitely harder to shear'. These heavier sheep were often more wrinkled, 'like the bellows of a concertina', requiring more care and exertion. Increased wool density had reduced tallies from an average 100 a day in 1891 to 70 in 1907, a fall confirmed by shearer Mathew Grogan, whose shearing experience stretched back to 1878. He claimed that the machines made shearing more strenuous. 'You are stooping all the time with the machine, and with the [hand] shears you generally sharpen them each half hour and stand up straight. With the machines you might shear half a dozen without straightening yourself up, and it gives you a backache more than with the shears, and the vibration of the machine shakes your whole system.' Grogan said that wrinkly sheep were tougher on the blades. It was difficult to get the wool close to the skin cleanly off. 'The skin stands up in bars round their necks and over their faces. They cannot see out of their eyes in many instances with the wrinkles.' Through a shearing life of nearly thirty years Grogan had been the classic itinerant. He had never had a settled home, 'except the occasional use of my father's and mother's'. In the off season he resorted to fencing, roadwork, 'any piece work'. He had lately acquired a little bit of land.[27]

To refute the AWU's evidence James Yates, the Queensland manager of the Federal Sheep Shearing Company, was an important witness. Yates

'A modern Australian shearer' with pushbike, swag and companion, *c.* 1900. *Tyrell Collection, National Library of Australia.*

represented the new middleman in the pastoral industry, the shearing contractor, who had emerged, in the AWU's eyes, as another hindrance to obtaining fair rates for the workers and recognition of the union as their sole representative. Yates told the court that the Federal Sheep Shearing Company was just three years old, but already had fifty Queensland stations contracted. He claimed that machine shearing had resulted in higher tallies. A good average team could average 100 a day. Yates also claimed that organisers visiting sheds and preference for unionists would cause trouble, with organisers making political speeches and non-unionists victimised. Justice O'Connor, referring to the AWU's reps visiting sheds, commented to Yates: 'I do not see that I can shut it out'.[28]

Indeed. After nearly twenty years, the pastoralists' determination to shut the AWU out had been undermined in the Arbitration Court. O'Connor handed down his decision on 20 July. The AWU's claim for rates was only marginally unsuccessful: 24s per 100 was the new shearing rate; 22s per 100 in Victoria and South Australia. Shearing rams attracted double rates. Wool-rollers, piece-pickers and penners-up got 30s a week; all other shed-hands, and all in Victoria (except the north-west) and south-east South Australia, received 27s 6d. A cook received 35s, but if shearers contributed to his wages, then he would receive 4s from each shearer. Weekly hours were set at forty-eight hours a week and work was to stop at midday Saturday. Shearers could refuse to shear wet or cancerous sheep, and if wet weather or broken machinery delayed shearing then the shearer would receive a free ration for the first day, and 10s a day thereafter. All parties were bound against the threat of fines to uphold the terms of the award, which would expire in June 1910.[29]

The *Pastoralists' Review* claimed that a 20 per cent increase in shearing rates was 'penal'. It was a grave injustice, and all other objections to the new award – even the payment of weekly wages to shed-hands – paled into insignificance. As far as Macdonell was concerned, the AWU 'came of age' in 1907. He told the 1908 AWU conference that the union's membership had jumped from 30 000 to 39 000 nationally, with workers attracted to the pastoral industry by the award's generous terms. Macdonell congratulated the pastoralists for allowing the case to proceed on its merits. 'They helped to establish the kind of court Labor has always been clamouring for, and to which it would always be loyal.' O'Connor's decision was not the only reward for loyalty. Macdonell told the conference that even this decision had been overshadowed by Justice Higgins's decision in the Harvester case, and the 'far reaching consequences' of minimum wage justice which Higgins defined in his seminal November 1907 judgment. His decision established the principle of a fair and reasonable minimum wage (which he set at 7s a day). It was the

tangible expression of the justice which Higgins had told Victorian AWU
members at St Arnaud in 1900 they should seek as due recognition of
their labours.[30]

## Membership Growth and Amalgamations

The years 1908 to 1914 were characterised by expansion for the AWU.
With peace prevailing in the shearing sheds after the 1907 award, the
AWU's leaders renewed their efforts to build an even more powerful
union. This period saw several key amalgamations which would make the
union a dominant force in the Australian labour movement for the next
half-century or more. Although unions were restricted by rules – under
State and federal industrial legislation – from enrolling members outside
their industry, amalgamations provided a means of circumventing this
restriction, as long as the members of the amalgamating unions approved the merger. AWU membership grew strongly as a consequence of
amalgamations in the pre-war period, reaching over 60 000 by 1914. It
was a diverse membership, in mining, the sugar industry, the pastoral
industry; but it was still essentially a bushworkers' union. That the Australian workforce still had a relatively large non-urban component, and
that the AWU had a virtual organising monopoly of these workers, can
be gauged by noting that by the outbreak of the Great War in 1914
almost one in eight of all Australian unionists were members of the
Australian Workers Union.[31]

First steps were small. Reaching into yet unconquered territory, the
1908 conference decided to organise in Tasmania and Western Australia,
efforts which only slowly paid dividends. By 1910 the WA Branch had
only 1000 members, and Tasmania 600. Similarly, efforts to broaden the
AWU's coverage to include almost the full range of agricultural
occupations also met with frustration, not least due to the sustained
hostility of employers. In August 1908 the Victorian Pastoralists Union
warned members that the AWU was seeking federal award coverage for
permanent station-hands, and urged members to gather employment
statistics for shed-hands and general station-hands, in anticipation of any
AWU application. But the AWU also needed time to organise and gather
information for an award. During this period the union decided to assist
the organisation of the Rural Workers Union and fruit-pickers around
Mildura, in much the same way that the AWU had encouraged the
General Labourers Union in the early 1890s. A year later, however, Macdonell explained to the 1909 conference that 'it was a big undertaking
to get all the rural workers into an organisation of that kind, and no
great success had attended the work'. Later at the conference Arthur
Rae moved that the AWU seek amendments to the Commonwealth

Conciliation and Arbitration Act to enable the union to cover any category of agricultural worker. He said that 'the great majority of AWU men were general labourers when not following the pastoral industry, and it seemed anomalous that they only had the Union protection for a certain period of the year'. Interestingly, Macdonell opposed the motion, noting that if the AWU's coverage were to be 'spread right round' then 'it would be almost impossible for one man to obtain the necessary knowledge of all the sections embraced and do justice to the whole at the same time'. In his view, the AWU was 'doing pretty good work' in catering effectively for pastoral industry workers. But it was not enough for a majority of conference delegates. They passed Rae's motion 14:10.[32]

Donald Macdonell would not live to see the AWU reach beyond the pastoral industry. On 26 October 1911 he died of cancer at the age of 49. Macdonell had been in poor health for several years, no doubt worsened by the enormous workload he carried. After the election of the first NSW Labor Government in 1910, he had been given the portfolios of Chief Secretary and Agriculture, although illness compelled him to relinquish most duties by early 1911. Friends and enemies alike mourned Donald Macdonell. Tom White, another Bourke official who succeeded him as general secretary, described him as a 'man in a million'; his 'commanding personality' had built a truly national AWU. Even the *Pastoralists' Review* conceded his great skills. 'A clever speaker, concise and straightforward, and level headed and level-tempered withal – qualities of inestimable value in the making of a true politician.' Both Henry Lawson and Mary Gilmore celebrated Macdonell in their work – Gilmore with 'Donald Macdonell' in *Marri'd and other verses*, and Lawson in the short story 'That pretty girl in the Army'. In 1914 the AWU commemorated Macdonell's role by naming its new Sydney headquarters at 321 Pitt Street in his honour.[33]

A new Pastoral Industry Award brought down by Justice Higgins in the Federal Arbitration Court in October 1911 proved a mixed result for the AWU. The shearing rate was standardised at 24s per 100 for Queensland, New South Wales, South Australia and Victoria, reflecting Higgins's penchant for a simplified minimum standard. The main beneficiaries of the new award were the shed-hands, who were granted 37s 6d a week. On the other hand, Higgins refused to include Tasmania within the scope of the award, as there was no evidence provided by the AWU of a dispute existing between employees and pastoral employers in that State. Higgins also refused to consider claims concerning station-hands, again because of lack of evidence concerning a dispute with individual employers. Despite these setbacks, the AWU regarded the award as a successful result.[34]

The AWU still faced the constant day-to-day struggle to achieve fair and reasonable rates of pay (where award conditions did not apply) and reasonable working and living conditions. The standard of hut accommodation for rural workers and the policing of the regulations governing those standards was a source of continued frustration. In New South Wales, Western Branch delegate J. Andrews told the 1912 Convention that in the area he had travelled last year 'there was hardly a hut complying with the Act', while a Central Branch delegate reported seeing huts 'which had been used as fowl houses and pig houses, and no fumigation had been carried out'. With a Labor government in power, prospects for innovative legislation for hut accommodation in New South Wales appeared bright. Despite some initial encouragement from Minister for Labour and Industry Beeby, the ensuing legislation was so emasculated in the Parliament – many rural workers were exempted from its provisions – that the Bill was eventually shelved. The AWU had long felt that the Labor Party was too city-oriented. The 1906 conference had rejected a motion that political funds, then sent by members to the AWU branches, should be sent directly to the Political Labor League. In Macdonell's view such a move would only encourage the PLL's worst habits. 'He thought the [PLL] executive, largely composed of city women and men who were entirely ignorant of country conditions, was the worst possible body to control such a fund.' In 1912 these prejudices seemed to be confirmed, and the *Worker* lamented the 'betrayal' of bushworkers and said that the McGowen Government's actions called for 'the severest censure'.[35]

By 1912 the AWU had a new general secretary, Edward Grayndler. Veteran Bourke Branch official Tom White, who had replaced Macdonell, had died within a year of him. Grayndler, a former shearer, NSW organiser for the Union and secretary of the Victoria-Riverina Branch, had only arrived in the AWU federal office in Sydney in 1911 to assist the ailing Macdonell with Arbitration Court work. Forty-five years old when he assumed office in 1912, Grayndler would consolidate the AWU's reputation for a commitment to well-researched arbitration claims over the course of the twenty-nine years he served as general secretary.[36]

Grayndler did not share Macdonell's resistance to amalgamations, and by 1913 the AWU had amalgamated with the Queensland Amalgamated Workers Association, the Rural Workers Union, the Carriers Union and the Rabbit Trappers Union. Of these the AWA was the largest and the most influential. The AWA began in 1907 as an organisation of miners and railway navvies. Under the leadership of E. G. Theodore and William McCormack, both of whom subsequently became Queensland premiers (and, in Theodore's case, a future federal treasurer), the union expanded to include a number of North Queensland bush unions comprising miners, sugar workers and labourers. In terms of internal union politics, the AWU–AWA amalgamation was undoubtedly eased by

The pre-First World War AWU leadership. The group includes: Tom White (front row, far left), Frank Lundie (front, third from left), Donald Macdonell (front, fourth from left) and W. G. Spence (front, with pith helmet), John Barnes (middle row, far right), Edward Grayndler (back row, far left), Frank Richardson (back, third from left), and Arthur Rae (back, far right). Francis ('Frank') Isaiah Richardson (1866–1937), was a foundation member of the ASU, AWU Executive Councillor, Organiser with the Victoria-Riverina branch (1902–36), and staunch ALP activist. His long career in the union – and his presence in many early AWU photos – now seems an ironic comment on the union's zeal for a White Australia. It is an irony made poignant by the great affection expressed for him by his AWU colleagues on his death in 1937. *AWU Collection.*

both Theodore and McCormack transferring much of their considerable ambitions from the AWA to the Queensland Parliament, to which they were elected in 1909 and 1912 respectively. However Theodore remained as Queensland AWU State president 1913–16, and McCormack was branch vice-president 1913–15.[37]

The 1912 AWU Annual Convention had debated a resolution to enlarge 'our field of operation by embracing all kindred organizations'. Many delegates could see merit in the proposal. One, confirming the 'bushwork' links which cut across industrial coverage, complained that he had to join as many as four unions to earn his living in the 'off' (non-shearing) season. There were other delegates, echoing Macdonell's concern, who baulked at the inclusion of those engaged in work other than strictly rural industries, and wanted to exclude organisations such as the AWA and the United Labourers Union of South Australia, whose coverage included the likes of platelayers and navvies. Only those industrially allied with the AWU, they believed, would ensure a closer unity which would be to the advantage of members. Some needed to be convinced that expanding coverage would not prejudice the AWU's status before the Arbitration Court. Legal advice confirmed that because of an 1911 amendment to the Commonwealth Conciliation and Arbitration Act passed by the Fisher Labor Government, the AWU's status would not be endangered as a consequence of amalgamation. Before 1911 there had been a prohibition on craft unions obtaining federal registration, and given the plethora of unions in Australia in the early twentieth century – as many as 700 in 1915 – much confusion about what criteria constituted a 'craft' union or an 'industrial' union. From 1911, combined craft and industry unions, and unions covering diverse industries, were free to seek federal industrial registration, thus alleviating the concern that an amalgamation with other unions might expose the AWU to a cancellation of its registration under the Act.[38]

Despite the concerns of some AWU members, in 1913 a membership plebiscite resulted in an overwhelming Yes vote across all four unions. In Queensland, the three AWU branches were consolidated into one and the organisation was subdivided into five districts along existing AWA lines. The first branch secretary of the new Queensland AWU branch was W. J. Dunstan, ex-shearer and Adelaide Branch president, brought in to Queensland as an AWU buffer against the influence of the headstrong AWA leaders McCormack and Theodore. It was clear that Dunstan presided over the largest AWU branch, with the widest industrial coverage of any State branch. Under the Constitution the states and the Commonwealth shared responsibility for industrial relations. Industrial rules and coverage could vary between the systems, and under Queensland State industrial law the AWU's rules were much wider in scope than in the other States or federally, largely because of the AWA's wide coverage of industries outside the pastoral industry, and a wide geographical coverage; the AWA had virtually an organising monopoly in North Queensland, for example. The amalgamations saw national membership increase to over 62 000. Figures provided to the Commonwealth industrial registrar in December 1913 showed that the AWU had 62 034 members: Queensland, 22 231; New South Wales, 21 088, Victoria, 10 987, South Australia, 5517, Western Australia, 1291 and Tasmania 920. The potential for amalgamations seemed limitless. The Australasian Meat Industry Employees Union and the Federated Sawmill and Timberyard Employees Union had also sent representatives to the 1913 conference; they were both considering joining with the AWU at some later stage. Spence spoke of the 'big step' which the amalgamating unions had been taken, a step which marked the departure from the 'narrower operations of purely craft unionism'. The AWU, he thought, 'was coming in measurable distance of the full scope of its title'.[39]

The AWU–AWA amalgamation would also change the AWU in ways other than the strict industrial nature of the union. According to Theodore's biographer Ross Fitzgerald, 'the basis of AWA organisation was much more autocratic than the AWU, whose branches maintained a fair degree of autonomy. It was also effectively simple: leave all decisions regarding organisation and industrial action to the central executive. According to Theodore, a union organiser's primary responsibility was "to get the money for the union tickets. That's all any union organiser worries about. Get the money and run"'. Hence Theodore and McCormack insisted that under the terms of the AWU–AWA amalgamation, the new Queensland AWU would adopt the more centralised structure of the AWA, while the rest of the AWU would retain its more autonomous branch network. Dunstan, pragmatic and able, emerged as the ideal manager of this centralism. As the Queensland Branch grew more rapidly in membership than the other States, and its proportional representation increased at the national union level (at the Executive Council and Annual Convention), the Queensland approach would soon be transferred across the union through the influence of its officials, notably, Clarrie Fallon and later Tom Dougherty.[40]

Despite the optimism engendered by the amalgamations, there were gathering clouds in the distance. The years immediately before the outbreak of the Great War witnessed a worsening relationship between the AWU and the Holman Labor Government in New South Wales over the issue of States' rights. The Fisher Labor Government held referendums in 1911 and 1913 seeking an increase in Commonwealth powers as they applied to Commonwealth–State relations on industrial and economic matters. On each occasion, Premier Holman adopted a 'states' rights' position and urged a No vote. This brought him into direct conflict with trade unions, which saw increased Commonwealth powers as the only answer to effective federal intervention in the economy. The AWU was well represented in the federal parliamentary party and was itself organised along federal lines. Not surprisingly, the union condemned Holman. General secretary Tom White told the 1912 AWU Annual Convention that the failure of the 1911 referendum 'was to a large extent due to the action of some of the New South Wales State Labor Party who ... caused a split in the ranks of Labor, and gave our opponents one of the strongest arguments they could adduce against it'.

White insisted that the AWU had been 'vitally affected' by the failure of the referendum as the decision thwarted attempts to increase the scope of the Arbitration Act to settle disputes. The *Worker* referred to the State Labor Government as 'State insects'. At the 1911 AWU Annual Convention, delegates unanimously carried a resolution which in part called on the Political Labor League to request Holman 'to retire from the Political Labor movement and fight it from outside and not from within'. Holman waited until the conscription crisis of 1916 to oblige the AWU's 1911 appeal. The AWU, which Holman once represented as an organiser, would be one of the few New South Wales unions which survived the devastating consequences of that split, and the subsequent 1917 strike.[41]

CHAPTER 6

# One Big Union

*The Conscription Crisis and the WIUA Challenge, 1914–20*

## War and Conscription

The outbreak of the First World War provoked an immediate response from the Australian trade union movement. Of the 54 000 recruits who enlisted in the first five months of the war, 43 per cent were unionists – far in excess of the proportion of unionists among adult males. In *The Story Of Anzac* Charles Bean observes that 'by April 1915, there had been enrolled 12,000 shearers and station hands, members of the Australian Workers Union'. The pages of the *Worker* profiled some of the AWU members who had volunteered. Distinguished among them was Albert Jacka, a Victoria-Riverina Branch member, who won the Victoria Cross at Gallipoli and the Military Cross at Pozières on the Western Front for conspicuous bravery. Many others did not outlive their heroic efforts. The *Worker* of 14 October 1915 printed an appeal from a Mrs Watson, in desperate need to contact her bushworker husband to tell him of their son's death as a result of wounds received at Gallipoli. Another report noted that an AWU ticket had been picked out of the mud of the Pozières battlefield. At the 1916 AWU Annual Convention, one delegate referred to the large number of AWU members who had 'crossed the great border' and the many AWU members 'who had gone to Gallipoli and whose bones were lying there'. The 1917 Annual Convention was told that of a total membership of just over 70 000, almost 30 000 were in the armed forces – so many that there had been talk of raising an AWU division, a proposal apparently raised with Defence Minister George

117

Pearce but which went no further (in the First World War a division
consisted of 18 000 men).[1]

As AWU members volunteered their lives for what they deemed as
their duty for King and Country, the AWU held another front line in a
battle at home: the campaign against conscription. The conscription
issue was debated within AWU ranks as early as August 1915, when the
*Worker* published an interview with several prominent members of the
labour movement on the question. One of those interviewed, William
Morris Hughes (who was to become Labor prime minister one month
later), indicated his opposition to the introduction of conscription for
overseas service. Within a year, Hughes, on his return from a visit to
England and France where the Allied Command had pressured him for
additional commitments of Australian troops, expressed concerned at
the fall-off in recruiting and announced that a referendum would be
held on the question of compulsory military service.[2]

At the 1916 Annual Convention of the AWU, a motion from Queensland and western New South Wales to oppose conscription received
unanimous support. An Interstate Trade Union Congress in May 1916
declared an 'uncompromising hostility' to conscription. Nevertheless on
26 August Federal Cabinet agreed by a majority of one to support
Hughes's proposal. The parliamentary Labor Caucus also fell in behind
the decision. However, Hughes had miscalculated the level of support
from the labour movement. Conscription was emphatically rejected by
the Victorian Trades Hall and the Sydney Labour Council and he was
expelled by the NSW ALP. In New South Wales Labor Premier William
Holman, the ex-AWU organiser, had his party endorsement withdrawn,
along with eight other parliamentarians.[3]

The conscription referendum was scheduled to take place on Saturday,
28 October 1916. From the end of August, the anti-conscription campaign gained momentum, led by the AWU through the *Worker*, published
weekly, with a special anti-conscription edition issued on the eve of the
referendum. Each week a torrent of anti-conscription material poured
forth, dramatised by the often brilliant political cartoons of Claude
Marquet and Mick Paul. The attack was led by Henry Boote, who had
taken over as *Worker* editor in 1914. Boote had a background with labour
newspapers in Queensland stretching back to the 1890s, and he had no
doubt that conscription was repugnant to the spirit of Australian Labor:

> The whole trend of Australian policy was to build up a self-reliant nation, cap-
> able of its own defence in case of attack, and free to act under all circumstances
> as an enlightened and sovereign people. Our Defence Acts were framed to
> protect us from invasion. The theory that Australian defence means the compul-
> sory deportation of our citizens' forces to foreign battlefields is entirely new, and
> diametrically opposed to the spirit and letter of all our defence measures.

## THE "CASE" FOR LABOR.
### (By W. M. Hughes).

First Conscription Referendum, 1916. The 'Case' For Labor, a mordant parody of Hughes' 1907 articles of the same name. Claude Marquet in the *Australian Worker*, 5 October 1916. *AWU Collection.*

The spectre of European militarism loomed, a repugnant reminder of the 'old world' which many Australians hoped they had escaped. The war was pulling them back to the age of the press-gang. Declining wartime wages and working conditions, which steadily eroded domestic morale, and fears of a mass importation of Asian labour to replace men dragooned into the armed services, also fanned working-class alarm at the prospect of conscription. On 26 October the *Worker* reported an increase in circulation of 31 500 in just three weeks. The AWU gave priority to the campaign over all other matters. An Executive Council meeting resolved on 24 September that until the end of the campaign the whole effort of the union would be directed towards defeating the question through the ballot box.[4]

AWU general secretary Ted Grayndler believed the union enjoyed strong rank-and-file support over its conscription stand. On 26 October Grayndler wrote in the *Worker*:

> Every representative meeting of AWU members where-ever held, in any of the States, has opposed conscription. In the camps, in the shearing sheds, at Local Committee meetings, at Branch meetings, at Convention, and at the Executive Council the decision has been the same. Thousands of members write from all parts of the Commonwealth endorsing our action; and, yes, from the very trenches at the front, AWU men write and encourage us to stand together and keep Australia as free as when they left it, and do our utmost to prevent conscription being fastened on this young nation.

The AWU could not claim universal support for its opposition to conscription, and dissidents emerged from within the heart of the union. Both AWU president W. G. Spence and his son-in-law and manager of the *Worker*, Hector Lamond, supported Hughes. At first Spence had indicated opposition to conscription, telling the NSW PLL in June 1916: 'In reply to your request as to my views I am *opposed to conscription* [emphasis added]. I think that Australia has done well and is still doing all that can reasonably be asked in this terrible struggle'. Two months later, however, Spence voted in favour of Hughes's proposal to introduce conscription. Spence was subsequently interrogated at a meeting of the AWU Executive Council on 22 September. He was asked if he was prepared to sacrifice the interests of the AWU by supporting Hughes. He replied that he did not see it as a question of sacrificing the union. He could not alter his views as he looked upon the conscription issue as the 'biggest question'. The Executive Council subsequently resolved to suspend Spence and on 31 October 1916 he tendered his resignation from the AWU. Hector Lamond also resigned as business manager of the *Worker*. The Worker Board of Control had insisted that all staff support the AWU's anti-conscription campaign. Mary Gilmore could not do so. She

Second Conscription Referendum, 1917. 'I'll Have You!' Billy Hughes and the chains of conscription. Claude Marquet in the *Australian Worker*, 13 October 1917. *AWU Collection.*

was ambiguous about conscription, and torn between her admiration for Billy Hughes and the labour movement's rejection of him. She avoided confronting her mixed feelings in the pages of the *Worker* by taking annual leave during the referendum campaign period. Nevertheless, her attitude would not be forgotten by her colleagues, and she was pressured again by the *Worker* board during the 1917 federal elections and the second referendum campaign in November 1917, when she wrote more enthusiastically against conscription, largely by directing her attack against the wealthy, whom she said were not sharing the burden of the struggle.[5]

Some AWU members suggested that Hughes and Lamond took advantage of the fact that Spence was ill at the time and 'tricked' him into voting for conscription. Spence seems to have been solidly committed to an anti-conscription position at least until June 1916, and his character and experience do not suggest that he would have been an easy mark for 'trickery'. The fact remains that somewhere between June and the Cabinet vote in August, Spence altered his position on the question and reiterated his support for Hughes before his own union one month later. Hector Lamond had helped Spence to write *Australia's Awakening* (1909) and the *History of the AWU* (1911). He was a strong pro-conscriptionist and became honorary general secretary in New South Wales for the Yes case in the first conscription campaign. We can only assume that he would have discussed the issue with Spence, and that Spence evidently concurred with Lamond's views.[6]

There is no doubt that the AWU's anti-conscription campaign played a critical role in securing a No majority of over 82 500 in the October poll. In November 1916 Henry Boote rejoiced at the news that the split in the federal parliamentary Labor Party had led to Hughes walking out of the Caucus, resulting in the formation of the conservative Nationalist Party in January 1917, with Hughes as leader and prime minister, and Spence vice-president of the Executive Council. Former Adelaide Branch official Alexander Poynton was also among the Labor MPs who walked from the Caucus room in support of Hughes, holding several ministerial positions in Hughes's subsequent administrations. Boote called for an immediate federal election to throw out Hughes's illegitimate coalition, but in May 1917 the voters massacred the Labor Party instead – then, in December, promptly defeated another attempt to introduce conscription, by a larger No vote than that recorded at the first referendum. The people evidently felt that Hughes could best lead an effective war effort, but they denied him the power to send conscripts to the carnage in Europe. Boote's harsh judgement of Hughes reflected the intense division in society created by Hughes's insistence on demanding a second referendum: 'The vanity of the miniature Nero has unbalanced his reason. He fancies himself a despot of divine right, and in the excess of his megalomania all who oppose him are traitors and rebels who may count themselves lucky to escape a white wall and a firing squad at dawn'. While Hughes emerged from the conscription crisis as a Labor villain, Boote was fêted as one of Labor's heroes, both for the *Worker*'s anti-conscription efforts and for his campaign for justice for the twelve members of the Industrial Workers of the World wrongly accused by Hughes of treason and plotting sabotage of Australia's war effort. He had been fined for breaches of the War Precautions Act for his part in the anti-conscription campaign, and his efforts on behalf of the IWW twelve brought him a futher conviction for contempt of court. Nevertheless, Boote was instrumental in securing a royal commission in 1920 into the IWW case, after which ten of the twelve were acquitted (Boote's campaign for justice for the IWW men was supported by the AWU's Executive Council in September 1919, despite the union's otherwise fierce opposition to IWW policies). But these victories came at a price. Boote, writing in April 1917, believed Hughes's 'judas-like' treachery had set back 'the great change in the social system' he craved for his country.[7]

The conscription campaigns exposed many hidden tensions in Australian society. An undercurrent of the anti-conscription campaigns was an economic motive which identified conscription as 'a move by exploiters to inhibit the struggle of workers against war profiteering'. Instead of conscripting workers, the abundant wealth of the rich should be dragooned into the cause. For many workers the government's secret agenda was a reduction in wages and a dismantling of hard-won working conditions. George Fern, an AWU Central Branch organiser, related in the *Worker* a conversation he had with a farmer he met while travelling between Narromine and Trangie. The farmer told Fern he saw the benefit of conscription as a means by which 'we could offer the men 5s per day to take our crops in, and if they refused it, we could ring up the police, who would get in touch with the local military camp, Dubbo, and have the men yarded to the colors, and a sufficient number of men who had been trained would be sent along to take the crop in at conscription wages'. The greater No vote obtained in the December 1917 referendum may well have reflected heightened suspicion that this kind of cynical manipulation was the real motive behind much conservative support for Hughes. Certainly, the experience of the 1917 strike in New South Wales, which ran its bitter course between August and October, could have only hardened resistance to any measure which would exacerbate the suffering of many working-class families.[8]

## The 1917 Strike

By 1917 war weariness was taking its toll among Australians. The slaughter seemed endless on the Western Front; a deterioration in living standards and rising prices impacted most severely upon the working class. Governments were seduced by the cost-saving and efficiency claims of the new techniques of 'scientific management' as higher costs and falling revenues dominated departmental balance sheets. Government employees, who received less pay than their private sector counterparts and were denied recourse to federal arbitration, were increasingly embittered with their lot. All these factors tumbled into the industrial turmoil in New South Wales between August and October 1917: the Great Strike, triggered by the implementation of a new costing system involving the use of cards to time work performed in the workshops of the NSW Department of Railways and Tramways. The nature of the scheme itself was anathema to the employees. The government fuelled the dispute by its refusal to negotiate the introduction of the scheme with the unions. By the end of the first week of the strike about 10 000 workers had withdrawn their labour. Other unions then became involved and by late October almost 97 500 workers were on strike, over a third of the State's union membership. By the time the dispute ended, about four million working days had been lost in New South Wales and the union movement had suffered a devastating defeat at the hands of a con-servative NSW Government which deregistered the striking unions and refused to re-employ many strikers. In the railways and tramways, government and employers encouraged the formation of scab unions to step into the vacuum created by deregistration.[9]

The AWU did not participate in the strike. Each edition of the *Worker* during the strike contained an official notification to AWU members, issued by general secretary Grayndler and NSW vice-president Bailey, instructing them not to cease work unless told to do so by the union's Executive Council, and reminding them: 'Any of our members in employment can most effectively assist the great body of men now battling for industrial democracy by levying themselves voluntarily to assist in supporting the wives and children of their fellow-unionists'. The Labor Party's Fighting Fund was publicised in each issue of the *Worker* with calls for contributions, and Boote's powerful penmanship was also brought to bear in morale-boosting reports of the strike's progress. The AWU's Railway Workers Industry Branch struck a voluntary levy to assist strikers and their families. Grayndler justified the AWU's non-participation in his report to the 1918 Annual Convention:

> Some attempts were made to embroil the AWU in the strike. When appeals failed to secure the end sought, threats were made by irresponsible persons to call out AWU men. As it was impossible to get your Executive Council together, your President and myself met in Melbourne and determined to keep the AWU free from participation in any sympathy strike, as we considered that the only effective help that our Union could render was that of financial assistance to those who were in need and suffering as a result of the strike and lockouts that followed.

The AWU contributed over £4000 of the £7000 contributed towards the strike fund, a far from insubstantial contribution to the needs of striking workers left without an income. Perhaps too, the AWU officials were concerned that any involvement in the strike would have prejudiced the newly won coverage for station-hands under the 1917 Pastoral Award, an application which was still before the Arbitration Court when the strike began, and which the AWU had been seeking since 1911. Certainly, the strident voice of IWW-style radicalism would have fallen on deaf ears, as indeed the strike leaders rejected the IWW's inflammatory rhetoric.[10]

What impact did the AWU's absence have in the eventual outcome of the dispute? In the opinion of labour historian Ian Turner the AWU's absence was critical: 'the front of the AWU and the other mass unions, created in the 1916 political crisis, was seriously weakened by the refusal of the AWU to be drawn into the struggle'. Perhaps that refusal was born in a memory of the long defeats of the 1890s. The leaders of the AWU in 1917 were almost entirely men with personal experience of the calamitous industrial defeats and severe unemployment of the period 1890–1904. They had seen unions built by years of hard work unravelled in a few days' confrontation with the state. The unions which were defeated and deregistered by the NSW Industrial Court in 1917 took years to rebuild – and only after the intervention of the law, when the Engineers' case in 1920 paved the way for registration of unions of state-employed workers under the Commonwealth Conciliation and Arbitration Act, and the pursuit of federal awards. Several of the revived unions were just beginning this process, with new federal awards, in 1924, seven years after the strike. NSW Labor Council secretary E. J. Kavanagh realised in December 1917 the damage wrought to the trade union movement by the strike: 'prior to the strike Trades Unionism had reached the highest pinnacle it had ever reached in this country. It took just twenty-seven years of hard work to bring it to that state of perfection. It was built up by arbitration and knocked down in twenty-seven days by direct action'. The defeats of the 1890s prodded the AWU towards the seductive amelioration of arbitration. The 1917 strike compelled a new generation of union leaders to measure their ideals against the incremental margins conceded by the industrial courts.[11]

## One Big Union

There is no doubt that the AWU thrived while many other unions collapsed. The period 1915–18 saw the AWU continue to grow through amalgamations with other unions. The AWU extended its influence into other areas of industry while maintaining its domination in the pastoral field. Successful amalgamations with the railway construction workers in New South Wales and metalliferous (non-coal) miners nationally saw the AWU move a step closer to its goal of representing all Australian workers as the 'One Big Union' – moulded in its own image.

The AWU Annual Convention held in early 1915 considered amalgamation between the AWU and the Amalgamated Meat Industries
Employees' Union (AMIEU), the Railway Workers and General Labourers Association of New South Wales (RW&GLA), the United Labourers
Union of Victoria (ULU) and the General Workers Union of Western
Australia (GWU). The meatworkers were a large and well-organised
union, particularly in Queensland, and Theodore was keen to secure the
amalgamation. But there was resistance within the AMIEU to merging
with the AWU, and despite some State branches indicating support for
the move, its opponents were able to defeat the amalgamation on the
grounds that the AMIEU would be swallowed up by the AWU. The AWU
had better success with the other unions. The ULU and the GLU were
small unions of construction workers, and they moved quietly into the
AWU. It was the amalgamation with the RW&GLA, however, which had
major significance for the AWU's coverage in the construction industry.
It added about 15 000 new members and gave the union its first major
industry branch, formed into the Railway Workers Industry Branch. In
1917 the Rockchoppers and Sewer Miners Union became a section of the
RWIB and the quarrymen were soon to join them.[12]

Construction workers comprised a mostly itinerant workforce in railway
and road construction. In New South Wales their main employers were the
large public sector organisations or their private contractors: the Public
Works Department, the Metropolitan Board of Water Supply and
Sewerage, the Sydney Harbour Trust and Government Railways and
Tramways. They were mostly pick-and-shovel men, although there was
scope for on-the-job skilling and specialisation in such areas as rock-
chopping and sewer mining. The work was physically demanding, with
dangers from shifting rock and earth, from blasting and from silicosis. The
Railway Workers and General Labourers Association, known as the
'Navvies Union', had a relatively large membership, reaching nearly
17 500 by 1914, making it the second largest in New South Wales after the
AWU. It had much in common with the AWU. It was in many respects
another bushworkers' union: men who might otherwise work in woolsheds, on farms or as miners might readily turn to railway construction.
The union officially favoured arbitration and saw direct action as a last
resort, although some RW&GLA officials feared AWU post-amalgamation
domination. RW&GLA organiser George Bodkin, apparently attracted by
the career opportunities available in the larger AWU, led the opposition
to the doubters, arguing that only the AWU offered the industrial strength
to organise nationally. The amalgamation was approved in 1915 after the
AWU agreed to allow the navvies their own industrial branch and
autonomy within the AWU. George Bodkin emerged as the new branch's
secretary.[13]

The success of the amalgamation of construction workers with the

AWU was followed by an amalgamation with the Federated Mining Employees Association (FMEA), an organisation of metalliferous miners (non-coal) formed in 1911, as the federally registered extension of the old Amalgamated Miners Association (AMA), except at Broken Hill, whose miners, more radical and industrially isolationist by nature, preferred their own local organisation. There had been moves among metalliferous miners to join with the AWU since 1903 when the Mt Lyell Branch of the AMA in Tasmania made unsuccessful overtures to the union to go in as a branch. In Queensland metalliferous miners had been members of the Amalgamated Workers Association, which also amalgamated with the AWU in 1913. The FMEA's coverage included New South Wales, Victoria, Tasmania, South Australia, and by 1916, Western Australia. Hence the AWU gained over 10 000 new members and the coverage of metalliferous mines nationally. At the end of 1917, the AWU advised the Commonwealth industrial registrar that the union had a total 86 499 members. It must be stressed that by contrast, most other trade unions were much smaller in membership and were often only State-registered organisations. In 1918 there were 767 State and federally registered unions around Australia, most of which were numerically very small. In New South Wales, several of these had been deregistered following the 1917 strike, and although their deregistration was rescinded afterwards, they continued to flounder, with low membership, as they sought an effective means of restructuring as federally registered organisations, either through amalgamations or through the elusive temptations of the One Big Union movement.[14]

As with the AWU's organisation in the pastoral industry in the late nineteenth century, union realignments in the metal-mining industry prompted a hasty employer response. On 17 May 1918 the first ordinary general meeting of the Australian Mines and Metals Association took place in Melbourne. The association, whose Board of Directors resembled a Who's Who of mining industry barons, was formed the previous year at a meeting of representatives of the principal gold and base-metal mining companies and related industries, in order to 'better protect the interests of such employers throughout the Commonwealth'. The association's first annual report reported that metal mining had suffered as a result of labour shortages and acute price increases due to the impact of wartime conditions. 'The pressing demand for labour has emboldened unions to make frequent and in most cases, unreasonable demands for higher wages, shorter hours and easier conditions of work.' The report went on to say:

> The Federated Mining Employees' Association is now merged or at least controlled by the Australian Workers' Union, and an application is before the Industrial Registrar from the Australian Coal and Shale Employees'

Federation for permission ... [to] extend its membership to employees engaged [*inter alia*] in metalliferous mines. In common with other employers interested this Association, on behalf of its members, opposed the application which was the subject of recent prohibition proceedings in the High Court. It is undesirable that power to control the whole of the primary industries of Australia should be placed in the hands of these two large unions...

Clearly the formation of the Australian Mines and Metals Association was, at least in part, a response to the AWU's absorption of the metalliferous miners.[15]

The AMMA was right to fear the determination of the AWU to build a powerful industrial empire. At the 1915 Annual Convention it was resolved to amend the union's rules to include as the first object of the AWU: 'To advocate one big union of Australian workers'. Since 1913, the union's pastoral base had broadened to include miners, railway and general construction workers, timber workers, bakers and shop assistants, although the three last categories were restricted to Queensland. In 1917, the Rockchoppers and Sewer Miners Union and the Quarrymen's Union joined as sections of the Railway Workers Industry Branch, and the small Kurrawang Firewood Workers Union amalgamated with the AWU in Western Australia. Moreover, decisions were taken at the convention in that year to make Darwin a branch of the union and to extend the operations of the AWU into Fiji and, except for legal complications, the AWU would have formally amalgamated with its New Zealand counterpart, the New Zealand Agricultural and Pastoral Workers Union, led by Grayndler's brother, in 1918.[16]

The AWU was not alone in pushing for the creation of One Big Union. In the wake of the war and industrial defeat, many unionists believed a more effective way of organising the entire labour movement lay in restructuring existing unions as sections of a giant umbrella organisation. In 1918 a conference of unions decided to support the establishment of the Workers Industrial Union of Australia (WIUA). Defying the defeat of 1917, the OBU aimed not merely to reorganise the trade unions: its architects sought the transformation of Australian society. The workers, 'the very life of all industry', should own and control the industries in which they laboured. To overcome the power of the capitalist class they had first to reform themselves. 'The trade unions foster a state of affairs which allows one set of workers to be pitted against another set of workers in the same industry, thereby helping defeat one another in wage wars.' Therefore all existing unions had to be persuaded to link arms in the OBU. But the biggest union of them all, the AWU, loomed as the OBU's biggest obstacle and ambitious rival.[17]

The AWU and the Labor Party were to prove the greatest hurdles for the budding OBU to surmount, the AWU because its officials feared their union would be submerged and their positions of power in the labour movement destroyed, and the politicians because they feared the consequences of revolutionary trade unionism for their electoral prospects. Ernest Lane, brother of William and an AWU member in Queensland, claimed that the AWU regarded the OBU as 'an unscrupulous poacher on its preserves and a revolutionary menace to the sane moderate Labour movement'.[18]

In 1918 Henry Boote observed that many AWU members hoped that their union would become the centre of the OBU and that the 1919 Convention would support the formal establishment of the WIUA. But by April 1919 the AWU leaders were in open opposition to the WIUA. The first indications of a break came in March, when New South Wales Labor leader Storey accused OBU supporters of seeking to impose their

Commanding the fleet. The AWU steers the One Big Union movement. Some unions preferred not to sail with the AWU. Jim Case in the Brisbane *Worker*, 1918. *AWU Collection.*

objectives on the party. Some weeks later, in an attempt to soften the antagonism developing between the AWU and the OBU, the NSW OBU Executive wrote to Grayndler asserting that its organising secretary, Jock Garden, had been misreported in the press and that the fledgeling WIUA had no intention of recruiting individual members or holding ballots among unionists, especially the AWU, without the consent of their union. The AWU response was hostile. The Executive Council met and announced in a 'manifesto' to the membership that it had unanimously decided to abandon the WIUA and pointed to the fact that its Preamble was virtually indistinguishable from that of the IWW, which was akin to 'madness, direct action, sabotage, dissention, disruption and destruction of the Union Movement'. The Executive Council also reaffirmed that the AWU maintained its commitment to arbitration and political action through the Labor Party. The councillors also curbed the editorial independence of the *Worker*, criticising Boote for supporting the radical OBU and insisting that the *Worker* support AWU policy and the ALP platform. Boote was also instructed to allow Grayndler to vet any articles which might conflict with AWU policy.[19]

The 1919 State Labor conferences were the scene for the next clash between the ALP and the AWU on one hand, and the WIUA's supporters on the other. Victoria had rejected the bid by the WIUA advocates to have the party adopt the OBU Preamble in favour of Blackburn's 'socialist objective', while in New South Wales the party's objective also proved to be the central issue. A. C. Willis from the Miners Federation proposed that it should be 'the establishment of a State of social democracy, in which the entire means of wealth production shall be owned and controlled by the community of workers industrially organised'. He went on to argue that the party platform should be cleansed of everything which assumed the continued existence of capitalism and that this new objective should be the sole focus of the forthcoming electoral campaign. AWU officials and the parliamentary party voiced the strongest objections to Willis's proposal and his motion was lost 127:112. In AWU ranks, Arthur Rae was the most prominent dissenter. He supported the change, saying that it should be possible to distinguish the Labor platform from that of their opponents 'without a microscope'. The defeat of Willis's proposal prompted the militants to walk out of the conference the following day. The AWU responded to Rae's dissent in September 1919 by removing him as a union delegate to the NSW Labor Council and as a director of Labor Papers Limited.[20]

At the 1920 AWU Convention, president Arthur Blakeley made it clear that the AWU was now determined to lay sole claim to the One Big Union mantle. He reported that the Executive Council had considered the WUIA scheme and had decided that 'it was not in the best interest of

the AWU to endorse the . . . scheme of industrial organisation'. Recalling
that it had failed miserably in the land of its birth, America, Blakeley went
on to describe the scheme as 'a dream scheme of Industrial Utopia, and
it is utterly impracticable to apply it to Australian conditions'. The AWU
constitution, Blakeley said, was 'the only basis upon which can be built
that One Big Union which we all so ardently desire'.[21]

Despite the leadership hostility, the 1920 AWU Annual Convention
revealed a significant proportion of delegates sympathetic to the WIUA.
The AWU's Western Branch was a stronghold of this support. Western
Branch secretary John Cullinan endorsed the new organisation, as did
Arthur Rae. In May 1919 the Executive Council condemned both the
Western and Railway Workers Industry branches for paying OBU affiliation
fees. In June 1920, exasperated by the Western Branch's continued defi-
ance, the Executive Council merged the branch into the Central Branch.[22]

Despite the hostilities, both sides made fitful attempts to reach a
compromise. At the 1921 AWU Convention, a letter was received from
the OBU under Garden's signature requesting that he and Willis be
permitted to address the Convention regarding the linking up of the
working class in the OBU. The AWU responded by informing the WIUA
that the Coal and Shale Miners, the Seamen, the Waterside Workers and
the newly registered Australian Railways Union were conferring with the
AWU with a view to amalgamation The result was the convening of an
industrial conference in March 1921 at which negotiations took place
between the AWU, the Miners, the AMIEU, the ARU and the WIUA.[23]

By early 1921 Garden was apparently convinced that the AWU could
command the rural departments of the OBU without challenging the
OBU's identity. The March 1921 conference resolved to establish an
Australasian Workers Union with preamble and structure similar to the
WIUA, but with a White Australia membership clause and provision for
tight central control over industrial action. While the industrial Left was
highly critical of these initiatives, they were by now convinced of the
necessity of working within 'reactionary' unions. Thus, with the birth of
the Australasian Workers Union, the WIUA was laid to rest. The new
union was, in essence, an AWU-run One Big Union. The AWU held a
membership plebiscite on the question of the OBU/AWU which resulted
in a vote in favour of 18 694 to 3889. The new organisation's inaugural
convention was held in February 1922, attended by representatives of the
AWU, the WIUA and the Waterside Workers Federation (the ARU and
the meatworkers having second thoughts). AWU president Arthur
Blakeley was elected president and acting AWU general secretary, John
Barnes, the general secretary of the OBU/AWU.[24]

Within a year, the urge for change was dissipated by technical hitches
and delays, and a common fear among the various union officials of a

loss of power and prestige. Constitutional difficulties encountered with the OBU/AWU meant that the various individual unions might have to be dissolved and reconstituted, a potential outcome which caused some alarm in AWU leadership circles in June 1923, as it was seen as a threat to award coverage. The Executive Council declared that the onus lay with the OBU Provisional Council to alter its rules to enable the development of the OBU to proceed, while clarifying the legal status of the existing unions. But the Miners Federation had become increasingly suspicious about deregistration, fearing marginalisation as a component of an enlarged AWU. By late 1923 revived sniping between the AWU and the miners effectively laid the OBU/AWU to rest.[25]

Was the AWU the villain in the demise of the One Big Union? There is little doubt that its devotion to arbitration and its strong commitment to White Australia made consensus difficult. Moreover, the AWU retained its own strong empire-building ambitions, which the union would not set aside in favour of the OBU. Vere Gordon Childe had few illusions about AWU motives and why the union succeeded in undermining the radical OBU objective. In his classic 1923 study of the Australian labour movement, *How Labour Governs*, Childe offered this assessment:

> The AWU wanted itself to become the One Big Union by simply absorbing other organisations, retaining the power in the hands of the existing hierarchy of officials in the pastoral section ... The AWU section was supported by the politicians under Storey and Catts, who were smarting under the continual interference of the [OBU] Section, and saw that a return to political power was impossible if the revolutionary aims of the OBU were included in the Labour platform. Their ranks were swelled by the more conservative craft unionists who had no time for industrial unionism.

The AWU's hostility to the radical OBU reflected the coalitionary nature of the labour movement. This was further complicated by the pressure imposed by democratic politics. In order to govern, the Labor Party had to appeal to small selectors, the middle class – a range of opinion often hostile to the aims of industrial unionism. The AWU, with its broad rural background, was itself the product of this coalitionary inertia. Historian Joan Simpson cites Henry Boote's pamphlet *OBU: Why It Failed* and his criticism of 'the apathy, indifference and ignorance of the mass of workers'. If workers had been 'intelligently alive to the urgency of Greater Unionism, and determined to have it at any cost, no Court could long impede the way'. While there is no doubt that such apathy was a factor, it must be recognised that over 18 000 AWU members took the trouble to vote Yes in the plebisicite on the issue, a substantial result, considering that voter turn-out in union ballots has traditionally been very low. Whatever general apathy existed, there can be little doubt of the specific hostility of the AWU's Executive Councillors. It was in many ways a pyrrhic victory; for during the 1920s it would be the AWU which was marginalised in the New South Wales labour movement, largely as a result of its attitude to the OBU ideal and the fear of domination the AWU's sheer size aroused among other unions. It seemed that the radicals might yet prevail in the contest for control of the Labor Party.[26]

# CHAPTER 7

## Ourselves Alone

*Splendid Isolation, Industrial Growth and Working Life, 1920–29*

> I don't know if the cause be wrong,
>    Or if the cause be right –
> I've had my day and sung my song,
>    And fought the bitter fight.
> To tell the truth, I don't know what
>    The boys are driving at,
> But I've been Union twenty years,
>    And I'm too old to 'rat'.[1]

In the early years of the new century a young learner shearer, E. L. Barnes, slept by the fire in the barracks provided at one of the Riverina stations he was working. 'I found I was in an excellent position to hear the old hands talking – and some of their stories were worth listening to.' By the fireside Barnes absorbed the myths and mateship of the shearing shed, and the AWU. 'The original organisers of this union ... were very sagacious men. They knew that, although they had to fight for anything that was worthwhile if they did not fight fairly they would lose in the long run. The AWU used all its weight – that of being the most powerful union in Australia at the time – to bring into being the Federal Arbitration Court. Although they have considered this court's findings not fair at times, they have always abided by its decisions.' While some 'radicals' opposed piece-work, 'wiser elements have prevailed'. The AWU was 'kept strong and healthy by being composed of members who are naturally self-reliant'. Piece-work was the embodiment of the AWU's robust independence: 'This competitive interest, which made the work of shearing sheep more like a game than otherwise, drew into the union ranks the most intelligent and competent in the country – for there is no place in the ranks of the shearer for the loafer who watches the clock and waits for pay day – and so an organisation was built up which is the envy of the organisers of other unions.'[2]

By 1922 the minstrel of the AWU myths which Barnes had absorbed so well was listening to the last call of 'mother bush', as he called it, in a final exhausted poem, 'On The Night Train'. Henry Lawson, worn out by the

134

struggle with himself and with a world which had often dismissed him, died in Sydney on 2 September 1922. In the *Worker*'s Women's Page his old friend Mary Gilmore eulogised him. 'In the early days and before the frame of the Labor Movement was set, he was not only our singer but our prophet; and in his prophecy he sang the men he knew – the landless man, the outback man, the Faces in the Street.' During the decade 1910–20 the AWU's industrial coverage moved a long way from the shearing shed, but not the emotional bonds of mateship. In 1912 Lawson celebrated AWU mateship in one of his 'bush union' classics, *The Old Unionist.* He recalled the bitter strikes and the gloomy depression days of the 1890s:

> The fighting, dying *Boomerang*
> Against the daily press;
> The infant *Worker* holding out;
> The families in distress;
> The sudden tears of beaten men –
> O you remember that ! –
> Are memories that make my pen
> Not worth the while to rat.

The AWU myth was fully formed, but it was not necessarily self-renewing. By 1920 the AWU leaders were so concerned that their own officers might well 'rat' that the Convention compelled them to sign a pledge confirming their unyielding loyalty to the union and their refusal to join any industrial or political organisation 'opposed to the policy of the AWU'. Ardent supporters like E. L. Barnes were mirrored by active dissidents like Arthur Rae, who had emerged as a critic of the AWU leadership and a supporter of the radical OBU ideal favoured by the Miners Federation and the NSW Labour Council. Rae's refusal to sign the pledge led to his expulsion from the AWU. Other AWU officials simply found it difficult to stomach the insult and humiliation implied by a signature on a scrap of paper. They made their views clear during the acrimonious debate on the pledge at the 1920 Convention, where several officials urged its 'cancellation'. Delegate John Cullinan from the AWU's Western Branch (in New South Wales), another OBU supporter, signed the pledge 'under protest': 'if it was essential that a pledge of this kind should be signed in the AWU, verily the rot had set in, and the sooner the "white ants" got it the better'. Queensland delegate Moir retorted that it was little different from signing the ALP pledge; Queensland Branch secretary Dunstan agreed, and wondered, 'anyhow, what was wrong with a pledge when a man was straight and intended to be straight?' Ernest Lane gave him an answer. He objected to the restriction on joining other organisations; the pledge 'gave the Executive Council more power than they ought to have'. Nonetheless it was a

power the Executive Council was determined to have, and after a series
of divisions and votes on amendments the pledge was incorporated into
the AWU's constitution.[3]

For Ernest Lane, the debate on the pledge was typical of many of the
debates he took part in at AWU conventions during his years in the
union. The outstanding feature for Lane was what he called a consistent
determination of the 'old guard' to covetously protect the AWU institutions from the infiltration of progressive organisations 'and to persecute
and suppress all those whoever or wherever they might be, who had the
temerity to question the infallibility of the AWU or to challenge its
supremacy as the greatest Union in Australia'. Lane, who was active in
the Queensland AWA and AWU from 1913 until 1926, was unable to
recall any major issue debated at Convention 'covering a period of eight
years that Grayndler, Barnes, Blakeley, Dunstan, Lambert, Bailey and
their henchmen did not score a victory'. In his reminiscences, *Dawn to
Dusk*, Lane concluded: 'There was always a strong militant minority to
advocate a more virile working class policy for the AWU and to
endeavour to break down the sectional hostility and bitterness of other
unions which then, as now, seemed to be a bedrock principle of the
organisation machine. But it was all in vain. We found the citadel of
bureaucratic control and dispensation of favours was too strong and
unscrupulous'.[4]

Vere Gordon Childe agreed. In *How Labour Governs* Childe asserted
that AWU structures were designed to reinforce the passing of union
control into the hands of few senior officials. Delegates to Convention,
the AWU's supreme decision-making body, were almost entirely officials
who could use the advantages of office to secure election. The three
newspapers controlled by the union, the *Australian Worker*, the *Westralian
Worker* and the *Worker* (Brisbane), were also used to suppress rank-and-
file criticism: 'the columns of these papers are not really open to publish
correspondence from members who have complaints to make displeasing to the official clique'. The AWU officials also spent an inordinate
amount of time seeking parliamentary preselection from the Labor
Party, which was itself often dominated by AWU officials. 'Everywhere the
AWU has provided a ladder whereby the ambitious unionists have sought
and often attained parliamentary honours.' Unlike some AWU critics,
however, Childe understood the AWU's often-criticised support for
compulsory arbitration. 'The union's adherence to arbitration, for
example, may only be due to the superiority of that method for settling
industrial disputes and improving conditions. Certainly the union's
experience of the alternative in the nineties had not been encouraging.'
In 1920 members had voted 16 138:10 157 to maintain AWU support for
the arbitration system. This was an unusually high voter turnout for such

a plebiscite, the relatively strong 'anti-arbitration' vote indicating the disappointment in the post-war period among the AWU membership – and in the labour movement generally – with Australia's industrial system. But as Childe realised, perhaps the AWU found it difficult to jettison a system it had fought hard to achieve, and with which its members were now so familiar.[5]

The seventeen-year struggle from 1890 until the winning of the Pastoral Industry Award in 1907 had left its mark on the union and the nature of its leaders. These saw themselves as practical men with little time for dissent (ironically, it was Arthur Rae who complained in the 1890s about 'ignorant' members who failed to understand how the union should be run) or foreign ideas – those troublesome twins which seemed to spring forth suddenly from the ferment of the Great War, in the divisive conscription crisis, the Great Strike, the One Big Union fiasco and the rise of communism in the Soviet Union. The dissident voice in the AWU, muted in the pre-war years, was now given form, an identity shaped by radical if not revolutionary criteria. Childe's *How Labour Governs* seemed to clarify criticism of the AWU, explaining its experience – and failings – in the context of the development of the Australian labour movement and testing its performance against a standard of industrial radicalism well understood in Europe but almost unknown in Australia, where a craft-divided and weakened union movement was only beginning to develop effective national organisation through federal union structures and, in 1927, the formation of the Australian Council of Trade Unions.

Despite the apparent ease with which the leadership controlled the AWU, the 1920s were a turbulent time for the union. The AWU stood resolute in its commitment to arbitration and a White Australia, a stand which exposed it to the rumblings of internal discontent and in direct opposition to many militant unions affiliated with State Trades and Labor councils, particularly in New South Wales. As the pledge debate indicated, the AWU imposed a severe discipline on those who violated union policy and principles, and punishments were permanent. This code reinforced the leadership and buttressed its culture. The processing of items for the agenda for annual conventions flowed unhindered from all areas but were chosen and ranked by the general secretary, although all were published in the *Worker*. Such practices did little to placate the more militant sections of the membership and contributed to the establishment of groups such as the Bushworkers Propaganda Group which Arthur Rae, despite his expulsion, was active in organising. Rejecting militancy and jealous of its status as Australia's leading union, the AWU, which in 1920 seemed so dominant in labour movement affairs, was by 1930 isolated from and rivalled the fledgeling ACTU. This isolation evolved partly from choice and partly as a consequence of the AWU's rejection by the dominant factions in the labour movement, particularly in New South Wales, a rejection precipitated in many ways by the aggressive and ambitious Jack Bailey.[6]

### The Rise and Fall of 'Ballot-Box' Bailey

The architects of the AWU's dominance of New South Wales Labor between 1916 and 1923 were the AWU's Central Branch president, John Bailey, and branch secretary William Lambert. Bailey, a hard-fighting shearer who had been active in the AWU since the turn of the century, has been described as 'the unchallenged dictator of NSW Labor politics' under whose direction 'the NSW Branch of the AWU maintained an iron discipline over the State's Labor movement, the union seeking to expand in order to dominate both the political and industrial wings and so further the political careers of its leaders'. Lambert became lord mayor of Sydney when his fellow aldermen, under the direction of the Bailey-controlled ALP executive, elected him in 1920. In 1922 he became MHR for Cook, which he represented for many years. Bailey's and Lambert's rivals were the industrial groupings of the Sydney Labor Council, tagged the 'Trades Hall Reds', under the leadership of Jock Garden, who became Labor Council secretary in 1918.[7]

With the OBU threat largely laid to rest, Bailey seemed ready to crown his career with a leading role in the NSW Parliament. Labor won office in 1920 and Bailey, while retaining his positions in the AWU (in addition to the Central branch presidency, he was also NSW Branch vice-president), was elected Member for Monaro. However, he was rejected for a ministerial position by the Caucus. He became consumed with a thirst for revenge, determined to destroy the parliamentary leadership of John Storey and, when Storey died suddenly in 1920, his successor James Dooley. Bailey also continued his attempts to manipulate parliamentary preselections and to agitate over the sectarian issue, attacking the parliamentary Labor Party as a party dominated by Catholics. Such destabilising behaviour, together with a successful Red-baiting campaign by Labor's opponents (which used the adoption of the socialist objective at the Interstate Conference in 1921 and the parliamentary party's association with the Labor Council to imply an association with communism), ensured Labor's demise at the 1922 election. The Dooley Government secured only 38.5 per cent of the vote, its worst result since 1907. When federal Labor lost the election in the following year, the party could no longer ignore the worm in the apple, and pressure mounted for a restructuring of NSW Labor.[8]

The New South Wales electoral system, then based on multi-member electorates, provided ample opportunities to corruptly influence party preselections. As Hagan and Turner observe, by the early 1920s 'there were almost endless allegations of forged ballot papers, multiple voting, ballot box stuffing, "crook" ballot boxes and impersonation. Most of the accusations pointed back to the Baileyite Executive'. J. H. Catts MHR, who had two preselection wins declared void, complained that 'the whole machinery for the selection of these candidates in New South Wales is at the unfettered discretion of this corrupt junta at Macdonell House [the AWU's headquarters]'. At the NSW ALP Conference in 1921, conference chairman Bill Lambert gagged Catts on a number of occasions when he attempted to provide evidence to delegates of his public allegations that 'the Labor movement is in serious danger of being overwhelmed with illicit money. Our great and glorious movement is being dragged in the mire of selfishness and corruption'.[9]

The 1923 NSW ALP Conference finally agreed to establish a committee to hear allegations that Bailey and others had engaged in ballot-rigging. It was alleged that Bailey had been instrumental in securing ballot boxes with a removable panel so as to facilitate vote tampering in the 1920 Sydney electorate preselection. The sensation of the conference was provided by Albert Willis, who must have had the memory of Bailey's role in the OBU defeats in his mind as he dramatically produced one of the suspect ballot boxes on the floor of conference and tapped it. Uproar followed as a concealed removable panel fell to the ground. The subsequent inquiry found Bailey guilty and he was expelled from the ALP.[10]

A flurry of inquiries and allegations followed. The AWU decided to hold its own inquiry, which unanimously concluded that there was no reliable evidence to connect Bailey with the fraudulent ballot boxes. Using this finding, the AWU applied pressure for a federal ALP inquiry, and after several abortive attempts former AWU official and Queensland Premier E. G. Theodore was chosen by federal Labor (and approved by the AWU) in 1924 to conduct a fresh inquiry. Theodore's appointment prompted Grayndler to proclaim that 'Bailey was at last before the fountain of Justice'. Theodore promptly stunned the AWU when he announced that he found the charges against Bailey proven. Theodore took on the inquiry to further his political ambitions. He had already decided he would make his run for a federal parliamentary seat in New South Wales at the 1925 elections and his aspirations for the federal ALP leadership depended on strong support from the New South Wales labour movement, from which Bailey was now irrevocably alienated, and therefore expendable. With Bailey's fall went AWU domination of the NSW ALP, and the union would not have any real influence again in local party affairs until the mid-1950s.[11]

Bailey's rejection by the Labor Party was not immediately reciprocated in AWU circles. In the 1925 Central Branch ballot Bailey and his supporters won every executive position. In the true Bailey tradition, the NSW AWU then began a national campaign against Theodore and Willis. In 1929 Bailey instituted libel proceedings against Willis and the committee on the 1923 report and was awarded £4500 in damages. Bailey and his supporters were finally disowned by the AWU in 1933, when the Executive Council reasserted control over the fractious NSW AWU by abolishing its internal branches and creating one NSW Branch with five zones.[12]

The collapse of AWU influence in the NSW ALP was reflected in the adoption of the so-called 'red rules' by the party in November 1926. In order to strengthen his position, NSW Labor Premier Jack Lang, with the assistance of a broad coalition of unions, set in place a collegiate voting system which meant that no one union could dominate the party's conference. In return for strengthening Lang's position, the rules were relaxed to allow members of the Communist Party to also hold membership of the ALP.[13]

The AWU saw the red rules as a direct attack on the union. The AWU believed the rules gave small unions the same voting strength as the AWU, with its large membership. *Worker* editor Henry Boote told the AWU's 1927 Convention that the 'Red Rules' were 'a concerted attempt . . . to fundamentally change the Labour Movement and reduce the AWU to political insignificance'. Boote was convinced that the entire episode was a conspiracy by Willis and Garden to allow communists to infiltrate the party in New South Wales, and he implored delegates to organise and defeat the rules before 'those people' succeeded 'in impregnating the Movement with principles absolutely alien to Australian sentiment'. Boote's appeal was unfulfilled. The AWU's bitter opposition to Lang led it to support the 'federal' NSW ALP Branch after the Lang Labor split of 1931, but this did not restore the union's influence in political affairs, as all of Lang's labour movement opponents remained in the wilderness until the federal Labor Party intervened and broke Lang's grip on the NSW Labor Party in 1940. In many respects, the New South Wales unions which had been frustrated by the AWU's opposition to the OBU now took their opportunity to marginalise the once dominant industrial giant.[14]

In South Australia, the AWU's influence rose as a result of the massive conscription split in the United Labor Party (the name under which political Labor had originated and organised since the 1890s in South Australia). As a result, long-serving Adelaide Branch secretary Frank Lundie (secretary since 1900) effectively controlled the SA Labor executive, although this strong industrial influence and power within the Labor machine did not translate into a parliamentary career for Lundie, as he failed in election bids for the Senate and the local House of Assembly. Nonetheless as ALP historian Ross McMullin observes, 'as a vital contributor of members and funds, the AWU provided many party office-bearers and pre-selected candidates'.[15]

In Western Australia, another sparsely populated State dominated by rural and mining industries, the local AWU's influence was primarily expressed through its journal, the *Westralian Worker*, which also served as the official voice of political Labor in that State, indicating the strong ties between the party and the union. Between 1917 and 1928 future Australian prime minister John Curtin was the editor of the *Westralian Worker*, and politically, his time with the paper did his future career no harm. His biographer describes Curtin's relationship with the union, and in doing so also reveals the apparently seamless relationship which had developed in many States between the AWU and the Labor Party: 'The Worker was mainly an AWU journal and Curtin's editorship identified him again [Curtin had briefly worked as an AWU organiser in Victoria in 1916] with this powerful union. From contacts with members of the AWU he increased his experience of the Labor movement, gained a position on a union and the state Labor Executive and kept important contacts with Labor men in other states'.[16]

In Victoria this symbiotic relationship was personified in John Barnes. A shearer and itinerant bushworker, Barnes had joined the Amalgamated Shearers Union in 1887. He was Grayndler's successor as secretary of the Victorian-Riverina Branch until 1913, when he was elected as a Labor senator from Victoria. He remained active in the AWU as he pursued his parliamentary and machine career in the ALP, serving as a member of the Victorian ALP executive throughout the 1920s. From 1924 until his death in 1938 Barnes also served as the AWU's general president. He entertained no doubts about the mutual benefits of this relationship. In his presidential address to the 1925 AWU Convention, Barnes intoned the mantra which soothed generations of AWU stalwarts, that their union was a vital instrument of Labor. Labor was the AWU. What, Barnes rhetorically asked, did the AWU do with the huge revenues generated from its mighty membership base? Australia-wide each year, it spent £33 000 on organisers, £22 000 on newspapers, £5000 in sustenation fees to Labor Party executives, resulting in Labor representation in Parliament and federal awards. The AWU sustained business concerns in the *Worker* newspapers worth, he estimated, £170 000, 'invaluable to the Union because of the work they did for it and the Labor Party generally'. Some in the Labor movement failed to understand this. The OBU had failed because of their opposition. Barnes expected opposition from employer organisations 'but none from kindred ones'. At times AWU leaders like Barnes seemed sincerely bewildered at the hostility, and perhaps jealousy, which the AWU attracted.

This perceived hostility and envy bred a fierce defensiveness and pride from the AWU leadership.[17]

### The OBU Aftermath: the Creation of the ACTU

Despite the setbacks in implementing the One Big Union ideal, many union leaders continued throughout the 1920s to search for ways of creating an effective national trade union organisation. The All Australian Trade Union Congress in August 1926 voted unanimously in favour of a motion from Jock Garden for the establishment of a central body 'to deal with all matters of industrial concern'. The 1928 AWU Annual Convention rejected an invitation to affiliate from the new Australian Council of Trade Unions. Boote criticised the ACTU's links with the Pan Pacific Trade Union Secretariat, which posed as an independent organisation but had strong connections with the Profintern, the international trade union organisation sponsored by the Soviet Union. Boote had taken a prominent role in the campaign to broaden the outlook of AWU members in the early war years and had preached that Labor's fate depended on its unbridled embrace of the international movement. He was now convinced that communism was to blame for the divisions in the labour movement. Convention passed a resolution which was clearly meant to demonstrate to the ACTU that the AWU could live without it.

> That [ACTU Secretary] Crofts be advised that when the A.C.T.U. can inform the A.W.U. that the Unions connected with the A.C.T.U. had fulfilled their 1921 Congress pledges as to the Labor Daily levy of 10/- and the formation of the O.B.U., consideration may be given to the application. Also, that Mr Crofts be informed that the A.W.U. has been fighting for years for a universal 44-hour week in Australia, and already it has been successful in the State of Queensland. Further that he be informed that the A.W.U. is strenuously fighting against the Federal Government's suggested arbitration legislation.

The ACTU's affiliation with the Pan-Pacific Secretariat also conflicted with the AWU's unassailable commitment to the White Australia Policy. The secretariat embraced the principle of non-discrimination on the grounds of race. In 1927 the AWU reaffirmed its White Australia stand with a new rule spelling out the racial eligibility requirements of potential members, and Asians and 'coloured' peoples were excluded by simple omission. Boote, an ardent supporter of the White Australia Policy, led a prolonged campaign in the *Worker* during the late 1920s to expose the Pan-Pacific Secretariat's non-racial principle as a communist plot to undermine restrictions on Asian-Pacific labour. Grayndler told the 1930 AWU Annual Convention that the Secretariat's desire to remove racial barriers would be 'an open door for the coloured hordes of the North Pacific'.[18]

Immigration was an issue high on the AWU agenda during the 1920s. The 1923 Convention resolved to make representations to Federal and State governments to discontinue existing immigration levels until there was an improvement in industrial conditions and unemployment. Two years later, Convention protested against Federal Government action which allowed 'large numbers of Southern European migrants' into Australia at a time when employment was scarce. By 1926 Convention was concerned about the 'southern European menace' and resolved, in concert with other unions, to make it known to 'representative bodies' overseas the 'deplorable' circumstances in which new arrivals found themselves. The AWU was sure that 'the continuous influx of migrants must have detrimental affects upon the Australian working-class movement'. The 1928 Convention demanded that the Federal Government abandon the immigration system on the grounds that it was socially unjust. While the AWU had little influence with the Bruce Nationalist Government, the shattering effects of the Great Depression, if not the AWU's trenchant defence of the White Australia policy, evidently had an effect two years later on an ACTU Congress searching for answers to the employment crisis. The 1930 Congress ceased affiliation with the Pan-Pacific Trade Union Secretariat and resolved by an overwhelming majority to support the White Australia policy. This change of heart did not impress the AWU. It would be another thirty-six years before the AWU affiliated with the ACTU.[19]

### Enemies Within: Rank-and-File Unrest

As the union grew during the 1920s so did dissatisfaction among its rank and file. There were pockets of dissenting members who failed to share the AWU's zeal for the arbitration process, preferring direct action. They were increasingly frustrated by the dominance of the officials, and sought greater rank-and-file participation in the operational and policy-making machinery of the AWU. This disenchantment culminated in formation of the militant Pastoral Workers Industrial Union in the early 1930s.

The origins of the PWIU can be found in the Bushworkers Propaganda Group. In 1925 several AWU members, under the name of the group, submitted a list of resolutions to the annual convention of that year. The thrust of the resolutions was not disclosed in the Convention Report, but during the Convention debates it was revealed that the group had threatened to refuse to take tickets in the AWU and would deposit their money with the Trades and Labour Council if their demands were not met. Central Branch secretary George Buckland warned that the group was not just attacking his branch but 'the whole of the officials of the organisation'. Convention declared the group 'a bogus body, and inimical to the working-class Movement' by 18 votes to 6. In his 1924/25 Central Branch Annual Report, Buckland again railed against the group with particular reference to the treachery of a shearer, W. J. 'Trucker' Brown, for refusing to take tickets. Buckland thought members should refuse to work with Brown and his ilk until they had regained their 'industrial manhood' and described the group as 'an asset to the boss, a menace to the welfare of our members, and an instrument to be used to gain office for a few office-seekers'.[20]

Discontent was not restricted to pastoral workers. In 1928 the Railway Workers Industry Branch held a Rank and File Conference. In a preface to the official report of the 1928 Conference, Rank and File executive secretary J. F. Murphy explained that the movement 'had been forced into being by the appalling conditions on many jobs and the traitorous conduct of well-paid AWU officials'. The AWU Executive Council subsequently suspended several members of the RWIB for holding an unauthorised conference and advocating the dissolution of the RWIB. The Executive Council also declared the 1928–29 RWIB ballot for positions void on the grounds of irregularities and corrupt conduct by officials. A number of senior RWIB office-holders were suspended and subsequently dismissed from the union, including the branch's long-serving secretary, George Bodkin, who had so keenly advocated AWU–RW&GLA amalgamation in 1915. This 'Rank and File Movement' also attracted the ire of Clarrie Fallon, the Queensland Branch president, who reported to the 1927 Queensland Branch delegates meeting that it appeared 'to have been expressly designed to weaken the AWU by employing every possible means to destroy the confidence of members in officials elected by the members themselves'. Fallon concluded: 'There is a very close analogy between this so-called Rank and File Movement and the now defunct Machine Shearers' Union of infamous memory. Members would be well advised at all times to regard with suspicion glib-tongued individuals claiming to represent any organisation the origin of which is clouded in mystery, who promise to provide a panacea for all industrial and social evils'[21]

Meanwhile Fallon was confronted with unrest in his own branch. In the Queensland sugar industry a dispute flared which sorely tested the leadership's ability to manage a body of members, in this case cane-cutters, roused to breaking point. The Central, Southern, Northern and Far Northern Districts of the Queensland Branch all had coverage of sugar industry workers. At the South Johnstone Mill near Innisfail in the Far Northern District a serious dispute erupted in 1927. The Queensland Government had recently transferred the mill to the ownership of a primary producers' co-operative. Like many new owners, the co-operative managers were determined to do things differently. They sacked the staff and compelled them to reapply for their old jobs. Curiously, some of the more outspoken unionists were not re-employed, and preference was not extended to long-standing employees. The AWU members decided to strike, and they were eventually joined by other unionists. Attempts to settle the dispute were abruptly torpedoed when the mill resumed with non-union labour in June. The AWU State Executive belatedly endorsed the strike, eager to contain it to the South Johnstone area. Tension mounted after 5 July, however, when a picketer was shot dead by an unknown assailant. Another attempt was made to settle the dispute by arbitration; the court proposed the re-engagement of all former hands and all field workers on rates equal to those which had applied in the previous contract. The AWU and the mill management accepted the arrangement but the strikers rejected it overwhelmingly – 310:28. They refused to work with non-union labour, and wanted them dismissed. The AWU was losing control of the situation, an outcome confirmed as the dispute became a bitter brawl between Premier Bill McCormack and the Australian Railways Union, the union which remained most determined to encourage the militancy of the strikers by refusing to handle 'black' sugar. The former AWU leader had been overseas when the dispute began. On 29 August McCormack took personal control of the Railways Department and, in an attempt to isolate the ARU, ordered the dismissal of all ARU men from 3 September, agreeing to reinstate them only if they pledged to obey the instructions of the Commissioner. When McCormack was advised that it was unlawful to discriminate against one particular union, and that the department had no records of ARU membership, he extended the ultimatum to all the department's 18 874 employees. This was an offer the ARU's leaders could not refuse, and both the strikers and the AWU – itself faced with a deregistration threat from the Arbitration Court over the dispute – were also coming under renewed pressure. On 12 September the defeated strikers returned to work.[22]

At the AWU Annual Convention the following year, AWU president John Barnes attempted to rationalise the untenable postion the AWU found itself in when confronted with the intractable McCormack Government, presided over by a former AWU vice-president.

> During this year, industrially you have only had one outstanding incident; that was the South Johnstone fight, which involved our membership. Not a great number, it is true, but there were very important issues at stake in that struggle, and our people, trained and skilled in industrial warfare, felt confident that they could carry on the fight to a successful end with the least harm all round. And though others butted into that fight, and complicated matters to some extent, I

am glad to say we came out of it with very great credit to the members of this Union who had the responsibility of handling the affair.[23]

The South Johnstone strike had in fact embarrassed the AWU, caught between the militancy of the ARU and the unexpected hostility of the Queensland Government. The legacy of the dispute had other repercussions:

> The humiliating defeat of the 1927 strike fuelled the tendency of Queensland unions to jettison militancy and the direct action tactics of the syndicalists. Although large sections of the labour movement had been alienated from Labor by McCormack's handling of the dispute, they were paradoxically driven to electoral opposition in continuing the struggle. The anger of the ARU and other disaffected sections of the labour movement translated into the defeat of the McCormack government at the 1929 election and its replacement by an administration that owed nothing to the labour movement.[24]

The defeat of the McCormack Government delayed the fulfilment of the political and industrial ascendancy which the Queensland AWU had been seeking since the amalgamation of the AWA and the AWUQ in 1912. In the 1930s Clarrie Fallon would realise the imminent ambitions of the AWU machine, in an alliance with a reinvigorated Labor Party, and its influence extending across the national AWU. Over the next thirty years the consequences of this ascendancy would touch everyone involved in the struggle for the control of the Australian labour movement.

### Industrial Relations and AWU Structure

During the 1920s the AWU built on the solid platform of amalgamation secured during the previous decade, by attaining a 50 per cent increase in its membership by 1929 – before the onset of the Great Depression saw this impressive growth collapse. Queensland was the fastest-growing branch with its membership increasing from 32 800 in 1921 to over 51 000 by 1929. In all, the AWU claimed a membership of 102 400 by early 1921, broken down into the following branch structure:

| | |
|---|---|
| Adelaide | 10 500 |
| Victoria-Riverina | 14 000 |
| Queensland | 32 800 |
| Central (NSW) | 14 000 |
| Railway Workers | 9 000 |
| Western Australia | 4 600 |
| Western Australia Mining | 3 300 |
| Tasmania | 3 500 |
| Darwin Branch | 300 |
| New Zealand | 10 000[25] |

New industries were added apace. By 1924 the Central Branch (NSW) had extended its operations to include about 2000 former members of the Factory Employees Union, almost all workers employed at race tracks and on golf links, as well as all employees of vegetable market gardens. In 1926, Central Branch was also granted State award coverage for rural workers, permitting it to apply for awards in the pastoral, horticultural, agricultural, dairying and forestry industries. In 1928 the Queensland Branch reported on the finalisation of its amalgamation with the Milling, Baking, Cooking and Allied Trades Union, giving it coverage in flour-milling, bread-making, the manufacture of biscuits and confectionery, pastry-cooking and employees in hotels, clubs, restaurants and boarding houses throughout the State. The Victoria-Riverina Branch added wool-classers (as did also Queensland, South Australia, Western Australia and Tasmania) and the Survey Employees of Victoria. In 1923 the union received a boost for its coverage of construction workers when the High Court ruled that the Commonwealth Arbitration Court could make awards for State instrumentalities, thus opening the way for the AWU to apply for federal awards for navvies employed on roads, railways and waterways. By the early 1920s the AWU operated 220 awards, both federal and State, throughout Australia. Of State awards, 123 were in Queensland, fourteen in Western Australia, thirty-six in South Australia, thirteen in Victoria and thirty-three in New South Wales. So buoyant was the mood among AWU officials that Victoria-Riverina Branch secretary Jack McNeill predicted 'that the day is not far distant when the AWU will be operating in South Africa and the United States of America'.[26]

Despite this brave and slightly bizarre prophecy, the AWU was finding it difficult enough to spread its influence around the margins of Australasia, let alone the globe. In the post-war period the AWU had tried to organise a Darwin Branch in Northern Australia. In 1921 these members joined the North Australian Industrial Workers Union and the AWU Branch effectively ceased to exist. Subsequently the NAIWU amalgamated with the Northern Territory Workers Union. Although the AWU effectively ceded its functions in the Northern Territory to local unions (in an unusually passive gesture, the 1929 Convention voted 'not to interfere' in the Northern Territory) it continued to operate in the Territory in connection with the extension of Commonwealth Railways from the south to central Australia, although as the local Territory unions eventually became part of the Federal Miscellaneous Workers Union, the AWU lost coverage of Territory uranium and other metal miners.[27]

Tenuous links with New Zealand pastoral workers, established in the late 1880s, were also severed in the 1920s. In 1921 a New Zealand branch, with a listed – and probably exaggerated – membership of 10 000 is included in the Convention report as a branch of the AWU. This followed

a 1919 plebiscite of members of the New Zealand Workers Union, which
approved amalgamation with the AWU. New Zealand delegates were
even sent to the 1921 AWU Convention. In 1924, however, the NZ
Workers Union voted to affiliate with the Alliance of Labour (the local
equivalent of the ACTU) in New Zealand. The alliance saw the amalgamation with the AWU as a threatening 'one big union' scheme and one
which would give Australia control of the NZWU, a fear apparently
shared by NZWU leaders. With the NZWU affiliation with the alliance,
the union severed all formal ties with the AWU.[28]

There was little reason for celebration in the Tasmanian Branch, which
had been in a chaotic condition since 1918. The branch secretary, James
Mooney, died in office in 1919 and his successor, James McDonald,
discovered that the books had been neglected. Like many AWU officials,
however, McDonald was also a Tasmanian MP and his parliamentary
duties called upon much of his time. No annual report or balance sheet
was produced for 1919/20, prompting federal intervention. A committee
set up by the AWU Annual Convention to inquire into the branch recommended that temporary control over its affairs be given to the Victoria-
Riverina Branch, which controlled Tasmania from 1924 until 31 May
1927, when the Tasmanian Branch was re-established with T. M. Jude, a
former secretary of the Victoria-Riverina Branch Mining Section, as
secretary. By 1929 the branch had a membership of over 6000, and Jude
was able to claim that it 'held its own financially'.[29]

Despite the strong membership growth evident in the Central Branch
and Queensland during the early 1920s, Victoria-Riverina branch
secretary Jack McNeill complained in 1922 that membership had 'fallen
off' because of decreased expenditure on public works by the Victorian
Government. The mining industry had slumped (see pages 156–8); there
was resistance among Melbourne quarrymen and construction workers to
enrolment, despite the efforts of two organisers. McNeill ruefully
commented, 'but in Melbourne, as in all cities, it is a difficult matter to
enrol into trade unions those who benefit most from the operation of
Unionism'. Like his mate and fellow Victorian John Barnes, Jack McNeill
was an ex-shearer with over twenty years' experience as an AWU official.
He retired as branch secretary in 1923 to enter federal politics, and was
replaced by James Meehan. Unlike other AWU officials keen to extend the
unions' reach beyond the pastoral industry, it seems McNeill never quite
made the adjustment to organising ungrateful city workers.[30]

Perhaps the most bitter of AWU recruitment efforts in the 1920s were its
attempts to enrol Newcastle steelworkers. In the wake of the 1917 strike,
many industrially battle-weary unions considered that amalgamation with
the mighty AWU was the quickest way to circumvent problems posed by
deregistration, hostile management and the rivalries of management-

sanctioned 'scab' unions. For these reasons New South Wales officials of the Australian Railways Union contemplated amalgamation with the AWU; so did the Newcastle Branch of the Federated Ironworkers Association. Their union had been industrially crippled by deregistration after the 1917 strike. BHP management had established a company union to squeeze the FIA out. In the middle was the AWU, with a small steelworks membership through its coverage of construction workers. In 1918 Newcastle FIA officials approached Grayndler, asking the AWU to sign up their local members. Grayndler was not interested: the AWU wanted to 'swallow the whole Ironworks industry'. Grayndler inadvertently surrendered his best chance of AWU domination of the steel industry. In 1922 the AWU attempted to undermine the FIA at the steelworks by agreeing to below-award pay rates for its members at BHP. The company had closed the steelworks in April 1922 in an attempt to impose a 10 per cent wage cut which had been denied in the NSW Industrial Court. The AWU's intervention galvanised the FIA leadership against the AWU. Grayndler may have hoped that the below-award offer would finally see off the FIA (union membership at BHP was by then divided between the AWU, the Company Union and a small FIA membership), but both the AWU and the FIA saw their membership levels at BHP decline in the 1920s. Many steelworkers remained outside unions, intimidated by an aggressive 'divide-and-rule' strategy applied by BHP management. This strategy was short-lived, however, because it was so implacably hostile: in 1927 the NSW Industrial Court granted the FIA a preference clause for the steelworks award because of BHP's intransigence. A legacy of hostility between the AWU and FIA endured into the 1950s.[31]

The AWU and the Australian labour movement in general had to battle anti-union political forces throughout most of the decade, with first the Hughes then Bruce-led Nationalists commanding the Government benches in Canberra. Justice Higgins, who had a series of clashes with Prime Minister Billy Hughes, resigned from the Arbitration Court in 1920, citing the enactment of the Industrial Peace Act as the trigger for his decision. The Act, he claimed, undermined 'the influence and usefulness of the Court' – which was precisely Hughes's intention, as he sought power to establish special tribunals to facilitate direct Federal Government intervention in industrial disputes. Writing in the *Worker* on 4 November 1920, Boote railed against the Hughes administration and the campaign launched by various employer organisations to get rid of the AWU's old friend:

> Because Justice Higgins loved his country, and interpreted the law with a scrupulous sense of justice; because he was animated by a broad sense of humanitarianism, which gained for him wide public approval; because he

committed the crime of having done his country great service, and was universally respected for having done so, his enemies saw to it that his position was made intolerable, leaving him no other choice but to quit the office he had held, with such high honor, for 13 long years.[32]

Higgins reciprocated these warm feelings. In 1917 he congratulated the AWU for maintaining its socially integrating role, fighting for members without the fearful taint of militancy: 'My experience with this union is that during the past five years and before that, they have assisted the peace in the industries in which they are connected – the leaders have done so very handsomely – I know this – that the Union leaders have done their best to avoid trouble'.[33]

The capricious meddling in the affairs of the Arbitration Court indulged in by Billy Hughes was a reminder that all the fair laws and systems in the world could be undone by the intervention of vested interest groups. Such difficulties marked the AWU experience in the 1890s, and were still at work in the 1920s.

### The Pastoral Industry

The one Australian export which dominated world trade, the wool clip, maintained its primary place in world production, with its share of the total averaging almost 25 per cent in the four years 1926 to 1929. In the 1928–29 season Australia produced a quarter of the world's wool of all kinds and half the total supplies of pure merino. Between 1920 and 1930, Australian sheep numbers increased from 86 million to almost 106 million, with the quantity of greasy wool produced increasing from 625 million pounds in 1920–21 to 937 million pounds in 1929–30.[34]

While the 1920s proved a reasonably prosperous time for Australian woolgrowers, the 1917 Federal Pastoral Industry Award had not been received enthusiastically by the AWU, and dissatisfaction with the decision continued among shearers and shed-hands into the new decade. The Queensland Branch made one of the first moves against the award when it requested the 1920 AWU Annual Convention to allow Queensland to seek an award for the shearing industry from the State Arbitration Court. Branch secretary Bill Dunstan told members that there was major concern over the Federal Court's decision to apply a flat rate for all of Queensland, saying that while it may be 'an exceptionally good award for the settled portions of Victoria' it was 'a scandalous award for the far western and northern portions of Queensland'. Dunstan also believed that with a friendly State government in power, a state award would also ensure that the Queensland pastoral industry secured a 44-hour week. Convention agreed and the Queensland Branch applied to the State Industrial Court for an award. This was eventually granted despite the concerted attempts of the United Graziers and the Pastoralists Federal Council to block the move on jurisdictional grounds. In June 1920 the *Pastoral Review* rebuked the court president, Mr Justice McCawley, for making the award, noting that he chose to 'sacrifice the other States' to industrial disruption at the expense of securing industrial peace in Queensland and that he 'took full advantage of the congestion in the Federal Court and the long delays that ensue in having claims dealt with to justify his own action in duplicating a Federal award by the introduction of a State award'. The award gave the Queensland shearing industry a 44-hour week and aggregate increases in the vicinity of £226 250 together with retrospective payments of about £20 000, for the 6500 industry employees. Station-hands, in a separate award, had rates increased by 7s a week, and a prohibition was placed on the employment of coloured aliens. The attractive terms of the award also entrenched an idea of Queensland as a distinctive and industrially successful part of the union, particularly in the pastoral industry, where the other AWU branches felt the pressure to keep up with Queensland.[35]

The loss galvanised the pastoralists. In the *Pastoral Review* of 16 April 1921, the New South Wales Graziers Association (reflecting the signing up of cattle owners, the PUNSW had changed its name in October 1916) announced proposals for the amalgamation 'of the numerous organisations representing the interests of primary producers in Australia'. The *Review* noted that it had always advocated such a step, 'and with the growing strength, increasing organisation, and absorptive policy of the AWU during the last few years, it has become more necessary than ever'. But the Graziers Association's efforts were premature; the response of rural employers to unions remained fragmented in the 1920s and 1930s.[36]

If the AWU thought the 1917 Federal Pastoral Award was unsatisfactory, the 1922 award must have been an even greater shock. In a departure from the Harvester Judgment of 1907, which the AWU believed would ensure that no rate of pay would be fixed at a rate lower than that indicated by the statistician's figures, Justice Powers reduced the shearing rate from £2 to 30s, shed-hands from 90s to 60s and others in the industry by like proportion. The AWU Executive Council protested the decrease and issued a fighting policy in terms of the award applying in Queensland. As a result of the union's protest, the judge found that he had erred in part and increased rates to 35s to shearers, 75s to shed-hands and proportionately to others. But the AWU remained defiant, and the Graziers Association was granted orders restraining the AWU from strike action. Nevertheless the strike that followed was described by Central Branch secretary George Buckland as 'the greatest struggle we have had with employers since 1902'.

The campaign resulted in the AWU winning the whole of South Australia, but in New South Wales, Victoria and Tasmania only a small percentage of sheep were shorn under AWU recommendations. Adelaide Branch secretary Frank Lundie may have presided over one of the smaller AWU branches, but any branch presided over by the aggressive Lundie was unlikely to be meek. In his report for 1922 Lundie claimed that the branch had won 'all but four sheds for Queensland rates' in South Australia, although around Broken Hill in New South Wales (an area administered from Adelaide) the union was not so successful, 'as the Wool Kings, with the aid of a few ex-shearers who are now homestead holders ... were able to carry on and shear all the small holdings'. With a tone of disgust Lundie complained that 'New South Wales, Victoria and Tasmania did not put up any fight at all'. Barnes attributed the loss to insufficient numbers of the rank and file following the AWU's direction to 'stay at home' and was of the opinion that a month would have been enough to have won the struggle. Blakeley, the retiring AWU president, on the other hand, considered that the great factor operating against the success of the strike was Australia's 40 000 unemployed. By 16 October 1922, the *Pastoralists' Review* was reporting that about 800 sheds in New South Wales were shearing in accordance with the new award provisions and that the strike could be regarded as practically at an end. Shearers as a body, the report said, 'are not whole-heartedly behind their leaders in their illegal repudiation of the Arbitration Court; only by intimidation and false propaganda have the union bosses retained any semblance of discipline over their members, and even many of these are loyally working under the Federal award'. Some months later the Graziers Association of New South Wales noted that the AWU had advised its members to engage upon the terms of the award (although it should be noted that the AWU continued to press for an award variation and negotiations with pastoralists) and jubilantly declared that the union 'has frankly admitted the very severe reverse which it suffered by the attempt of its executive to force an illegal policy upon its members last season in direct opposition to their previously expressed wish, and has also freely admitted that its membership numbers have been very greatly diminished'. AWU membership declined from an estimated 102 400 in 1920–21 to 96 899 in 1922–23. While not all of the reduction in membership can be attributed to the pastoral sector (mining was also in severe decline), the unrest in 1922 must have been a factor in membership decline during this period.[37]

In 1926 the NSW AWU, following the success of the Queenslanders, sought the approval of the Lang Labor Government to approach the State Arbitration Court for a New South Wales State award. The Lang Government agreed and amended the State Arbitration Act accordingly. Central Branch then immediately applied for State awards in the pastoral, horticultural, agricultural, dairying and forestry industries. In 1928, however, the NSW Graziers Association and the Federal Pastoralists Association sought a new federal pastoral Award to render the State award ineffective. The new federal award slightly increased rates for shearers and shed-hands, but these rates were still less than the State award rates. Other conditions were altered which favoured employers. For instance, station-hands were required to advise employers in writing of their AWU membership otherwise they were not entitled to award rates. This move was a blow to New South Wales shearing industry workers. As most pastoralists were members of the Graziers Association of New South Wales, the State award henceforth had little application for AWU members. The AWU was still trying to overcome the contradictions of a dual federal–state industrial relations system when the Great Depression intervened in 1929.[38]

Ironically, by the 1920s, the pastoralists who had bitterly resisted the intervention of the state in the pastoral industry in the period before 1907 now seemed as committed as the AWU to the arbitration system. When the Bruce–Page Government threatened in 1929 to withdraw the Commonwealth Government from arbitration altogether, the *Pastoralists' Review* intimated that pastoralists would probably request that the shearing industry be kept under the Federal Arbitration Court as the New Graziers Association 'fears that if separate State awards are to be made for shearing it will lead to industrial discontent and perhaps to serious trouble'. The *Review* hailed the success of arbitration in the industry: 'Both sides have shown a willingness to confer amicably' and with the exception of 'two serious strikes since 1907 the awards of the court have been faithfully carried out'. The pastoralists evidently saw such advantages in maintaining a good relationship with the AWU that in 1925 the secretary of the NSW Graziers Association, J. W. Allen, met with Buckland and offered to help facilitate an early hearing of arbitration claims. Allen's sudden concern for the AWU may have been prompted by fears that the AWU leadership might be overthrown by the more radical Bushworkers Propaganda Group, a most displeasing prospect for the pastoralists, who had already spent forty years getting used to the AWU. Allen also offered to assist the AWU to 'eliminate the revolutionaries'. Buckland responded that the AWU felt at this stage it should deal with 'extremists' in its own way.[39]

### The Bushworker's Life

What sort of a life was it for a pastoral worker in Australia during the early twentieth century? Poor accommodation was a long-standing grievance for many rural workers, although the enactment of the Lang

Government's Rural Workers' Accommodation Act in New South Wales in 1926 was expected to make life somewhat more bearable. Historically, the effectiveness of accommodation legislation depended on how well it was policed. Rural workers were often faced with the prospect of living conditions which were cramped, unclean and unsanitary. It was not uncommon for shearers and shed-hands to be offered accommodation previously enjoyed by dogs and pigs. The new Act provided the air space allocation for each worker's sleeping compartment to be doubled to 480 cubic feet, disallowed upper bunks, required sleeping quarters to be divided into compartments with not more than two occupants in each, prohibited the use of sleeping quarters for the cooking of food and the serving of meals and required that baths be provided where sufficient water was available. The legislation also provided for the appointment of additional inspectors to supplement police in ensuring compliance on the part of pastoralists. Within a year, however, AWU Central Branch reported that 'there had not been the observance of [the Act] we expected ... in many cases no attempt to comply ... innumerable exemptions.' Nevertheless, the newly appointed inspectors had been 'most assiduous' in trying to enforce the Act.[40]

Riverina shearer James McIntosh told a Commonwealth Arbitration Court hearing in 1926 that he thought accommodation 'all right' in some places but 'poor' in others. Over twenty years he had come across only three baths in shearing accommodation and observed that most huts were unlined and usually without a fireplace. Samuel Turnbull, a shearer for thirty years, complained of a station at North Wyoe where shearers were provided with mattresses 'made of new chaff bags filled with grass'. William Sims, another thirty-year veteran of the sheds, demonstrated the precariousness of the position of shearers' 'rep'. Shearing at Malaraway in New South Wales, Sims was instructed by his shed to complain to the AWU about the substandard accommodation. An inspector subsequently visited the shed and ordered the owner to comply with the Accommodation Act. The owner asked the source of the complaint, to which Sims answered that he had laid it. The owner then made it known that he did not 'want Sims on my station again'. Giving evidence in a case before the Arbitration Court brought by the AWU against the Pastoralists Federal Council and others in 1922, Tasmanian AWU Branch secretary Roy Cole, a shearer since 1906, described accommodation in that State as the 'worst of all in Australia. In some instances roofs were made of palings, men huddled in small rooms, with straw lying upon the floor and there were no bunks in some instances ... you can count the stars through the ceiling above'.

Shearing had other occupational hazards. James McIntosh warned of the menace of burr and thistle in the Riverina: 'thistle can get into one's hands so he can't even carry a sheep out. In the Riverina a man has to wear gloves. If burrs get into combs they can make the machine fly out of a man's hands ... apt to cut the shearer or the man next to him'. Frank Lysaght recounted the danger of prickly pear: 'thorns go through the clothes into the skin, scratch into the flesh and fester. Some have had to leave the shed and seek medical attention'.

Life was no easier for station-hands, whose duties might include mustering, crutching and dagging, lamb-marking, dipping, drenching, care of windmills and pumps, repairing and straining fences, gate-making, replacing gate posts and hanging gates, breaking and handling young horses, milking and killing stock, treating scabby-mouth sheep and sheep with foot rot. Thomas Ryan told the 1917 Station Award hearing that his duties as a station-hand were 'equally as hard as mining or navvying'. He worked from 7 a.m. to 5.30 p.m. Monday to Friday with an hour's break for lunch. On Saturday he was required to work from 7 a.m. until 4 p.m. As it was common for pastoral workers to be accommodated some distance from the station, their day was often longer than officially recognised. Some were better off than others. Samuel Jamieson, married with three children, was allowed the use of a cow. If he broke it in, he could have the use of it until it was twelve months old. This provided milk and the opportunity to make a little butter. Although his wages were paid on an 'unfound' basis, he was given half a sheep per week, between 28 and 30 pounds' weight, which he had to kill and dress. He lived in an old dilapidated five-room weatherboard house about 6 miles from his station. This gave him the opportunity to tend a small vegetable garden and room to run a couple of pigs and some poultry which he had managed to acquire.

Bill Hall worked as a station-hand on properties in northern New South Wales and southern Queensland during the late 1920s, travelling to jobs by jumping trains, carrying his 'cigarette swag' of rolled-up clothes and blanket. As he remembers, 'train jockeys' were still common in the 1920s. Sometimes he could ride in the brake van with a friendly guard; others were not so tolerant, and the swaggies would resort to hiding under the tarpaulin covers of the goods vans. Hall could earn around £2 a week for station work: up at 5 a.m. to tend the shearers' cooks' fire, milking and rounding up cows, chopping wood and fencing. He also remembers the strict pecking order of the station: the managers at the top with their attendant jackeroos, who were the sons of pastoralists absorbing the rituals and techniques of station management, young men who 'always echoed the boss', as he recalls. The station-hands never mixed with the jackeroos, who always ate with the boss. The shearers ate in their own accommodation and had their own cook. They also tended to be more unionised than the station-hands, the itinerants near the bottom of the social scale, fed on freshly killed meat and dried fruit ('no green vegies') and housed in bare timber and wrought-iron sheds. Right at the bottom of the scale were Aborigines, whose employment on the stations was not always tolerated by the white shearers and station-hands, despite AWU policy, established in the 1890s and re-affirmed at the 1916 Convention, that Aborigines had to be employed on equal terms with white members. Hall remembers one station near Brewarrina in New South Wales where the Aboriginal workers were unwelcome because the station-hands feared that they would undermine pay rates. 'The aborigines that worked as station hands weren't paid award wages ... so there was a distinction between the union blokes and [them] which shouldn't have been, of course, but it was there none-theless.' But an AWU organiser, Sam Brassington, compelled the white workers to allow the Aborigines to be employed at the station. The realities of the social hierarchy of pastoral stations were somewhat different from union declarations and award decrees.

Itinerant shearers had a number of expenses to meet from their wage. They had to provide their own tools and food and meet travelling costs. By the 1920s, flocks had become smaller and shearers needed to travel to more sheds than they had done in the past. Travel was generally by rail or hired car or truck. James McIntosh observed that railway fares in Victoria had become more expensive and had increased twice since 1917. He had had to use a hire car to travel between sheds from Quimong and East Woondooke – he travelled with three others to defray the cost – but it had cost him 12s 6d to travel 15 miles. There was little option as he would have lost a day if forced to walk. Samuel Turnbull noted it had cost him 10s to travel 6 miles in a hired lorry. Accommodation and meals were also becoming more expensive, he observed: 'A few years ago I could get second class accommodation at country hotels for 4/- per day. Now I cannot get it anywhere for less than 8/- and in most cases it costs 10/- to 12/-'.[41]

### The Metal-Mining Industry

The Australian mining industry had been declining since 1907. The virtual exhaustion of Australia's richest and most accessible mines and higher costs in production, transport and labour were given for the collapse of Australian mining. The Armistice spelt the end of the copper boom. By 1920 the four smelters of Queensland's Cloncurry copper belt were idle. The value of pure copper fell from £136 a ton in 1917 to £75 a ton by 1921.The Mount Morgan Gold Mining Company, which by the 1920s depended more on copper than gold, was also in decline, and by 1927 the company was in liquidation. By early 1919 Great Cobar, the largest mine in the New South Wales copper centre at Cobar, had closed.

Soon only the Mount Lyell mine in Tasmania remained, saved by new smelting technology. The collapse in the copper price was accompanied by similar slumps in the production of other metals. Queensland gold-fields continued their pre-war decline and by 1930 mined a bare £30 000 in gold. In New South Wales some large and numerous small mines ceased operations. The Mount Boppy and Mount Hope mines closed and the towns in the New England area north-west of Sydney were abandoned. In 1930 the only goldmine to pay a dividend in Victoria was the small Rose, Thistle and Shamrock mine at Harrietville. In Tasmania, Mount Bischoff and Zeehan mines closed and the fertile goldmine at Beaconsfield was flooded. Australia mined 24 per cent of the world's gold in 1903 and 2 per cent in 1929. In most years during the 1920s, Australia's metals earned barely a third of the sum they earned in the period 1906–8. In all, more than 100 000 people were forced to leave mining towns. In North Queensland thousands went to sugar farms and small ports. AWU reports of the 1920s are littered with gloomy news about the state of mining in all areas. Metalliferous miners were among the lowest-paid workers in New South Wales, 'notwithstanding the skill required, and the onerous and dangerous nature of the work'. Central Branch reported membership of the Mining Section at 1300–1400 com-pared with 4000 a few years previously.[42]

By the end of the decade, eight out of every nine ounces of gold pro-duced in Australia were mined in Western Australia, but even production in the rich 'golden mile' at Boulder, south of Kalgoorlie, and nearby Coolgardie, had also significantly collapsed. Seventy-five thousand workers were employed in Western Australian goldmines in 1900 and thirty years later their number had been reduced to 6000. Many left the goldfields to search for work in the wheat belt, or returned dejectedly to the eastern States. After the amalgamation with the FMEA in 1917, the Western Australian mining membership was large enough to justify the establishment of a WA Mining Branch of the union, separate from the traditional AWU branch in the State, which organised the rural and construction membership. It was a branch which periodically displayed an independent streak. In 1920, when the AWU membership had voted in a plebiscite to maintain union support for the arbitration system, the WA Mining Branch had voted 496:296 in favour of abandoning arbitration, a relatively low voter turnout (branch membership was approximately 3300 at the time) but a fair reflection of the membership's views. Miners, like shearers, were usually paid piece-rates, or some form of direct contract payment between themselves and the company. At least in good economic times, many miners probably felt that they could do better through direct bargaining with the company, rather than through arbitration structures defined in distant cities. Some branch members

were not employees at all, but worked under the tribute system, which
was a strong feature of the Western Australian mining fields, particularly
Boulder, in the inter-war years. Tributers subleased a portion of the mine
from a mining company, paying the company a royalty on ore won and a
further charge for supplies and services. Tributers would often employ
other miners to work for them, thus providing a saving on labour costs
for the 'host' mining company. Just as some shearers saw themselves as
independent contractors, perhaps with their own small selection, many
miners had a similar self-image. It is unlikely that those miners who were
tempted by the idea of big profits through the tribute system would have
felt that the arbitration system had much relevance for them. As Patrick
Bertola indicates, the AWU had little success in winning better terms
from mining companies on behalf of tributers in the early 1920s. High
unemployment on the Western Australian goldfields had left the AWU
Mining Branch financially – and industrially – weakened. Indeed, the
AWU Executive Council temporarily assumed control of the WA Mining
Branch in 1922 because of the financial 'incompetency' of its officials.
Poor performance by the branch would have undoubtedly contributed
to members taking a harsh view of an arbitration system with which the
union was so strongly associated.[43]

A 1921 dispute at Mount Morgan is a telling example of the difficulties
which the union faced in its relations with mine owners during the
decade, and indeed the vagaries which could plague the underground
mining industry. In March 1921, Mount Morgan mine management
informed the unions that wages now accounted for 45 per cent of the
company's expenses. The only way to reduce costs was to reduce wages
by 20 per cent. The mine had not paid a dividend since April 1920 and
the company was experiencing an acute liquidity problem. Queensland
Branch president W. J. Riordan and organiser J. C. Lamont called mass
meetings of members which endorsed their recommendation to refer
the proposal to the Arbitration Court and ask the government for
assistance. The company closed the mine 'for repairs' on 24 March and
told its employees that unless its terms were agreed to, the mine would
not reopen on 5 April, the date the renovations were due for completion.
An AWU deputation met the now Premier E. G. Theodore and the
Member for Mount Morgan, James Stopford (also a former AWU
official), on 1 April. In the meantime the company sought to withdraw
an earlier application for a consolidated award for Mount Morgan from
the Arbitration Court. Riordan countered by seeking a court order to
have the company's books examined by two accountants to verify the
supposed losses. Riordan said the company withdrew the award claim to
pressure the workers to accept the 20 per cent reduction in wages. He
reminded the court that the basic wage was already 4s less than for other

Hard work if you can get it. Working the Mount Morgan Mine, Queensland 1913. Working conditions remained heavily manual until after the Second World War. *National Library of Australia.*

industries and the hours far longer. The AWU then put forward a counter-proposal that the company should issue deferred certificates for employees on minimum wages accepting the 20 per cent reduction, to be redeemed in more prosperous times. The company rejected this proposal. A mass meeting of AWU members voted 726:547 to reject any reduction in wages. At the end of October, a full bench of the Arbitration Court granted the company its 20 per cent reduction. Despite still being 'locked out' of the mine by the company, AWU members met again on 4 November and rejected the court's decision, with only four dissenters. Finally, in February 1922, the breakthrough occurred, prompted by government intervention on behalf of the AWU. The government freight rate concession was increased to a maximum of £1100. The company agreed to allocate the benefit of the freight concession among employees by the addition of 13s a week per employee to the award rate. After a 322-day lock-out, the mine finally reopened. Three years later it was closed again after a serious underground fire, which may have been a result of continuing industrial unrest. The mine was closed for several years.[44]

As important as an adequate living wage was for miners, the AWU was also concerned about the health risks associated with mining. Lung diseases, often generically referred to as 'Miners' Phthisis', and mineral poisoning were common complaints and death was a common result. South Australian Branch secretary Frank Lundie reported in 1920 that 'a considerable number of AWU members' had suffered lead poisoning at Port Pirie smelters, 'with many deaths'. The biggest killer of mine workers was dust. For many years the insidious effects of deep shaft mining and silicosis (dust inhalation causing lesions and thickening of lung tissue, and further complications such as tuberculosis) were poorly understood, and it was only gradually that efforts to curb its incidence were introduced. Drilling techniques introduced in the 1870s produced a continuous shower of dust. Ventilation systems were often poor. In the early 1900s, it was estimated that of Western Australian goldminers, one in four displayed symptoms of silicosis. Geoffrey Blainey wrote:

> How many lives had been cut short by the fine dust of Australian mines cannot be counted, but the number must have exceeded ten thousand. Ironically once the menace was seen it could easily be curbed by playing water on the dust and by ventilating the deeper workings. However, many miners ignored their water jet and many companies owning deep shafts on narrow leases recoiled at the expense of providing ventilation.

Pressure from unions during the 1920s gradually prompted State and federal government action to alleviate what has been described as a silicosis epidemic in the Australian mining industry. In 1921 the Commonwealth Government established the Industrial Hygiene Division within the Department of Health. It was specifically charged with addressing the silicosis problem in the mining industry and lead poisoning at Port Pirie. In 1923 the WA Government passed the *Miners' Phthisis Act* to provide for compulsory medical examination of the State's mining workforce. In 1925 miners' phthisis was included in the schedule of diseases in the WA Workers' Compensation Act. In 1928 the AWU in New South Wales was successful in bringing the 'miners' complaint' under the umbrella of the Workers' Compensation Act. Similar legislation followed in Tasmania, Victoria and Queensland.[45]

There were many dangerous practices for mine workers to contend with. In a series of Commonwealth Arbitration Court proceedings during the 1920s and early 1930s, AWU metal miners simply but eloquently described their working conditions. Joseph Cahill of White Hill was employed at the New Chum Syncline mine in Victoria as a shift leader in shaft sinking during the early 1930s. This dangerous work involved riding up and down mine shafts, some of which were over 300 feet deep, in a 'bucket'. The 'bucket' was below when the charge used to blast the rock was fired, which meant the occupant had to rely on being raised – very quickly – to the surface. Cahill was paid 16s 6d a day. Ernest West, a miner for ten years and married with two children, was employed at Tasmania's Mount Lyell mine as an underground machine operator at a rate of 12s a week plus the basic wage for Queenstown, which was £3 2s 6d. West described how the exhaust of the machine caused a 'fog' which mixed with oil and, along with smoke, was breathed in by the operator. The cold water, another underground problem, and the 'fog' penetrated the skin and caused chills. He suffered from rheumatism and had lost seven shifts in the last twelve months because of illness. He paid £1 a week from his wages for accommodation for his wife and family and had 'trouble making ends meet' with what was left.

William Bowman had thirty years' mining experience and was employed as a spitsman in the flotation plant at Mount Lyell (flotation was the new technology which kept the Mount Lyell mine open by separating ores and slag more efficiently). Bowman explained how watching the 'changing' for the different ores and chemicals with which he worked, including cyanide and lime, strained his eyes. He had also worked in the crushing section which he described as 'energy intensive' – he started this work weighing 11 stone 3 pounds and ended it twelve months later a stone lighter. Jack Harigan was a tank hand, which required him to handle sharp-edged copper. Although provided with gloves, the copper cut right through them. He had recently sliced a finger through to the bone, forcing him to take time off work. He had also been employed as a tank cleaner. Duties involved drawing cathodes out of cells and washing out the blistered copper which had passed through them. He would then empty all the solution from the tank to approximately one foot from the bottom and mix, with a hand scraper, all the 'gold slimes' on the bottom of the tank; the 'slimes' comprised gold, silver, lead and some other metals. The problem here was being splashed with this residue which, in his experience, was unavoidable. Harigan recalled that a singlet 'would not last a fortnight'. The mine superintendent had suggested wearing wool. Harigan's view was that this would have been too hot – not to mention utterly futile as a means of protecting his health.

Michael Kinsell was a refinery worker at Mount Lyell. He described how his work was hard on his clothing and affected his hands. He had 'come off night shifts and placed a basin of water alongside the bed with Condy's Crystals before I could get to sleep, on account of those fumes which are very bad'. Constipation was a 'side effect' of his duties and he suffered sweating and burns from splashing acid. A green colour oozed from his skin when he perspired and he had difficulty keeping food down while on the job – 'if I eat anything but tomatoes I am sick, on account of the fumes'.

Eric Reece, a future organiser of the AWU's Tasmanian Branch and Tasmanian Labor Premier (1958–68, 1972–75) was employed at Mount Lyell during the early 1930s. Reece provided a graphic description of his work, charge wheeling to the furnace:

> A 'charge' comprises three carts of concentrates, an amount of silica, lime, slag, and coke, and throughout the last few weeks I expect an average of 46 charges has passed through the furnace in every eight hours. It is necessary for four men to keep that amount of material up to the furnace, and on what is called the 'raw concentrate' and three men are engaged for six hours, and for the other two hours a man has to put it in wheeling the silica, lime, slag and coke. The wheeling is split up by four men, and three men are engaged in the raw concentrate end and an extra man spends two hours and then changes with a man on the concentrate end. There is a change over and a break for every man during the shift.
>
> It is necessary for a man to load the cart of concentrates, wheel a distance of about 50 yards to the furnace and tip it, before he returns for another charge, in ten minutes. The weight of the contents of the cart would be between 1400 and 1500 lbs … a comparison has often been made between what is a fair load for a horse and what is a fair load for a man to pull. A horse, under a competent driver, will not be asked to pull more than about one ton; therefore it must be quite apparent that 1400 to 1500 lbs seems a quite unfair load for a man to pull under practically the same conditions.

Reece also described flue-cleaning:

> After the furnace has stopped its run, it is the duty of the flue cleaners to open up the doors, go into the flue and shovel the material out. The flue dust, as you will understand, contains a big percentage of acids and, as a man perspires in the hot flue, the flue dust settles on his clothing and skin, and when it settles on the skin it causes an itch. It has the effect of rotting his clothing. Clothing lasts no time in the flues. The nails of boots are turned into copper and last a very short time. In fact, we are always advised when we go into the flues to try and pick out the oldest clothes we have, because they will not last.

Washing and changing facilities were poor or non-existent at many mines. Often water was not available and miners would have to travel unwashed and in wet clothes to their homes, several miles from the workplace. George Stackpoole, a Victorian miner, lived 4 miles from the mine and had no washing facilities. Samuel Grieben, a miner in the Gippsland area of Victoria, worked at ore-getting on the stopes (the mine face at the end of a shaft) with a hand hammer and drill. Although this was very dusty work there was no change house at the mine, 'not even a shed', although twenty or thirty men were employed there. His clothes were always wet because of water constantly dripping on him while working. He had to walk 3 miles back to his tent each day in his working clothes. Robert Davies of the Culupula Mine had to travel 18 miles a day back to his digs without a wash, although he was able to dry his clothes on a boiler at the mine.

Miners with families often found it impossible to find adequate accommodation near their place of work. It was not unusual for wives and children to live in rented accommodation in the nearest major town or city, while the miner had to pay for his lodgings closer to the mine site or pitch a tent. He sometimes had to pay for transport to and from the mine and to have food and other provisions brought up to his lodgings meant that he always paid higher prices. Grieben's provisions had to be brought up from a town 32 miles away.[46]

## The Construction Industry

The construction industry had the grim distinction of sharing similar health and safety problems with the mining industry, and not just the most obvious dangers associated with handling explosives or constructing timberwork in tunnels and so on. Silicosis was also a problem in the construction industry. AWU members in quarrying, sewer construction and rock-chopping were all exposed to silicosis-inducing work practices. Of 716 Sydney construction workers tested for silicosis in 1924, 123 exhibited symptoms; 38 of these had also developed tuberculosis. In 1927 a compensation scheme for New South Wales construction workers suffering from silicosis was established.[47]

Sewer maintenance workers were required to walk in sewers up to their waists in water. In smaller sewers, according to an AWU organiser's evidence during an Arbitration Court hearing in 1926, a man was dragged along on 'a sort of plank, on his back, and he looks up at the roof to see if there is any defect'. Evidence was also given of the dangers inherent in the introduction of new machinery, in the use of which workers were often poorly trained. For example, one member had strained his heart and died while using a new $\frac{3}{4}$ hundredweight jackhammer during the conversion of the St Kilda Esplanade tramline.[48]

Peter Sheldon observes that construction work in the years 1910–19 was often 'dirty and dangerous'. Conditions improved little in the following decade. The nature of the industry retarded efforts to alleviate working conditions. As Sheldon comments, construction workers were usually itinerant single males, signed on by a contractor for a particular job, then moving on to something else. Work was often disrupted by poor weather or a lack of materials. None of these factors facilitated unionism. As noted earlier, Victoria-Riverina Branch secretary Jack McNeill was frustrated in 1922 by the apathy of Melbourne construction workers, who perhaps could see little benefit in paying union dues for a job which might only last a few weeks or months.[49]

Railway bridge construction, Sydney 1924. Still a strongly manual process, but some labour-saving technology is evident – as is the rear-end of a more traditional horse and dray on the extreme left. *National Library of Australia.*

## Working the Riverina

Unlike the male-dominated occupations in pastoral, mining and construction work, one in six workers in the fruit-picking industry were women. John Dwyer, an AWU agent in Mildura in 1924, told an Arbitration Court hearing that of the 3270 AWU members in the industry in the fruit-picking regions of New South Wales and Victoria, 555 were women. In many cases employers preferred women workers because it was believed that their nimble fingers enabled them to pick more. They were also considered to be better at pulling out and tying up in the pruning season. Women were employed at the same rate for picking as male employees. Awards and agreements in the industry, as a rule, provided for equal pay for equal work although, according to Dwyer, the award current for 1924 contained, through 'inadvertence', a provision that women be paid less than men for pulling out and tying up. The majority of women workers were local residents. Fewer itinerant women workers came to Mildura because of the lack of accommodation.

Following regular bushwork routines, fruit-pickers were drawn to the work from the mining fields of Broken Hill and Cobar, from Melbourne, and from the Victorian pastoral centres of Warrnambool, Casterton and Coleraine. Others came by river from Renmark, Adelaide and Swan Hill,

Euston and Balranald. Some travelled down from Sydney. Those from Broken Hill generally drove down by cart; others came by bicycle or train. Many male workers travelled with their wives and some were able to find accommodation in Mildura. Others resided in surrounding districts and came into Mildura each day. Those workers unable to obtain accommodation camped in tents pitched near where they were working.

Workers had to buy their own food. Some of the stores in Mildura would deliver for an additional charge. The delivery charge on bread was 2d a loaf and an extra 1d a pound for meat. The climate in Mildura in the summer was extremely hot, with temperatures ranging from 90° to 96° and 112° to 115°, making the keeping of perishables difficult. The salt meat delivered to them was sometimes tainted and had to be discarded. Because of this, some families were forced to turn to an expensive diet of tinned fish. High rent was also a burden on fruit industry workers. Dwyer reported that a survey of married permanent male workers indicated that the average rental for a four-room house was 25s a week and in some cases as high as 30s a week. Out of forty-nine permanent hands employed at one property, there was accommodation for only twenty-three of them. Wages for pickers ranged from about £4 a week when the fruit-picking 'was on' in full swing, down to £3 17s 6d during quieter periods. John Case, who was married with eight children had, by 1924, worked as a fruit-picker in Mildura for sixteen years. On these wages, he said, he was unable to buy much meat and needed to purchase an average of twenty loaves of bread a week at 1/2d a loaf. He paid 10s a week rent for a house with only two 'good' rooms, the kitchen being all trellis work. He also paid 25s a week for wood in the summer and more in the winter. Workers had to provide their own clothes and, if involved in pruning, their own shears. Generally there were no sanitary arrangements on the blocks where picking took place. The fruit-picking industry also had its own health and safety hazards. Cyanide was used in fumigation and pickers were sometimes forced to drink irrigation water, which induced dysentery.

Dwyer suggested that many permanent workers were frightened to give evidence to a court or tribunal or to go near the union office or union delegate through fear of recrimination (which presumably accounts for the unfortunate fact that no women – or men – fruit-pickers gave evidence to the 1924 hearing). Workers were also disadvantaged by the contract system of employment. In numerous instances the AWU found that the contractor, who was not permitted to be a member of the AWU, would not observe award rates and conditions. They would merely accept a contract at so much a dry ton and engage the pickers.

The fruit-preserving and packing industry, another major employer of women, also came under the umbrella of the AWU. In late 1922 the AWU entered into agreements with the Water Conservation and Irrigation Commission and the Murrumbidgee Irrigation Company for the regulation of this industry in the Leeton irrigation area. Soon afterwards, a dispute arose in the factories over pay rates: the female employees in the canning factory demanded increases which management had refused. The women stopped work and were supported by other employees. They resumed work two days later after a promise of arbitration of the dispute by an arbitrator appointed by the Department of Labour and Industry. The arbitrator decided the increased rates should be paid and awarded a fortnight's retrospectivity. Central Branch secretary Buckland commented: 'By their display of solidarity at Leeton the girls really set an example which could well be emulated by the male members of our organisation'.[50]

For many AWU members, like the members of most other unions in blue-collar industries, working life in the 1920s was physically onerous and often unnecessarily dangerous. It was not simply the predatory instincts of capitalism which embedded these conditions; ignorance of problems such as chemical handling, together with wilful neglect, left workers exposed to hazards which the tedious strictures of the law were often slow to remedy.

CHAPTER 8

# A Union that Battles

*The Great Depression and the Rise of the Queensland Branch,*
*1930–39*

The Wall Street crash in 1929 set the economic, social and political agenda for Australia and the rest of the world for the next decade. The price of Australia's precious commodities wheat and wool, already in decline, fell steeply after the crash – by more than 50 per cent by the middle of 1931. The evaporation of overseas loan funds forced governments to reduce expenditure, particularly in the public works sector where cuts are estimated to have put 200 000 people out of work. Unemployment rose from 9.3 per cent at the beginning of 1929 to 25.8 per cent by early 1931. The free-fall in prices for rural produce and the slashing of public works budgets had a disastrous impact on AWU members. Although the pastoral and construction industries were hit particularly hard, the AWU's coverage of such a diverse range of occupations meant that the union was exposed to the full force of spiralling unemployment. Total AWU membership achieved a level of about 160 000 in 1928, but by 1930 this figure had been cut by more than half. The Queensland Branch, the largest, had boasted a membership of 42 764 in early 1930. This fell sharply to 22 418 within two years. In New South Wales, membership collapsed from 35 000 to 5000 in 1932.[1]

Government response to the economic crisis drifted between confusion and arbitrary gestures. In August 1930 Sir Otto Niemeyer, a representative of British financiers, told Australia's politicians that their governments borrowed too much, spent too much, and promoted heavily protected and inefficient industries. This statement of the obvious, couched in patronising language about the unreasonable

Two fundamental tenets of the AWU ethos, *c.* 1930: arbitration and anti-communism. The solid bushman of Will Donald's 1929 *Australian Worker* cartoons calls on workers to rally against the Bruce Government's threat to remove the Commonwealth from regulating industrial relations. The second cartoon exhorts the Labor Party to emulate the AWU and wield the big stick of expulsion to drive out the communist menace. *AWU Collection.*

optimism of Australians and their need to understand their role in the empire economy as a tolerable source of raw materials, incited an outburst of indignation, scapegoating, and a plethora of contrary plans. Meanwhile in January 1931 the Commonwealth Arbitration Court, in the apparent belief that further depressing the economy must be good for it, reduced the basic wage and all margins for skill by 10 per cent. *Worker* editor Henry Boote was outraged:

> Thus is democracy defeated by a judicial triumvirate created for that purpose by the crafty haters of democratic rule. Thus are the victims of capitalistic greed compelled also to bear the penalty of capitalistic incompetence ... The edict of the Court is as illogical as it is ruthless, as fallacious as it is insolent. No Government representing the great Labor Movement can tolerate it without dishonour.

The Scullin Government was willing to tolerate it. Ted Grayndler described the government's listless acquiescence to the harsh terms of the Premiers' Plan, as advocated by Niemeyer and Commonwealth Bank governor Sir Robert Gibson, as one which 'will further add to unemployment, as with wage reduction and lesser spending power, all kinds of services and occupations will be necessarily curtailed'. The responses of the labour movement to the depression, however, were as fractious and disjointed as those of the politicians. AWU strategies were coloured by difficult relations with the broader labour movement and by internal opposition to the leadership, from rank-and-file dissidents who sought a militant response to the economic crisis inflicting so much suffering on the Australian working class.[2]

### The War against Lang

In February 1931 NSW Premier Jack Lang began to undermine the Federal Labor Government of James Scullin with a strategy for repudiating overseas loan repayments, opening an ideological and factional divide which pitted Lang against Scullin and federal Treasurer Ted Theodore. The former AWU official and Queensland premier had little time for Lang's ill-conceived populism. Theodore wanted to stimulate economic activity through an expansion of credit and spending on public works. The first battle of this short but unpleasant war occurred in March 1931 when the ALP Federal Executive, and the NSW Branch controlled by Lang, split over the loans issue. The AWU affiliated with the 'new' NSW Branch of the ALP established by the Federal Executive. Most other New South Wales unions remained affiliated with Lang Labor. The AWU had fallen out with the Lang Labor machine in the late 1920s, losing the battle for control of the NSW ALP. The AWU's Executive Council also rejected

the Lang Plan and declared its opposition 'to any one state dictating
a policy for the Federal Labor Party in opposition to that laid down by
the Federal Conference and Federal Executive. We deplore the action of
the NSW State Executive in endeavouring to do so'.[3]

Henry Boote had a particular dislike for Jack Lang. Since the controversy over the 'red rules' in 1927, Boote had regarded Lang's control
of NSW Labor as dictatorial, and would often say so in the *Worker*. But
Lang and Boote shared a violent aversion for the 'Money Power', the
shadowy reign of omnipotent private banks and international financiers
whose money Lang was so keen to disparage and so happy to spend.
Boote had been regularly blaming the Money Power for many of society's
ills since 1911, when he first began writing for the *Worker*: 'The despotism of the Lords of the Purse is one that penetrates into every home, and
extracts its due from the leanest households. There is no escaping from
it. The very infant in the cradle is meat for the ravernous maw of the
Money Power'. The Premiers' Plan was the Money Power at full feast.
'The organisations of Labour, both industrial and political, regard this
plan with invincible repugnance. The product of book-bound experts, of
the Money Combine, and of Nationalist politicians, it is as thoroughly
reactionary in its conception as it will prove to be calamitous in its
results.'[4]

Nevertheless in June 1931 the AWU Executive Council voted to express
its heavily qualified support for the plan, although it was 'definitely
opposed' to further cuts in wages, pensions and social services, cuts
fundamental to the plan's intention to reduce public expenditure and
promote 'sound finance', an admirable and, in the context of an international depression, quite gratuitous aim. The AWU recognised that
Theodore's alternative plan was thwarted by the banks and a 'reactionary' conservative-dominated Senate. In a final indication of the union's
distaste for the Premiers' Plan, it was decided that 'no publicity be given
to the resolution'.[5]

The Executive Council had little power to resist the Premiers' Plan or
Lang's domination of NSW Labor. Lang's stranglehold on the New South
Wales labour movement was only beginning to tighten and by November
his divisive influence had split the federal parliamentary Labor Caucus.
The federal Lang Labor group, led by Jack Beasley, brought down the
Scullin Government with a no-confidence motion. Scullin had refused to
investigate charges – no more than political scuttlebutt – that Treasurer
Ted Theodore was corrupting the unemployment relief scheme in New
South Wales to benefit political supporters in his Sydney electorate of
Dalley – supporters opposed, coincidentally, to the Lang Labor machine.
Former Scullin Cabinet minister Joe Lyons, who had quit the Labor Party
in May over the government's handling of the economy, emerged as

prime minister following the December 1931 elections, leading a conservative United Australia Party Government. Labor would not have to
implement the Premiers' Plan after all.[6]

On 22 December 1931 federal Labor MP and future prime minister
John Curtin wrote to his old friend Henry Boote, lamenting Labor's fate:
'We have gone to dusty death'. Curtin, caught up in the electoral rout of
the divided Labor Party, had lost the Western Australian seat of Fremantle.
Now he turned again to the AWU, hoping that Boote might intercede with
Grayndler to find him a job. Curtin also toyed with the idea of moving back
east to fight Lang. He told Boote, 'I somehow do not like to leave the next
few years to the cannibals who live on their own species, and hanker for a
go at them'. Eventually Curtin took a job as the sporting writer with the
*Westralian Worker*; he could have had the editor's job if he wanted it, but he
refused to displace the incumbent, Fred Gates. At the 1934 elections
Curtin regained the Fremantle electorate for Labor.[7]

In the *Worker* of 23 December Boote flayed the 'base treachery' of the
Lang faction. As a journalist, Boote reserved particular scorn for the anti-
Labor press. 'For sheer political dirtiness and barefaced misrepresentation
the campaign launched against the Government by the Sydney "Daily
Telegraph" would be hard to beat.' The AWU leadership well realised that
a powerful press could influence the nation's political agenda. They had
only to recall the role of the *Australian Worker* in the 1916–17 conscription
crisis. Even in the midst of the depression they were determined to expand
the AWU's influence through the revival of a daily Labor newspaper, the
*World*, the former Hobart *Daily Post* which Labor Papers Ltd had purchased
and relaunched as the *World* in 1918, and which collapsed in debt in 1924.
It should have been a warning: in April 1931 the Executive Council asked
the directors of Labor Papers Ltd – in effect, the AWU leadership – to re-
establish the paper so that the AWU could be a 'rallying point for Industrial
Organisation in the Commonwealth' and to support the policies of the
ALP. Reviving the *World* would also mean that the AWU could confront its
rivals, the ACTU and the Lang machine.[8]

The influence of the *Australian Worker* had already been challenged by
the *Labor Daily*, established in 1924 by the Miners Federation precisely for
that purpose. The *Labor Daily* was also supported by several other NSW
Labor Council affiliates. Confirmed AWU enemies Jack Lang and NSW
Labor Council secretary Jock Garden also served as *Labor Daily* directors,
and in 1931 'the skilful publicity' of the *Labor Daily*'s writers and
cartoonists 'helped create the larger-than-life [Lang] legend' – to the
chagrin of the marginalised AWU. The decision to revive the *World* was
taken at the same Executive Council meeting which condemned the
Lang Plan and decided on affiliation with the Federal Labor Party
branch in New South Wales. The *World* proved a poor depression-era

weapon against the Lang machine. It first appeared on 26 August 1931 and closed on 14 November 1932, generating a £60 000 debt for Labor Papers Ltd, and forcing the directors to offer bargain Macdonell House rents to meet the repayments. In the crowded Sydney newspaper market, at the height of the depression, the *World* could simply not attract sufficient advertising to pay its way, let alone make a profit. Most of those unions which had invested in Labor Papers subsequently sold their shares to the AWU's Queensland Branch 'at less than face value'. Labor Papers Ltd and the AWU struggled with the debt until the early 1960s.[9]

In prompting the ill-considered revival of the *World*, Jack Lang inadvertently did his old enemy Ted Theodore a favour. In 1932 Labor Papers Ltd asked the former treasurer to report on options for the failed newspaper. Like Curtin, Theodore had lost his seat in Federal Parliament at the 1931 elections, defeated by a Langite. Disillusioned with politics, he had his eye on a business career; he had a partner in a young Frank Packer. Theodore told the AWU officials that they should sell the *World* to Packer and himself, at a bargain price. Grayndler and president John Barnes, who by late 1932 were desperate to unload the *World* and its debts, were said to have arranged the terms with Theodore in a Melbourne pub while the former treasurer plied them with drink. A £1 banknote was used as a rudimentary contract to confirm the details, and was signed by the three men.[10]

The *World* deal, like many commercial ventures with which unions are associated, generated an enormous controversy in the labour movement, leading to heavy financial loss and recriminations. The 'sale' arrangements soon became a deal by Theodore and Packer's Sydney Newspapers Ltd to lease the *World*'s printing presses and space in Macdonell House. Early promises by Sydney Newspapers Ltd to publish a new daily newspaper to replace the *World* – and save the jobs of 280 staff – were also shelved. Theodore and Packer had quietly done a deal with Sir Hugh Denison's Associated Newspapers Ltd – of which Frank's father, R. C. Packer, was managing editor – not to use the *World*'s presses to produce a Sydney daily newspaper, which would compete with Associated's *Sun* afternoon newspaper, for three years. In exchange, Frank Packer and Theodore got £86 500 for doing nothing. The *World* staff lost their jobs, and the AWU wore the opprobrium of the sackings, and further embarrassment in 1933 when Jack Lang, who harboured as much enmity for the Packer family as he did for Theodore and the AWU, exposed the deal with Associated Newspapers in the NSW Parliament, and some other dubious share transactions with which the Packers' companies had been involved. Debate at the 1933 AWU Convention had already disclosed that while Packer and Theodore had leased the printing equipment at rock-bottom rates, the union was left with a huge redundancy bill – up to £10 000 – for

the *World*'s staff. The minutes of Labor Papers Ltd reveal fitful and
unsuccessful attempts during the 1930s by the directors to negotiate better
terms with Sydney Newspapers. As late as February 1939, Labor Papers was
still struggling with a cash-flow crisis; the company had a £25 000 overdraft
with the bank but still needed an additional £3000 to tide them over the
current month – this for a company whose main activities, thanks to the
collapse of the *World*, were primarily restricted to managing Macdonell
House. Meanwhile, Macdonell House throbbed to the unlikely sound of
the production of an innovative new magazine, the *Australian Women's
Weekly*, established in 1933 by Sydney Newspapers Ltd. Unable to produce
a daily newspaper, the company had found a lucrative use for the *World*'s
equipment. The huge financial success of the *Women's Weekly* led in 1936
to the creation of Consolidated Press Ltd, the publishers of the often
virulently anti-Labor *Daily Telegraph* which Henry Boote so detested. E. G.
Theodore was the first chairman of directors of Consolidated Press. The
*World* deal had been the second occasion on which the AWU had trustingly
asked Theodore, a former official, for advice – the first had been over the
Bailey ballot-box affair – and it was the second time that the union might
rightly have felt bemused at the result.[11]

Theodore was not the only magician to entrance AWU officials in
the grim depression years. In 1930 Harold Bell Lasseter walked into
Macdonell House and captivated that hard man of the AWU, Central
Branch president Jack Bailey, with a tale of gold. He had found a rich reef
of gold in Central Australia, Lasseter breathlessly told Bailey, but owing
to a surveying miscalculation he could not locate the exact site. He
needed funds for an expedition to find the lost reef. Bailey agreed to
provide AWU funds to finance the expedition and establish the Central
Australian Exploration Company, of which Bailey was the honorary
chairman. According to Ion Idriess's 1931 book *Lasseter's Last Ride*,
'prominent people became interested, and £5,000 was raised within a
few hours to float a company'. Idriess added that 'the directors ... would
receive no remuneration for services rendered'. It was said the company
was more interested in solving 'Australia's financial crisis'. Lasseter's
party set out from Alice Springs later that year to find the reef, but
dissension among the searchers – largely fostered by a suspicion that
Lasseter had no idea where he was going, and possibly had never been in
Central Australia before in his life – led Lasseter to strike out on his own,
determined to find his gold. He found a lonely death instead.[12]

Bailey himself was about to be cast into the wilderness. Politically,
'Ballot Box' Bailey was a liability in the world of NSW Labor. The Executive Council also believed that the Central Branch was mismanaged,
something perhaps indicated by lavishing funds on wild prospect-
ing schemes. In early 1933 the Executive Council, at the behest of

Queensland Branch secretary Clarrie Fallon, decided to close the Central and railway construction branches and establish a combined NSW Branch, with former Victoria-Riverina Branch secretary Jack McNeill brought in as NSW Branch secretary (McNeill had lost the federal seat of Wannon at the 1931 elections). Bailey had apparently been smitten with the idea of joining Lasseter's expedition – Fallon no doubt wished that he had gone – and between 1933 and 1938 Bailey joined the many hopefuls beguiled by Ion Idriess's book and took off for the bush, lured by the chance of finding Lasseter's legendary gold. In 1938 he almost made a comeback as NSW Branch president, but the Executive Council, determined to keep the irrepressible Bailey at bay, declared the election void. Bailey died in Sydney in 1947.[13]

There was also trouble in the *Worker* office in the early 1930s. Both Adelaide Branch secretary Frank Lundie and Henry Boote cultivated an enduring hostility to Mary Gilmore over her reluctant support for the union's anti-conscription stance in 1916–17. Boote may have also seen her as a potential rival as *Worker* editor. During the 1920s her 'Women's Page' frequently became a smaller column, with Boote pleading poor paper supplies. In 1928, with the arrival of Tim Donovan as *Worker* manager, Gilmore's enemies began to speak out against her. The AWU Convention considered a resolution from some Victorian members urging the union to guarantee Gilmore a full page, 'and thus bring into the lives of women and children more sunshine'. Lundie responded with a strident attack on Gilmore, describing her as 'an out and out conscriptionist'. Gilmore angrily demanded an apology and threatened resignation. While no apology was forthcoming, her full page was restored in early 1929. Within a year, however, she was removed as a full-time member of the *Worker* staff, and merely described as a 'contributor'. Faced with this continuing hostility, Gilmore resigned on 6 February 1931. The subsequent edition of the *Worker* brusquely advised readers that Mary Gilmore was 'no longer connected with the "Worker"'. She later claimed that this curt dismissal made her feel like 'an embezzler'. It was certainly an ungracious farewell for a woman who had made a pioneering contribution to the *Worker*, and the 'sunshine' – and at times cold truth – which Mary Gilmore had provided for many thousands of *Worker* readers since 1908.[14]

## Challenge In The Pastoral Industry

Of all the industries under the umbrella of the AWU, the wage-reduction decisions of 1930–31 struck particularly hard at pastoral workers. Following an application by graziers in July 1930, Justice Dethridge cut rates and wages in the Federal Pastoral Industry Award. Shearers and crutchers suffered reductions of 20 per cent, cooks 10 per cent and wool-pressers 15 per cent. For example, shearers' rates fell from 41s per 100 to 32s 6d per 100. The 10 per cent basic-wage decision cut the weekly wage of shed-hands, wool-scour workers, station-hands, cooks and pressers. A further decision of the court in May 1931 saw station-hands' wages reduced by a total of 20 per cent.[15]

Working life in the pastoral industry in the 1930s was harsh, un-rewarding and often lonely. Ernest Mathews had been a station-hand in South Australia since 1906. During the 1930s he was employed at Kalabity Station in the north of the State and his duties involved looking after six paddocks – a total area of 114 square miles populated by 2900 sheep and little else. He earned £2 5s 6d a week with keep. He lived in a hut with basic amenities, about 26 miles from the station, although he could keep in touch by telephone. Stores were brought up by truck or buggy and hygiene took a back seat in the process. Up to three items of food were carried in one bag; for example, tea placed in the bottom gathered by a string tie, then currants with the bag gathered again by string, then some other item. Often the carrier would pick up sheep skins at various camps and these would be slung in the back on top of the ration bags. It was not unusual for the flour to have been partly eaten by mice before it arrived at Mathews' hut. Rations did not include butter or fresh vegetables and station-hands had to make alternative arrangements with local providers for these items – if they could. Mathews was required to work fifty-eight hours a week and to do any emergency work on Sundays should the occasion arise. During shearing he had to work all day Sunday mustering, sometimes mustering 2500 sheep on his own. He was given fourteen days' holiday a year but worked on public holidays. He generally worked until three in the afternoon on Saturdays, often later. In the winter, Saturday afternoon was reserved for bread-making, leaving Sunday free for washing and cleaning the hut. As the depression added further burdens to the many pastoral workers who would be familiar with the experiences of Ernest Mathews, it was little wonder that some would be sympathetic to complaints that the AWU was not doing enough for them, and be drawn to calls for militant action.[16]

Following the 1930 Dethridge award the AWU set up a special com-mittee to examine the decision and consider the options available to the union. Frank Lundie believed the AWU was fighting an uphill battle, with a system stacked against them. 'Either the Judge is utterly unfitted for the duties imposed on him in the Arbitration Court or he is biased against the workers. I think it is the latter.' The special committee deliberated for over a week, attempting to develop an official response to strike camps which had been established at Moree, Collarenabri, Walgett and Brewarrina, New South Wales districts in which about 1000 shearers were on strike. Central Branch secretary George Buckland appealed to members to 'meet the position with a little patience and be guided by the Union in any action that it may advise'. Finally, the *Worker* of 30 July 1930 published a manifesto by the AWU Executive Council, which decided to have a bet each way: 'That whilst asserting the right of our individual members to bargain for rates above the minimum rates prescribed by the Dethridge Award any member who accepts employment in terms of the Award is not offending against any principle of the Union'.[17]

This ambiguous response sent out a confused message to pastoralists and AWU members alike, although it was not untypical of trade union responses generally to the pressures generated by the collapse of industry and the barrage of wage cuts which hit all workers in 1930–31. On one hand, organisers in New South Wales were reporting a general resumption of work after the manifesto, while the *Pastoral Review* of August 1930 claimed that 'at least some of the AWU officials actively encouraged the men to refuse to work at the new rates'. Other members took matters into their own hands. The *Worker* warned of attempts to form another bogus union by 'well-known disruptionists' who were 'striving to create disunion and dissention'. This 'bogus union' represented an ambitious challenge to the AWU. The Pastoral Workers Industrial Union, which had evolved from the activities of the same AWU dissidents who supported the Bushworkers Propaganda Group in the 1920s, characterised itself as a 'fighting organisation' aiming to 'combat the activities of the Graziers and Arbitration Court, the Capitalist Class, and their lackeys, the reactionary AWU officials'. The PWIU's industrial militancy went hand in hand with a close ideological affiliation with the Communist Party of Australia, and a style particularly intolerant of the Labor Party and its supporters, whom both the PWIU and the CPA derided as 'social fascists' (following political direction from the Soviet Union, communist parties around the world in the early 1930s attacked Western labour parties and trade unions as 'class collaborators' with the capitalist system). The PWIU also attracted the support of Laborites sympathetic to its criticisms of the AWU, and to the embarrassment of the union, the PWIU's inaugural president in 1930 was ALP Senator Arthur Rae, the former AWU organiser and general secretary (1897–98) who had been denied AWU membership in 1920 after he had refused to pledge his undivided loyalty to the prevailing union leadership.[18]

Concern – if not panic – over the participation in the PWIU of such a prominent former official as Rae may have prompted the AWU's approach to the NSW Graziers Association to undermine the influence of the PWIU and the dissident strikers. The Graziers Association and the AWU agreed on an exchange of information, with the graziers indicating which sheds had returned to work at the new rate, while the AWU advised the graziers of any sheds requiring additional labour. AWU officials also publicly said that the old award could be restored if the strike was called off, a highly optimistic assessment which encouraged many shearers to return to work. Simultaneously the graziers' own aggressive efforts, including prosecutions of strikers under the enduring Masters and Servants Act, also discouraged prolonged militancy.[19]

The PWIU fared no better in Queensland, where it was also active (the PWIU appears to have been unable to organise effectively in the other States, although its southern New South Wales activists would have worked sheds in Victoria and South Australia). In November 1930 the Queensland Industrial Court announced a reduction of 10 per cent in the State pastoral award. In terms of shearing this meant a cut from 40s per 100 to 30s per 100. Consistent with their southern colleagues, the Queensland Branch of the AWU responded to calls for action from Western District sheds by cautioning against strikes and appealing for faith in the arbitration system. But the faith of the branch officials was stronger than that of the rank and file, and by December 1930 a number of sheds in Longreach, Barcaldine and Emerald were on strike. The PWIU published a Queensland edition of its regular newsletter, the *Rank and File Bulletin*, attacking the government, graziers and AWU official-dom as well as identifying and exposing shearers engaged in strike-breaking. In response, the Queensland AWU refused to authorise the strike and branded the PWIU a communist front organisation, bent on destroying the AWU and the Queensland labour movement.[20]

Many Queensland shearers were won over by the PWIU's militant stand against both the pastoralists and the AWU hierarchy. The com-munist paper *Workers' Weekly* reported the signing by the PWIU of a majority of shearers in Toowoomba, Hughenden, Charleville, Longreach and Goondiwindi (reports in part substantiated by police information provided to the Queensland Government). During the strike Alf Kain was a shearer at Emerald, and recalls that PWIU activists 'Trucker' Brown and Bert Buckley signed up almost 400 local shearers, enabling the PWIU to claim an active presence in the area for some years.[21]

Despite these initial successes, the PWIU's position was undermined by the Queensland Government, concerned at the strike's effect on the depressed Queensland economy. The government ensured that strike-breakers were railed into western Queensland from other parts of the State and from New South Wales under heavy police escort. In Emerald, a pitched battle between police and striking pastoral workers led to a number of arrests, with some shearers gaoled. The *Pastoral Review* of 16 February 1931 reported that an engine-driver had been stoned by a crowd at Barcaldine and that authorities at Emerald had discovered that spikes had been removed from the railway line. In the meantime, many

sheds were able to complete shearing, with strike-breakers working
under police guard. In a final attempt to regain the initiative, the PWIU
pinned its faith on the transport unions declaring the wool 'black'. The
Australian Railways Union had willingly given financial and moral
support to the striking shearers but baulked at direct involvement unless
the other railway unions could be relied on to assist. Any hope of this was
shattered when the leadership of the Australian Federated Union of
Locomotive Engineers ordered its members not to become involved in
the dispute. The failure to gain the direct involvement of the rail unions
resulted in the strike being called off in April 1931.[22]

By the end of 1932, pastoral workers in the southern States were
granted small increases in rates with the basic shearing award standing at
£1 7s 3d per 100 (unfound), £2 14s 6d a week (without keep) for station-
hands, and shed-hands receiving £4 16s a week (without keep). Slight
increases were again awarded in 1936 with shearing rates rising to
£1 12s 6d per 100 and shed-hands' wages reaching £5 6s 6d. The *Worker*
lamented the court's failure to recognise the injustice of the decision but
warned against impetuous strike action – Boote sardonically observed
that the PWIU had 'decided parasitically' to accept the court's decision.
Nevertheless the *Worker* of 29 July 1936 carried a warning that PWIU
circulars were appearing in sheds urging members to support a strike
levy. This call apparently failed to excite much response. A month later
AWU president Barnes was citing the PWIU itself as a source that its
membership now totalled a mere 483. There was no strike, and the AWU
persevered with applications for increased rates through the Federal
Arbitration Court. By 1938 the AWU was granted an award which
increased shearers' rates to £1 15s per 100 and shed-hands' wages to £6 a
week. Station-hands were awarded £3 7s a week.[23]

Ultimately, the PWIU failed to make sufficient inroads into the AWU's
power base to seriously threaten its status among pastoral workers. In
January 1932 Queensland Branch organiser Jim Lough confidently
announced: 'I can now say, after four months of touring this district and
visiting all the sheds possible, that the bogus outfit is now dead and will rise
no more under that title'. PWIU membership never exceeded 2000. The
PWIU was also torn between its industrial activities on one hand and its
strict adherence to CPA direction. The Communist Party promoted the
PWIU and when it finally disbanded in 1936, it did so on party orders: the
CPA, following a new Soviet edict, embraced a 'popular front' strategy of
collaborating with social democratic parties and laborist trade unions – the
types only recently vilified as 'social fascists'. The PWIU had apparently
outlived its political usefulness, although a core of dissident AWU
members remained willing to challenge the union leadership. They could
claim a couple of scalps. Powerful Queensland Branch secretary Clarrie

Fallon was not impressed with the way New South Wales officials Jack Bailey and George Buckland had dealt with the PWIU challenge. And Fallon was wasting little time in placing his stamp in the national union. As Clyde Cameron observes, 'Clarrie Fallon had put his finger on the union's [NSW] trouble when he declared that the formation of the PWIU was the direct result of grass roots dissatisfaction with the leadership of Buckland and Bailey. Their poor leadership played in to the hands of the militants and therefore into the hands of the communists'. Fallon's unhappiness led to the reorganisation of the NSW branch in 1933.[24]

The AWU's problems with Lang and the PWIU were largely confined to New South Wales, a key State in the politics of the labour movement, but not necessarily crucial to the AWU's national influence. ALP historian Ross McMullin notes that during the 1930s 'that giant union dominated the party in Queensland, South Australia and Western Australia, and also in the federal sphere. At least half the federal parliamentary Labor Party during the Scullin Government was at some stage connected to the AWU'. In Western Australia, the AWU was also close to the Willcock Government and dominated the WA ALP's General Council. *The Westralian Worker*, the paper owned by the local AWU, was also the chief labour voice in the State. Aside from the important pastoral industry and public works coverage, the AWU had a strong block of 6000 members in the eastern mining fields centred around Kalgoorlie. Gold prices rose during the mid-1930s and after several strikes stretching over three years Western Australian goldminers defied the lingering effects of economic depression and won a shorter hours campaign in 1938 – a 44-hour week for surface mining and a 40-hour week for underground. In South Australia, Frank Lundie, 'the Industrial King of Adelaide', dominated the local labour movement until his death in 1933. In his thirty-three years as Adelaide Branch secretary Lundie had built the AWU into the State's largest union, with a series of amalgamations extending the AWU's coverage into fruit-picking, quarry works and construction. He developed a strong AWU influence in the State ALP branch, a tradition maintained by his successors.[25]

The Victoria-Riverina Branch struggled throughout the 1930s. Unemployment among its membership was high; in 1930 membership was around 14 400, but had fallen to 4845 by the middle of 1932. Those fortunate enough to be employed were subjected to work rationing and wage reductions. The bulk of State Government work was being financed by unemployment relief money and some men were getting only three days' work a week. By mid-decade the branch had made some progress in securing improvements in awards and wage increases, for construction and sewer workers, as well as for some members in the mining industry. By 1936, Branch secretary W. B. Dale was able to announce the success of the branch's application to vary the mining industry award to encompass several companies not previously embraced by the award and to predict a 'much better' outlook for the industry in the coming year. Dale retired in 1938 and in the following year incoming branch secretary Dave Gunn reported a slow improvement in wage levels and the securing of improvements in leave and holiday entitlements. By 1940 membership had recovered to reach 7528, only half the total of a decade before.[26]

In Tasmania, a depression-induced collapse in membership was compounded by continued decline in the mining industry, a severe problem for the branch throughout the previous decade. Low metal prices (except for gold, always popular with investors in times of economic distress; but gold was not a significant Tasmanian metal) and the closure of some mines, and an acute downturn in the public works sector, were the main contributors to unemployment and loss of members. The election of the Ogilvie Labor Government in 1934 provided the kind of government-directed economic stimulus from which the AWU's members might benefit. The Ogilvie Government expanded hydro-electric projects and the paper-making industry, and unemployment relief works such as road construction were implemented – all industries covered by the AWU. By 1938, branch secretary W. H. Nicol was able to report that AWU activities in Tasmania 'have been extended throughout the State, with the result that new fields have been explored and Agreements or State wages Boards have been brought into operation to cover workers in industry not hitherto provided for'. Increased wages and a 44-hour week had been obtained for members in the Carbide Works, the Country Shire Councils, quarrymen and the Railton Cement Works. By the following year membership had risen to a record 5197, compared to 2750 three years earlier.[27]

### The Reign of 'the Red Terror': the Queensland Branch, 1930–39

The key to the AWU's national political influence was based in its strong grip on the Queensland labour movement. Between 1920 and 1950, four out of six Queensland Labor premiers came from AWU ranks: Theodore, McCormack, Cooper and Forgan Smith. In the first Forgan Smith Government in 1932, of the ten-man ministry nine had a strong AWU background. In effect Premier William Forgan Smith, and State ALP president and AWU State secretary Clarence George ('Clarrie') Fallon governed Queensland together, and in many ways they did so well, with the kind of expansionary policies which E. G. Theodore had wanted to implement in Canberra. In 1938 Forgan Smith maintained that Queensland had 'the highest wage system, the best conditions of labour and the lowest unemployment' in Australia. These were conditions fostered within a strongly rural State economy which Forgan Smith nurtured, much to the delight of the rural-based AWU. In 1932 Forgan Smith declared, 'primary production is the natural occupation of mankind'. It was very much a guided agrarian democracy. Both Forgan Smith and Fallon believed in ruthless command and unquestioning loyalty.[28]

Clarrie Fallon had been blooded industrially and politically in the canefields of central Queensland. He was a tough and astute operator who began his AWU career as a Central District organiser in 1921, based at Bundaberg. In 1927 he moved to the Northern District, and was elected district secretary in 1929, and soon after became branch president. By 1932 Fallon was branch secretary, ruling AWU meetings more by a studied and often menacing silence than by the blustering display of temper often preferred by his thrusting lieutenants, Joe Bukowski and Tom Dougherty. In other respects he did not fit the image of the burly AWU organiser. Tall, thin, red-headed and intense, he gave an impression of concentrated intelligence and sullen hostility. His colleagues dubbed him 'the red terror'. Terrorism could take many forms. Tom Dougherty recalled that a Fallon favourite would be to move unexpected and patently ridiculous resolutions at branch executive or delegates meetings and closely observe those assembled to see whether or not they would all support the motion. If they did he would be satisfied and later move the resolutions' recission. In Fallon's view, the true test of loyalty was not to have someone support you when they believed you were right, but to have someone support you when they believed you were wrong.[29]

Command was built upon unremitting control of the machine. During the depression the AWU was able to consolidate its influence and position within the ALP even as the ALP's membership levels experienced a steep decline during the period of economic crisis. Between 1925 and 1932, ALP membership declined by over two-thirds (9720 to 3144) and the number of branches was reduced from 294 to 197. The reduction in membership forced the party to be even more dependent on the AWU's organisational support. The regional organisation of the AWU into South-east, Western, Central and Northern districts served both an industrial and political purpose. AWU organisers would often recruit members to the party, and during election time AWU organisers would undertake official ALP duties, acting as canvassers and booth workers. The AWU's fleet of vehicles was made available to campaigning ALP candidates, and Forgan Smith and his ministers recognised this crucial aid with diligent appearances at the Queensland AWU's delegates meetings, the annual assembly of the branch officials.[30]

The AWU's power in political circles was also enhanced by the decline of the number of unions affiliated with the ALP. Affiliates declined from seventy-one in 1926 to fifty-nine by 1935, thus increasing the difficulty for anti-AWU forces of forming a coalition. Their position was further exacerbated by the fact that the AWU's old enemy and the obvious leader of any anti-AWU opposition, the Australian Railways Union, was outside the ALP since its disaffiliation from the party in 1926, after Premier Bill McCormack, with the support of the AWU, compelled ALP members to sign a pledge that they were not members of the Communist Party. Many remaining affiliates experienced a substantial loss of membership during the depression, which also reduced their representation at conventions and on the Queensland Central Executive. Although AWU membership declined by 54 per cent between 1927 and 1932 (in comparison with an overall Queensland union membership decline of 30 per cent), the AWU increased its membership by 136 per cent between 1932 and 1935 compared to an overall union increase of 42 per cent, giving the AWU an impressive numerical superiority. This was important in terms of the union power at Labor-in-Politics Conventions, the annual conference of Queensland Labor, at which the number of delegates from each union was determined by union membership levels.[31]

By 1935, Queensland Branch membership had recovered almost all the depression-induced losses, rising from 22 418 in 1932 to 53 547. For this renewal Fallon gave thanks to Forgan Smith, and his government's refinements to the previous conservative administration's unemployment relief scheme. The new Labor Government opted to cover relief workers under the appropriate industrial award. The AWU was the chief beneficiary of this change because the union covered the unskilled occupations primarily required for the public works jobs on offer.[32]

The Queensland AWU also dominated the policy and direction of the national union. With over 53 000 members the Queensland Branch could boast thirteen delegates to the 1936 Annual AWU Convention; New South Wales membership was a paltry 6600, entitling the branch to only two delegates. Western Australia took second place to Queensland with three delegates. Queensland's thirteen delegates easily outnumbered the combined total of nine from all other branches. Ten years later, in 1946, the Queensland Branch was able to claim twelve delegates' positions compared to a combined total of fourteen from the other branches.[33]

The Queensland Branch rules ensured that Fallon could always send reliable delegates to the AWU Convention and to fill the various positions within the branch. Rule 64 provided that candidates had to provide proof of at least two years' continuous membership and to satisfy the branch executive that they were fit to hold the position and were of 'good behaviour generally' before a nomination would be accepted. As the dissident Membership Rights Committee stated exasperatedly in a 1936 pamphlet, *Ballot Dodging in Queensland, the Case for a Democratic Ballot in the AWU*: 'There are none so hard to satisfy as those who do not want to be satisfied'.[34]

The Membership Rights Committee had been formed by AWU members at Innisfail to redress the disqualification of five financial members who nominated for positions in the 1936 ballot for the Queensland Branch executive. At the centre of the dispute was the omission of F. C. Broad from the list of endorsed candidates for the position of branch president, despite the fact that the returning officer declared the nomination in order. Broad's supporters claimed that he was never given the opportunity to prove his fitness to the branch executive, nor was he told that qualifications were necessary for his nomination to be endorsed. Broad was evidently a popular local figure, having topped the poll as a Labor councillor in recent Johnstone Shire Council elections and, it seems, would have been formidable opposition for the incumbent president, J. C. Lamont. As well as Broad's omission, a number of candidates for district secretary and organisers' positions were also denied nomination. Peter Atkinson was rejected as a candidate for organiser and Far Northern District representative. Atkinson, a cane-cutter and Mossman local commiteeman, had collected levies for strikers at South Johnstone in 1927. The fact that of the thirty-one organisers employed in the Queensland Branch only fifteen were elected led some AWU members to the conclusion that the branch was appointing organisers, where it was permissible within the rules, as a means of evading elections. The Innisfail Membership Rights Committee believed that Far Northern District organiser Joe Bukowski 'has gone south for his reward'. Bukowski had been appointed as an organiser in the Northern District, the cradle of many future Queensland Branch secretaries, as a reward for his support of the ruling clique, having taken 'a leading part in the attempts to break the ranks of the South Johnstone cane-cutters to stampede them back to the disease-stricken fields, when they were on strike'. Bukowski, their pamphlet alleged, threatened his critics in a bombastic manner and attempted to disrupt meetings by starting fights and brawls among AWU members if it appeared that the vote would fall contrary to the official line.[35]

Broad eventually got his case to court in December 1936. Mr Justice R. J. Douglas held that the branch executive had not acted in a bona fide way in deciding that Broad was not a fit and proper person or lacked the ability and fitness for the position of branch president. Fresh elections were called. Broad polled only 3496 votes against 6098 for Lamont, who also outpolled Broad in each district except the Northern.[36]

There was a move at the 1938 Queensland Branch annual delegates meeting for ballot boxes to be supplied at every job, or at least for adequate facilities to be provided to allow members to record their vote. The practice was to provide large envelopes, which Fallon said 'was the best means of achieving what they desired'. To provide ballot boxes at every centre would have been 'utterly impracticable'. A suggestion that ballot papers be issued with a copy of the *Worker*, to facilitate voting opportunities for isolated bushworkers, was also dismissed by Northern District organiser Tom Dougherty: 'each worker gets a ballot paper and envelope'. The meeting decided that present arrangements were adequate.[37]

### The Queensland Sugar Industry

The AWU's Northern District, centred around Mackay and Townsville, was an active breeding ground of both senior AWU officials and dissidents. Perhaps it was the thrill of contest: Fallon, Dougherty, Bukowski and Edgar Williams all passed through the area. During the 1930s life on the north Queensland canefields was exhausting, dangerous and, given depression-inspired wage cuts, underpaid. Canecutters often worked on a contract basis, and 'were not an easily tapped political or industrial source. Scattered in barracks, along roads, and up bush tracks and headlands, they were difficult to contact or organize. *En masse* they appeared once a year on sign-on day ... Time meant money to a man paid on contract, not hourly rates'. Like construction workers or any number of bushworkers' jobs, canecutters were difficult to organise and prey to exploitation. These were conditions which favoured both industrial militancy and communist agitation.[38]

The AWU also complicated its relationship with canecutters by its attitude towards the large numbers of Italian immigrant workers in the local industry. Italians had first come to the northern canefields in numbers at the end of the nineteenth century as a result of a government promise to rid the industry of Kanaka labour. By 1930 almost 24 000 Italians had settled in Queensland, most of them in the north. The AWU was not pleased, as the Queensland *Worker* indicated in 1925. 'The Federal Government has betrayed Australian workers by encouraging Mediterranean scum to overrun the country ... [It was] responsible for this dago invasion ... and the influx of this breed.' Commonwealth government legislation and a series of Queensland inquiries and legislative strictures were implemented to curtail Italian immigration. Non-English speakers who wished to become cane farmers were required to take a dictation test. The AWU attempted to protect its British-Australian members by refusing 'cutting' tickets to Italians and engaging in negotiations to establish a 75 per cent Australian to 25 per cent immigrant quota system for both farmers and millers. In June 1930 a 'preference' agreement was signed by the AWU, the Australian Sugar Producers Association and the Queensland Cane Growers Council. The

A predominantly Italian cane-cutting gang, Macknade Mill, Queensland
c. 1930. After lobbying to remove Melanesian (Kanaka) labour from the
Queensland sugar industry in the early twentieth century, further AWU
attempts to diminish competition for Anglo-Celtic members were defeated by
the introduction of Italian labour in the 1920s and 1930s, and the post-Second
World War mechanisation of cane harvesting. *Noel Butlin Archives, Australian
National University.*

AWU consistently argued that its objections to the Italians were economic
and not xenophobic (a distinction perhaps not evident to the Italians,
particularly if they were greeted by AWU officials with the same elegance
as the 1925 *Worker* comment). For example, clause 11 of the agreement
provided that field hands (excluding cutters) who could not read the
sugar award should be paid in cash in the presence of a government
official. The AWU feared that by breaching awards, accepting deferred
pay or working solely for board and keep, the Italians would lower the
living standards of Australian workers.[39]

   The AWU's control of the canefields membership was seriously challenged by a series of strikes in 1935, incited by a rank-and-file campaign
to eradicate Weil's disease, an affliction which hit over forty canecutters
in the 1934 cutting season. The disease was spread by rats in the
unseasonally wet conditions prevailing in the fields, and could result in
fever, muscular pains and intense headaches. Several patients suffered

internal haemorrhages and vomiting, and two died. Medical experts argued that the cane should be burnt before harvesting to sterilise it. But this also had the effect of lowering the sugar content, and the growers objected.[40]

There followed a series of unauthorised strikes in the Northern District canefields, with communist activists using the issue to heighten discontent with the AWU. The union was, however, active in attempting to obtain court orders to compel growers to burn the cane before harvesting, although sometimes the members took matters into their own hands. As sporadic strike action persisted at various canefields, on 22 August 1935 the Townsville Chamber of Commerce asked Premier Forgan Smith to intervene, complaining of the AWU's inability to control events. Fallon said that the AWU had not sanctioned strikes. In September the Queensland Government made it an offence to induce or incite any person to take part in an illegal strike and imposed a fine of £100. Fallon told Innisfail cutters that by persisting with the strike they could have their contracts cancelled and be fined for contempt of court. Faced with this pressure, the strikes ceased in early October.[41]

In January 1936, Northern District secretary Beecher Hay told the Queensland Branch delegates meeting that 'the dispute was not a strike in the ordinary sense, in that it was not an attempt to improve conditions of employment, but it was very definitely an attempt to give effect to the instructions issued to the "Key Men" of the Mischievous Minority from the Communist Hall, Sydney, with the object of undermining and, if possible, destroying the influence of the AWU'. His Far Northern District counterpart Bushnell thought it significant that 'once the fear and intimidation exercised by this crowd [the Communists] was removed the men concerned took full advantage of the first opportunity and returned to work', and 'in retrospect they know that they were misled, and it is safe to predict that it will be many years before the union-smashers will be able to put the like over again'. Yet part of the final resolution carried by the strikers at Tully on 7 October read: 'We repudiate the slanders of the AWU officials that our leaders are disruptors who led us into defeat. We affirm our unbroken confidence in the strike committee. We the sugar workers of the Tully area, declare the AWU officials to be strike breakers, organisers of scabs, and agents of the bosses'. Some good came of the dispute: on 21 July 1936 the AWU won a case in the Queensland Industrial Court compelling owners to burn cane before harvesting.[42]

### 'A Union No Man Could Put Down': the AWU's Fiftieth Anniversary

Fallon had consolidated his grip on the AWU by the late 1930s. General secretary Edward Grayndler was increasingly infirm and, at 69 years of

age in 1936, heading reluctantly towards retirement, spurred by Fallon's
impatient ambitions. Although Grayndler doggedly held on until early
1941, the union seemed increasingly to be governed by Fallon's whims
and obsessions. Each year at the annual delegates meeting at Dunstan
House in Brisbane Fallon would redefine the role of the union and the
appropriate role of the assembled organisers and district secretaries, who
largely constituted the meetings' delegates. He lectured young organisers on attending to correspondence and reliability; they must always
uphold the prestige of the union. In turn, they honoured their elders. A
precocious organiser, Bill Edmonds, who had recently entertained a high
opinion of himself as a unionist, now understood he had a lot to learn.
'After his experience of Delegates Meeting he had developed a new
outlook and he was determined to go back to his work a better unionist
and a better organiser.' Fallon was devastated by the loss of his son Jack
in an RAAF flying accident in 1937. He channelled his grief into a
resolution adopted by the 1938 delegates meeting for a wide-ranging
royal commission to investigate the administration of the RAAF. Four
years after his loss, Fallon still demanded the government establish a
royal commission. Despite this tragedy, the delegates did what they could
to shelter and mollify their leader. When Fallon was attacked by often
unspecified outsiders – in the press, by other unions or communists – the
delegates would rise to defend him. At the 1941 delegates meeting, held
at the height of wartime anti-Italian feeling, Fallon gave a spirited
defence of his conduct towards Italians in the northern canefields in the
1930s, after an attack in an unnamed newspaper against him. There were
accusations that Fallon had pandered to the Italian section of the community. Fallon reeled off example after example of his tireless pursuit of
cane farmers who were breaching award conditions.

> I attempted to grapple with this problem, and because I did so I became a
> target for attack from people who were exploiting the Italians. I say that I
> played a stronger part in resisting what came known as the foreign influx than
> any other man in the Commonwealth.
> Delegates: That is true.
> The Branch Secretary: I earned the detestation of Italian people, not
> because I was concerned about their nationality – or where they came from,
> but because at that time they represented a definite menace to the industrial
> conditions and wage standards of wage-earners.

Northern District secretary Tom Dougherty led an outpouring of praise
for Fallon, and he was followed by fifteen of the twenty-four assembled
delegates. The meeting expressed its confidence in Fallon's 'sincerity,
honesty and integrity' and condemned the attacks against him. Fallon, in
response, cast his mind back to long line of AWU officials who had been

castigated for their principled stands in the past. He even forgave Spence; 'even if he did fail in the evening of his life', Spence, Fallon said, had made an immense contribution to the labor movement. He exhorted delegates to read *Australia's Awakening*, which recorded Spence's trials as an AWU pioneer. Fallon could sympathise with Spence. 'Labor will always be subject to attack and falsehood. Someone had to carry the baby, even if it breaks his heart. The man who is carrying on to-day is just incidental to the Movement. If his family is shamed by those who attack him, that is incidental to the movement.' A year later, Fallon was presented with a gold cigarette case at the 29th delegates meeting, in honour of ten years' service as branch secretary. In response, the man who had declared that he did not believe in 'isms' and foreign ideologies revealed how he was so vitally nourished by his own ingrained value system, handed down the generations of AWU leaders. Thanking the delegates for their valuable gift, Fallon said 'he sometimes thought that the nicest word in the English language was the word "mateship". It seemed to crystallise all the manly and fine things to be found in real men when they were associated'. The presentation was made on behalf of the delegates by Dougherty and Central Districts secretary Joe Bukowski, the new generation venerating – and awaiting the retirement of – the old.[43]

The AWU's fiftieth anniversary in 1936 was commemorated in an almost ecclesiastical manner, with officials leading a number of pilgrimages to the resting places of former comrades. Convention delegates stood before the grave of AWU pioneer Donald Macdonell on 2 February 1936. On arrival at the grave at Stuart Mill in Victoria, 'the St. Arnaud band played a number of appropriate airs, during which the assemblage stood in reverent silence'. President John Barnes concluded his address with a eulogy written for Macdonell by Roderick Quinn, the last verse of which ran:

> He has mounted his horse and smiled farewell,
>     And rides where the shadows fall;
> Honor him, men of the Western sheds,
>     Honor him – honor him, all.

Grayndler described Macdonell as 'the most charming gentleman I ever met. To me he was one of God's chosen men'. Others were less deserving, or outcast. Convention simply decided to put a railing around Temple's grave. A pilgrimage was made to the Ballarat memorial honouring those killed during the storming of the Eureka Stockade in 1854, an event William Guthrie Spence claimed to have witnessed as a young boy. Homage to Spence was conspicuous by its absence. In AWU mythology, he had ceased to exist, despite Fallon's absolution. Within a few years many of the AWU elders who stood in reverence by the graves would themselves be gone. Barnes died in 1938 and the 1944 AWU Annual Convention solemnly announced the passing of Jack McNeill, who had served as secretary of both the Victoria-Riverina and NSW branches. General secretary Grayndler, and vice president and Victoria-Riverina Branch secretary Dave Gunn also died in 1943.[44]

In the manner of the poet laureate, Henry Boote provided some dutiful doggerel for the anniversary, published in a special golden jubilee edition of the *Worker*. It captures the confident mood of the leadership as they prepared for the tasks which lay ahead, and gloried in the AWU's stoicism, bred by fifty years of lonely struggle.

> Unequalled has been its fraternal career
> From the hour of its birth to this Jubilee Year,
> On the job, in the shed, in the mine and the field,
> New rights it has won and old wrongs it has healed.
> And so let us all in its victory rejoice,
> And tell the whole world with one harmonised voice,
> That great was the day when in Ballarat Town
> They started a Union no man could put down,
> A Union that battles, and always wins through;
> Up, up with its standard! – the A.W.U.[45]

CHAPTER 9

# A Wonderful Machine

*War, 1940–49*

## The AWU and the ALP, 1940–49

The outbreak of the Second World War brought fundamental change to the way work was organised in Australia, particularly after the entry of Japan into the war in December 1941, posing an imminent threat to Australia. Central to the Curtin Labor Government's domestic policy response to this crisis was a series of new regulations under the National Security Act, which greatly increased the Commonwealth's control of the workforce. All industries were declared essential or non-essential for the war effort, and employment was regulated accordingly. This disrupted the AWU's control of its membership in several industries, already hard hit by military mobilisation. By the early 1940s, 39 per cent of primary industry workers, 20 per cent of miners and 48 per cent of the building and construction sector workforce were in the armed forces. Over 50 000 workers also served in the Civil Construction Corps, which carried out major works for war purposes within Australia. These men were under the control of the director-general of the Allied Works Council, who had extraordinary powers to regulate their working conditions under the National Security Act. The director-general was former treasurer E. G. Theodore, and as most CCC workers were AWU members, Theodore had the opportunity to renew his rocky relationship with the union. The AWU's industrial problems also affected the union's relationship with the ALP; it was tested further by the Curtin Government's decision in 1943 to introduce military conscription for operations in the South-West Pacific theatre and the employment of prisoners of war in AWU industries.[1]

The AWU entered the war firmly supporting the federal Labor Party. As federal ALP president, Fallon had been a key player in federal intervention into the NSW ALP, which cleared out the Communist Party members who had sought to take advantage of the vacuum created in the party by the slow but sure collapse of Lang's control of the branch. Fallon presided at two Unity Conferences convened to restructure the NSW ALP. The first was held in August 1939. Promises of unity were soon undermined at the following March 1940 NSW ALP Annual Conference, at which a small group of communists and ALP sympathisers exercised enough influence to have conference pass the notorious 'Hands Off Russia' resolution. The resolution reflected prevailing CPA defeatism: that the war was of no interest to the Australian working class, and that Labor should resist any hostile action against 'any country with which we are not at war including Soviet Russia'. The Soviet Union had just signed a cynical non-aggression pact with Nazi Germany, and in September 1939 the two countries divided Poland between them, hardly the most elegant expression of the yearning by the Comintern for peace. The outrage which followed the adoption of the 'Hands Off Russia' resolution prompted another federal ALP thrust into New South Wales. Fallon presided at another Unity Conference in August 1940 which reaffirmed support for federal Labor and agreed to the restructuring of the NSW ALP executive.[2]

Communists were not the only supporters of the 'Hands Off Russia' resolution; *Worker* editor Henry Boote also supported it. Since the mid-1930s he had become quite outspoken in his endorsement of some causes unpopular with the AWU leadership. In the late 1930s he echoed the CPA's 'popular front' line by supporting collective security against fascism, and he was a harsh critic of the ALP's isolationist policy (a stance which may have also been stirred by his loathing of Lang, an ardent isolationist). Boote's support for the 'Hands Off Russia' resolution brought him into conflict with the AWU hierarchy, and he threatened to resign when they suppressed his article supporting the resolution. In his private diary, Boote described the federal ALP's intervention in New South Wales over the resolution as 'a cowardly surrender to the capitalist press and politicians, in my opinion, and to the anti-red and Catholic Action reactionaries'. On 26 May 1940 the Executive Council voted to endorse ALP policy on war and defence, and offered the Menzies Government the AWU's co-operation 'to bring Australia's war and defence effort to as high a state of efficiency as is practicable at the earliest possible moment'.[3]

Although Clarrie Fallon usually displayed little tolerance for AWU dissenters, Henry Boote was another matter. Fallon had a high regard for Boote. Despite the 'Hands Off Russia' affair, Fallon told Boote in late

1940 that he was 'writing better than ever'. On several occasions he
implored the 75-year-old Boote to stay on as *Worker* editor, despite Boote's
belief that it was time to retire. Some of the subtleties of their
relationship have been preserved in a diary Boote maintained between
1940 and 1943. Although Boote had regularly seen Fallon in the Sydney
AWU office (the *Worker* office was upstairs in Macdonell House) and at
annual conventions, it was not until 1940 that he worked closely with
Fallon, who was in Sydney frequently as acting general secretary, as the
Executive Council continued its efforts to persuade the ill and ageing
Grayndler to retire (see below). Boote found that Fallon confided in
him. In December 1940 he noted in his diary: 'Am surprised to find that
Fallon seems to like talking to me ... I certainly don't push myself upon
him. He calls me down to his office'.[4]

During 1940–41 Fallon and Boote frequently discussed the problems
besetting the federal Labor Party. Labor was confronted by the dilemma
of seeking office in wartime in its own right, or joining a government of
'national unity' with the conservative United Australia Party under R. G.
Menzies' prime ministership, a course being urged by the ambitious ALP
MP and former High Court judge H. V. 'Bert' Evatt. Fallon and Boote were
also concerned that party leader John Curtin was not tough enough for the
job. According to Boote, Fallon said in 1941 that Curtin's prime
ministership could be 'a bloody calamity'.[5]

Boote and Fallon agreed that Evatt's support for a coalition with
Menzies had to be discouraged. Boote was also a confidant of Evatt's and
his diaries reveal repeated contact with Evatt, as the future Labor leader
sought Boote's advice. In late 1940 Evatt told Boote that he didn't
'favour' a coalition government, but it was 'inevitable' if Labor did not
risk office on its own. Boote noted crisply, 'I denied the inevitability'.
Boote found Evatt 'passionately desirous of office' in early 1941, an
ambition which some in the AWU and the labour movement found
unseemly. To such criticisms Boote retorted that although Evatt was 'too
swayed by personal ambition and capitalist press flattery', this stage
would pass, 'and he'll be a distinguished member of the Party and a big
Australian'. Fallon had less patience with Evatt. Both Curtin and Evatt
addressed the January 1941 AWU Convention. Fallon, according to Clyde
Cameron, ordered delegates to humiliate Evatt with a cool reception
while cheering a dispirited Curtin with rousing applause. Evatt was also
compelled to sit and endure a blistering attack from Fallon on 'unspecified persons' in the ALP advocating a coalition government with
Menzies.[6]

Although the AWU was pleased when Labor assumed office in October
1941 (the Menzies Government fell after losing the support of key
independents in Parliament), both the union and Boote broke with

the Curtin Government over defence policy. As early as April 1939, the *Worker* expressed concern about the introduction of military conscription when it criticised the Federal Government's proposal to compile a compulsory register of the workforce as 'a preliminary step to conscription'. In June 1941 the Executive Council instructed, on a motion from Fallon, all AWU officers around Australia to prepare to combat any move 'to foist conscription for overseas service upon Australia'. AWU fears were confirmed in November 1942 when Curtin proposed that conscript

## LOOK OUT, AUSSIE !   DANGER AHEAD !

This Will Donald *Worker* cartoon from 1940 reflects AWU fears that the outbreak of the Second World War would lead the conservative Menzies Government to introduce conscription. Ironically, it was the Curtin Labor Government which reintroduced conscription, for service in the South-West Pacific, in 1943. *AWU Collection.*

troops of the Australian Militia, established for the defence of Australian territory (Australia's principal army was the Australian Imperial Force, a service drawn from civilian or Militia volunteers), be permitted to fight in the South-West Pacific theatre of operations. Boote believed that such views were the product of 'the growth of a Fascist-minded military caste' in Australia. Boote wrote in his diary: 'this meant conscription for service overseas. Labor movement staggered. Labor's enemies delighted ... my position would have been impossible had AWU favoured the proposal, but transpired that both Fallon and McNeill [NSW Branch secretary] oppose the move'. He added that 'many Labor politicians and trade unionists will follow the Labor Government wherever it may lead them'. Ironically, the Australian communists who opposed the war effort before the German invasion of the Soviet Union in June 1941 had now changed their tune, as Boote wryly observed: 'The communists have come out as fierce conscriptionists. They have conscription in Russia – that settles the matter for *them*'. Curtin argued that while American conscripts were engaging in ferocious island-hopping battles, Australian conscripts should be available to secure the Japanese-held areas side-stepped by the US campaign to bring the war closer to mainland Japan. The January 1943 AWU Annual Convention passed a unanimous resolution affirming its faith in voluntary enlistment and declaring 'our implacable hostility to conscription for military service outside Australian territories'. The ALP's Federal Conference, meeting almost simultaneously with the AWU Convention, decided to support Curtin's stand, although the party had been rent by bitter controversy before the conference. The Queensland Branch of the ALP, dominated by Fallon, was the only ALP branch to oppose conscription at the Conference. The *Worker* also ran a vigorous campaign against using conscripts outside Australia during January 1943, but this faded in the face of the ALP Conference decision.[7]

Fallon's relationship with the ALP worsened over the next eighteen months. In June 1944 he resigned the federal ALP presidency over the government's management of the Civil Construction Corps. The AWU wanted compulsory unionism for CCC workers, and improvements to their working conditions, but under wartime regulations the director-general of the Allied Works Council, Ted Theodore, had extraordinary powers which could circumvent customary award rights and conditions. Strike action was virtually outlawed. Theodore's robust organisation of the CCC provoked complaints from several unions. In late 1942 Boote described the CCC as 'Theodore's conscript army', and believed that Theodore 'has more power than any member of the Government'. Several unionists in the CCC had claimed that they had been victimised by Theodore. Despite the tensions between the AWU and the government over the CCC issue, few thought it sufficient to warrant Fallon's sudden resignation, which was also attributed to his enduring anger with the Curtin Government over the conscription issue. For his part, Henry Boote suspected that Fallon's hostility was a little more complicated. Fallon seemed 'to be disconcerted with the Curtin Government on many matters'. Fallon, he wrote in the same diary entry, was 'a strange man. Sometimes remarkably clear-headed. At other times flies into senseless passions and makes himself thoroughly detested by all who come in contact with him'. Boote thought that Fallon's worst instincts were exacerbated by alcohol. In January 1943 Fallon was reported to have said that he was sorry the AWU had ever supported the Curtin Government, then later tried to deny that he had made the statement. Boote observed, '[Fallon] probably made the statement when drunk and was ready to kick himself for it when sober'.[8]

The employment of prisoners of war, particularly in the fruit industry, also incited AWU protest. The 1942 Convention debated the decision to employ prisoners of war as labourers in the fruit industry, fearing it would deprive fruit workers of employment and fair wages and conditions, and constitute a menace to the country. The government had said that POWs would be used only when existing labour resources were unavailable. The AWU relented, and agreed to the use of POWs if all other avenues of securing labour had been exhausted.[9]

The AWU leadership believed that they were entitled to expect a great deal from the ALP in return for the devotion provided by the union ('a wonderful machine'), which was made available for the perennial re-election of political Labor in Queensland, and, it was hoped, across Australia. Branch president Beecher Hay reminded the annual Queensland delegates meeting in 1942 that the AWU had played a 'very prominent part' in the recent re-election of the Queensland Labor Government. The printing presses and the influence of the *Worker*, the fleet of motor cars, the telephones, the willing organisers, 'every part of that wonderful machine, which is controlled by the Branch Executive of the Australian Workers Union, was set in motion and directed by the Branch Secretary towards the defeat of the enemies of Labor'. All, he noted, for less than 6d per week from each male member, and around 3d for women and juvenile members. Hay declared that 'our policy in regard to the Labor Movement, to Arbitration as our industrial method, etc., has been developed and defined, the machinery necessary to give effect to this policy has been brought to a state of perfection'. And then, set in bold type in the minutes, Hay added:

> Every member, every rep., every committeeman, and every official must recognise that 'no man liveth unto himself', and that his job is an important cog in the great machine, which can do so much on behalf of humanity.

Such was the hope that laborites had of the trade unions they had built. For his own part Beecher Hay was about to learn how that great and wonderful machine could be directed, in all its pitiless force, by the branch secretary against anyone who defied the code of loyalty which bound the AWU leadership together.[10]

### The Man who would be King: the Rise of Tom Dougherty

By 1941 Fallon had become acting general secretary of the AWU as well as remaining Queensland Branch secretary. Refusing the £1000 a year salary (the general secretary of the AWU was the highest-paid union official in Australia), Fallon had taken on the extra position in June 1940 as a consequence of a prolonged illness afflicting the 73-year-old Ted Grayndler. In late 1940 Grayndler resumed duty, although it was quite clear that he was far from well. He rejected several approaches to resign. The opening of the 1941 AWU Convention was postponed until after lunch while the Executive Council discussed Grayndler's obstinacy. Fallon, as usual, worked out the decisive tactics. When the Convention resumed, Fallon asked for the general secretary to present his report. Grayndler's explanation that he did not have it ready because he had been on sick leave prompted Fallon to move successfully that Grayndler be directed to prepare the report and to deliver it at Convention the next day. As expected, the report was inadequate – Boote observed in his diary, 'Grayndler's unfitness to act made painfully obvious' – and Fallon convinced Convention to recommend that Grayndler stand down. Grayndler finally agreed after Fallon recruited Henry Boote to propose to him that he receive a salary for life while he wrote the history of the AWU (a task he failed to begin; Grayndler died in Melbourne in 1943). Indeed, he wanted Boote to do it for him, a task Boote did not relish. 'The time left to me now is not enough for my own work.' Grayndler, Boote ruefully noted, could now do nothing on £500 a year. The machine that Grayndler helped to forge was left to the fractious contest of his ambitious colleagues. For the moment Fallon seemed in complete control. Of the 1941 Convention, Boote's diary entry for 28 January records: 'Attended Convention again. Proceedings very dull. It's a one man show. Fallon absolutely dominates it; delegates are nauseatingly subservient to him. Left at noon and made for home'.[11]

The meetings of the AWU's Executive Council between 1941 and 1944 reveal a pattern of infighting, as several officials competed for the general secretary's position. Fallon, accustomed to supremacy, was unusually vexed: should he stay in Queensland or assume full control in Sydney? Either course could encourage his rival, Queensland Branch president Beecher Hay, or his ambitious lieutenant, Northern District secretary

Tom Dougherty. In April 1941 Fallon, 'in the strictest confidence', told Boote of his quandary. Fallon thought the general secretary's position 'largely useless'; the real power was presumably in Queensland. Although he would like 'the present state of things to continue', Fallon did not want Hay in head office. 'He was a good lieutenant, but would make a weak and pliable leader.' Or perhaps one that Fallon could not control.[12]

Beecher Hay had followed Fallon's career path, from Central District organiser in 1927 to the Queensland Branch's leadership nursery, the Northern District, where he had been district secretary since 1934. Hay had been Queensland Branch president since 1938, when he had taken over from J. C. Lamont, who had been appointed to the Queensland Transport Commission. In 1940 Fallon described Hay as 'one of the greatest men the Movement ever produced', a man who had struggled in his early years to provide for his family as a canecutter, navvy and miner. At successive Queensland delegates meetings Hay had returned this warm praise. In January 1941 he joined the chorus recognising Fallon's courage in taking on unscrupulous canegrowers in North Queensland. Within a few months Hay was testing for weaknesses in Fallon's control of the union.[13]

At the June 1941 Executive Council meeting Hay lodged but then abruptly withdrew a nomination for the general secretary's position, after his resolution that the general secretary be based in Sydney was defeated (its passage would have forced Fallon to choose between the position of Queensland Branch secretary and general secretary). The numbers were not yet there for Hay. But an identical resolution was passed by the Executive Council in June 1942, a decision due to come into force at the end of the 1943 Convention. Unfortunately for Hay, the fact that the resolution succeeded a year later did not mean that the numbers had swung his way. Clyde Cameron says that before the June 1942 meeting, Hay discussed the issue of the general secretaryship with Tom Dougherty, then Northern District secretary in Queensland. Dougherty agreed to support Hay's move to again put the motion. Dougherty, however, had secretly forged an alliance with Fallon. Dougherty would take the general secretary's position in Sydney; Fallon would remain in Brisbane. Queensland was his power base and whoever controlled Queensland controlled the AWU. Although Hay's motion was carried, Cameron said that he would never forget the look of terror on Beecher Hay's face, that of a man who knew he was for the 'high jump' as an AWU official. The June 1942 Executive Council meeting was the first attended by two future rivals, Tom Dougherty and Adelaide Branch secretary Clyde Cameron. They each profited from the dilemmas facing Beecher Hay and Clarrie Fallon: Cameron by a compelling lesson in the nature of AWU power politics, Tom Dougherty as a direct beneficiary of the game.[14]

AWU Convention, 1947. The post-war leadership – and rivals – emerge. Delegates include (seated from left): Queenslander Gerry Goding, long-serving Victorian secretary 'Brahma' Davis, Tom Dougherty, and general president Vic Johnson. Standing: South Australian secretary Clyde Cameron (front row, third from right); Queenslanders Joe Bukowski and George Pont (standing between front and back row). Immediately behind Pont is an ageing Clarrie Fallon. *Noel Butlin Archives, Australian National University.*

Beecher Hay was not quite finished. At the 1943 AWU convention in Ballarat Fallon tendered his resignation as general secretary. There were two nominations for the position before Convention, Dougherty and Beecher Hay, and each received 15 votes. Convention's solution to the impasse was to instruct the Executive Council to appoint the general secretary. This course of action was decided by the narrow vote of 16:14. At the AWU Executive Council meeting held immediately after the Convention on 17 February 1943, a ballot to decide the matter was won by Hay, 6:3. Neither Hay nor Dougherty, who were both present, recorded a vote. Fallon's grip on the union was apparently weakening.[15]

Dougherty did not give up. In June 1943 both Hay and he renominated for the job for the following year, 1944–45. When the ballot results were announced to the 1944 Convention, Dougherty received a majority of 4543 votes over Hay. Queensland carried the day for Dougherty, delivering him 11 159 votes and only 3054 to Hay, Dougherty's Queensland tally representing almost half of the total national vote cast. Interestingly, NSW Branch delivered Hay 2266 to Dougherty's 614, a result that Dougherty would not forget. On the fifth day of Convention, Hay, armed with a legal opinion, announced that he would challenge the validity of the elections. Hay considered several thousand votes should be declared invalid because they were not accompanied by the prescribed certificate 'or because they had been recorded at various centres, collected by individuals, and taken down and "dumped" in the box at the AWU office'.[16]

But Hay had already made a terrible mistake. The pressure on him was undoubtedly immense, so much so that he had neglected to produce a balance sheet and an annual report to Convention. Hay told Convention that 'through stress of work he had not had an opportunity so far of even examining the proof of the first portion of his report, which had been sent out, nor of looking into the financial statement properly. He wished to discuss the financial statement with the Auditor before bringing it down'. It was an act of political suicide. Of this failure to produce his reports, president Vic Johnson ruled at the Convention that Hay could no longer occupy the position of general secretary. The Executive Council, convened later that day, immediately appointed Dougherty to this position.[17]

Hay took the question of Dougherty's appointment and the ballot irregularities to court and asked for an order directing the union and its executive officers 'to observe the rules of the union' and reinstate him. In August 1944 the Federal Arbitration Court refused Hay's applications. Justice O'Mara found there had been ballot corruption ('in some instances bundles were found in the box in the Australian Workers Union office in Brisbane and it was impossible to identify the bundle with any shed or gang') but considered it would be 'perpetuating a futility' to order a new ballot. In November 1944 Hay was expelled from the AWU after it was found that while general secretary he had withheld from the Executive Council complaints concerning alleged malpractices in regard to the 1943 NSW Branch ballot (see below). His appeal to the Arbitration Court against this decision was also unsuccessful. *Tribune*, the Communist Party organ, commented: 'The Executive Council has now removed all danger of Mr. Hay beating Mr. Dougherty by expelling him from the union – one of the safest means of winning an election yet discovered'. At the 1945 Convention it was decided to conduct ballots for the general president, general secretary, Executive Council and branch officials every three years, instead of annually. *Tribune* saw this move as giving the AWU leadership 'further protection against rank and file democracy'. Beecher Hay subsequently obtained employment on the Sydney waterfront as a tally clerk.[18]

### The Purge of the NSW Branch

At the age of 41, Tom Nicholson Pierce Dougherty had climbed to the top of the AWU empire. Born in Bollen, Queensland, in 1902, he had tried his hand at a variety of bush jobs, even working a New Guinea rubber plantation for a time. From 1921 until his appointment as an AWU Northern District organiser in 1932, Dougherty had worked the Mackay canefields. Tanned, strong, tall but slightly stooped from his labours, Dougherty had made his way up the Queensland AWU ranks, becoming Queensland Branch president in 1943. Along the way he had exchanged the rough gear of the sweating canecutter for a flash white suit and white shoes. But there were hurdles still to be jumped. Sydney-based as general secretary, Dougherty was confronted by hostile NSW Branch officials, who had the capacity to both disrupt his control of the union and his involvement in the NSW Labor Party, where it soon became obvious that Dougherty intended to make his mark. With Fallon's aid he set about the reconstruction of the branch and the purging of its officials, a task which had fitfully preoccupied the Executive Council since the removal of Jack Bailey in 1933.

The NSW AWU Branch had grown strongly since the depression. By 1944 secretary Con Bowen reported a membership of almost 19 000. Bowen had recently been elected to replace Jack McNeill, the veteran official who had died in June 1943 at the age of 75. The branch's various departments were flourishing, and new ones developed. Apart from traditional pastoral and mining coverage, the branch boasted a Factory Department which covered workers in soap and candle-making, paper-milling, margarine and vegetable oil manufacturing, nut food making and laundries. The revival of the local mining industry also increased membership and prompted the formation of a Mining Department in 1940 and a new Mining Industry Award. A Construction Department was created following the amalgamation with the United Labourers Union in April 1941. The amalgamation boosted branch membership by 5000 and entrenched coverage of all civil construction work throughout the State, including railway works, roads, channels, weir construction, sewerage work and bridges. The ULU had also covered forestry work. Branch secretary McNeill thought it 'one of the best amalgamations . . . since the amalgamation of the AWU and the AWA in Queensland in 1913'.[19]

The death of McNeill and the dispute over the general secretary's position provided an opportunity for a new group of NSW AWU officials to challenge the domination of the federal AWU and the Queensland Branch. Bowen led a group of left-wing activists, some of whom had opposed the AWU leadership since the PWIU days of the 1930s. In mid-1944 members of the NSW Branch Executive, including Bowen, took action in the Equity Court of New South Wales over the issue of branch autonomy. They claimed that the NSW Branch was not subject to the constitution and rules of the Australian Workers Union. The Executive Council responded to the NSW Branch court application by declaring that the branch had not complied with Executive Council instructions. It would assume direct control of the branch 'with a view to reconstruction'.[20]

Dougherty alleged that three members of the NSW Branch executive were active supporters of the Communist Party. Dougherty maintained that one of them, Leo King, was the head of the Communist Party's Agrarian Branch, while C. G. Connors and E. Irvine had actively assisted and collected funds for the party. All three had been recently identified in *Tribune*. The NSW executive contended that it was defending the interests of branch members against an 'unwarranted attack' by Fallon and Dougherty. Moreover, allegations of communist control were a 'bogey'. This ploy, the executive claimed, 'flogged to death by Goebbels, Hitler, Togo and other fascists', was now being employed by 'Dougherty and Co. to confuse the minds of the members as to the real issue of the dispute. It is a fight for the autonomous rights of the New South Wales Branch members'. The executive accused Dougherty and Fallon of seeking to remove elected officials and replace them with 'a set of Yes men'. Dougherty, it was alleged, was concerned about the forthcoming ballot for the position of general secretary in which he was up against Beecher Hay 'and may think Yes men controlling the New South Wales Branch would be helpful'. Using the courts to assert their independence proved as frustrating as Beecher Hay's appeals for redress. In September 1944 the NSW Equity Court affirmed the rules of the federal AWU and rejected the NSW Branch executive's contention that the branch was a trade union in its own right. Justice Roper held that the branch was not an independent trade union within the meaning of the NSW Trade Union Act but merely part of the registered AWU.[21]

The Executive Council moved swiftly to take over the branch. On 19 September 1944, the council called before it J. Moss, Con Bowen, T. Dalton, L. King, O. Hearne and C. Connors to answer charges that they attempted to break the branch away from the union, failed to observe the directions of the council on the question of the ballots, failed to comply with the AWU loyalty pledge, and misused branch property and funds. All pleaded not guilty then addressed the council on each of the charges. Connors was the one exception. He too pleaded not guilty but when asked by the president if he had anything to say in reply to the charges, he retorted, 'I think it would be a waste of words, as I think this is a farce'. Connors refused to withdraw this statement and he was dismissed from the meeting. The Executive Council subsequently found all charges proven and all were expelled from the union. Tom Ledsam, a member of the AWU since his former union, the Railway Workers and General Labourers Association, amalgamated in 1915, was appointed NSW Branch president pending elections, and Bill Wilson, an organiser with the AWU on the South Coast (and a winner of the Military Medal in the Great War where he had served with distinction in Gallipoli and France), was appointed branch secretary, along with the requisite number of delegates and organisers. Ledsam and Wilson were subsequently confirmed in their positions at a ballot held the following year. Despite the fact that Bowen appealed his dismissal as far as High Court action in 1948, he was unsuccessful in being reinstated. Of the High Court's decision, Dougherty felt it was highly satisfying for the Executive Council, saying that the judgment 'will establish for all time the right and authority of Federal organisations in regard to Branches'.[22]

Dougherty's problems were not over. He would still find himself plagued by obstinate NSW Branch officials until another purge ran its course in 1951. And during the late 1940s Dougherty developed a poisonous rivalry with his mentor, Clarrie Fallon. George Pont, the Far Northern District branch secretary in Queensland and a friend of Dougherty's, offered this succinct assessment: 'Dougherty was a man who must be on top and so was Fallon and they went from buddies to real enemies'. Executive Councillor and Adelaide Branch secretary Clyde Cameron also found himself at odds with the new general secretary. The Executive Council's treatment of Beecher Hay 'cut across my grain. I just could not abide this kind of behaviour and I made my position clear by what I said and the way I voted'. Cameron also dissented from the decision to remove Con Bowen as NSW Branch secretary.

Dougherty never forgave me for supporting Bowen and for the other things I did contrary to what he wanted. The differences between us became worse in 1946. As Secretary of the Adelaide Branch, I encouraged my Organisers to support the rank and file in their out-of-court action to get a forty-hour week in the shearing industry. They succeeded, and the forty-hour week was largely a fait accompli before the Court formally approved it. But, in keeping with the AWU's slavish adherence to arbitration, Dougherty did not just remain neutral, but actually carried on a relentless campaign against the shearers who were involved in the action.[23]

## Industrial Issues in the Post-War Period

Industrially one of the more important issues for the AWU during the late 1940s was the campaign for a 40-hour week, and renewed unrest among rank-and-file membership in the pastoral industry over pay. One of the difficulties for the AWU was the fact that there had been no new pastoral award since 1938 because of the wartime policy of 'wage-pegging'. This had meant that the AWU had been required to seek improvements by variations to the existing award. Although some wage relief was obtained in 1945 when pastoral workers received increases under the 1938 award, it was not until 1947 that Dougherty finalised the preparatory work for a new award. Shearers, however, began to take industrial matters into their own hands – a common pattern across many industries in the immediate post-war years, as frustrated workers struggled to boost low wage levels and improve conditions. By March 1945, shearers were already on strike in Queensland and there were moves afoot to extend the dispute into New South Wales, with branch secretary Wilson warning that 'bogus outfits' were trying to bring about a stoppage further south. Defence committees began to spring up in some areas, seeking mass meetings of New South Wales pastoral workers to consider supporting their Queensland counterparts, who were claiming an increase in rates of 15 per cent. Names such as Bowen and King, former NSW Branch officials expelled after the Dougherty purge, were linked with these rank-and-file groups. The AWU hierarchy was quick to deny any involvement in the pastoral strike in either State. By early March it was claimed that almost all sheds in Broken Hill, White Cliffs and Wilcannia were idle because of the strike in New South Wales, although there were signs in Queensland that the strike was breaking, with reports that shearers in many sheds had resumed work, particularly in the south-western districts. Sheds in the central west had carried resolutions opposing the strike. Nevertheless sporadic strike action continued, even after June 1945 when a new pastoral award increased rates to 45s per 100 to shearers in New South Wales, Victoria and South Australia (3s 9d higher than the previous rate) and an increase from £5 10s a week to £6 a week for shed-hands. Rates in Western Australia and

## STRANGE BEDFELLOWS.

The Chifley Government's 1945 decision to dramatically increase European
immigration to Australia prompted some calls to include limited Asian
immigration – a view quickly attacked by the *Worker*. This cartoon targets
Liberal backbencher Eric Spooner and communist FIA secretary Ernie
Thornton as enemies of a White Australia, which a 1944 *Worker* editorial
referred to as 'the most outstanding political characteristic of this country'.
*AWU Collection.*

Tasmania were slightly lower, while Queensland pastoral workers had
enjoyed new rates under a separate State award since May 1945. The *Worker*
carried reports throughout the remainder of 1945 alleging that
communist-sponsored rank-and-file disruption campaigns were being
channelled through 'phoney' rank-and-file defence committees.[24]

Concurrent with its application to seek an increase in rates, the AWU
lodged an application to decrease hours from forty-four to forty hours a
week. This occurred at the same time as the Printing and Kindred
Industries Union filed a similar claim. The Commonwealth Arbitration
Court, sensing a general application by industry for a 40-hour week,
reserved judgment on both claims. Hence the AWU claim was delayed by
a general industry case for a reduced working week. Rank-and-file unrest
prompted Fallon to put a successful motion before the 1947 AWU

Annual Convention that members throughout Australia refuse to accept employment in the shearing industry after 15 March 1947 except on the basis of a 40-hour working week. During the debate, Dougherty went to some pains to stress that the AWU's 120 000 membership must receive their instructions from the union on the matter and any decision must represent the desire of the rank and file. This was partly a reaction to the ACTU's public claim that it was the only organisation which should speak on the 40-hour week issue, but also a response to rank-and-file unrest – and the defiance of him implicit in Cameron's encouragement of the rank-and-file campaign in South Australia. Following a compulsory conference between the AWU and the pastoralists, a 40-hour week was secured in June 1947. The Commonwealth Arbitration Court applied the 40-hour-week decision across all industries from 1 January 1948.[25]

Since becoming Adelaide Branch secretary in 1941, Clyde Cameron had set about building the branch with considerable energy and determination. Membership of the Adelaide Branch increased from around 7500 to almost 13 000 when Cameron resigned to enter Federal Parliament in 1949. Organisers were instructed to call at properties 'off the beaten track' and, for the first time, to enrol permanent station-hands as members. The branch also recruited in previously neglected industries: the Adelaide Cement Works, Mount Lyell Fertilizers, and among local government workers. Effort was also put in to enrolling railworkers employed by the Commonwealth Railways (this was the only Australian rail system where the AWU had coverage of operating staff. Elsewhere, the AWU only covered rail construction staff). Cameron also negotiated the amalgamation of the State-registered Tile and Pottery Employees Union with the AWU, extending the union's coverage into potteries and brickworks. During Cameron's tenure, the branch revived its activities in the SA Labor Party. Cameron became State ALP president in 1946.[26]

As a consequence of the impact of the Second World War, the Victoria-Riverina Branch was forced to face many of the same problems encountered during the previous decade. Unemployment among branch members, most of whom were engaged in construction work, was high on account of the curtailment of many construction activities because of the lack of available capital. The CCC absorbed some construction workers, creating further frustrations for the union, as these workers effectively, if temporarily, slipped from their control. Similar restrictions also meant a reduction in the mining membership, as many of these men were required for defence work. Discontent among branch membership was fuelled by low wages and inferior conditions, particularly in the case of pastoral workers (see below) and workers in the fruit industry. Industrial action resulted in the achievement of a 44-hour week and improved pay and conditions in the fruit industry by 1944, and in the

case of the Corowa and Rutherglen districts, 100 per cent membership
coverage of permanent hands. The end of the war saw a gradual improvement in wage rates and conditions in most industries during the second
half of the decade. Branch membership increased from a little over 7300
in 1945 to around 14 000 by the end of the decade. Branch secretary
Dave Gunn died in office in 1943 (he had been secretary since 1938) and
was succeeded by Jim Macpherson, who served until 1946 when Harry
'Brahma' Davis was elected to the position. Davis served until 1968, and
emerged as a key figure in the controversies which engulfed Victorian
Labor in the 1950s. Davis was also general president of the AWU from
1949 until 1964.[27]

The demands of the war economy led Tasmanian Branch secretary
Nicol to report in June 1943 that the branch had passed through a
period 'fraught with many difficulties'. Membership had declined to
4748. Some progress had been made. Improved conditions, allowances
and marginal increases had been obtained for the mining sector, while
additional annual leave, marginal rates and wage loadings were secured
in the carbide-manufacturing industry award. Employers in the rural
industry had stoutly resisted branch endeavours to organise rural workers, but the union prevailed for the most part, with particular success in
the hop industry, where an award was established. In the mining
industry, all Tasmanian mines continued to operate throughout the war,
although hampered by reduced labour. In the post-war period, as in the
1930s, political intervention again benefited the Tasmanian AWU. In
1946 the Cosgrove Labor Government began to prepare a large-scale
program of public works, creating a demand for construction workers.
The government also supported an AWU application for a 40-hour week
in the Hydro-Electric Commission, the Forestry Department, the Public
Works Department, the Department of Mines and other government
departments engaged in construction work. The branch was also successful in negotiations for improved conditions in other industries,
including the marine boards and butter and cheese manufacture.[28]

Tensions emerged in the relationship between the AWU and other
unions in the immediate post-war period. Rivalry had existed between the
Artificial Fertilizers and Chemical Workers Union and the AWU since the
1920s, when an agreement was made whereby the AWU would desist in
enrolling members in the industry in Victoria and South Australia. As the
industry was for all intents and purposes confined to those two States, the
AWU had effectively left the field to its rival. With the advent of the Second
World War the industry was revitalised and spread into New South Wales.
Although it was never previously spelt out in the agreement, the AWU
interpreted it to mean that it had exclusive coverage in that State (and as
indicated above, Cameron revived enrolment of workers in South

Australian fertiliser companies in the 1940s). The position was aggravated by a merger agreement between the AFCWU and the Federated Iron-workers Association, the communist-controlled steel industry union to which the AWU had had a strong antipathy for some years. The AFCWU brought matters to a head in 1942 by serving a log of claims on companies operating in New South Wales which were already subject to AWU-administered awards or agreements. Communist Party official Eric Aarons established a party branch at the Timbrol chemical plant at Rhodes in Sydney where he was employed as an industrial chemist. A campaign was launched to fully unionise the plant and to replace the AWU coverage with that of the more militant AFCWU. The AFCWU application eventually came before the NSW Industrial Commission and the AWU intervened, claiming that the companies were adequately covered by awards and agreements obtained by it. The issue was further complicated in 1945 with an application by Imperial Chemical Industries to extend the Federal Chemical Award to its works in Botany, New South Wales. This application had the consequence of seeking to restrain the AWU from proceeding with a claim for an award for New South Wales before the Industrial Commission. Tensions erupted late in 1946 when a strike began in the ICI Botany plant involving 300 workers but throwing a reported 8000 out of work by February 1947. The dispute was finally resolved in August 1947 when Mr Justice Kelly of the federal Arbitration Court confirmed the AWU's right to cover chemical workers in New South Wales. Intermittent strike action continued at Botany over the next few years, which the AWU claimed was communist-inspired.[29]

For the duration of the Chifley years (1945–49), the AWU stood as a bastion against communist activities in Australia's unions. Senior figures in the Labor Party were concerned at the increased number of unions with communist officials and the strong influence of communists at the 1945 ACTU Congress. Hagan estimates that 'party members exercised a strong influence on executives of unions whose members numbered about a quarter of Australian unionists'. This is despite the fact that CPA membership was in fact declining, and continued to do so throughout the post-war years. Nevertheless, the impression of communist menace, dramatised by Soviet expansion in Eastern Europe, increased throughout the late 1940s. In 1945 the ALP decided to establish industrial groups within trade unions, to disseminate ALP propaganda and to assist pro-ALP candidates in union elections. In January 1945 Fallon made it clear that with fascism on the run in Europe and the Pacific, the next struggle for laborites and democrats would be with the Communist Party, who wanted to establish a Nazi-style dictatorship in Australia. 'Unionists, you must awaken from complacency and assist active unionists, including your leaders, to defeat the enemy within . . . This is something you cannot leave

to your Labor parliamentarians or your job rep. or union official. It is up to
you – think it over!' It was an emotionally charged atmosphere, fuelled by
an unprecedented number of industrial disputes through which, as one
labour historian has observed, the CPA believed they could win working-
class support away from the ALP. In the steel industry in 1945, and in
Queensland in the meat industry (1946) and the railways (1948),
prolonged and bitter strikes occurred, characterised by accusations of
communist manipulation. The two Queensland disputes encouraged the
formation of ALP industrial groups in that State. AWU Southern District
secretary Joe Bukowski was involved in the early co-ordination of the
industrial groups in 1948 and became State secretary of the industrial
groups in 1950.[30]

The most politicised of these disputes were in the coalmining industry,
where the AWU's mining industry coverage provoked demarcation disputes with the Australasian Coal and Shale Employees Federation (often
known as the Miners Federation). In South Australia and Victoria
coalmining was covered by the AWU, and in other States there was
frequent potential for mischief. In 1948 one of these disputes flared over
the AWU's organisation of sixty workers employed in the construction of
the 2.8-mile Kemira Tunnel between the Mount Kembla and Mount
Keira collieries. The ACSEF retaliated by attempting to enrol AWU
members at Leigh Creek (an open-cut coalmine in South Australia,
where by another obscure twist in the complexities of Australian trade
union demarcation, the AWU had coverage), Mt Isa and Captains Flat (a
silver mine in New South Wales). The AWU's Executive Council decided
in September 1948 to concede coverage of the Kemira workers to the
ACSEF (despite the fact that the men were engaged in construction, not
mining work), on the stipulation that the Miners Federation provide
equal pay and conditions, and desist from attempts to organise workers
in metal mining. The ACSEF rejected this compromise and began a
stoppage which escalated into a statewide dispute, resulting in the im-
position of severe coal restrictions. Court action in March 1949 awarded
coverage to the AWU. The issue smouldered throughout the year, before
the AWU finally agreed to concede coverage to the ACSEF. Meanwhile,
the 1949 coal strike intervened.[31]

The AWU was not directly involved in the month-long dispute triggered by the Miners Federation over a range of industrial demands. The
strike crippled power supplies for industry and domestic use during a
harsh winter (in the late 1940s all power supply was based on coal), and
the hand of the Communist Party, some of whose members were
prominent ACSEF leaders, was detected manipulating the dispute to
challenge the working-class appeal of the Chifley Labor Government.
The government took a tough line with the Miners Federation, gaoling

some of its leaders and imposing stiff fines. Historian Tom Sheridan suggests that the AWU also played a major role in defeating the coal-miners, maintaining that 'it was the threat posed to their jobs by this old enemy that was probably most persuasive in the minds of miners when they decided the strike was lost'. AWU coverage of coalminers in Victoria and South Australia posed a continual threat to the ACSEF in New South Wales and Queensland. The strike opened the way for the AWU to permanently increase its presence in coalmining across Australia, as the ACTU and the NSW Labor Council refused to sanction the strike. The NSW Labor Council's Land Transport Group of unions voted on 14 July to move coal which had been mined before the strike, a decision attacked by the Miners Federation but which was carried out by members of the NSW ARU and AFULE. As the dispute worsened, the Chifley Government considered using either AWU members or troops to resume mining and break the strike. Dougherty was never one to miss an opportunity to extend AWU coverage, and he warned that 'if we go into the mines, we will be in them for all time'. On 2 August Chifley chose the troops, and by 15 August the strike had ended.[32]

### THE WRECKERS

The bitter 1949 Coal Strike. 'The Wreckers' identifies a Press-Tories-Communist conspiracy against a Labor Government bound for progress. *AWU Collection.*

The struggle against communism was also cited by the AWU leadership in maintaining its opposition to ACTU affiliation, despite occasional rank-and-file appeals to join the peak council. A delegation from the ACTU addressed the 1943 AWU Convention. The principal AWU objections were the financial cost of affiliation and a loss of the power and prestige inherent in splendid isolation. At the 1949 Convention, these same objections were again cited, but Dougherty also claimed that communists exerted undue influence in ACTU forums, despite conceding that there were some 'good people' in the ACTU. Dougherty was winding up to full rhetorical roar when Fallon abruptly moved that the question be put. 'If the matter was allowed to be discussed further it might be that good people associated with the ACTU would be antagonised.' It was an obvious shot at Dougherty's robust debating style.[33]

### The Fall of Fallon

Since his appointment by the Executive Council as general secretary in January 1944, Dougherty had moved relentlessly to assume personal control of the AWU. He was a cunning student of that master of control Clarrie Fallon, his mentor, who had probably hoped to neutralise the ambitious Dougherty by encouraging his desire to become general secretary. Perhaps Fallon had in mind the model of the ageing Edward Grayndler, unable to challenge the domination of the Queensland Branch from Sydney, the home of the federal office, and a NSW Branch which, after the turbulent 1920s and the domination of local Labor affairs by Bailey, had lapsed into a weakened role within the AWU and the New South Wales labour movement. But Dougherty was also a Queenslander, with his own supporters in that most powerful branch, and he was determined to challenge Fallon's authority in Queensland, on the Executive Council, and in New South Wales, where he planned to emerge as the leading AWU identity. Indeed, with grim purpose Dougherty had brought the NSW Branch to heel – only to underestimate Fallon's ability to play rivals against each other. Bill Wilson, the NSW Branch organiser brought in to replace Con Bowen as secretary, showed no more inclination than Bowen to work in Dougherty's shadow, an irritation encouraged by Fallon. In 1949 Fallon persuaded Wilson to contest the general secretary's position. In his last effort to maintain supremacy, Fallon had over-reached himself. Despite polling well in the north Queensland canefields – Fallon's fiefdom – Wilson was defeated by Dougherty by a margin of 3000 votes. This was as close to defeat as Tom Dougherty had come since his frustrations with Beecher Hay in 1943. Dougherty was not grateful for the experience, and Wilson's time as New South Wales secretary was about to run out. In September 1949 the Executive Council decided to assume control once more of NSW Branch affairs and investigate allegations of ballot irregularities in the NSW Branch elections. A resolution from one delegate encouraging Dougherty and Wilson to meet and discuss the differences between them, and hence promote harmony within the AWU, lapsed for want of a seconder.[34]

Fallon was increasingly isolated, and it weighed upon him. In May 1949 he wrote to Henry Boote after a testimonial held for Boote in Melbourne. Fallon had lavishly praised Boote as 'Australia's greatest writer', although Boote had put down his pen in March 1943, when ill health had finally forced his retirement after twenty-nine years as *Worker* editor. Boote was grateful for Fallon's warm words. Fallon felt they were barely enough. 'No language of mine could even begin to express what I feel about the men and women who changed the circumstances in which people lived, from what they were in the years that are gone and what they are today.' Fallon told Boote that while in Melbourne (Boote had been too ill to travel) he had made a pilgrimage to the graves of John Barnes, Edward Grayndler and John McNeill. By Barnes' grave he saw the Cootamundra wattle planted by McNeill. Barnes, McNeill and another AWU official and Labor senator, Andrew McKissock, had made a pact that as each died, the survivors would plant the wattles by the other's graves, and friends would perform the duty for the last of trio. To Boote, Fallon reflected that 'I sometimes wonder whether some of us who are charged with the responsibility of carrying on the good work where they left off are worthy of the honour. I sincerely regret to have to admit that I doubt it'. Henry Boote died in Sydney on 14 August 1949. Within six months, Fallon would also be dead. As Beecher Hay had told the Queensland Delegates Meeting in 1942, no one was greater than the union. Now even Fallon, that most vital cog in the wonderful machine, was worn out.[35]

The AWU's Executive Council gathered in Sydney in January 1950. It was a poisonous atmosphere, debate given over almost entirely to the NSW Branch ballot investigation. Several NSW Branch officials were questioned about alleged ballot irregularities; after a long evening session on the second day of the council meeting, 10 January, the delegates dispersed. Fallon and Queensland Branch president Harry Boland returned to the hotel room they were sharing and sat up for many hours talking. At half past three they had a final smoke, and Fallon suggested they should get some sleep. Boland remembered: 'A little later I heard a peculiar noise. I jumped up and put the light on, and Mr. Fallon had then obviously taken the stroke. His voice was very inaudible, although I did understand some of his remarks; but he finally went into a coma from which he never recovered'. Clarrie Fallon died at 4.15 p.m. the following afternoon. He was 63 years old.[36]

Clyde Cameron claims that Fallon died of fright. Dougherty had 'put the whisper round that he was going to have a full-scale enquiry into the balloting procedures in Queensland'. Southern District secretary Joe Bukowski, who might have been expected to support his boss, Clarrie Fallon, had thrown his support behind Dougherty. Bukowski allegedly threatened to expose Fallon's attempts to manipulate Queensland votes in the 1949 general secretary's ballot. He demanded that Fallon reverse this manipulation in favour of Dougherty, a reversal which Cameron says was the deciding factor in Dougherty's victory over Wilson. At the AWU convention in late January, Bukowski obliquely alluded to 'irregularities' in southern Queensland during the elections; and at the Executive Council meeting on the day after Fallon's death, Dougherty moved that all the recent AWU State and federal ballots be investigated by a com-mittee of the Executive Council. This move seems to have been quietly set aside, except in New South Wales, where Dougherty remained determined to remove Wilson. This payback was finally settled in 1951, with the election of Western Australian MP and former AWU official Charlie Oliver as NSW Branch secretary. The NSW Branch was again restructured, and Wilson was exiled to the new Leeton district office. With Fallon's death, the urge to investigate Queensland lost its appeal.[37]

One obituarist believed that a mystery died with Clarrie Fallon: 'the mystery of the enormous influence he wielded over the Australian labour movement. What he said today became government policy tomorrow'. Temple, Macdonell and Grayndler had built a great industrial union, but it was Fallon who drew all the nascent political instincts together, focusing the union's authority on exercising influence over Labor Government leaders in Queensland and Australia. With these leaders he traded control and industrial peace – stability, the bedrock of prolonged political power. Queensland Labor Premier Hanlon recognised the loss. 'We always took it for granted that in the storm and stress of industrial and political struggle he would be there, firm as a rock, in defence of the great Union and Party to which he dedicated his life.' Prime Minister Ben Chifley described him as a personal friend, and 'valued his advice'. Dougherty dismissed him as a 'hard worker'. Within the union Fallon was often aloof and menacing. Overt conflict was minimised, driven into fear and acquiescence. But whatever knowledge of these mysteries Fallon passed down to his ambitious pupils, Tom Dougherty and Joe Bukowksi, subtle manipulation was a lesson entirely lost on them. Throughout the 1950s they would fight their enemies with few restraints, two men who thought they could seize control from within the political bonfire they inflamed. Clarrie Fallon was buried in a Brisbane cemetery on 14 January 1950. According to his wishes he was buried alongside his son Jack, killed in an aircraft crash thirteen years before.[38]

CHAPTER 10

# Anxious to See the Light
## National Politics and Industrial Organisation, 1950–59

### The Reign of 'Tom the Terrible': the AWU and Labor Politics

With the death of Fallon and the removal of NSW Branch secretary Bill Wilson, Dougherty was finally able, after six years in the job, to exert unrestrained authority as general secretary. In Charlie Oliver, Dougherty had finally found a candidate with whom he felt he could share power in New South Wales – or at least one who would not challenge his authority. An AWU member since 1923, Oliver resigned his position as the Labor Member for the Western Australian State seat of Boulder (in the Kalgoorlie goldfields) to take up the NSW Branch secretary's position in 1951. Like many AWU officials Oliver was a physically imposing, ambitious man. He left his family behind in Western Australia to cross the continent and pursue a new career in the union hierarchy. He would spend nearly thirty years (with a few spectacular interruptions) as NSW AWU secretary, marked by great political guile and often furious faction fighting, within both the ALP and the union.[1]

Dougherty's rise to power occurred at a time of increasing conflict in the labour movement over the anti-communist push led by the ALP's industrial groups. Many industrial groupers welcomed the Menzies Government's Communist Party Dissolution Bill in 1950, while others in the labour movement were fierce opponents of the legislation's assault on civil liberties. The AWU leadership juggled a seemingly contradictory stance of being implacably hostile to communists (to the extent that they were barred from holding office, and indeed membership of the union) while opposing the legislation. The Bill was successfully challenged by several communist unions in the High Court; Menzies resorted to a referendum in 1951. Dougherty urged AWU members to vote 'No'. He also expressed strong support for the work of the industrial groups. 'Menzies and Fadden [Country Party leader and deputy prime minister] have never once lifted a little finger to swat one Communist, although they are now frantically trying to out-rival each other in robbing Labor's industrial groups of the credit due for the progressive decline in Communism in recent years'.[2]

In some respects Dougherty's attack on Menzies was an effort to shore up a divided ALP, which found itself caught between aggressive anti-communism (through its own sponsorship of the industrial groups) while officially opposing the referendum, only narrowly defeated in September 1951. Vociferous anti-communism was also a useful weapon for Dougherty to employ against his enemies in the ACTU and key ALP State branches, power centres which competed with the AWU leadership for authority in the labour movement. In September 1950 Dougherty attacked the ACTU in the *Worker*, claiming that communist-led affiliates to the peak council dominated ACTU policy-making. Dougherty described the 'pro-Communist' ACTU executive members as 'back seat drivers' shaping ACTU policy on the Communist Party Dissolution Bill and support for the communist-dominated World Federation of Trade Unions. Mutual AWU–ACTU hostility re-emerged in March 1951, when the federal ALP Conference proposed to include AWU representatives – Dougherty and general president H. O. Brahma Davis – on the Federal Labor Advisory Committee, a liaison body between the political and industrial wings of the movement. ACTU secretary Albert Monk said that the ACTU might have to 'retire' from the committee; including the AWU would 'place a premium on trade union isolationism'. In a swipe at Dougherty's *Worker* barrages, Monk added that the AWU had helped communism by refusing to join the ACTU. In July the ACTU withdrew from the committee, and the ALP quietly closed it down. Its fate was a reflection of a labour movement in which consultation was increasingly being replaced by hostility and division.[3]

In the NSW ALP the AWU leadership was also having difficulty exerting influence. Frustrated ambition contributed to Dougherty's fierce antagonism towards the NSW ALP executive, led by branch president Jack Ferguson, the secretary of the NSW Branch of the Australian Railways Union and also federal ALP president. In the mid-1940s, not long after his arrival in Sydney as general secretary, Dougherty had sought Labor nomination for the NSW Legislative Council – a reward for service often claimed by local union officials. Dougherty's overtures were rejected by the executive, and thereafter Dougherty maintained a prominent public campaign to force the ALP to honour its policy pledge to abolish the Legislative Council, whose members were not demo-cratically elected but were appointed by the government of the day. Dougherty was also determined to have revenge on Ferguson. An oppor-tunity emerged in the early 1950s. Ferguson and his mentor, federal Labor leader Ben Chifley, were increasingly uneasy about the threat to party unity posed by the activities of the industrial groups. In his 1951 presidential address Ferguson told the federal ALP Conference that too many ALP members believed that hatred of communism was the only condition of good party membership. Ferguson had also supported the 1951 decision by the SA ALP to disband industrial groups in that State. The local party branch claimed that the groups were picking favourites among ALP candidates, a natural extension of ALP factionalism (which increasingly characterised the groups' activities in all States) but one at odds with the groups' charter. It was a decision largely engineered by Clyde Cameron, the president of the ALP's SA Branch. The former AWU State secretary was now a federal Member of Parliament, and his opposi-tion to the groups was another sore point with the AWU leadership.[4]

With the death of Chifley in 1951 Ferguson was exposed to his enemies in New South Wales, where a coalition of the AWU and other disaffected pro-industrial group unions was moving to assume control of the ALP executive. In the lead-up to the NSW ALP Conference in June 1952 Dougherty periodically attacked Ferguson in the *Worker*, describing him as a defender of the perks enjoyed by NSW MLCs. Ferguson responded that Dougherty had once tried very hard to become an MLC, and was now a 'saboteur', trying to extend AWU domination of the ALP Australia-wide. Dougherty intended to sponsor a resolution at the June Conference that the Legislative Council be abolished; however, Ferguson evidently concluded that he had already lost the struggle with the AWU and the other pro-grouper unions unhappy with his performance. In April 1952 he resigned all union, party, and parliamentary positions to take up the NSW Labor Government's offer as chairman of the NSW Milk Board.[5]

The heated 1952 NSW ALP Conference saw the 'AWU–Grouper faction' ticket take control of the NSW ALP executive. A *Herald* corres-pondent concluded that as a result of the Conference ballots, the AWU now dominated the NSW ALP. Dougherty was poised to become 'the most powerful figure in the Australian political labour movement'. At the previous federal ALP Conference the AWU had sixteen out of the total twenty-four delegates; the New South Wales result could give them twenty delegates. Those who feared the AWU juggernaut hoped for a revolt against this domination, but 'these hopes may not be realised if the AWU can benefit by the mistakes made during its era of power from 1916 to 1927, and hasten slowly'. The era of calm in the labour movement appeared to be over. 'Some in the ALP fear a split'.[6]

The most cataclysmic of Labor's splits was now developing, as the struggle over communist activity in the union movement reached a critical point. Dougherty and the AWU had been consistent supporters of the industrial groups, and benefited from supportive leaflets distributed under the name of the industrial groups to AWU members in the union's 1946 and 1949 elections (the NSW ALP executive later claimed that these were organised and paid for by Dougherty – a breach of AWU rules, as candidates in AWU ballots were banned from canvassing for votes). But a gulf gradually opened between the groups and the AWU, just as group supporters were at the height of their influence in Victoria and New South Wales. Increasingly, this success alienated the AWU. In Victoria tensions between AWU Branch secretary 'Brahma' Davis (his nickname reflected his pugnacious, bull-like physical build, and perhaps his negotiating style) and the ALP led to the AWU's disaffiliation from the Labor Party in mid-1954, over a mixture of industrial frustration with the Cain Government (it refused to increase margins for government construction workers) and disputes with the Victorian ALP executive, where the AWU had, before the breach, been able to exert little influence.[7]

Labor leader H. V. 'Bert' Evatt addresses the 1952 AWU Convention. General secretary Tom Dougherty and general president 'Brahma' Davis are seated right. At the time both Evatt and the AWU supported the industrial groups. *Noel Butlin Archives, Australian National University.*

In New South Wales, Dougherty's expectations that the elimination of Ferguson in 1952 would see him emerge in a leading role in the NSW ALP were dashed. Indeed, in June 1954 both Dougherty and Oliver refused to renominate for the NSW ALP executive, a culmination of several months of increasingly critical statements by Dougherty concerning the activities of the groups, and other differences between the AWU and the NSW ALP executive, indicative of the AWU leaders' inability to influence the party machine. In 1953 Dougherty was thwarted by the executive in an attempt to win aldermanic preselection for the Sydney City Council, as part of an apparent move to become the lord mayor of Sydney. In early 1954 the AWU's restrictive membership rules provoked a controversy in New South Wales, with the NSW Labor Government, ALP Branch secretary Bill Colbourne and several union leaders expressing embarrassment at the AWU's determination to deny membership to Asians, communists and 'new applicants whom it considers undesirable'. The government complained that the AWU was undermining its efforts to promote compulsory unionism in the State; secretary Charlie Oliver was even charged with breaching ALP rules over compulsory unionism, although the executive ultimately backed down. Dougherty commented that 'the AWU will not lightly sacrifice the principles of its constitution forbidding the enrolment of Communists or Asiatics'.[8]

For many groupers (and others in the labour movement), the AWU was the epitome of an old style of unionism, autocratic and intolerant of dissent. The groupers had opposed these characteristics of the communist-controlled Federated Ironworkers Association. Rising pro-group union officials like Lloyd Ross, the secretary of the NSW Branch of the Australian Railways Union, and Laurie Short, who assumed control of the FIA as national secretary after a long and bitter campaign against incumbent national secretary Ernie Thornton, were both members of the NSW ALP executive, and had been strong advocates of democratic practices in unions and of generally modernising union organisation. This commitment was put to the test in November 1953. The NSW ALP executive agreed to a request to reform the industrial group which had been active in the Transport Workers Union, a union run by pro-ALP officials over whom hung allegations of corruption and ballot-rigging. As the executive explained in a subsequent statement, 'there cannot be one standard of conduct for ALP officials and a different standard for others ... Communists can be successfully fought in the Unions only when members can rely on honest administration from the opponents of the Communists'.[9]

The executive's decision converted Dougherty and NSW TWU secretary Barney Platt into implacable enemies of the industrial groupers.

The decision opened the possibility for AWU dissidents to call on the NSW ALP to establish a group in the AWU, in a manner similar to the reformation of the TWU group. This 'interference' in the internal affairs of the AWU was something that Dougherty would never tolerate, and the AWU leadership moved quickly to declare their hostility to any suggestion of establishing an industrial group in the AWU. In January 1954 the AWU Convention stated that it was opposed to the formation of any group of members, including industrial groups, within the union. The convention also affirmed its 'confidence in the Constitution and general rules of the Union and the manner in which they are being administered'. NSW Branch secretary Charlie Oliver said that the AWU had never needed the help of an industrial group to fight communists in the union, adding: 'we have done an excellent job for the people and we will continue to do it ... [This motion] will make it clear to everyone that this Union at least does not want interference from groups of any kind'. This nervousness was also reflected at the June 1954 Executive Council meeting, where the Convention decision was reaffirmed and a warning issued to all AWU officials that if anyone supported an attempt to form an industrial group that official would be dismissed immediately. In July 1954 Dougherty tentatively suggested in the press that when a group won control of a union from communist officials that group should then be disbanded. *News-Weekly*, the voice of the Catholic Social Studies Movement (which provided, under the leadership of B. A. Santamaria, significant logistical support for the industrial groups), patiently responded that Dougherty was not completely 'on the ball': such an action would merely drive the communists underground. Dougherty's dilemma was that having so strenuously supported the anti-communist activities of the industrial groups in the past, he could not turn on them too aggressively without some credible justification.[10]

On 5 October 1954, federal ALP leader H. V. 'Doc' Evatt provided Dougherty with the opportunity he had been craving. After sustaining the narrow – and unexpected – defeat of the 1954 federal election, and the subsequent traumas of the Petrov Royal Commission on Espionage, Evatt dramatically issued a statement, in part at the urging of Dougherty, attacking his perceived political enemies. Evatt accused a 'minority group of [ALP] members' of disloyalty to the labour movement and his leadership. He added: 'It seems certain that the activities of this small group are largely directed from outside the Labor Movement. The Melbourne *News-Weekly* appears to act as their organ. A serious position exists'. Evatt's targets were the Catholic Social Studies Movement and industrial group supporters in the NSW and Victorian ALP executives. Evatt also singled out several Labor federal parliamentarians, who, in varying degrees, had been critical of Evatt's erratic performance as party leader, and his obsession with the Petrov Commission, at which members of his personal staff had come under scrutiny for their associations with Soviet diplomats.[11]

Events now moved very quickly, and with equal speed Tom Dougherty sought to guide the hand of official vengeance towards his own enemies. On 20 October Dr Evatt stood on a table in the federal ALP Caucus room to watch his ally Eddie Ward list the names of his tormentors as they voted in a division to 'spill' the party leadership (the motion was acrimoniously defeated). On the same day, the front-page headline of the *Australian Worker* proclaimed: 'Santamaria unmasked – mastermind behind industrial groups – cloak and stilletto [*sic*] methods exposed by General Secretary T. Dougherty'. Dougherty dramatically revealed selected highlights of a private speech delivered in early 1953 by Santamaria, 'The Movement of Ideas in Australia', which had outlined the changing nature of the anti-communist struggle in Australia. This speech is in many ways a perceptive analysis of the labour movement at the time, but in his prophecy Santamaria had failed to take account of Tom Dougherty. The speech having never been previously published (and indeed, Santamaria's own behind-the-scenes role in aiding the industrial groups had only been publicly revealed in a newspaper article on 28 September 1954), Dougherty could now sensationally 'expose' Santamaria, lashing him for allegedly belittling the political legacy of Ben Chifley (the so-called 'Chifley legend') and for conspiring to use the industrial groups to capture the Labor Party for his own sinister purposes. With a single press statement Evatt had lifted the AWU's reversal of support for the groups from the realms of self-interest to a fight to save the soul of the Labor Party.[12]

From late 1954 and into the new year, the *Worker*, widely distributed outside the AWU (thousands of copies of the Santamaria exposé were also printed and distributed in pamphlet form), maintained a barrage against the groupers, and stridently defended Evatt's leadership. Dougherty emerged as a key Evatt ally, and the leader of a group of twenty-two rebel unions which coalesced to fight the NSW ALP executive. At a meeting in November 1954 they called for the removal of 'outside influences' from control of the ALP; they wanted the ALP Federal Executive to investigate the NSW Branch. Several unions in Victoria, including the AWU, made a similar assault on the Victorian ALP executive. In New South Wales the 'rebel' unions' statement was signed by Dougherty and Oliver, Barney Platt (TWU), Fred Campbell (ETU), R. H. Erskine (Textile Workers) and R. J. Williams (Builders Labourers). These 'rebel' unions formed the core of what would soon become the Combined Unions Steering Committee, the political organisation of the industrial Left in New South Wales Labor.[13]

At the January 1955 AWU Convention Dougherty took aim at his enemies in the NSW ALP executive. He accused Short, Ross and Jack Kane, the assistant secretary of the NSW ALP (and former TWU official) of being the leaders of a Movement cell in the party, who launched a cowardly attack against Barney Platt for political purposes. Dougherty's broadside was a welter of disparate slurs, delivered in a typically blustering style. He offered this assessment of the Movement:

> I want to say this: That 'The Movement' obviously cannot be a Sectarian Movement. Have a look at the conglomeration of misfits, go-getters and ambitious men, some of whom were Communists not so long ago, fellow travellers, and Liberals who should be in the Liberal Party, and general nonentities that comprise this secret organisation known as 'THE MOVEMENT'.

Dougherty rejected suggestions by his critics that he was fanning religious sectarianism, claiming that many Catholics were disturbed by the activities of the groups. One after the other delegates spoke in equally hostile terms about the Movement and its alleged activists in the ALP. Brahma Davis maintained that the Movement ran the Victorian ALP, and that senior Victorian ALP officials had been 'out to get me' since the late 1940s. Queensland Branch president Joe Bukowski explained that he never been a genuine group supporter (despite the fact that he had served as the Queensland secretary of the industrial groups), but that Dougherty and he 'decided I would coast along [with the groups] for the purpose of ascertaining what they did and how they did it and their approach to all these things'. It had been rumoured that the Movement had tried to encourage Bukowski to run against Dougherty. A NSW AWU organiser, J. S. Bielski, claimed that ALP federal MP Stan Keon (who would split from the Labor Party in 1955) made such an approach to him. Clyde Cameron recalls that when Dougherty published his October 1954 attack on Santamaria, 'it was customary for the *Worker*, which was published by the Queensland Branch of the AWU, to pick up any major article printed in the *Australian Worker* and reprint it in its own issue, but on this occasion, that did not happen. That worried Dougherty and I was suspicious too'. Edgar Williams says Dougherty 'put the waddy onto Bukowski and said, "You've got to give them [the groups] away", and Joe gave them away. It was either that or his job'. At the January 1955 AWU Convention Bukowski duly recanted, along with his fellow officials. Into this solemn ritual only Queensland branch secretary Harry Boland introduced a note of humour. Expressing his distaste for the language of the resolution they were debating (which referred to the groups' 'standover tactics' and 'unscrupulous methods'), Boland nonetheless supported the Convention resolution to oppose the groups – with an ambiguous twist. He concluded his remarks with 'a little story':

Many years ago there were two Irishmen walking through the hills, and they decided to camp out in a cave for the night, and found a grizzly bear there. Pat and the grizzly got into combat, and Pat called on Mike, who said, 'Do you want me to help you hold him ?' Pat said, 'No. I want you to help me let him go.'

That applies to a lot of people associated with the Labor Movement and associated with this Union. They are anxious now to see the light. God bless them, I hope they see it.

When the delegates eventually voted to support Evatt and fight the Movement and the groupers, only Charlie Golding, the WA Branch secretary, dissented. He told Convention that the AWU should fight communists, not the industrial groups. Of Tom Bourke and Don Willesee, federal ALP parliamentarians whom Dougherty had attacked as Movement members, Golding said 'both men were his personal friends and he did not believe they were members of a movement trying to destroy the ALP'. Golding's objections were overwhelmed.[14]

After the Convention, Santamaria, Short and Kane rejected the assertions made about them by Dougherty. Kane commented: 'the spectacle of the AWU bureaucrats pontificating nonsense to each other for days on end would be comical were it not for the possibility that constant repetition might lead some people to give credence to their irresponsible allegations'. The NSW ALP executive considered taking action against Dougherty, but decided to await the NSW ALP Conference scheduled for later that year, which had the power to expel him from the party. According to one source, the executive did not want to act prematurely 'and make a martyr of him'. The AWU's Executive Council met in February and condemned 'sectarian mongers', including 'certain clerics and others' trying to prevent the AWU from fighting Santamaria's 'foreign movement'. The AWU's abrupt withdrawal of support for the groups sparked some unintentionally ironic comments, demonstrating the depth of the realignment that was taking place in the labour movement. *Tribune*, the journal of the Communist Party, welcomed the 'important truths' which it believed Dougherty had revealed about the industrial groups, and praised the AWU's 'progressive stand'. *News-Weekly*, on the other hand, commented: '[the] current hand-in-hand walking-out together of the AWU and the Communist Party bears resemblance in certain respects to the Ribbentrop–Molotov alliance that started World War Two. Remember how Ribbentrop finished up?'[15]

In the period late 1954 to mid-1955 Dougherty emerged as the single most powerful trade union official in New South Wales, and possibly Australia. He was a convenient champion for the embattled Evatt, taking a sword to Evatt's political enemies and using Evatt's name to punish his own. Evatt appreciated the AWU's efforts. In January 1956 he addressed the AWU's Annual Convention, and told the assembled delegates: 'In that fight nobody contributed more than the Australian Workers Union, and I see here to-day men associated with that struggle; men like your President, Mr Davis; Mr Dougherty, your General Secretary; men like Mr Bukowski, like Mr Oliver in New South Wales, and like Harry Boland'.[16]

The degree of co-operation between Dougherty and Evatt in this period became extraordinary in January 1955, when it was suddenly revealed that the two men had applied for one each of the two Sydney and two Melbourne television licences recently made available by the Federal Government. They had done so, they explained, on behalf of the ALP and the AWU, of which they were trustees, but without consultation with anyone else in the labour movement. Dougherty defended the applications on the grounds that Evatt and he were attempting to ensure that organised labour had a say in this vital new communications technology, and to stop the capitalist media – and foreign interests – from totally dominating the licences. While

'EVATT: "Hand up the W and the U, Tom".' *News-Weekly*'s comment in January 1955 on the close political bond between Labor leader Evatt and Dougherty. Evatt substitutes the L and the P of ALP with the initials of the AWU. *News-Weekly*.

these were worthy aims, their applications were poorly prepared, and as Evatt's biographer notes, made more in opposition to the other applicants than as a properly financed and structured submission. And the timing of the applications, albeit a factor which neither Evatt nor Dougherty could control, was appalling. The licence application hearings were in late January to early February 1955, just as the storm in the party was building to full fury. Unsurprisingly the applications were unsuccessful, and TV ownership in Sydney came to be dominated by the anti-Labor Con-solidated Press, owned by Sir Frank Packer, the media empire which had so greatly benefited from the *World* deal in the early 1930s.[17]

While Dougherty's efforts may have shored up Evatt's leadership in early 1955, it had not yet cemented the AWU's control of the ALP machines in Victoria, New South Wales and Queensland, and hence national control of the labour movement. In 1955 two opportunities emerged to build AWU influence in the party: the annual Conference of the NSW ALP, and the party's National Conference in Hobart. Dougherty was to wield a key behind-the-scenes role in the factional intrigues of the labour movement throughout 1955, but it should be stressed that although other prominent AWU officials were members or delegates to various ALP decision-making bodies, Dougherty himself was not. He was not a member of the ALP's Federal or NSW executives, nor was he a delegate to the ALP's National Conference. He was able to wield great influence either through direct access to Evatt, through other AWU officials who served in the ALP machine, or through common cause with the coalition of interests which was emerging within Labor to back Evatt's leadership.

The ALP Federal Executive decided to intervene into the affairs of both the NSW and Victorian ALP executives, and break the domination of the industrial groupers in those branches. Dougherty travelled to Melbourne to lobby the Federal Executive members during their crucial meeting in late 1954. The Federal Executive apparently wanted to balance the power of the groupers on the two State executives with representatives from other power centres within the labour movement, including the AWU, but in the angry and uncompromising atmosphere of the party in 1955 this relatively moderate aim was submerged beneath an often viciously personal power struggle. As the March Federal Conference – the ALP's supreme decision-making body – loomed, where the numbers would be available to settle the dispute one way or another, the Victorian groupers decided to boycott a special State Conference to be held in February 1955, before the federal meeting. They feared that they would lose control at this Conference of the delegation to be sent from Victoria to the Hobart Federal Conference. So when the participants assembled in Hobart for the Federal Conference two rival delegations from Victoria demanded recognition: the 'old' pro-grouper delegation, which had been elected at the Victorian Branch's

June 1954 Conference, and the 'new' anti-grouper delegation elected at
the February special Conference. The Federal Conference chose to recognise the 'new' delegation, and in protest at this decision seventeen Federal
Conference delegates decided to boycott the Conference. The party was
split, and a split in the federal and State parliamentary caucuses, and
purges and resignations of party members, would soon follow. The Hobart
Conference also confirmed a Federal Executive decision to withdraw
official ALP endorsement of the industrial groups. The AWU remained
firmly behind Evatt. Of the seventeen 'pro-grouper' delegates to boycott
the conference, five came from Queensland, including Premier Vince
Gair. His support for the groupers would not be forgotten by the
Queensland AWU. The only delegate from Queensland who refused to
join the boycott was Harry Boland. Victorian AWU Branch secretary
Brahma Davis was one of the 'new' Victorian delegates. The AWU
leadership also participated in the purges and anti-grouper campaigning
which followed the Hobart Conference. When it was revealed in the press
that the Federal Executive proposed to intervene into the affairs of the
NSW ALP, this course of action was attributed to charges made against the
NSW ALP executive by Dougherty.[18]

The six New South Wales delegates at Hobart had all voted to join the
boycott, and were all members of the NSW ALP executive. They had
already launched their own counter-attack against Dougherty, a pamphlet
entitled *Labor Nails The Rebels' Lies*, which refuted Dougherty's 'nebulous
and unsupported' allegations against the executive and individuals like
Jack Kane. The pamphlet also alleged that Dougherty and his supporters,
during the 1949 elections, had 'fraudulently' identified themselves in
election material as receiving the endorsement of the 'ALP industrial
groups', a charge hotly denied by Dougherty. Charges and counter-
charges were also repeated at a series of anti-executive rallies addressed by
both Evatt and Dougherty in mid-1955, despite a Federal Executive ban on
public statements on party affairs. A few days before the NSW ALP's
Annual Conference in August 1955, Evatt and Dougherty addressed a 'pro-
Evatt' rally of 2500 in Sydney. The imminent defeat at the Conference of
the groupers was confidently predicted. Dougherty singled out both
Laurie Short and, ominously, Queensland Premier Vince Gair, for special
mention. Gair, he asserted, had 'led' the breakaway at the Federal
Conference. 'Have a look at Gair', Dougherty metaphorically suggested to
his audience. 'I say Gair should be sacked now.'[19]

The Conference was intended to be a moment of political glory for
Tom Dougherty, savouring the kind of victory which had been denied
him in 1952, when Jack Ferguson had resigned before the drama of the
Conference, and its ritual of sacrifice and triumph, could unfold. There
would be no anti-climax now. The groupers who had won with Dougherty

in 1952 assembled in 1955 to fight him. It was an opportunity Dougherty relished.

> It was a theatrical performance from its early moments when Mr Tom Dougherty, massively built leader of the pro-Evatt rebels, lumbered up to the delegates' dais at the back of the hall to make his first tactical thrusts.
> Dougherty, who saw victory followed by the attractive prospect of a purge of his enemies ahead of him, stood with his shoulders relaxed and sloping like a heavyweight waiting to go into the ring.
> His head was down and his eyes glared, and as his voice boomed through the conference hall he looked the perfect Hollywood conception of the ruthless local political leader.
> A day later he was fighting uphill, struggling to regain control of the conference which had begun to slip from his hands.

Whereas branch secretary Bill Colbourne's report had been received with a 'rousing reception' by the delegates, Dougherty 'was subjected to an almost continuous barrage of interjections when he spoke against the adoption of the report'. In the ballot for executive positions, the groupers were successful in continuing to dominate the branch, winning twenty-nine of the thirty-two available positions.[20]

The Conference result marked a decline in Dougherty's influence in national and NSW Labor politics. Those who wield the knife are rarely celebrated, even by their supporters, and as Dougherty defended Evatt, his leader was displaying a preference for a new and more subtle champion, ALP federal president Joe Chamberlain, who had emerged as a powerful national figure at the Hobart Conference, and who had presided over the purge of many of Evatt's leading enemies in Victoria and across the country. Increasingly, Dougherty's continued attacks on his enemies in New South Wales were seen as immoderate and unjustified. At the 1957 AWU Annual Convention Dougherty delivered a tirade – 'at times Mr. Dougherty leaned across the table and shouted to the delegates who were seated around the room' – against the NSW ALP parliamentary Caucus, whom Dougherty claimed were still dominated by the 'Santamaria movement'. The MPs were, Dougherty said, 'a bunch of go-getters, legal "experts", retired or not retired publicans, cranks and professors'. The next day the *Sydney Morning Herald* described Dougherty as 'Tom the Terrible', and used his outburst to claim that the purported solidarity of the New South Wales labour movement was a 'sham'. Ironically, New South Wales Premier Joe Cahill had been invited to address the Convention, and with characteristic diplomacy coolly replied to Dougherty's attack. Dougherty claimed to have been misquoted in the press, but defended his right to criticise the Labor Party.[21]

In New South Wales the conciliatory style of Cahill and Colbourne defined the party's recovery from the split. The tempestuous era in which Dougherty had emerged as a key player was now giving way to the reconciliation of the AWU with the ALP. Branch secretary Charlie Oliver joined a restructured NSW ALP executive as vice-president in 1956. Oliver formed an effective working relationship with secretary Bill Colbourne, a relationship strengthened when Oliver became NSW ALP president in 1960. In 1958 the *Sydney Morning Herald* reported the formation of a 'new Labor faction' with the co-operation of the AWU, ARU, Storemen and Packers, and the FIA. They proposed to purge the ALP executive of 'all left-wing elements', an ambition pursued with vigour and frustration ever since. It was the beginning of the modern factional alignment of NSW Labor, and in terms of AWU influence in NSW ALP affairs, the 1960s would be Oliver's era, and on local party matters Dougherty would generally defer to Oliver.[22]

In his report to Victorian Branch AWU members for 1955, Davis optimistically noted 'the work of the AWU and other unions in this state has borne fruit in the political field'. The 1955 federal elections, in which Labor had been decisively defeated by Menzies, had at least demonstrated that the voters 'do not want sectarianism or outside influences in the Labor Party'. Expelled ALP MPs such as Keon and Mullens, standing as 'Anti-Communist Labor' candidates in their old electorates, had been rejected, and ALP candidates elected. But two anti-communist Labor senators were also successful, providing the nucleus of the Democratic Labor Party which would be officially formed in 1956, and which would frustrate the ALP's efforts to win federal elections for another sixteen years. In terms of the Victorian ALP machine, Davis hoped that 'the continued loyalty of members to the union and to the official Labor Party, will strengthen and build up our political organisation to its former great influence and enable it to once again occupy the State Treasury benches'. The AWU's efforts to rebuild its influence in the Victorian ALP through the defeat of the groupers were thwarted. The split had devastated the non-left forces in the party, and a coalition of left-wing unions dominated the ALP from the late 1950s. Brahma Davis, who had complained of a lack of influence on the ALP in the late 1940s and early 1950s, was once again out in the cold.[23]

### A Changing Membership: Industrial Issues and Organisation

There was no outbreak of peace in Queensland, and the bitter 1956 shearers' strike would feed another traumatic Labor split the following year. Yet most of the diverse industries in which AWU members worked experienced little significant industrial unrest in the 1950s. This owed as much to the general prosperity and economic stability of the period as it did to the AWU's preference for industrial harmony. The early 1950s were also a time marked by the urge to expand and diversify Australia's post-war economy, and some of the biggest projects employed AWU members.

In 1950 there were 839 136 trade unionists in Australia – over 60 per cent of the workforce, more than there had ever been. Of these men and women, over 140 000 were AWU members, in a union with assets exceeding £2.5 million. In December 1950 the number of unemployed union members reached a record low: 0.7 per cent. During the depression, only eighteen years before, that unemployment rate had reached a crippling 30 per cent. The Australia of the 1950s was prosperous, and its economic activity more diverse, although many workers and their families remained scarred by memories of want and war. New manufacturing industries emerged; the first oil refineries were constructed; mining operations expanded, particularly in Queensland and Western Australia. In some of these industries AWU members would find lucrative employment, although in the rural industries, its traditional base, the workforce declined by 20 per cent over the period 1933–54, as station and farm operations were mechanised. By contrast, manufacturing industry employment rose by 10 per cent in the 1950s.[24]

The AWU had celebrated mateship in the 1890s, the cocoon of a closed world of white men. The world was less closed in 1950, and the nature of Australian industry was changing. Hovering around the AWU's bush kingdom were European immigrants, women, Asians, Aborigines. They were only a small part of the AWU's membership, yet their presence drew a mixture of hostility, confusion and, occasionally, empathy from AWU officials. The ships bearing thousands of Europe's refugees from war and political turmoil, and those simply seeking a better life, symbolised a world changing forever.

Australian unions in the 1950s found that it was not always easy to enlist immigrant workers, but as one commentator has observed, 'the unions had only themselves to blame for this reaction'. On the Snowy Mountains scheme, where AWU officials first encountered large numbers of 'New Australians', many European immigrants resented being compelled to join unions, and were angered by local unions who refused to recognise their trade qualifications. Union officials often made little effort to understand the problems faced by these workers performing onerous jobs in an unfamiliar environment. NSW Branch secretary Charlie Oliver did not believe that the New Australians made particularly good unionists, only joining 'because they felt they had to'. The AWU was also concerned that immigrant workers might erode local wage levels and conditions, and take jobs 'rightly' belonging to Australians. The AWU's 1950 Annual Convention expressed a strong objection to plans by the Federal Government to allow 40 000 British migrants into Australia, describing it as an attempt to introduce 'industrial conscription', undermining local award wages and standards. Nonetheless the AWU did make some fitful efforts to overcome these fears. Organiser J. S. Bielski dealt with immigrant workers' problems, often explaining industrial issues in the *Worker* in German, Polish and other languages. In January 1956 he echoed AWU concerns by emphasising the importance of union membership and the need to refuse to work for anything less than award wages and conditions. 'This is the way to win the hearts of Australian workers.'[25]

Bielski himself wearied of trying to win the support of the AWU leadership, and came to believe that he could do a better job on behalf of immigrant workers than Oliver. At the 1958 Convention he unsuccessfully moved three resolutions on immigrant issues. In response to a proposal that more space be given in the *Worker* for articles in foreign languages, Bielski received a tirade from the Polish-descended Joe Bukowski, who claimed that migrants had 'bankrupted' Queensland State Government Insurance with compensation claims and, more frequently than 'Britishers', went 'around the back door' to break awards. 'Why don't they assimilate?', Bukowski wondered. That Bielski had never really assimilated with the AWU leadership became obvious in February 1958, when Oliver, fearing his increasingly assertive behaviour, dismissed him for failing to attend an arbitration hearing.[26]

The sharp edge of the AWU's attitude to foreigners was expressed in its fierce support for the White Australia Policy. In 1956 the AWU's Annual Convention unanimously reaffirmed its commitment to a White Australia, claiming that the introduction of 'Asiatic labour' would lower Australian living standards and threaten national security, and would bring about 'a half-caste and piebald community, and therefore create evils and troubles of which the Commonwealth is fortunately free'. Dougherty attacked External Affairs Minister Casey for declaring the term White Australia 'offensive' (although the government continued to support the terms of the Immigration Restriction Act, which prohibited Asian immigration). Dougherty also noted that *News-Weekly* and the Communist Party supported a relaxation of White Australia, which he implied was linked to their mutual interest in undermining Australian democracy. *News-Weekly* retorted that Dougherty was living in the past. 'A policy that may have suited Australia's growing pains sixty years ago is no longer applicable. Australia is not part of Europe, but geographically in the Asian hemisphere. Any attempt to ignore that fact will have disastrous consequences'.[27]

Under AWU rules, White Australia was buttressed by a prohibition on Asian membership of the AWU. Women, however, were tolerated, at least in some circumstances. The 1956 Convention debated, at considerable length, the vexed question of allowing women to work as shearers' cooks.

One delegate felt that women were not qualified for the work, requiring, for example, the help of a man to butcher a sheep's carcass. They also took the 'cream' of the work which should be available to men. 'They did not go out into the back country or to the difficult sheds. They left that to the men.' No one at the Convention disputed the need to restrict female employment in the pastoral industry, but there was some confusion as to whether a blanket prohibition could be made to work in practice, or would be upheld in the courts. As AWU president Brahma Davis explained, the itinerant bushwork nature of the AWU rather perversely undermined male supremacy. 'Suppose you had a female working in the sugar or fruit industry and she became a member; when she completed that work she had the right to apply for work in any industry set out in that clause of the Constitution [rule 6, which provided for AWU coverage of males and females working in various nominated industries].' This additional work could include cooking for shearers. Hence the Convention simply decided to reaffirm a previous Executive Council decision, *discouraging* shearers from engaging women cooks.[28]

In various States the AWU had women members who worked in canneries or as fruit-pickers (not to mention shearers' cooks). The largest concentration of women in the AWU membership was in Queensland, where the AWU had coverage of catering and hotel workers (which was not the case in other States). Here the AWU had no hesitation in promoting equal pay for women, an application denied by the Queensland Industrial Court in November 1956, which ruled that 'the average male cook produced work superior to that of the average female cook' in hotels in Queensland's Northern and Mackay regions. AWU Queensland Branch secretary Joe Bukowski responded that the ruling bore little relation to the reality of hotel work in those areas, where of forty-two major hotels only four employed male cooks. The local hotels would have to shut down, he said, if the women decided not to turn up for work.[29]

In 1955 Aborigines were the subject of renewed AWU efforts to have them included under the terms of the Federal Pastoral Industry Award, although this aim was again frustrated by the fact that Aborigines were not Australian citizens, at least in the terms of the 1901 Constitution. The AWU had officially supported equal pay for Aborigines since 1891, when the Amalgamated Shearers Union conference voted to accept them as full members of the union, entitled to full union recommended rates. In 1916 the AWU Convention ruled 'that if members are found working with aboriginals who are not paid full rates they will be fined not more than £5'. In 1941 the Convention decided that Aborigines in the Pastoral Industry should be covered by the federal award. Queensland Branch secretary Clarrie Fallon told the 1942 Convention that 'his experience was that the aborigine was exploited because he was a first-class man and that he could be employed cheaply. He was quite convinced that if the Union was able to secure award rates for them they would still be employed on stations'. But in 1944 the Arbitration Court rejected the AWU's application: the court believed that the AWU's motivation was simply to 'make work for white employees'; if both Aborigines and whites received full pay, employers would prefer to employ whites. In his January 1956 decision, Commissioner Donovan also refused to bring Aborigines under the terms of the award, but by the post-war years both the unions' and the courts' attitudes were beginning to change. Donovan noted that 'this is a most controversial matter and I desire to hear further evidence and submissions as to whether the employment of aborigines should be covered by the Federal Award'. Federal constitutional discrimination was now the obstacle to equal pay; and perhaps the AWU's attitude had changed. In 1960 the Executive Council called for Aborigines to be granted full citizenship rights and in 1964 the AWU tried once more to include them in the federal award, with the Federal Council for Advancement of Aborigines intervening to support the application. The council's representative, Dr Barry Christophers, said that discrimination on the basis of colour was morally indefensible; Dougherty told the commission that 'fully competent aboriginal workers had been exploited'. But the application was again rejected, although the AWU had better luck with the Western Australian Farm Workers Award in 1964, a new State award which incorporated equal pay for Aborigines. Aborigines were not included under the Federal Pastoral Industry Award until 1968, after the 1967 referendum ended constitutional discrimination against Aborigines.[30]

## Construction and the Snowy Mountains Scheme

The most ambitious of the development schemes instigated in the post-war years was the proposal to harness the waters of the Snowy Mountains to provide electricity for Victoria and New South Wales and irrigation for the farms along the Murray and Murrumbidgee rivers. The Snowy Mountains Scheme was enthusiastically welcomed by the AWU, as its members would be principally employed in this vast civil construction project. In January 1950 organiser Vic Kearney reported in the *Worker* that sixty members attended the first AWU meeting on the site, at Kiandra, 'a spot on the map' 26 miles from the nearest settlement at Adaminaby in southern New South Wales. The initial work focused on the construction of the Kiandra camp and access roads through the rugged foothills of the Snowy Range. 'All men are housed in tents, and the rough ends of constructional camp life existed in their rawest state at the time of my visit.' There were complaints about this roughness from members. However Kearney found the local

engineers and managers responsive to union calls for improvements in
amenities before the coming winter, and the overall impression was an
eagerness to get on with the job. Standing in Kiandra camp, 'within the
folds of the hills', Kearney felt the union traditions associated with the
scheme, and the role AWU members had played in developing Australia.
'So was the standard of the AWU erected on this outpost of the Snowy
Mountains Scheme and not far removed from the old gold diggings of
years ago, when a fragment of early Australian industrial trade unionism
was nurtured.'[31]

The scheme was very ambitious, and over twenty-five years (1949–
1974) $820 million was spent constructing seven power stations, 80
kilometres of aqueducts, 140 kilometres of tunnels and sixteen large dams,
in an area of about 3200 square kilometres. During the life of the scheme,
100 000 men and women were employed by the Snowy Mountains
Authority. During the late 1950s 5000 workers laboured at various sites
along the length of the project, which one AWU organiser described as a
necklace of power stations and tunnels. It was difficult and often
dangerous work. Tunnelling was the most dangerous of the jobs, with the
use of explosive charges greatly increasing the risk for underground
miners. As with many other jobs undertaken by AWU members, the Snowy
scheme workers were also paid bonuses for quick progress, adding to the
risk of accident (bonuses were common in mining and construction
projects, as were piece-work rates in mining and shearing, which also
encouraged speed). The tactics attributed to American tunnelling
contractors were also questionable, themselves offered bonuses by the
Snowy Mountains Authority for quick completion of tasks. 'Tunnelling
crews ... were pushed harder and harder until they were regularly setting
new world tunnelling records. Three deaths for every mile of tunnel was
considered acceptable by the Americans. As they were keeping just under
this, they imagined themselves beyond reproach.' A hundred and twenty-
one workers were killed in accidents on the Snowy Mountains Scheme,
despite some imaginative efforts to reduce the accident toll, including the
introduction of 'safety ballots'. Employees with an accident-free record for
three months were eligible to enter the ballot to win a £50 bonus.
Management believed that the ballots led to substantial falls in accident
rates, providing a competitive inducement to take extra care on the job.
Yet this competitiveness seemed to be contradicted by the temptations
offered to get the job done as quickly as possible.[32]

Despite the AWU's difficulties in representing its new immigrant
members, the union demonstrated characteristic skill in easing industrial
problems at the various Snowy scheme sites before they became major
disputes – a skill frequently attributed to Oliver and Justice Stanley
Taylor, the industrial arbitrator for the project – and in winning better

pay deals and substantial compensation payouts for the workers injured
during the course of the 25-year project. The AWU was successful in
securing an impressive range of allowances and over-award payments
which substantially boosted pay packets: underground and wet places
allowances, height money, dirt money, distant places allowance, danger
money and shift allowances. The accommodation was provided free of
charge and a camp allowance covered meals.[33]

Construction projects were a major employer of AWU members in all
States, but this was particularly so in Tasmania, where of 7800 branch
members, 3000 were employed under the Federal Construction and
Maintenance Award. The path of European development in Tasmania was
typified in the industries in which AWU members worked. The construction of the Electrolytic Zinc works at the Rosebery mine in the 1920s
prompted the need for electric power to refine the zinc. In the 1950s, the
E-Z works used one-third of the electricity generated by Tasmania's Hydro-
Electric Authority to efficiently extract zinc from ore, a process which had
long frustrated mining engineers. The road network which did so much to
expose the wilderness of Tasmania to these ruthless changes was built and
maintained by the Department of Main Roads. All these organisations
were major employers of AWU members. By the 1950s, mechanisation had
greatly increased the scale of physical change in Tasmania. As Tom
Dougherty explained to the Arbitration Commission in 1958, the days of
the pick-and-shovel man in major construction projects were over. 'It
is now big machines, powerful machines, great gorges being closed –
dammed – and most of the work is being carried out in the most in-
accessible parts of this rather rugged continent, up in the mountains,
down the deep valleys ... the men who work in this industry must work
under most severe climatic conditions for long periods of the year.'
Dougherty cited the example of Poatina power scheme in Tasmania,
where construction workers were battling to maintain schedules and keep
unsurfaced roads open despite torrential winter rain. 'They are opening
up an area which has never been touched excepting for the Hydro-Electric
Authority deciding there was a medium through which they could control
water and power which would be to the benefit of the people and business
of Tasmania.' In 1958 the environmental complications of this development were not the AWU's concern. Dougherty's responsibility was for the
workers who were called on to fulfil the HEC's ambitions, to cope with the
physical demands and dangers. The AWU had applied for increased
margins and new entitlements (for example, three weeks' annual leave,
increased camp, travelling, meal and even an altitude allowance for
workers in the Victorian Alps) for construction workers in Victoria and
Tasmania. On 25 August 1958 the commission granted a range of increases
with an 8.5 per cent increase in margins for skill over and above the basic

wage (approximately £13 a week in 1958, although it varied from State to State), but it would only grant three weeks' leave to workers on seven-day shifts.[34]

## The Mining and Oil Industries

During the 1950s, approximately 27 000 (non-coal) miners worked over 2000 mines and quarries across Australia. They mined metals like bauxite, copper, gold, lead and zinc; non-metal minerals like sand, gypsum, limestone and the deadly blue asbestos of Wittenoom in Western Australia; they quarried for stone and river gravel. Nearly all these miners were members of the AWU. In 1952 the industry employer organisation, the Australian Mines and Metals Association, reported that 'it is gratifying to be able again to record that industrial relations in the metalliferous mining industry have been characteristically cordial. There have been minor disputes but most have been unimportant and all have been short lived'. It was a calmness which prevailed throughout the decade, with mineral prices and wage levels generally buoyant.[35]

A multitude of State and federal agreements covered the mining industry. The main federal award was the Gold and Metalliferous Mining Award. In 1952 the AWU successfully applied for an increase in margins. Following the new award, basic-wage rates ranged from £9 to £11 a week with an average margin for skill of an extra £1 a week. But the AWU was unsuccessful in an application for a 35-hour week for underground miners in Victoria and Tasmania, a longstanding claim of all Australian mining unions. The union also unsuccessfully argued for a special bonus for its members, 'to allow employees to share in the prosperity of the industry'. Commissioner Donovan, despite recognising that miners had often been sacked or called on to accept wage cuts when metal prices were depressed, refused this application, arguing: 'It would be necessary to cover the activities of undertakings mining gold, wolfram, copper, tin, lead, silver and zinc. Some of these metals are sold by the ounce, some by the unit, and in the case of wolfram by the ton. It would be impossible to draw up a clause to implement the claim'. There were precedents however, and Donovan was responsible for one of them: the Wool Value Allowance in the Federal Pastoral Industry Award (see ch. 11). There were also State awards providing prosperity bonuses: at Broken Hill, the lead bonus paid to Mount Isa miners, and the industry allowance paid to miners in Western Australia. Despite this setback, the union continued to press individual mining companies for profit-sharing agreements, and Dougherty reported in 1953 that two unspecified Tasmanian mining companies had agreed to such payments (their anonymity was perhaps due to an unwillingness to set an industry-wide precedent).[36]

Western Australia had long been a centre of strong AWU domination of mining industry coverage, and the branch had its own Mining Division to service 6000 miners engaged in goldmining. In the 1950s most of these men worked the mines around Kalgoorlie, Coolgardie and Murchison (the vast iron ore deposits of the Pilbara and the Hamersley ranges were not substantially worked until the 1960s). The reports prepared by Mining Division secretary Fred Collard frequently emphasised the importance of safety procedures. In May 1958 he urged both members and their employers to heed Mines Department warnings concerning the firing of faces, with the men often resuming mining operations too quickly after the firing – or, more dangerously, firing before the allocated time. Apart from the immediate risk of death, silicosis and other dust-induced disorders were exacerbated by working in the unsettled dust thrown up after a firing. In 1959 Collard wrote a series of *Worker* articles on the dangers of silicosis and asbestosis, the disease which would extract a fearful toll from the blue asbestos miners at Wittenoom Gorge. Despite the advances made in dust control and medical examinations in the 1920s, Collard could still ruefully observe that 'far too often in Inspectors of Mines reports we find comments such as those following: "Ventilation to be stepped up in this workplace" ... "Water sprays to be turned on"'. The effects of these slack standards – the product, as Collard observed, of both management and worker apathy – were plain. The incidence of tuberculosis, a complication of silicosis, was more prevalent among miners than other members of the community. Other deadly complications of silicosis developed later in life. Such was the case with asbestosis, a poorly understood disease, as Collard conceded: 'although I have not been able to procure very much on the disease of asbestosis, it does seem to me from what I have read that Asbestosis has a quicker disabling effect or advances much faster than does Silicosis'. In fact the disease quietly did its damage in many miners over a long period, with accurate diagnosis not being made until long after the worker had left the mining industry.[37]

The realities of working beneath the ground did little to allay the optimism felt by the AWU (and many others in the community who benefited from mining activity) about the outlook for the industry. In the 1950s new mining and oil fields expanded the opportunities available to AWU members. In 1955 bauxite deposits were discovered at Weipa, on Queensland's Cape York; uranium was discovered at Mary Kathleen in 1954, 50 miles from Mount Isa, in western Queensland. Australia's first aluminium smelter commenced operations in 1955 at Bell Bay in Tasmania. By 1953 the nation's first oil refineries were under construction at Kurnell, near Sydney, and Kwinana, south of Fremantle in Western Australia, although all the crude oil refined at these sites was imported.

An oil strike at Exmouth Gulf, 700 miles north of Perth in 1953, failed to
yield significant quantities of oil. It was not until the early 1960s that local
oil and gas deposits at Moonie in Southern Queensland and in the waters
of Bass Strait proved commercially viable. AWU leaders rubbed their
hands together at the prospect of coverage of this new industry, with
Dougherty reminding the 1954 Convention that the AWU had sole
coverage rights of oil industry workers. In 1953–54 the AWU moved
quickly to obtain a State-registered agreement with Caltex, to cover
workers at Kurnell, and the first federally registered agreement for the
industry, covering workers at the Shell refinery at Corio, Victoria.[38]

The post-war mining of uranium produced some ambiguous responses
from the AWU. Between 1949 and 1961 AWU members extracted
uranium ore from the appropriately named Radium Hill in South
Australia, and in 1953 Eric O'Connor, the AWU's South Australian
Branch secretary (the name had been changed from Adelaide Branch in
1951, when Dougherty restructured the NSW Branch), said that the
project loomed large in importance for Australia – and the AWU. This
did not stop the union from mounting a protracted campaign for a 35-
hour week for underground miners and two men to work each drilling
machine. The Commonwealth Government, which owned and managed
the project, refused these claims, but the new award in 1954 did provide
for a 37-hour week, which O'Connor said 'made industrial history' as the
shortest working week for underground miners anywhere in Australia (it
narrowly edged out the $37\frac{1}{2}$ hours previously awarded in Western
Australia). Within a year O'Connor's attention turned to concerns about
the health hazards that might be associated with the mining and treatment of uranium. Despite union concerns for members at the uranium
treatment plant at Port Pirie, the Arbitration Court did not believe that
any special factors operated and 'chose to regard the work at the plant as
similar in practice and circumstance to work of a somewhat similar
nature in the established chemical industry'.[39]

AWU concerns over uranium mining were heightened by the union's
coverage of construction and maintenance workers at the Woomera
rocket-testing range and at nearby Maralinga. O'Connor concurred with
the view expressed by the 1956 AWU Convention, which decided to
oppose the testing of nuclear weapons in Australia. During the debate,
Dougherty commented: 'we do not know what is going on in Australia.
All we know is that Britain, or the British Commonwealth of Nations has
decided that a certain part of Australia is to be used for research and
experiment in regard to guided missiles and the explosion of atomic
bombs'. Australia, Dougherty said, was an ill-informed party to the
possibility of global nuclear holocaust. He was not totally opposed to
atomic energy, however. 'Why not use scientific brains to turn atomic

energy into peaceful channels for a better way of life for the human race?' To that end, the AWU invited Professor Harry Messel from Sydney University to address the Convention, and after his plea to take a positive attitude to the potential of nuclear power, the AWU decided to con-tribute funds to Messel's Nuclear Research Foundation, and Dougherty took up a position on the foundation's board of governors in 1957. The AWU took a practical attitude to atomic energy. Its members mined uranium; if nuclear power stations were constructed in Australia, as Messel advocated, then AWU members would build and maintain them. Nor did fears of nuclear war prevent the AWU from securing the 'excellent' Remote Areas Award for its Woomera members in 1959. The AWU leadership rarely passed an opportunity to expand the union's areas of coverage, particularly as Australia's industrialisation moved into more technologically sophisticated areas, away from the industries where employment levels were falling in the face of mechanisation, for example in sugar and in the pastoral industry. As Charlie Oliver noted in 1957, he 'thought much more could be done to channel nuclear energy in our industrial life'. However, Australia never embraced nuclear power, and in the late 1970s the labour movement began a rather fitful process of banning uranium mining in Australia, a ban which, like many such edicts, was endlessly qualified at stormy union and ALP conferences.[40]

CHAPTER 11

# The Meaning of Mateship
*The Shearers' Strike and the Split in Queensland, 1956–59*

Immigration, women workers, new industries: Australian society was changing, while the AWU adhered to its old ways and its proud independence. A man who seemed to embody these traditions was Rochus Joseph John Bukowski, who became the president of the AWU's Queensland Branch in January 1951. In his first presidential address he associated himself with these traditions, the marks of his tribe: 'In the Australian Workers Union organisation the way is open for all men to rise to the topmost rungs of the ladder'. In bushwork from the Gulf of Carpentaria to Grafton, Big Joe Bukowski, tall and physically powerful, had risen through the ranks, 'learning the true meaning of mateship, and learning, too, that those who abuse it are not worth their tucker'. He came to office realising that the AWU faced a renewed challenge from its old foe, the Communist Party, and 'their treasonable, anti-democratic practices'. He saw the AWU surrounded by enemies and jealous rivals. 'We know little or nothing about the future, except that it is fraught with grave industrial, political and international dangers.' The AWU was also sensitive to its perceived rights as the embodiment of the Australian Labor tradition. Bukowski asserted that the AWU, and perhaps himself, did not receive just recognition:

> I think that this union should be consulted more often than it is, and that its opinion should be sought on every possible occasion. In view of our history, I think we can claim to have played a major role in the formation of the ALP, and that we have been the keystone of that political organisation.

In 1950 the AWU leadership seemed poised to secure its claim as Aus
tralia's leading trade union, rivalling the influence of the ACTU and
dominating the affairs of the Labor Party. There would be no greatei
beneficiary of this rising power than the AWU's Queensland Branch,
which claimed nearly half the union's overall membership: 58 000, oui
of a total of approximately 140 000. In all, a massive 81 per cent of men
and women workers in Queensland were unionised, and 75 per cent of
them were politically affiliated, through their unions, with the ALP.
Queensland *was* Labor, or at least so it seemed. Within a few months,
stretching from late 1956 until early 1957, those traditions would be
shattered, leaving the AWU marginalised in the Queensland labour
movement until the early 1980s.[1]

### The 1956 Shearers' Strike

Although most industries in which AWU members worked were
industrially peaceful in the 1950s, the pastoral industry, more exposed to
fluctuations of the international economy, experienced industrial turmoil. These fluctuations were not always bad news for local growers. With
the outbreak of the Korean War in 1950, prices paid for Australian fine
wool on the international market reached record levels, with the United
States Government purchasing large quantities for lining the uniforms
of their troops, fighting amid the severe winters of the Korean front. In
1949 the price stood at 76d a pound; in September 1950, it reached 225d
a pound, and 375d a pound in March 1951. The AWU leadership
ensured that their members shared in this largesse, and in April 1951 the
*Worker* proclaimed that the new shearing rate awarded by the Commonwealth Arbitration Court was also a record, topping the £7 per 100 level.
There were also significant increases for shed-hands, crutchers and
station-hands; the top shed-hands' wages, for example, increased from
the 1948 award level of £9 4s 1d to the new rate of £17 8s. The increases
flowed from the new Wool Value Allowance proposed by the AWU and
accepted by the court. Unfortunately, the court also recognised that
basing the allowance rate on the market value of wool could also be
applied to cut shearing rates and pastoral industry wages.[2]

In 1952 falling wool prices, coupled with Australia's first post-war
recession and credit squeeze (the banks drastically restricting access to
loans) prompted moves by graziers to cut shearing rates and shed-hands'
wages. But this application, along with another in 1953, failed to persuade the Commonwealth Industrial Court to cut rates and wages. In late
1955 the determined graziers finally broke through. In September 1955
Grazier Associations from all States (except Queensland, where industrial jurisdiction resided with the Queensland Industrial Court) applied

to cut shearing rates by £1 14s 6d to £5 11s 6d per 100, while the AWU
sought to increase the rate to £10 per 100. The graziers' advocate, W. De
Vos, argued that a 30 per cent decrease in wool prices over the previous
two years justified the application. 'The industry is no longer in a
position to pay rates to employees based on prosperity. The prosperity on
which those rates are based no longer exists.' While the Wool Value
Allowance was measured by the court at a rate of 85d a pound, the actual
rate at the wool market was 55d a pound. De Vos also produced Rural
Bank of New South Wales estimates to show that producers' costs were
exceeding wool prices. Dougherty retorted that since 1949 graziers had
enjoyed unprecedented returns. He also claimed that while wool prices
had fallen, on his estimate, by around 12 per cent over the last two years,
they sought a 17 per cent reduction in wages. Dougherty also said that
the 'untold wealth' saved by graziers by the use of myxomatosis against
rabbits was another reason why a decrease in wages was unjustified
(Dougherty argued that the elimination of rabbits led to bigger wool
clips). The protracted hearings dragged on into the New Year, with
Commissioner Donovan reserving his decision until February 1956.
Growing AWU concern at the progress of the case was reflected in the
increasingly prominent editorial space given to it in the *Worker* in the last
months of 1955, gradually displacing the regular front-page attacks
Dougherty had been launching on his enemies in the labour movement
since late 1954.[3]

Meanwhile, in Queensland, events had been moving with greater speed,
and pre-empted the federal arbitration decision. In November 1955 the
Queensland Industrial Court cut shearing rates by 10 per cent, effective
from 1 January 1956. The judges of the court commented that 'we think
the obvious decline in the prosperity of the industry should be shared by all
sections of the industry'. At £7 14s 3d per 100, Queensland had the highest
shearing rates in the country, but now Queensland shearers saw their rate
fall below that applying in the southern States, to £6 18s 6d per 100. The
Queensland AWU responded by recommending that shearers refuse to
work under the new rates. Dougherty told the federal hearing that
Queensland shearers hardly felt it worth their while to go out shearing, a
pointed remark given the decision Donovan was due to hand down. On 16
February, Donovan announced that shearers' rates in all States except
Queensland would be cut by 5 per cent from 5 March, bringing their rates
in line with Queensland rates. It was a reduction of 7s 6d; shed-hands'
wages were unaffected. Donovan applied the decrease in terms of the Wool
Value Allowance, arguing that he 'couldn't compel owners to pay bonus
payments in 1956 based on 1952 wool prices'. On 23 February the AWU's
Executive Council called on members to refuse to work under the new
rate. Commissioner Donovan's decision was, in the AWU's opinion,

'unjust, unfair and illogically arrived at [and] has materially damaged Federal arbitration'. Dougherty was instructed to inform Donovan of this opinion at the first opportunity. About 50 000 shearers, shed-hands, wool pressers and cooks in New South Wales, Victoria, Western Australia, South Australia and Tasmania were now, to all intents and purposes, on strike – unless they could find work on stations where the owner or the manager was willing to pay the old rate. It was a return to the shed-by-shed industrial warfare of the 1890s.[4]

The rhetoric also had a familiar ring. In January the *Pastoral Review* accused the Queensland AWU of holding the industry to ransom. On 3 January, at a station near Hughenden, in the heart of central Queensland's rich wool region, the station manager refused to sign a group of shearers at the old rate, and they promptly walked off the station, declaring it 'black'. It was the first confrontation of an industrial war that would last until October. At Charleville an AWU organiser claimed that six sheds had started at the old rate; the Queensland United Graziers Association responded that all its members stood firm, and would only accept shearers at the new rate. The UGA claimed that 'very substantial' numbers of sheds were working at the new rate. UGA president William Gunn optimistically declared that the strike was 'breaking down'. However, the dispute spread beyond Queensland after 5 March, when the new rate applied in the southern States. Without a trace of irony, or at least some recollection of the catch-cry 'freedom of contract!', the *Pastoral Review* bitterly criticised the AWU for attacking arbitration 'nationwide'. The AWU had 'dishonoured an agreement and defied the law'. The *Review* hoped that the AWU rank and file wouldn't follow the union's example and defy the court. Perish the thought.[5]

Across Australia, shearers and graziers renewed the battle of the woolsheds. In March, Queensland graziers flew 200 scab shearers and shed-hands from southern States to work at seven central Queensland stations. A reporter who travelled with them on the plane recorded that 'the shearers and shedhands, all of them young men, sat grim and silent. When the plane arrived at Charleville they were told to go straight to waiting cars and to ignore anyone who tried to stop them'. Trying to stop them proved a time-consuming task for AWU Western District secretary Watson and his organisers. Based at Longreach, they patrolled hundreds of sheds around Longreach and Hughenden. At many stations they visited, the manager or owner refused them entry, despite the fact that they could produce written authorities under the Queensland Conciliation and Arbitration Act giving them the right to enter any place where union members were working. At several stations they were assured that physical force would be used against them if they attempted to enter the shearing shed. At one station, Uanda, however, organiser McKitrick was able to get access to the shearers working at the new rate. He reported to Watson that 'this team is not what you would call an intelligent lot and seem to have no real reason for being there ... but seem to be under the influence of the employer'. The shed rep told McKitrick, rather lamely, that 'if the sheep were not shorn they would be all dead and there would be no sheep to shear next year'. At least some of the men who travelled from the southern States to shear as scabs in Queensland also subsequently wondered why they went. The shearing contractors Grazcos, and other contracting companies and state Graziers Associations, enticed southerners north with the promise of good work at award wages (new rates) and all expenses paid, despite the fact that many of these men had little or no shearing experience. Many of the men who signed up were advised to use assumed names. Reg Readon of Braidwood in New South Wales signed on as 'Reg Magnusson'. He was flown to Longreach then transported by car to Maneroo Station. He was quickly disillusioned. 'I left the shed because I do not like the conditions we are working under. I thought everything was alright when I came to Queensland. After arrival and when I found out what the position was, I had to work to get sufficient money to return to NSW. I was a learner shearer and signed as a shearer ... Most Maneroo men came from Melbourne and the cost of plane service to land them at Longreach was £1,140.'[6]

Among several Melbournites who travelled to Maneroo station was William Rayner ('Bill Mathews'). He signed on as a shed-hand ('I have worked in the Industry for about 4 months since coming out of the Army'), and throughout his journey north, and while at the station, he was kept well away from any potential contact with AWU officials. At his hotel room in Brisbane, 'Grazcos had pickets on all doors to see we did not get through. I endeavoured to get over town but was stopped on every occasion'. At Maneroo Station the manager told the arriving workers that 'there are two locked gates; we do not want to cause any trouble between you people and the Union'. But there were apparently some consolations for the inconveniences. 'On arrival at Maneroo we were given cold beer free.' Rayner endured two and a half weeks' enforced isolation at Maneroo, but not before he and the other 'visitors' fell out with management over a refusal to shear wet sheep. The Boss of the Board cursed their ingratitude. 'That is the greatest bastard of an act to put on after paying you double time for Monday. The sheep are not even wet.' Finally, feigning illness, Rayner made his way to Longreach and reported his dismal experiences to the AWU. Like many other promises made to him by the eager graziers and their agents, the offer of free beer proved illusory. He told the union, 'Wages statements shows [sic] entries made for purchase of cordials. This is in fact Melbourne Bitter Ale and I was charged 6/- per bottle ... Eleven shearers were doing about

900 sheep per day. The food was far from good and not up to shearing shed standard'. Many unionists felt little sympathy with the scabs who tried to take their jobs, and there were occasional outbursts of brawling between scabs and strikers, particularly in Queensland, where the strike went on for several months longer than in the southern States. In Blackall, a group of thirty new-rate shearers who came to town for a drink were asked to leave the town after a confrontation with old-rate shearers. An estimated crowd of 300 farewelled them with 'get out of town, you scabs!' But not all scabs, or potential scabs, were judged harshly; strikes attract both the opportunists and the simply desperate. In September Watson reported to branch secretary Joe Bukowski the case of Clifford Eric Meharg, a 16-year-old from Brisbane who had been battling to support himself and his mother, who was struggling to pay back rent and hire-purchase payments on furniture. He had been lured west by the promise of £17 a week wages. He was given rail fare to Longreach from the Brisbane UGA office, 'and informed he would be met at Longreach and looked after for all times if he was prepared to stick to his job'. At Longreach he was in fact met by a local railworker, who advised him to visit the local AWU office before doing anything else. After talking to Watson he decided to return to Brisbane, his fare paid this time by the local strike committee. Watson asked Bukowski if a job could be found for him. A week later Bukowski told Watson that 'he has been found a job under the Sawmilling Award; and should now be all right'.[7]

In New South Wales the Bourke strike committee made a shrewd choice when they put Neil Byron on as their organiser at the beginning of the strike. According to him, 'we had only two sheds that escaped us in Bourke and they were both flood bound. We tried to get them to knock off but they had them too well trained – cockies' sons'. Some scabs were easier to get at. When trains arrived at Bourke station, Byron would stride along the platform, yelling, 'Anybody for Grazcos?' Eventually the graziers got wise to this, and told the scabs to get off further down the line at Byrock. Not to be outdone, Byron and a carload of AWU members chased them there, only to find that they had missed them, and the locals either didn't know which way they'd gone or were unwilling to tell the AWU loyalists. Such was the case with one local couple until their small child pointed in the direction of Brewarrina: 'Yes daddy, I've seen them, they went this way ... We had to inspect all the bloody gates to Brewarrina ... and we found them at a shed about ten miles out of Brewarrina. They were just ready to start shearing and we put on a bit of demo, went into town and got a few of the boys, and the owner sacked them all'. Both sides indulged in 'stretching' the law in order to prevail during the dispute, and sometimes the law was stretched a long way. At one point several truckloads of 'black' wool were hijacked and burnt just outside

Bourke. Neil Byron was charged and convicted with malicious damage. 'I couldn't get a job anywhere after the '56 shearers' strike. The cockies were in the court; as soon as they found me guilty, the cockies went 'hooray!' ... I couldn't get another job in the town, orders were out through Grazcos and the union was no help, and I went to an old chap who had a vegetable garden.' Byron worked at the vegetable garden outside Bourke while maintaining his position as local AWU committee secretary. But Byron, who had been a Communist Party supporter since the 1940s, was out of favour with the AWU leadership. 'The union didn't want me as the bloody rep.' Nevertheless he continued to look after the local members until ill health forced him from this post in 1965.[8]

Reg Mawbey, then a young shearer who later served as an organiser under NSW Branch secretary Charlie Oliver, believed that Oliver played an important role in the strike. 'Charlie was out among the shearers', Mawbey recalls, 'meeting them and talking to them and putting the proposition that we shouldn't have an all-out stop, we should just say we'll shear your sheep if you pay us the old rate'. Mawbey remembers Oliver's ability to sway a difficult meeting. 'He had some pretty terrible meetings. You always had a group that wanted an all-out strike, and Charlie used to be able to swing the meetings ... he said you're not dealing with a strike in the normal sense of having a factory [where] you can picket the gates. We've got 40 000 gates in New South Wales to picket.' Following Oliver's tactics, Mawbey says that 'I never walked out of any place where they didn't get the old rates'.[9]

Errol Hodder believes the decision by the AWU to agree to work, providing old rates were paid, was 'a master stroke'. Hodder was a 15-year-old learner shearer in Roma in southern Queensland when the dispute began, and soon became involved in the waiting game played by the local strike committee. 'What we were determined to do was not to vacate the shearing halls and let the scabs take our work from us. We agreed to work providing we got the old rate, and we paid a 10 per cent levy in strike funds.' This way they could support members placed in financial difficulty by the strike. If shearers had unilaterally refused all work, 'I don't think that strike would have lasted very long at all'. The men could get by with at least some work at sheds willing to pay the old rate, but such a strategy could only succeed if members could afford to hold out for a prolonged period. Hodder comments: 'I guess to some degree your cost of living might have been less, but basically you wouldn't find people with the same financial commitments that they have today, in terms of a capacity to run a strike for ten months'.[10]

In Victoria, another chapter was being written in the traditional struggle between Western District graziers and their shearers and shed-hands. On 21 April thirty AWU members met at the Casterton Fire

The conditions of the shearing industry of the mid-twentieth century were little changed from those of the late nineteenth. Shearing shed technology, like that at Benangaroo, NSW (above), had not changed since the introduction of Wolseley's shearing machine in 1888 and shearer's tucker (below) followed an established tradition of presentation and content – seen here at Wanbanumba Station, Young, NSW. *National Library of Australia.*

Station, and sent an 'urgent request' to the union to meet with the graziers. The Casterton Branch members, who worked both the Western District of Victoria and south-east South Australia, also expressed their frustration at the vagaries of the arbitration system, resolving that AWU representatives meet with graziers 'outside the arbitration system to settle this dispute'. Branch members were also determined to ensure that anyone who worked at the new rate would be blacklisted. They wanted action taken against the contractors Austral Shearing for applying the new rate, an offer which must have enticed some shearers. Austral Shearing sent out telegrams to the shearers on their books, and John Tuffnell, a Casterton shearer, received the following temptation in May 1956:

> Just a short note re shearing. Would you care to accept a pen starting in July at Heds Corner and continuing down to the South East. We will be paying current award rates as instructed by all the owners.
>
> At present there are over 350 men working at these rates in SA and more and more are offering for work every day.
>
> Please let us know as soon as possible.

Apparently John Tuffnell succumbed. On 19 May the Casterton strike committee placed his name on the blacklist.

Months after the strike ended, the Casterton strike committee was still trying to establish the identity and breaches of scabs in their area, and resolved that 'no member of the AWU work with anyone that worked at scab rates during the recent dispute'. Brahma Davis did what he could to help them, and in August, a month after the strike was settled outside Queensland, told the committee what he knew about two scabs who had worked various stations around Hamilton, including one owned by the Nareen Pastoral Co.: 'It is interesting to note also that one of the members of Nareen Pastoral Co. is J. Malcolm Fraser who appears to be the Federal Member who came out strongly supporting the shearers at the beginning of the dispute and who subsequently changed his views.' Casterton members were angry with Davis's Victoria-Riverina Branch over the matter of the blacklist, indicating the depth of feeling the strike had engendered in their local region. They wanted the branch to forward to them a list of scabs for Victoria, New South Wales and South Australia, but the branch office advised that this would be 'dangerous'. When the strike was settled on 28 June, the union agreed to lift all bans and limitations; any continued action against scabs would prejudice the union's arbitration case for an increase in pastoral award rates. Enemies were now, if not friends, at least parties the union could live with. 'There is nothing to prevent the men concerned shearing for Austral, or Grazcos and certainly the Union would not penalise the men for doing so. I think the matter should be left to the

judgement of the men individually at the present stage.' This did not satisfy
all Casterton members. In October a motion was put to censure 'our
officials' for lifting the bans and limitations on scab shearers and
contractors. But an amendment was carried supporting the union's action
and recommending carrying out local bans to 'try to win members from
"black" contractors'.[11]

The AWU and the graziers continued to exchange claim and counter-
claim over the number of sheds working at new or old rates, but it was
clear by mid-year that the graziers could not decisively break the union's
support among the shearers. In June the *Pastoral Review* described the
situation as 'complex and chaotic'. They cursed a lack of Federal Government intervention to aid their cause. Immediate government action was
required 'to avert widespread unemployment and a complete breakdown
of the arbitration machinery'. In March, Commissioner Donovan had
inserted an anti-strike clause in the Federal Pastoral Industry Award, but
this had little impact in the shearing sheds. Federal Labour and Industry
Minister Harold Holt complained that he needed to boost the Arbitration Court's penal powers in light of the boilermakers' case. In 1956 the
Boilermakers Society, a manufacturing industry union, challenged the
authority of the Commonwealth Arbitration Court in the High Court of
Australia. The High Court found that the Commonwealth could not set
up a court which had both legislative and judicial functions. This resulted
in these functions being split between the new Conciliation and Arbitration Commission and the Commonwealth Industrial Court. Meanwhile
the shearers' strike ran its course, and the *Pastoral Review* echoed the
pastoralists' rhetoric of the 1890s as it cursed the legal complexities
which beset graziers. 'It should, of course, be unnecessary for a government to intervene with directives in industrial disputes, but our
modern democratic state is so tangled with Federal, State and industry
wage-fixing tribunals – all created by politicians – [that] an industry itself
is frequently powerless to act effectively owing to a conflict between
different laws.'[12]

The boilermakers' case was not the only High Court decision to
influence the strike. In June 1956 the High Court ruled that in his
February decision to reduce shearing rates and wages, Commissioner
Donovan had exceeded his authority by extending his decision to
include non-unionists. The preference-for-unionists clause in the award
only entitled him to make an award for members of the Australian
Workers Union. This in turn had a devastating impact on the graziers'
efforts to defeat the AWU in the woolsheds. The effect of the decision
was that non-unionists – scabs – could not be paid the 'new' reduced
shearing rate. As the AWU's solicitor, Cecil O'Dea, gleefully explained to
*Worker* readers: 'This was because such employment [of non-unionists] is

governed by the [NSW] State Pastoral Award, which requires payment of the old rates. All non-unionists employed by graziers at the new 1956 rates have been employed illegally and in breach of the State Award, in which case graziers are exposed to prosecution at the instance of the AWU or of the state authorities'. Hence New South Wales graziers had no incentive to resist AWU claims: they could no longer resort to employing cheaper non-union labour. The shearing rate under the New South Wales award was £7 9s 6d, considerably higher than the federal award rate. The president of the Graziers Federal Council conceded that 'since there are no practical or legal means of distinguishing between unionists and non-unionists, the task of disproving a claim by a worker that he is a non-unionist is impossible'. Graziers would be forced to pay the old rate to everyone who sought it, including AWU members covered by the federal award.[13]

By the end of June, the graziers' resolve was worn away by the High Court, after months of inconclusive struggle in the woolsheds and on the wharves. A ban by storemen and packers had indefinitely postponed the Sydney wool sales; £2 million worth of wool was lying in store, unable to be shipped to buyers. Of an estimated 59 million sheep in New South Wales, only 12 million had been shorn since March. In desperation, the Graziers Federal Council applied on 6 June for an *increase* in the award shearing rate; they sought to apply a 10s basic-wage increase to the award. It was the first time in the history of Commonwealth arbitration that pastoral employers had made an application to increase rates and wages. The AWU insisted that they wanted the old rate or better. The 10s increase would only bring the shearing rate up to £7 1s 6d per 100. The increase was nonetheless granted by the Arbitration Court, but it was too late to head off the effects of the High Court's rejection of Commissioner Donovan's decision. The shearing strike finally ended, in all States except Queensland, with Donovan's decision of 28 June 1956 to bring the Federal Award into line with the NSW State Pastoral Industry Award: £7 9s 6d per 100.[14]

While the AWU had faced an industrial challenge in the pastoral industry on a scale not seen since the 1890s, a political threat to the leadership from internal militants did not materialise. AWU opposition to the ALP industrial groups and their supporters since 1954 ensured that the Communist Party supported the AWU's struggle with the graziers, while the union also enjoyed unprecedented support from peak councils such as the ACTU and the Queensland Trades and Labour Council. *Tribune* declared that 'the pastoral dispute reveals that the policy of the AWU is in a welcome process of change to meet the times'. The union was moving away from a 'slavish' commitment to arbitration, with many AWU officials attacking the arbitration system during the course of

the dispute. *Tribune* also sought to encourage greater rank-and-file participation. 'Local committees [should] be strengthened and transformed
into permanently functioning bodies.' *News-Weekly*, the industrial
groupers' champion, took a jaundiced view of this rapprochment between the AWU and its former left-wing enemies. In July the Queensland
AWU, appreciative of the support it had received from the Queensland
TLC during the strike, decided to affiliate with the TLC, from which it
had disaffiliated in the early 1930s, critical of its lack of 'appropriate'
representation (while other unions feared AWU dominance). The
Queensland TLC was militantly left-wing in outlook, and its secretary in
1956, Alex Macdonald, was a communist. *News-Weekly* described AWU
affiliation as 'one of the greatest industrial somersaults in Queensland's
industrial history'. The AWU was apparently content to affiliate, with just
8 votes at TLC meetings. 'Many trade union officials are asking whether
it is the price for Communist support in the Labor Party dispute.' In
Queensland, the fight between the supporters of the disbanded
industrial groups and their enemies began to blur with the tense stand-
off of the shearers' strike, which dragged on month after month.[15]

The support of the broad labour movement nationwide contributed
greatly to the AWU's success in the strike. Co-ordinated efforts, particularly in the transport sector, were sufficient to overcome the graziers'
efforts to shear their wool and transport it to market. Even if the station
manager could rally his neighbours – or scabs – to help shear his sheep,
he faced the logistical dilemma of transporting his 'black' wool to port.
On 27 February the Queensland TLC disputes committee voted to ban
all wool shorn by non-union labour, and the members of the Transport
Workers Union, the Australian Railways Union, the Storemen and
Packers Union, the Waterside Workers Federation and the Seamen's
Union would refuse to handle or ship it. The UGA bravely promised to
find alternative means of transporting their members' wool. In the other
States, Dougherty's ally in New South Wales, TWU secretary Barney Platt,
promised the support of his union, as did the TWU's Federal Committee
of Management. The Commonwealth Council of the left-wing Amalgamated Engineering Union, the largest of the manufacturing industry
unions, also promised that its members would withhold maintenance
from any aircraft which graziers might try to use to overcome road, rail
and sea transport bans (the national executives of the WWF, ARU and
the Seamen's Union had also promised support for the AWU). These
bans had the desired effect. In June the *Pastoral Review* described how the
'spotlight' of the union campaign was shifting from the woolsheds to the
wharves, where the AWU and their 'friends' in the transport unions,
'mainly communist wreckers', were bringing the wool industry to a
standstill. The tables of 1890 had finally turned. In 1956 there would be

no triumphant procession of graziers, protected by the forces of the state, to the Sydney wharves.[16]

In Queensland the dispute worsened as the year progressed. In April, the Brisbane wool sales were cancelled; 50 000 bales of wool were held at country rail stations and stores, unable to be shipped. It was estimated that the railways had lost £100 000 in freight revenue. Various attempts at negotiations between the UGA and the AWU broke down; Queensland AWU secretary Harry Boland and president Joe Bukowski were both fined £100 for their role in the 'illegal strike', as it had been defined by a decision of the Queensland Industrial Court. In May heavy rains fell across western Queensland, and sheep, which had not been shorn for seventeen months, died beneath loads of up to 23 pounds of long muddy fleece, and graziers complained of a massive financial loss through either lost stock or unsold, stockpiled wool. On 3 July, as the strike was ending in other States, the Queensland Industrial Court removed the preference-for-unionists clause from the State Pastoral Award, encouraging the UGA to begin a new drive for non-union labour, and even arranging for training learner-shearers (rather optimistically, given the time it would take them to acquire any degree of skill).[17]

As the economic difficulties in Queensland began to compound be-cause of the prolonged dispute, the unions fell out with Gair over his efforts, co-ordinated with the Menzies Government, to reschedule the disrupted September wool sales, and guarantee the delivery to buyers of wool shorn at the new rate. The government did not specify how this would be done (given the union bans), and the unions speculated that troops would be used. Dougherty declared that Gair would go down in labour history as the only Labor premier to connive with an anti-Labor Federal Government to undermine a union campaign. On 23 September a meeting of Queensland unions demanded that Gair 'get onside' with their campaign. Gair responded that while he would answer to the labour movement, 'I am not over-awed by the Communist dominated meetings at the Trades Hall'. He also announced he was convening fresh talks between the UGA and the AWU. These 28 September talks also ended in failure. While the UGA was willing to accept Gair's proposal to settle the dispute by a mutual acceptance of the new Federal Award rate of £7 9s 6d per 100, the AWU would not accept less than £7 13s 3d per 100, a shilling less than the rate which applied before the court's 10 per cent cut in November 1955. Bukowski told the meeting that 'the man shearing in Queensland was entitled to more than the man down below. There were broken spells in Queensland shearing, against good runs-through in New South Wales and Tasmania, and heavier costs of travel in this state because of the distances involved'. The failure of the talks meant con-frontation over the wool sales, which began on 2 October, with

£1 750 000 worth sold on the first day, none of which would be moved by striking storemen and packers. 'Hundreds' of graziers threatened to take matters into their own hands, and transport it from the woolstores themselves. Finally, on 4 October, Gair declared a state of emergency, and ordered the strikers to return to work, and in a secret ballot they voted to do so. Dougherty commented that 'Gair has shown that he is in collaboration with the enemies of the trade union movement'.[18]

On 9 October Gair issued a proclamation enabling the Industrial Court to reopen Pastoral Award hearings, and on 12 October the court increased the shearing rate to £7 11s per 100 – the highest rate applying in Australia. The next day, meetings of shearers at Longreach and Charleville voted to accept the increase and to end the strike, and the TLC voted to lift all bans. Bukowski also called for the removal of all 'free labour' (non-unionists) from Queensland shearing sheds, and no victimisation of any unionist involved in the dispute. The *Pastoral Review* complained that the Queensland Industrial Court had 'succumbed to the strong arm tactics used by the AWU'. By reopening the Industrial Court proceedings on 9 October, Gair had finally conceded his inability to extract a compromise from the AWU. The protracted nature of the dispute, and the increasingly bitter and intemperate exchanges between the unions and the government, left many in the unions believing that Vince Gair was an enemy of industrial labour. It was a judgement reinforced by several other protracted disputes and personal animosities. A few days before the strike ended one commentator observed that the dispute had moved a long way from a test of strength between the AWU and the graziers. 'The present strike is bound to be settled, but not the private war between Mr. Gair and Mr. Bukowski.'[19]

### Queensland: the 1957 Split

The key figure in the gathering crisis of Queensland Labor was Joe Bukowski. He seems to glower incredulously from old *Worker* photos, suspicious that the observer might not look at the world in precisely the same terms as Joe Bukowski. He had strong and simple ideas of right and wrong, friend and foe. Physically, he was the epitome of the Queensland AWU organiser, the tough enforcer of AWU rules whom Clarrie Fallon had hand-picked in the northern Queensland canefields in 1935. It was a reputation Bukowski relished, as the Queensland *Worker* noted. 'Mr. Bukowski has been in some of the toughest union spots in the history of the state and was responsible for cleaning up Communists who were attempting to get control of the sugar fields and the industry.' In this role Bukowski acquired a reputation as 'Midnight Joe' for his alleged habit of visiting recalcitrant agitators in the night and dispensing summary justice

The big men of the AWU at the Labor Day March in Brisbane, 1952 (left to right) Brisbane *Worker* editor Jack McCarter, general secretary Tom Dougherty, Queensland Branch president Joe Bukowski and Queensland Branch secretary Harry Boland. *Noel Butlin Archives, Australian National University.*

with his fists. With Fallon's encouragement he became the Southern District secretary in 1942, the largest and most powerful of the Queensland AWU's districts. He became State president in 1951, and in July 1956, at 55 years of age, he took over as Queensland Branch secretary upon the sudden death of Harry Boland. He also inherited Boland's position as president of the Queensland Labor Party.[20]

Harry Boland had a reputation as a likable and effective official, with a mischievous streak of Irish humour. As *Worker* editor Jack McCarter wrote in an affectionate obituary, 'you never knew whether he meant it or not'. Conciliatory by nature, he would try to sooth divisions within the union and the Labor Party. Life's harmonious ironies were somewhat lost on Joe Bukowski, and several of the senior AWU officials who served under Boland and Bukowski found the adjustment to the new boss difficult. Edgar Williams was the Northern District secretary when Bukowski became State secretary. 'We never saw eye to eye. Joe was a standover man.' Bukowski feared the rivalry of some of his colleagues, particularly Williams and Far Northern District secretary George Pont, from whom Bukowski had taken the AWU branch presidency in 1951. Williams recalls two unannounced trips Bukowksi made to his office in Townsville during the 1950s, apparently with the intention of finding some pretext for sacking Williams as district secretary. 'The train used to land in Townsville at six o'clock in the morning, and on both occasions I just happened to be walking along the platform and said, "Hello Joe, what are you doing here?" But his purpose in coming up was to sack me. That's how intense it was.' Gerry Goding, the Central District secretary, became AWU branch president in 1956. Of all the district secretaries, Goding was the closest to Bukowski, whom he says 'never asked anybody to do what he wasn't prepared to do himself. He was a hard worker'. Nevertheless, he saw a change in Bukowski once he became State secretary. 'In my opinion he was going to make the Union a one-man show and nobody else had a say.' There were those who did have influence with Bukowski, and in 1956 Jack Egerton, the Queensland secretary of the Boilermakers Society, and George Whiteside, the secretary of the Federated Engine Drivers and Firemen's Association, were both close to Bukowski, an allegiance forged in the co-operation between the AWU and the TLC in the shearers' dispute and fed by mutual antipathy to Vince Gair. George Pont saw it this way: 'I couldn't talk to Bukowski because he had then become friends with Egerton's crew and the Trades Hall ... They became bosom friends and nothing would take away the destruction of Gair. Nothing'.[21]

The prolonged dispute over union demands for the Gair Government to legislate to introduce three weeks' annual leave for Queensland workers finally broke the bond between the industrial and political wings of Queensland Labor, and paved the way for another disastrous Labor split. In February 1956 (an election year in Queensland) the three weeks' leave issue reached its first crisis point. The ALP's Labor-in-Politics Convention at Mackay (the Queensland ALP's Annual Conference) saw the unions take decisive control of the local party, to the virtual exclusion of Labor parliamentarians. The traditional alliance between the politicians and the AWU had fragmented: the AWU voted with the TLC unions in an anti-grouper alliance. Only three parliamentarians, including Gair, now sat on the Queensland Central Executive of the party. They faced eleven unionists. This was not the only problem posed by the Convention for the Gair Government. Some of the TLC unions, led by Egerton, were pushing for a showdown at the Convention with Gair on the three weeks' leave issue, demanding its immediate implementation by the government. Gair, irritated by these increasingly belligerent union demands for action, threatened to resign.[22]

George Pont was one of the Convention delegates sent to negotiate with Gair over the three weeks' leave issue.

> We met with Gair and Duggan, [who] was Minister for Railways and Deputy Premier. We argued the point for some time and Gair sort of gave in. Duggan jumped up and said, 'Mr. Premier, do you know what you've done to the budget for the Railway Department? You've killed the Railway, that actual three weeks annual leave will destroy the Railway'. I was sitting between Gair and Duggan and I turned to Jack. I knew Jack Duggan very well and I knew his politics, and right to the limit he was right-wing. I said, 'Whose side are you on, Jack?' just like that. And he turned around and did he get up me – 'I'll have you know that I'm as good a Labor man as ever drew breath in this country, but the Premier has just done something without consideration and he'll just destroy the Railway budget'. So we kept on arguing the point about it and all of a sudden Gair turned to me and he said, 'I'll introduce three weeks annual leave; come down to the pub and we'll drink on it.'

Pont recalls that Gair insisted on a face-saving resolution to be brought before Convention, and warned that he could not accept dictation about the timing of the legislation, a demand he repeated during the fiery debate on the issue at the Convention. Jack Egerton provided Gair with a clear indication of the gulf which divided political and industrial Labor in Queensland in 1956. 'There is much logic in what the Premier said, but the time for logic has disappeared ... we will not presume to direct the Government. But we will presume – and only because it is forced upon us – to direct the parliamentary representatives of the Australian Labor Party.' Eventually Convention adopted a compromise amendment put forward by Gerry Goding, the AWU's Central District secretary, requiring Gair to implement the leave entitlement in the first parliamentary session after the State election, due some time in 1956. Goding says his intention was to both defuse the immediate crisis and give Gair some breathing space. But he did not expect the parliamentary party to put off the reform indefinitely. 'Gair always said that he promised that he would implement the three weeks' annual leave when the economy was right but nobody had put on record who was going to decide when the economy was right.'[23]

As the shearers' dispute intensified throughout 1956, so did Bukowski's wide-ranging attacks on the Gair Government. On 1 October, as Gair threatened to impose a state of emergency to end the dispute, the Queensland *Worker* reported that meetings of shearers declared that they no longer supported the Labor Premier; and Bukowski made 'sensational' claims about Gair's alleged links with the 'Santamaria movement'. Bukowski said that given Gair's performance at the 1955 Hobart ALP Conference, he 'would not be surprised if the Premier broke with Official Labor' and joined the new DLP. Bukowski also alleged that Gair had received £12 000 from 'sources outside the Labour movement' to help

fight the May 1956 election. In December Bukowski also alleged in the
*Worker* that Gair intended to block any AWU candidate for the current
vacancy on the Queensland Industrial Court. Declaring that he was not
interested in the job for himself, Bukowski asserted the right of the AWU
to claim the job, and listed his own qualifications, citing the demands of
servicing 300 AWU awards. He concluded: 'I wonder could the Premier
handle them and at the same time satisfy the membership? Without being
egotistical, I'm sure I could do Mr Gair's job, and I'm sure that any high
official of the AWU could carry out the work of any Cabinet Minister'. The
antipathy between Gair and Bukowski was said to go back to the
playground of the Christian Brothers College at Rockhampton, where
Bukowski would torment Gair. Evidently Bukowski was still determined to
prove himself the better man.[24]

Gair, himself an obstinate man, was equally determined to uphold the
sovereignty of the Parliament. He had the support of his Caucus. After
the State election in May 1956, which Labor won comfortably, a worsening economic recession led to cuts in government expenditure. Faced
with these circumstances, on 26 September the ALP State parliamentary
Caucus voted 28:19 against introducing the three weeks' leave legislation.
Two days later both Bukowski and TLC secretary Alex Macdonald
attended the meeting organised by Gair in an attempt to end the
shearers' strike. Transport Minister Jack Duggan outlined the impact the
strike was having on the Queensland economy, emphasising that the
railways had lost £280 000 in revenue as the result of lost wool haulage.[25]

By early 1957 reasoned debate about the State economy or the timing
of the proposed three weeks' leave legislation became completely submerged beneath a welter of personal attacks, and conflicts over new
issues which intensified the crisis. Legislation covering controls on petrol
production and distribution and the administration of Queensland
University, of only marginal significance in themselves, became further
examples of Gair's failure to consult the party – at least in the opinion of
the already hostile Queensland Central Executive. Deputy Premier
Duggan (who was increasingly promoted as a successor to Gair) also
attracted party and union support by attacking the Petrol and Univer-
sities bills. Significantly, the Queensland AWU invited Duggan to address
its annual delegates meeting in January 1957 – an invitation usually
extended to the Premier. Of Duggan's address, the *Worker* noted, 'He hit
the nail right on the head when he said that any Labor Government
which imagined it could get along without the cordiality, assistance and
power of the AWU was only trying to have wool pulled over its eyes'. The
unity of the parliamentary Caucus was cracking. On 27 March the
Caucus voted for a proposal put forward by Duggan to hold a conference
on the three weeks' leave issue between the parliamentary party and the

QCE. However this conference failed to resolve the deadlock. Gair was apparently convinced that the QCE would not cross the line and expel him from the party. 'Certainly it wants to humiliate me, but it recognises the need for a Labor Government in Queensland.' On 18 April the QCE decided to summon Gair to a meeting on 24 April to explain why he should not be expelled from the Australian Labor Party for his defiance of the Labor-In-Politics Convention decision to legislate for three weeks' annual leave.[26]

Bukowski, in his role as Queensland ALP president, denied that the dispute over three weeks' leave was a personal vendetta between himself and Gair. All of his actions, he said, were guided by the majority decisions of the QCE. Some of Bukowski's colleagues in the AWU disputed the common sense of these QCE rulings, as George Pont remembers. 'I wasn't on the ALP executive but Edgar Williams was, and we decided that if they split the Labor Party in Government it would be a hundred bloody years before we'd become a Government again. We wanted to deal with him [Gair] but not to the extent of splitting the Government.' This view did not prevail. On 24 April the Queensland ALP Central Executive voted 35:30 to expel Gair.[27]

Both Gerry Goding and Edgar Williams voted against the motion, an unprecedented defiance of the AWU secretary (although technically, Williams was a QCE delegate from the ALP Convention, not the AWU). Edgar Williams encounted Gair at the entrance of the building (Dunstan House, which appropriately enough was also the AWU's headquarters) after the vote. '[Gair] shook hands with me and said, "I want to thank you for supporting me". I said, "Vince, I didn't support you, I voted against the ALP being split in half", and he dropped my hand like a dead fish and never spoke to me from that day on, excepting to be a bit nasty.' In better times both George Pont and he had visited Gair's home. But as Pont says, 'I never spoke another word [to Gair] from that day he split the Party'. Bukowski was undoubtedly angered by the defiance of his officials, and the *Worker*, announcing Gair's expulsion, carried the prominent page-one warning that 'the AWU is pledged to support ALP decisions and anyone who would attempt to breach that pledge is liable to be dealt with by the union and the ALP'.[28]

The expulsion of Gair led to a split in the parliamentary Labor Party, with twenty-five MPs – including eight Cabinet ministers – joining Gair's new 'Queensland Labor Party'. Duggan became ALP leader upon Parliament's resumption in June. The Gair Government was defeated in Parliament by the combined vote of the ALP and the Country–Liberal Party coalition, and elections were held on 3 August. Labor failed to regain office; Duggan lost his seat. The 'Queensland Labor Party' was reduced to a rump of seven, and thirty years of conservative government began. During the election campaign, Duggan enthusiastically promised to introduce three weeks' leave if elected to govern. Gair responded that 'Mr Duggan now poses as the champion of three weeks leave, but no one in the Cabinet and the Party was more opposed to such legislation at the present juncture than he was'. Gair claimed that Duggan changed his tune 'when big boss Joe and others started to wield the whips'.[29]

The lifelong habit of wielding the whip extracted a price from Joe Bukowski. He soon found the network of support he had built up with the TLC and the Labor Party beginning to crumble. Clyde Cameron, who had a wide range of contacts in the Queensland labour movement, says that Bukowski's behaviour became increasingly autocratic throughout 1958, particularly in his dealings with the TLC and the Queensland ALP, of which he remained president. 'He was issuing directives, threatening to sack people and trying to get rid of [ALP Branch Secretary] Jack Schmella.' He also clashed with the ALP over the party's decision to move out of Dunstan House, a decision which was prompted by Bukowski's insistence that ALP radio station 4KQ pay a higher rent for office space. The climax of a year of tension came at the ALP's Christmas party in December. Bukowski, who had been drinking, told the widow of a local ALP official that her husband had been a 'scab', during a minor industrial dispute. A heated argument broke out, with Bukowski threatening, and exchanging, blows with several people at the meeting. On 18 December Bukowski's membership of the ALP was suspended, and in turn Bukowski disaffiliated the AWU from the TLC and the ALP on 23 February 1959, claiming that the ALP executive was 'riddled with sectarianism, communist influence and inefficiency'. Clyde Cameron remembers that 'Jack Schmella and Jack Egerton were both delighted! They phoned to tell me what had happened saying they were glad the AWU had broken off its affiliation'. Only a few years before, Egerton had only been too pleased to cultivate Bukowski. His support against an intractable government was no longed needed; the AWU presence in the TLC was intimidating the smaller affiliates. The bond between Queensland political Labor and the AWU had been broken – at the cost of the Labor Government.[30]

Bukowski's hubris had been fed by a burning desire to assert his right to lead the AWU, and to lead the labour movement in Queensland. In his last years it had also been fed by an illness in body and spirit, reflected in repeated references to the onerous and stressful nature of his job in his speeches to the branches' annual delegates meetings in 1958 and 1959. Edgar Williams remembers when Bukowski told him that he was dying. 'I was down from Townsville and he said, "You've got to come down to the Southern District". I said, "No way, Joe, there is no way I'll come down [as Southern District secretary] while you're there". "Well", he said, "I'm going to die. If you want my job you've got to be here in the Southern

District to get it".' Bukowski had seen a specialist in Sydney, who had told him that he had a terminal illness. Williams accepted Bukowski's grim offer in late 1959, and in January 1960 he travelled to Brisbane for the delegates meeting. 'Five days later Bukowski went home, laid on the top steps and died.' Bukowski died on 20 January 1960, aged 58. His early death stunned the officials gathered in Brisbane for the delegates meeting. Edgar Williams succeeded Bukowski as branch secretary somewhat sooner than he had expected. 'I never had the opportunity of testing out whether his word would have stuck or not.' Perhaps it was just as well. Gerry Goding, whom Bukowski confided in, also knew that Bukowski was dying, and heard the bitterness which welled in him. 'He was going to destroy anything he could. He realised he was finished, and as he put it himself, he'd kill a lot before he went and he'd take a lot with him when he went'.[31]

Robert Murray has observed that 'men such as Dougherty and Bukowski seemed to have a strong sense that they were not attaining the same unquestioned power as Fallon, the man in whose shadow they lived'. During the late 1950s Bukowski liked to reprint flattering press stories about himself in the *Worker*, most of which praised 'Hard hitting Joe Bukowski, one of the really big men of Australia's trade union movement'. It was almost as if he didn't quite believe it himself, and was hoping that perhaps sheer repetition might confirm it. The 1950s had brought to a climax many of the long traditions and contradictions which had characterised the AWU and its relationship with the labour movement since the 1890s. In the course of those disputes many had trembled before the power of the AWU, but they did not always obey. And sometimes victory for the AWU's leaders was not always what it had promised to be, as Joe Bukowski found. The AWU resumed its isolationist stance in Queensland, just as it maintained independence from the ACTU, but its call in February 1959 for unions to join an anti-communist federation of unions fell on deaf ears. The AWU's SA Branch, which would frequently find itself at odds with the federal AWU in the 1960s, had already broached the unthinkable a year earlier by supporting a resolution at the Convention recommending ACTU affiliation. Dougherty reiterated the AWU's long-standing hostility to the ACTU, and his view again prevailed, but as one commentator noted in 1959, 'twenty years ago the AWU, with its isolationist policy, was able to set itself up as a rival to the ACTU and to wrest from the Liberal Federal Government equal concessions. Under later control much of this prestige has disappeared, until today the AWU operates more or less in the shadow of its previous political greatness'. During the 1960s the AWU would finally be reconciled to the ACTU, but the fight for the soul of its traditions would continue to be played out in the long vendetta of Clyde Cameron and Tom Dougherty.[32]

# CHAPTER 12

# Making the Truth Hurt

*The CMC, Mount Isa and Better Deal Challenges, 1960–69*

In 1960 political commentator Alan Reid described the AWU as a 'colossus'. Tom Dougherty presided imperiously over Australia's largest and wealthiest union with about 170 000 members and assets running into several million pounds. The Executive Council, Reid noted, was often flippantly referred to as Dougherty's 'College of Cardinals'. Comprised largely of 'the powerful, sometimes turbulent but (when their mutual interests are under fire) the aggressively defensive and toughly trained State Secretaries', his loyal 'college' added to the aura of invincibility surrounding the general secretary. In 1961 the Queensland AWU issued a special magazine celebrating the seventy-fifth anniversary of the AWU's formation, as the Australasian Shearers Union, in 1886. The publication reflected the AWU values which had endured down the years: the celebration of bushwork, White Australia, cradling the early Labor Party. Dougherty declared that the AWU stood 'pre-eminent as Australia's premier industrial union'.[1]

What did the national office of this mighty union look like? Wendy Pymont, who has served as private secretary to every general secretary since Tom Dougherty, started work for the AWU as a 15-year-old office junior in 1961. She remembers a dilapidated Macdonell House office in Pitt Street, Sydney, filled with second-hand furniture. 'Tom was great for putting up partitions and surrounding people', Pymont recalls, 'and everything got used. You never got anything new, because they'd wait for someone to move out and normally one of the tenants, if they left a table or a chair or a bit of a partition they'd come and put that up somewhere.

We never got new things, all the things we got were leftovers from all the tenants. We couldn't afford it'.

The union, or at least its related company, Labor Papers Ltd, had financial problems, a lingering consequence of the collapse of the *World* thirty years before. As a result the AWU occupied only a cramped suite on one floor of the eight-storey building. These days, national union offices are filled with industrial and administrative staff. In 1961 the federal AWU office had a staff of five, including three clerks. Dougherty 'was a kind of administrator', Pymont recalls. 'He spent a lot of time on the phone.' Bob Scott, an industrial officer, 'did everything else'. The federal office administered about twenty federal awards in 1961. A vast proliferation of State awards and agreements were handled by the branches. Pymont says that there was little automation in the AWU office, even by the standards of the time. Preparations for lodging a log of claims on 20 000 pastoral industry employers involved duplication, on a manually operated gestetner machine ('[Dougherty] wouldn't buy an electric one, oh no, they were too much') of 20 000 copies of a 50-page document. 'Everybody in the office used to take fifteen minutes on it, it took days and days to get it out.'

The union was Dougherty's life, to such an extent that by the late 1960s he was living in Macdonell House, his family having moved to Laurieton on the New South Wales north coast. As a result 'I had to do his shopping, buy his groceries, sew his buttons on'. Pymont recalls that Dougherty was active in the Sydney Masonic Lodge – 'he was into it seriously' – and that he had many friends in Sydney's Chinese community. Professor Harry Messel, the Sydney University nuclear physicist, was also a close friend. The Mandarin Club and the Masonic Club were popular Dougherty haunts. Pymont remembers a man who could intimidate, if only by reputation. As a teenager, she was a little awe-struck by him: 'I'd never met anybody quite so famous as him'. She recalls a young legal clerk, later a prominent NSW Labor parliamentarian, who 'used to actually quake in his boots' whenever Dougherty walked into the office. 'He was a big man, with a loud voice'. Yet she also remembers a kind, and later in life, lonely man. 'He was a great Australian. I wish I had known him as an adult; I was 27 when he died but you understand people as you get older.'[2]

The seventy-fifth anniversary was the high-water mark of the AWU leadership's unchallenged authority. Throughout the 1960s there was an intense reaction to the centralised control of the AWU by various dissidents in South Australia, Queensland and New South Wales, and indeed to Dougherty's power as general secretary. The link between these disparate expressions of dissent was Clyde Cameron, the former Adelaide Branch secretary and, since 1949, federal Labor backbencher, a man who believed the power of the AWU cardinals had to be restrained in favour of rank-and-file democracy, a man who, as the *The Voice of the Rank and File* (Cameron's dissident AWU journal) said in 1961, 'made the truth hurt'. Making the truth hurt resulted in a decade of fierce AWU infighting.[3]

## Cameron versus Dougherty

Clyde Robert Cameron was born at Murray Bridge in South Australia in 1913, the son of Robert Cameron, a shearer and founding member of the Amalgamated Shearers Union of Australasia. Cameron's mother was responsible for his early political education. She was a committed Christian, raised as an Anglican but later became a Quaker and embraced socialist principles. Cameron recalls that she would regularly raise political and social questions around the family dinner table. Cameron joined the AWU in 1928 when he became a rouseabout at the age of 15. He went on to shearing and was elected as an AWU organiser in 1938, becoming Adelaide Branch secretary in 1941. In 1946 he was elected president of the SA Branch of the Australian Labor Party. He won the federal seat of Hindmarsh for the ALP in 1949.[4]

According to Cameron, his dispute with Dougherty began when he failed to support the general secretary over a number of issues. Cameron was disturbed by the treatment meted out to Beecher Hay and the NSW Branch dissidents who defied Dougherty, leading Cameron to dissent from the Executive Council rulings which expelled Hay, Bowen and their allies. The Dougherty–Cameron tension was also exacerbated by Cameron's support for a rank-and-file campaign for the 40-hour week in 1946, and by several proposals from the Adelaide Branch to change the AWU's rules at the January 1950 Convention. (Although by then a federal parliamentarian, Cameron was still active in the AWU as vice-president of the Adelaide Branch and as a Convention delegate.) The most contentious of the changes proposed by the Adelaide Branch were a reaction to the 1940s purges; they were implicitly critical of Dougherty's control of the union. Although the motion was defeated, Cameron is convinced that these episodes marked the beginning of Dougherty's long campaign to seize any opportunity to engineer Cameron's expulsion from the AWU.[5]

In 1953 and 1957 Dougherty attempted unsuccessfully to develop grounds to expel Cameron, first over Cameron's failure to support Dougherty at a vote at the 1953 federal ALP Conference, and later over a claim that Cameron had provided journalist Alan Reid with 'untruthful' information about the AWU, including a story that Dougherty had obtained a £6650 loan at 1 per cent interest from Labor Papers Ltd for the purchase of a house. The minutes of Labor Papers Board of Directors meetings reveal that in July 1952 the board discussed buying a property 'which would suit the requirements of the General Secretary'. A price range of £6–7000 was deemed appropriate. On 17 April 1953 Dougherty purchased a Clovelly property (a beachside suburb of Sydney) at 2 Cliffbrook Parade from Labor Papers Ltd for £6676 6s 3d. Interest was set at 1 per cent, with quarterly rests in the repayments (the longer the period between calculating the interest on the principal, the greater the advantage to the debtor; hence quarterly rests were preferable to daily or weekly). He paid a £500 deposit and £9 a week repayments. Dougherty also paid a rental of £3 10s per week.[6]

A February 1953 board meeting also considered winding up the company. 'It was pointed out [that] the purpose for which the company was originally established, that is the publication of the Labor Newspaper, appeared to be no longer possible.' No final decision was made. Two years later the company was still in business, with directors' expenses set at a February 1955 meeting at £200 for the chairman and 110 guineas for other directors. Macdonell House expenses continued to burden the company. In 1958 Labor Papers Ltd spent £9000 on repairs and maintenance to the building. The ground and first floors had been vacant all year during negotiations to re-let, and then for a further period while the floors were renovated to suit the new tenants. The company showed an after-tax profit for 1958 of £991 16s 11d, which fell to £285 4s in 1959. Labor Papers Ltd was finally wound up in March 1966.[7]

The decisive clash between Dougherty and Cameron sprang from comments Cameron made in a speech in the House of Representatives during the Second Reading of the Conciliation and Arbitration Bill on 14 May 1958, a speech which returned to the debates at the 1950 AWU convention. Cameron described several deficiencies in the Menzies Government's legislation, particularly its failure to protect rank-and-file elected officials from suspension or dismissal by a union executive. While not mentioning a specific union, Cameron complained that it was no use having a court-controlled ballot 'unless there is vested in the persons so elected a right to remain in office untrammelled by the dictation of some czar at the top of the pyramid'. When asked if he was referring to the Australian Workers Union, Cameron was again vague, but explained that a certain union had rules which allowed the secretary to suspend, and the Federal Executive to dismiss, not only a rank-and-file elected official, but an entire State branch executive. He continued: 'It is true that the federal executive is, nominally, the body that does this, but, in practice, it is the tyrant at the top who actually makes the dismissals. The tyrant at the top of the pyramid, or whose wishes are carried out by the federal executive, adopts the usual Khrushchev method of giving effect to his dictates by the simple expedient of lopping off one official at a time'.[8]

Unsurprisingly, Dougherty drew the conclusion that the union Cameron was describing was the AWU and that he was the unnamed tyrant. In January 1959 the Executive Council formally charged Cameron under the misconduct rule and in July he was found guilty of the charge and was dismissed from membership of the union. The motion was opposed by the two SA Branch delegates (one of them was Cameron's brother Don, an SA Branch organiser), and the two Victorian Branch delegates. Cameron was given to understand that Brahma Davis, the Victorian Branch secretary, told his delegates that the charge against Cameron was 'an outrage' and that they ought to vote against it. Cameron decided to challenge the dismissal and eighteen of the union's rules in the Commonwealth Industrial Court on the grounds that they contravened the Arbitration Act and were invalid and unenforceable.[9]

On 30 November 1959, the Commonwealth Industrial Court found that nine rules of the eighteen challenged by Cameron were invalid. Another, which permitted the Federal Executive to take over a branch, dismiss its elected officials and appoint new ones, was declared inoperative, and five other rules dealing with AWU elections were considered by Chief Justice Spicer, on the the basis of the present conduct of elections by the AWU, not to conform to the secrecy provisions of the Commonwealth Conciliation and Arbitration Act. The court's decision was a real blow to Dougherty. He had sworn that he would get rid of Cameron 'come what may, legal or otherwise'. Dougherty was described as never having been seen as 'so overbearing and confident but he was riding for the biggest shock of this life'.[10]

Cameron's victory was incomplete. The judgment did not apply retrospectively, so the rule under which Cameron was expelled from the AWU was assumed valid at the time. Dougherty unsuccessfully appealed the November 1959 decision to the High Court, arguing that the Industrial Court had no jurisdiction to interfere in the internal affairs of the union. In the meantime, another court action in April 1960 resulted in Cameron's reinstatement as a member of the AWU and as vice-president of the SA Branch. The court decided that there was no material before the AWU Executive Council in July 1959 upon which 'reasonable men' could possibly reach the conclusion that Cameron was guilty of misconduct. The court's judgment was described at the time as sending 'a shock of amazement through union and labor circles through the country. The amazement was not at the judgement brought down, but at the political consequences'. Cameron's victories had dented the wall of autocracy which for almost fifty years had protected the centralisation of power in the AWU hierarchy.[11]

### The Council for Membership Control

Shortly after his expulsion Cameron announced to the AWU rank and file that he was establishing an organisation to fight the union's leadership. Called the Council for Membership Control, Cameron had planned its organisation, going so far as to have its letterhead printed, before he was expelled from the union by the Executive Council in July 1959. Dougherty responded to Cameron's push to 'clean up' the AWU by saying, 'Any organisation that Mr Cameron forms would be about the strangest ever, because he is no longer a member of the AWU ... I have no doubt about the loyalty of members to their elected officials'.[12]

Cameron set out to test that loyalty. On 16 August 1959 he addressed a meeting of about forty 'representatives and members of the AWU' at the Trades Hall at Broken Hill. Cameron spoke for two hours, alleging 'corruption, terrorism and tyranny within the AWU', and mentioned several members of the Executive Council of the AWU as the 'main perpetrators' of those actions. The meeting unanimously called for Dougherty's resignation and elected R. J. Hearne, a local AWU organiser, as the local representative of the CMC. In a circular letter issued by Cameron as honorary national secretary of the CMC, recipients were asked to distribute enclosed pamphlets explaining the court's finding on the AWU rules issue, and to seek financial assistance for the CMC from AWU members. The pamphlet also set out the objectives of the CMC: clean elections; protection for elected officials from dismissal for merely carrying out rank-and-file wishes; rank-and-file approval of all Industrial Agreements and Consent Awards made between the union and employers; closer cooperation with other unions whenever common interests were involved; reaffiliation with the Queensland ALP; affiliation with the ACTU; and organised support for candidates willing to fight for these objectives. The pamphlet concluded: 'Remember! The AWU is your union. It is not the private possession of a few power drunk individuals. Remember also that its paid officials are your *servants* and not your *masters*'.[13]

In February 1961 the CMC began publishing a newspaper entitled *The Voice of the Rank and File*, substantially written and edited by Cameron himself. The *Voice* vigorously pursued Dougherty, and the quest for a greater role for the rank and file in the conduct of AWU affairs. In its first issue, the editorial ran in part: 'In our opinion Dougherty has been the chief obstacle to the reforms which are needed to give AWU members a proper voice in the affairs of our union. It is for this reason that we give our kindly attention to TOM NICHOLSON PEARCE DOUGHERTY'. The campaign for cleaner ballots was a constant theme in the *Voice* between 1961 and 1963. Of particular concern was the AWU practice of requiring members to identify their ballot papers by a coupon which carried their respective membership numbers. In *Cameron v. The AWU* the court considered that AWU elections did not conform with the secrecy standards for union ballots provided for in Section 133 of the Conciliation and Arbitration Act. It was, however, open to members of trade unions, under the provisions of the Conciliation and Arbitration

# Growing Support For C.M.C.

## Publishes Own Paper

Rank and File support for the Council for Membership Control of A.W.U. ("C.M.C.") is quickening to such an extent that the C.M.C. is now able to publish its own paper.

OF THE RANK AND FILE

"The Voice of the Rank and File" (as the paper is called) will enable the C.M.C. to maintain regular contact with A.W.U. members all over Australia—the A.W.U. has about 140,000 financial members throughout Australia.

"The Voice" will actively campaign for A.W.U. affiliation with the A.C.T.U., constant loyalty to the A.L.P., the return of Labor Governments in both Federal and State Spheres, the right of A.W.U. members to determine Union policy, and to elect their officials and fill all Vacancies in a secret postal ballot free from corruption.

### LEADERSHIP

The paper will give leadership in political and industrial thought. It will set out to educate its readers on the principles of Socialism. It will show that in politics, choice is not limited to monopoly capitalism, or totalitarianism. There is another alternative — a vigorous and progressive Labor Party that will use socialistic means, democratically determined by the people, for ending the exploitation of man by man.

### TYRANNY

The C.M.C. is opposed to tyranny wherever it is found—whether it be in Government or in a trade union.

That is why it demands the repeal of those A.W.U. Rules which permit a Secretary to sack an elected organiser "if his services are not required" (Rule 59(d)) and for the Federal Executive to sack without notice and without trial any Secretary or member of an Executive (Rule 36).

Official Organ:
Council for Membership Control of A.W.U.,
Box 723 F, G.P.O., Adelaide.
February, 1961 — Price 6d.

# H.P. FOR ONLY 3 p.c.

S.A. Trade Unions have shown how to provide H.P. Finance at only 3 per cent. interest and at the same time pay a dividend of 5 per cent.

In his annual report to the 25 South Australian Trade Unions that have invested money in the Trades Union Hire Purchase Co-operative Society Ltd., the Society's Secretary, Mr. L. P. Noller, says, "We don't seek to make large profits. Our chief concern is to see that our members are given finance at the lowest possible rates."

The report goes on to state that the recent appeal to all unions to assist in providing £1,500 extra capital resulted in the subscription of more than £4,000 — increasing capital plus deposits to over £11,200. The Society has financed 256 transactions for goods valued at about £24,500.

Continuing, Mr. Noller reported that since the inception of the Society three years ago, it had made three successive profits, each one bigger than the year before. For the past two years shareholders had received a dividend of 5 per cent. The profit for last year, he said was £825 before tax.

### INTEREST REDUCED

"At the same time," said Mr. Noller, "the Society has progressively reduced the rate of interest to borrowers. Commencing in January, 1958, with a rate of 5 per cent. p.a. flat, the rate was later reduced to 4 per cent. and in July last, it was again reduced to 3 per cent. p.a. flat." This compares with the average rate of 10 per cent. flat charged by private H.P. Companies.

Mr. Noller reveals that in cases where the Society is able to buy at wholesale rates, it refunds the whole of the interest at the end of the hiring provided all instalments have been paid on or before the due date.

### PORT PIRIE

A.W.U. members at Port Pirie want their union to invest its surplus funds with the H.P. Co-op, so that A.W.U. members can enjoy the benefits of these greatly reduced interest charges. They sent a resolution to this effect to Annual Convention but "The Voice" can forecast its defeat.

# ANOTHER DEFEAT FOR MR. DOUGHERTY

In his campaign against Clyde Cameron, Labor M.H.R. for Hindmarsh (S.A.), Mr. Dougherty has suffered a long series of disappointments. First, Cameron succeeded in upsetting the "no canvassing" rule as well as eight other rules of the A.W.U.

Then Dougherty went to the High Court in an effort to prohibit the Industrial Court from making its order in Cameron's favour. He lost again!

His next set-back came when the Industrial Court declared that the Union had improperly expelled Clyde Cameron.

Not satisfied with these three defeats, he then decided to try his luck before the Privy Council in London. Mr. Dougherty briefed Mr. Eric Miller, Q.C., of Sydney, to go to London to put his case. But once again, he lost his case and the Union's money, when the Privy Council decided that Cameron was unlawfully expelled.

According to the "Nation", the first three cases will probably cost the union £15,000, and the Privy Council proceedings will run into another small fortune. Some of the members of the South Australian Branch Executive, whose names were linked with Mr. Dougherty's Privy Council appeal, knew nothing about their alleged application until they read of its failure in the daily newspaper.

CLYDE CAMERON, M.H.R.
SENIOR VICE-PRESIDENT
(S.A. BRANCH A.W.U.)

The *Voice*, the journal of the Council for Membership Control. The February 1961 edition was the first published by the CMC. *AWU Collection.*

Act, to petition the industrial registrar to conduct union ballots. A court-controlled ballot was conducted in 1964 for the position of general secretary which Dougherty won by a substantial margin against the CMC-supported W. L. Deuis. Deuis, a Broken Hill shearer, had previously challenged Dougherty in the 1961 ballot conducted by the AWU and lost by 3198 votes to Dougherty's 24 415. Deuis threatened a court challenge over the result on the grounds of irregularities in the ballot, a threat which may have had some bearing on the union's decision to agree to a court-controlled ballot three years later.[14]

The *Voice* pursued Dougherty relentlessly over a multitude of issues. The paper regularly reminded readers that Dougherty was the most highly paid union official in Australia, enjoying a salary of £4500 a year in the early 1960s. The March 1962 issue highlighted the fact that Dougherty had confirmed to Convention that year that £7500 in legal costs incurred in the Cameron case had been paid out of the AWU Fighting Fund. The CMC also took up the running in support of the campaign for a 35-hour week. In June 1963 the CMC observed that the AWU was leaving the fight for a 35-hour working week to the ACTU. The *Voice* reminded readers: 'AWU members have long since learnt that they must look to the ACTU for industrial reform'. Affiliation with the ACTU was a major plank in the CMC platform and a regular issue debated in the pages of the *Voice*.[15]

Dougherty tried several ways to encourage the wilful Member for Hindmarsh to concentrate on his parliamentary duties. The AWU Annual Convention of 1961 passed a resolution which prohibited any politician holding an official position in the AWU, to take effect by the end of that calendar year. Dougherty, speaking in favour of the motion, thought serving two masters incompatible: 'Should we wish to give our services and ability to the people of the Commonwealth and work in another capacity such as a politician, we should attempt to have ourselves elected through the different stages to that job. I honestly believe that you cannot combine the two and do a good job'. Dougherty himself was a member of the NSW Legislative Council and would have also been caught by this rule change. He maintained that this suited his campaign to abolish the chamber (and rid himself of Cameron), as he explained to the NSW Parliament: 'I am a Union official and have no intention of seeing my term out in this Parliament. I came in here to help carry out the pledge given to the Labor Party and work and fight for the abolition of this Chamber'. The NSW Labor Government subsequently supported a referendum to abolish the Upper House. It went before voters in April 1961 and was comprehensively lost. Dougherty, who had been the main sponsor of the Bill, was forced to resign from Parliament in order to retain his position as AWU general secretary. Cameron did not re-nominate as South Australian vice-president for 1962, being replaced by Eric O'Connor.[16]

The 1961 Convention also criticised the SA Branch in a resolution moved by the Queensland Branch secretary, Edgar Williams, Bukowski's successor. This resolution expressed 'concern' at the failure of the SA Branch executive to prevent the CMC committee being set up at Broken Hill (which although in New South Wales, had traditionally been included in the SA Branch boundaries), 'got up' by a 'self-confessed' communist, Jim Doyle, and of allowing a branch official (namely Clyde Cameron) to interfere with another branch. This referred to Cameron's attendance at meetings in south-western Queensland, where he was critical of the AWU and some of its officials. There was no debate; the motion that the resolution be referred to the Executive Council to take any action which they may consider necessary to 'protect the interests of the Union and the interests of the South Australian Branch' was carried unanimously. In the following year, Convention carried a further vote of no confidence in Cameron for his attacks on the union through meetings and through the *Voice*. Again it was left to brother Don to defend him, although it is somewhat difficult to accept that Cameron's activities were kept so clandestine that much credence can be given to his brother's assertion that so far as he knew, 'Clyde Cameron was not connected with the paper the "Voice" nor with any other attacks on the Union' (the Cameron brothers had some respect for Dougherty's enthusiasm for litigation; Clyde went to great lengths to conceal his personal association with the *Voice*, to the extent of only dealing with its printer, Messenger Press, through anonymous correspondence). The Executive Council declared the CMC and the *Voice* to be 'bogus', 'working against the interests of the Union and its members'. In April 1964 Dougherty forced Messenger Press through legal action to print a public apology in all major daily newspapers throughout Australia, and in the Broken Hill press and the two *Workers*, retracting any imputations of wrongdoing or irregularity against Dougherty in the exercise of the duties of his office. Messenger Press acknowledged it had 'recently been shown proof that the statements made in The Voice of the Rank and File disparaging Mr Dougherty should never have been made'.[17]

Meanwhile, a split had been developing within the ranks of the SA Branch leadership. Eric O'Connor, the long-serving branch secretary, began to to move against some of his own organisers. He did so largely at the behest of Dougherty, who had told O'Connor that these officials, principally Jack Wright and Don Cameron, were conspiring against him. In March 1964 O'Connor dismissed the popular Northern Region organiser, Jack Wright. A hundred and thirty AWU members at Port Augusta responded by calling for O'Connor's immediate resignation.

The meeting further resolved that if O'Connor failed to resign, or was not dismissed, by 23 March, then these members intended to 'dissolve partnership with the AWU'. The SA Branch executive acted swiftly and reinstated Wright. O'Connor refused to recognise the authority of this decision and appealed to the Executive Council. A further mass meeting in early April resulted in the withdrawal of the ultimatum to O'Connor contained in the earlier resolution, but only after State president Don Cameron and State vice-president Reg Groth assured the meeting that O'Connor was more than likely to be defeated in the ballot for State branch positions to be held in the middle of the year. The SA Branch elections held in July 1964 resulted in a reconstituted executive comprising, *inter alia*, Don Cameron as State secretary, Jack Wright as president, and Reg Groth and Jim Dunford as vice-presidents. Clyde Cameron claimed in his memoirs that 'we [the CMC] had captured control of the South Australian Branch in 1964', but Dunford declared to the AWU Annual Convention the following year that he was 'not associated with the CMC in any shape or manner'.[18]

Dougherty evidently agreed with Clyde Cameron's assessment of the 1964 election result. In January 1965 the AWU Annual Convention debated allegations that branch secretary Don Cameron failed to carry out certain of the rules of the union in relation to the conduct of the 1964 ballot. Convention carried a resolution which gave the Executive Council complete freedom of action in the conduct of an inquiry into the affairs of the branch. As far as Charlie Oliver was concerned, the imperative for the Executive Council was to cut out the CMC 'cancer'. 'The fact that there was a division in the South Australian Branch only meant added weight to their [CMC] activities.' The Executive Council decided that the recently elected SA Branch executive had indeed breached rules relating to balloting procedures and on 6 May 1965 dismissed all the elected officials, including Don Cameron, Jack Wright, Reg Groth, Jim Dunford, 'Rocky' Gehan and Mick Young. The Executive Council resolved to call fresh branch elections 'at such time as the Executive Council considers to be in the best interests of the Union and its good government'. Meanwhile it appointed officers from the WA and Queensland branches to administer the branch. Don Cameron, Groth and Wright were also expelled from the union. They promptly challenged the actions of the Executive Council in the Commonwealth Industrial Court in November 1965 and won. Clyde Cameron saw this court victory as one of the most significant defeats inflicted on Dougherty, and for many years after he and the SA AWU officials celebrated 'Smithers Day' on 29 November (named in honour of the presiding judge). Eric O'Connor had no cause to celebrate. In the wake of the defeat, Dougherty abruptly dumped him, leaving a rift between O'Connor and the Cameron brothers healed only shortly before

O'Connor's death in 1977. Reinstated branch secretary Don Cameron reported the year's events to his membership with considerable under-statement: 1965 was 'very eventful and one of great importance to this Branch'. Since the 1940s, the SA Branch had carefully walked a path of dissent from the Executive Council, and in 1965 a more assertive genera-tion of dissenters came close to complete defeat. Their survival ensured that the CMC maintained a support base in the AWU, from which renewed efforts to challenge Dougherty's control might be launched.[19]

### 'Head-On Impact': the Mount Isa Dispute

Mount Isa, progressing steadily since the days of the original discovery is today stepping up its rate of progress with undiminished optimism. And who knows, many a young Australian in the distant future will be able to thank his stars that one of his ancestors in a foreign land, decided to emigrate to this country and to establish himself as a new citizen at Mount Isa.[20]

Unrest in the Mount Isa mine in Queensland provided the greatest test for the AWU leadership during the 1960s. Rich in lead and copper, the Mount Isa mine had been worked since the late 1920s. The AWU covered about 70 per cent of the 4000-strong workforce. In the early 1960s, in-dustrial discontent among Mount Isa miners focused around the issue of bonus payments. Since 1937 the miners had received a 'lead' bonus in addition to award wages, the rate of which was tied to the world price of lead. In the eyes of the miners, the bonus, as Margaret Cribb observes, was important, 'for it was regarded in the [Mount Isa] community as partial compensation for the strains, stresses and cost of life in a harsh, isolated and difficult environment'. Like many Australian mining centres, Mount Isa was in a remote and arid region, a parched and starkly beautiful landscape of broken red hills and spinifex in western Queens-land. Mount Isa was a company town preoccupied with the fate of the mine and the good income miners and their families expected to extract from the hard work of underground mining. Many miners also came for the quick quid to be made from both the bonus and from contract work. As the 'Annual' produced in 1961 by the AWU's Queensland Branch observes, 'Men from almost every country on earth have flocked to Mt. Isa over the years. There have been Britishers, Americans, Lithuanians, Russians, Irishmen, Scotsmen, Italians, Germans, Poles, Finns ... one could go on indefinitely, and the Australian Workers' Union has been in the majority of cases their Union'. These itinerant miners, like their nineteenth-century forebears, could often be found in shearing sheds at other times of the year, or engaged in other forms of bushwork between spells down the mine. Hence labour turnover at Mount Isa was very high, a factor which complicated industrial relations for both Mount Isa Mines

Ltd and the unions. By 1951 the bonus had risen to a high of £17 5s a week, but with lower world prices this had fallen to £3 17s 6d in April 1959. Over the decade MIM had also cut lead production at the mine in favour of increased copper output, a change recognised in 1959 by the Queensland Industrial Commission. In line with the new production regime, the commission decided that the nexus with lead prices should be cut, and the bonus should be fixed at £8 a week.[21]

The Queensland political landscape had also changed. The Gair Labor Government had been destroyed by conflict with the unions in 1957. The Nicklin Country–Liberal Party Coalition was no friend of the labour movement, and in 1961 this became clear with changes to Queensland's Industrial Conciliation and Arbitration Act. A dual system was created with an Industrial Commission to arbitrate claims and an Industrial Court to hear appeals. The Act also restricted access to bonuses, describing them as 'payments in excess of a just wage'. The Act granted the commission power to reduce existing bonuses in awards but allowed no means of increasing them. Bonuses could still be created or increased, but this could only be done outside the award system, through direct bargaining between unions and employers. In fact the government's intention was to phase such bonuses out completely. MIM was unlikely to protest about the new legislation, and less likely to agree to further increases in the now fixed £8 a week bonus. MIM undoubtedly believed the existing bonus was more than generous. According to Geoffrey Blainey, 'shareholders whose willingness to invest had alone made Mount Isa profitable waited twenty-five years for the first dividend, and then in the following decade they got less in dividends than the employees got in lead bonuses'. Blainey says that many mining investors were anxious to stem the spread of bonus payments in the industry, and it seems that the Nicklin Government was sympathetic to these concerns. AWU Queensland Branch secretary Edgar Williams had his own views about the ramifications of the 1961 legislation for Mount Isa. He did not share the Nicklin Government's naivety about its ham-fisted attempt at industrial deregulation. Cutting off the bonus from the award system and award increases, Williams believed, would push 'those good supporters of arbitration into the "law of the jungle" and ... serve only the best interests of the Communist Party who are behind the move to destroy arbitration'.[22]

During the early 1960s the AWU made several claims on MIM for an increase in the bonus, which the company consistently refused. In November 1963 the AWU and the combined tradesmen's unions applied to the Industrial Commission for an increase in award wages of £4 a week, based on the prosperity of the company. But the Industrial Commission refused the application in August 1964, arguing that the claim simply amounted to the kind of bonus payment the commission was legally bound to reject. This knock-back was the last straw for the frustrated miners, and from this point the tactics of the local AWU rank and file and the union began to diverge. While the union mounted an Industrial Court appeal against the commission's decision, the men voted on 23 August to revert from contract work to wage work, a decision which would mean a wage cut of between £20 and £30 a week for them, but which would also have the effect of a 'go-slow', substantially reducing the mine's productivity. Mr Justice Hanger of the Queensland Industrial Court decided that this was little less than outright strike action. He refused to consider the AWU's appeal until the men resumed contract work. The AWU executive recommended to the Mount Isa membership that the contract ban be withdrawn to allow the appeal to proceed. This proposal was rejected by the rank and file at a mass meeting on 11 October. The men had been emboldened by a dissident group of rebel AWU members led by the new chairman of the AWU's Mount Isa Section Committee, Pat Mackie.[23]

Mackie was a 48-year-old New Zealander who had worked as an organiser with the Seafarers International Union in the United States and Canada. Always seen around Mount Isa in a trademark red baseball cap, this former wrestler, wharf labourer, fettler, ore gouger and rouseabout

Working a narrow stope at the Mount Isa mine, c. 1965. The harsh and remote working conditions of Mount Isa fed a spirit of industrial militancy. *National Library of Australia.*

arrived in Australia in 1949 and for a while operated his own lead mine in north Queensland. In 1961 he obtained a job with Mount Isa Mines as an underground timberman. In July 1964, as the bonus dispute simmered, he became chairman of the Section Committee.[24]

Pat Mackie's sense of grievance about the conditions faced by Mount Isa miners grew out of his own experiences on the job. When he started at Mount Isa in 1961, Mackie quickly came face to face with the harshness of contract work, and the demands it placed on the miners. These contracts were loose unwritten agreements between the shift bosses or a foreman and the men working under their control. The contract rate was fixed according to the difficulty of the particular task faced by a gang. And the faster a gang worked, the more they earned, as Mackie found on his first day on the job, when he was paired with a Finnish miner, 'Seppo', drilling the face.

> Seppo worked like a man possessed. He rigged up both our machines and had them drilling in no time. All I had to do was 'collar' the holes for him, with both hands, guiding the tungsten tipped point of the drill against the face of the rock until it bit far enough in to stay in the right place. After half an hour of breathing in the vaporous air and the oily exhaust from my machine I was gasping for breath. I felt I was drowning. The noise and the heat were so intense my whole body was throbbing, my head bursting. The weight of my sodden trousers, the heavy belt and light battery dragging low down on my waist added to my misery. I had never worked under such strenuous circumstances in my life, even as a ship's fireman.

Realising that he could never match Seppo's prodigious productivity – 'Seppo drilled four holes to my one' – Mackie joined an underground timbering gang, building bulkheads and frames to support the mine shafts. For a time Mackie earned good money as a timberman, but various changes introduced by management eroded the value of contract work, fuelling the grievance over the bonus, which had not been increased since 1959. And there were other needling grievances: Mackie's involvement in the AWU Section Committee sprang from irritation with MIM over the poor shower facilities provided for miners.[25]

Like many other Mount Isa miners, Pat Mackie was not Australian-born, and during the Section Committee meetings between July and October 1964 he quickly realised that language was a barrier to solidarity, and particularly their campaign to increase the bonus and to remove the injustices of the contract system.

> A Finn took the floor to complain, in incoherent English, about having had money chiselled from him by a foreman wrongly measuring the job he had done. Whilst he was battling on with the language trying to explain his problem, an impatient old Aussie jumped up and said, 'Oh sit down ya wog bastard and shut up!'

> The Finn replied, with great dignity and passion, 'Ve focken vogs, ve Union men too. Ve all pay Union dues all like you do. Ve got like you the same trouble, and ve must talk too of our trouble!'

Mackie organised interpreters to cater for as many of the language groups as he could – he estimates that there were forty-seven nationalities working at Mount Isa in 1964 – and by so doing tapped a previously unorganised force. 'New Australian workers would prove themselves outstanding, devoted Unionists; and, through their numbers would provide the dependable backbone to the whole struggle.'[26]

As this language problem indicates, Mackie and the AWU both struggled to manage a dispute which, in style and intensity, was unlike most of the disputes the AWU had had to deal with over the years, as Mackie's account of the 11 October meeting of Mount Isa AWU members reveals. Kevin Costello, the AWU's Northern District secretary, had come to Mount Isa to urge the men to return to contract work, essentially taking their campaign back to square one. Up to that point, the AWU's court claims on behalf of the bonus increase had met nothing but frustration. Nevertheless, the union was convinced that only gains won through the court would resolve the dispute. But when Costello recommended a return to contract work,

> instantaneously all hell broke loose. As one, the 1,000 odd hitherto silent men became a stamping, hooting, jeering mob. The roar from the open-doored theatre could be heard for blocks. Endeavouring to bring the meeting to order, I reached for the microphone to request them 'to give him a fair go'. Costello refused to let go of the mike and persisted in speaking into it thereby increasing the rage and the shouting. After minutes of bedlam he gave up.

The AWU had misread the mood of the miners, although Edgar Williams believed that this was largely due to Mackie's mischief. Williams believed that the October meeting marked 'the beginning of a lawless era ... the departure from all the rules. There was a fight not only on without, but within'. The actions of both MIM and the AWU after the October meeting ensured that Mackie's personal fate became hopelessly entangled with any meaningful resolution of the dispute. On 22 October Mackie was sacked by MIM for failing to appear for work at the mine, after he had been refused an absence of leave to attend to union business. From MIM's point of view, this clumsy attempt to get rid of the dispute's 'ringleader' completely backfired. Mackie believed that MIM wanted to end the dispute by prompting a walk-out by the miners, to end the debilitating go-slow. 'An illegal stoppage would be what they most desired, to invoke all the penal clauses of the Act.' On 25 October the men voted, at another rowdy meeting, to continue on wages work. They also carried no-confidence motions against both Costello and Williams. As far as the AWU was concerned, however, the meeting was illegal, as the men had refused to allow Costello to chair it. For this, and for his encouragement of the miners' determination to remain on wages work, Mackie was expelled from the AWU on 7 December.[27]

The day before his dismissal from the AWU, a rank-and-file meeting had made their faith in Mackie clear by demanding his reinstatement by MIM. Their breach with the AWU was also confirmed by a decision to affiliate the AWU Section Committee with the Mount Isa Labor Council, the organisation of the combined tradesmen's unions. The pressure on the Queensland Industrial Court, and the Government, was also beginning to tell. The Queensland Railways had already lost £250 000 in ore cartage as a result of the go-slow. On 10 December the Queensland Government declared a state of emergency and ordered the miners back to contract work. But another rank-and-file meeting on 13 December simply reiterated the men's previous demands. In response, MIM closed the mine on 16 December. That same day, the Queensland Industrial Court decided that the miners had effectively won the argument. The court set aside the Industrial Commission's original rejection of the AWU's claim and ordered the commission to reopen the hearing – a loud hint which the commission acknowledged on 24 December, awarding a £3 a week 'prosperity loading'. But it had come too late to solve the dispute. The miners insisted on a firm increase of £4 (one that could not be revoked if MIM declared, after the dispute, that the company could no longer afford the 'prosperity' payment), Mackie's reinstatement and a lifting of the state of emergency.[28]

By this time the Mount Isa dispute, as far as Pat Mackie was concerned, had become something more than a struggle over a bonus. 'It developed into a struggle pre-eminently for self rule and industrial legality, for the Union principle of loyalty to fellow Unionists and legally acknowledged Arbitration principle of "no victimisation".' The AWU also believed that the nature of the dispute had changed. As the *Queensland Worker* commented in February 1965:

> The dispute at Mt Isa is no longer an industrial dispute. The big part, and the main part, is Communist infiltration and Communist domination of sections of the trade union movement, particularly in big production areas that can be regarded as the essence of industries that are peculiar to the defence of the country.
> It is no different at Mt Isa. Indeed quite recently more positive identification of a Communist cell in Mt Isa has become known. The discovery of documents shows that the pipeline of the set up of a Communist cell in Mt Isa emanated in the first place from Adelaide.[29]

The 'Communist cell' emanating from Adelaide was in fact the AWU's way of describing the intervention of the Council for Membership

Control, which organised a rally at Mount Isa on 5 January 1965. In late
1964 Mackie became the secretary of the Mount Isa CMC branch, and
Cameron provided Mackie with as much assistance as he could. The
meeting was attended by most of the AWU's Mount Isa membership, who
expressed their confidence in Mackie's campaign and demanded the
right to elect their own local officials. The following day CMC representatives were denied participation at a compulsory conference called in
another failed attempt to solve the dispute. The pattern which typified
the remainder of the dispute, until the end of March 1965, was now set.
The rank-and-file representatives were largely frozen out of talks to settle
the strike. This was particularly true of Mackie, who had been declared
*persona non grata* as both an MIM employee and an AWU member. Yet
without the co-operation of these rank-and-file representatives, the strike
could not end.[30]

On 27 January the State Government intervened again by issuing an
Order-in Council which gave the police powers to remove from or forbid
entry to the Mount Isa field any person whose presence they considered
prejudicial to a return to work, and forbade the writing or printing or
speaking of any words or signs inducing any person to interfere with a
return to work. The Queensland Trades and Labour Council threatened
a State-wide stoppage over this order, and there were dramatic scenes as
two TLC officials were removed from a plane at Longreach, *en route* to
Mount Isa. The ensuing controversy prompted the government to withdraw the offending order on 1 February 1965. Attempts at conciliation
continued to founder on the demand for Mackie's reinstatement. Finally,
on 17 February MIM reopened the mine and offered to re-employ those
men who had been employees as at 14 December 1964. This prompted
the AWU to call on its members to return to work. At the same time,
AWU strike relief payments were withdrawn from those members who
refused to heed the call. At first the response was merely a trickle, but
numbers increased slightly each week despite the existence of a vocal and
threatening picket line. After an incident at the Star Gully barracks on
14 March, where an AWU member who had returned to work fought
with several strikers and two men were shot and wounded when a rifle
discharged, the State Government enacted legislation which outlawed
picketing and increased police powers to remove persons from the site.
This time, the government's action failed to attract the hostility of the
January order; a protest stoppage of all unions affiliated with the
Queensland TLC was cancelled because of lack of support. Mass
meetings of the AWU and craft unions agreed to return to work and the
dispute was effectively over by the end of March.[31]

Although the company had originally agreed to reinstate all workers
employed as at 14 December, it was to renege on this arrangement and,

after negotiations, eventually refused the re-employment of forty-five workers, most of whom were rebel AWU members. Edgar Williams rejected accusations that the AWU did nothing to assist these members and was adamant that the local organiser, Fred Sargent, had made representations to MIM on their behalf. The company steadfastly refused to reinstate them. These outcasts turned to the Queensland TLC for assistance. The Queensland Industrial Commission ordered the company to re-employ the men, noting that its refusal 'smacked of unwarranted discrimination'. Commissioner Taylor went on to say that he was of the opinion that the men had been refused reinstatement at the instigation of AWU officials. Taylor rejected the company's claim that it was merely a coincidence that the rejected applications were all from men who had incurred the displeasure of AWU officials, commenting: 'There is obviously complete agreement, down to the last man, between the company and the union as to the merits of the application'. The AWU vehemently denied the accusation and pointed to the fact that that no AWU official was asked to give evidence or comment on the suggestion of collusion. Edgar Williams told journalists outside the court: 'I deny that any AWU official discussed affairs with Mount Isa Mines outside the conference room'. The company appealed the decision to the president of the Industrial Court, Mr Justice Hanger. On 14 October 1965 the court found in favour of the company and ordered the commissioner's decision set aside. There was insufficient evidence to support the conclusion that the men were not re-employed at the instigation of the AWU. The full bench of the Supreme Court rejected an appeal from the Queensland TLC in December 1965.[32]

The dispute also had consequences for the AWU's relationship with the Labor Party. In July 1965 the Executive Council voted unanimously to withdraw all financial and other support from the federal parliamentary Labor Party until it was satisfied that it had the ALP's 'loyal support' over its handling of the Mount Isa dispute. This decision was provoked by the assistance given by two federal Labor MPs, Clyde Cameron and Dr Jim Cairns, to Mackie and the rebel union leaders in Mount Isa. The decision was viewed seriously by the ALP, for at least five seats in Queensland, the three seats in Tasmania, and one each in South Australia and Western Australia were in danger of being lost if AWU support was withdrawn. The AWU contributed about £30 000 a year to the federal Labor Party and State branches and during federal election campaigns provided the services of seventy-nine paid officials across Australia. The AWU demanded a written undertaking from the parliamentary leader, Arthur Calwell, that Labor Members and senators would refrain from interfering in AWU industrial affairs. Despite an initial rebuff by the ALP Federal Executive to the AWU's demand, an undertaking was eventually given and the matter settled in October 1966, two months before the federal election.[33]

The AWU made efforts to rebuild its position at Mount Isa. Two new organisers were appointed specifically to serve Mount Isa members, and both had worked in the mine. Lawrie Buckman replaced Kevin Costello as Northern District secretary (Costello and Edgar Williams had apparently fallen out after the dispute), and found there was much healing to do. The AWU was far from welcome among many of the rank and file and the CMC was still quite active, although Mackie had left the scene by April 1965, unable to overcome MIM hostility to his reinstatement. Buckman recalled that his early attempts to initiate meetings with the rank and file were 'pretty rough'. Members tried to snatch the microphone from him and take over the meeting and on a number of occasions he was told he 'wouldn't get out of town alive'. Buckman and the AWU had also to fend off attempts by the Broken Hill Barrier Industrial Council to extend its influence in Mount Isa, a niggling campaign encouraged by Cameron and the CMC. Yet Buckman persevered, introducing two-yearly agreement talks with MIM which involved local AWU representatives and more frequent meetings with the rank and file before logs of claims were drawn up. As Buckman observed, one legacy of the Mount Isa dispute was a recognition by the AWU of the need to involve the rank and file to a greater extent in decision-making. Some of the anomalies of the contract system were overcome by a new MIM award in June 1965. This award provided for a range of measures which boosted the income of Mount Isa miners, including a provision that marginal loadings and basic-wage loadings automatically increased with any increases in basic-wage rates and marginal rates. This 'double dipping' was, according to Edgar Williams, 'a tremendous industrial reform, as the Mount Isa Mines Limited Award is the only award of any Industrial Tribunal in Australia which makes such a provision'. For Williams, these gains were what unions achieved for their members 'simply through hard work, industrial conciliation and arbitration'.[34]

Edgar Williams would never concede that Mackie was a legitimate spokesman for the AWU's Mount Isa membership. Mackie, taking 'much pleasure in declaring the mine black', 'posing' in his jeep which he drove around the town, appeared to Williams as a shadowy, elusive foreigner, typified by the confusing way his name changed from Patrick Murphy to Eugene Markey to Pat Mackie. Mackie's experience was at odds with the hierarchical, patient work of the AWU. As Williams commented of Mackie in his book, *The Isa: Yellow, Green and Red*:

> There is little doubt that Markey-cum-Mackie [Williams refers to Mackie in these terms throughout his book] was versatile; that he was born in New Zealand and left there at the age of 16, so his experiences of life must have started early; that

he had been for a number of years a seaman at sea, and that for several years he had been an organiser gaining experience in the Canadian-American experience of 'head-on impact'. His philosophy or attitude seems to have been clearly expressed when he said to a union official, – 'That Williams guy has to abide by rules; I can say anything I God-damn please'.

By saying anything he 'God-damn pleased' Pat Mackie had talked himself into a fight much bigger than his own natural sense of grievance could easily manage, but for a brief historical moment a stranger in a red cap became the focus of a bemused Queensland society.[35]

### What to do about Lew: the Better Deal Team and the NSW Branch Dispute, 1967–70

By the mid-1960s Charlie Oliver seemed well entrenched as both NSW AWU secretary, and as president of the ALP's NSW Branch. In 1964 he had been re-elected unopposed to both positions. In 1967, however, his smooth control of the New South Wales labour movement began to unravel. Oliver was depressed by the NSW ALP's election defeat in 1965, and, at age 63, it seemed he might be heading for retirement. He heightened that impression by taking a long overseas trip after the defeat of the Renshaw Government. When he returned he found two organisers, Lew McKay and Reg Mawbey, willing to assume the reins of power as NSW AWU secretary. But Charlie Oliver was not thinking about retirement.[36]

Reg Mawbey was loyal to Oliver and Oliver made him acting branch secretary during his absence overseas. Of the gathering storm at home, Mawbey recalls that

when I become an Organiser [in 1964] and was situated in Dubbo, I took the place of a chap called Lewis George MacKay and we became good friends. Apparently, Lewis had ambitions that he wanted to be the Secretary and he came down to Wollongong and of course Lew and Charlie Oliver started to quarrel. I came to Sydney in 1965 and was made Secretary, and Charlie was overseas and Lew was bitter about that, that I'd got the job and not him. Lew started to become a nuisance ... and the Executive decided to do something with Lew.[37]

The tension between Oliver and McKay, the AWU's South Coast organiser, persisted until June 1967, when the NSW AWU Executive dismissed McKay from his organiser's position for his refusal to accept a transfer from the South Coast to Sydney, where he would come under Oliver's close supervision. Oliver felt that he could no longer accept McKay's challenges to his authority. 'He is the only organiser who ever attempted to set himself up as a separate part of the Union.' Thus began not only an intense factional dispute, but an almost legendary – and

frighteningly expensive – series of court actions, which persisted into the
1970s. As Mawbey recalls, 'that was the start of the big faction fight. The
Comms got interested in Lew and of course, Lew wasn't a Comm, I'll say
that, Lew thought that he could use them, well of course no-one could
use the Comms, in those days they couldn't. So anyhow Lew started up
the Better Deal thing, he went around town drumming up support, and
he was getting a lot of support'.[38]

The Communist Party newspaper *Tribune*, which was often well informed of the activities of AWU dissidents, later observed that the 'brawl
grew in dimensions to an open split and McKay initiated a South Coast
Representatives Committee which later linked up with the Sydney CMC
to form the Better Deal Committee in March 1967'. With Mawbey
apparently anointed as Oliver's successor, McKay looked elsewhere for
support. The Sydney CMC was founded by Daniel Leen, a former miner
from Captains Flat, and Nev Cunningham, a former seaman, in 1961–62.
They were to become integral members of the BDC.[39]

Despite the efforts of the BDC, the 1967 NSW Branch ballot returned
the Oliver team. However, McKay was not prepared to let the election
result – or his dismissal – rest. In the Commonwealth Industrial Court
McKay challenged the right of the branch executive to dismiss an
organiser, and the Full Bench by a 2:1 majority ruled in his favour,
deciding that dismissal power was vested in the secretary, not the full
executive. So Oliver sacked him again in December 1968. McKay also
sought a Commonwealth Industrial Court inquiry into the 1967 elections, alleging ballot irregularities.[40]

That Oliver was not entirely in control of events became obvious in July
1968, when the half-yearly meeting of NSW Branch members rejected
the branch's balance sheet and condemned the executive. The meeting,
attended by about a hundred members and dominated by McKay's
supporters, also 'viewed with grave concern the total disregard shown by
the executive' in the administration of the branch. Then on 27
November 1968 Clyde Cameron told the House of Representatives that
Oliver had recently written in the *Worker* that unnamed persons had
misled the Commonwealth Industrial Court's inquiry into the 1967
ballot 'by creating irregularities'. Cameron said that these allegations cast
doubt on the conduct of the deputy industrial registrar and his staff, and
also on Lew McKay, on whose behalf Cameron claimed to be speaking.
'Mr. McKay emphatically denies the false insinuation that he committed
a fraud, conspiracy or forgery of papers.' Cameron made it clear that
forged ballot papers clearly favoured Oliver's supporters in the ballot.
The pressure on Oliver began to tell. At the January 1969 half-yearly
meeting, held just before the AWU's Annual Convention, Oliver walked
out after again being confronted by McKay's supporters over allegations

of ballot-rigging. In an emotional address to Convention on 29 January 1969, Oliver thundered: 'The most amazing thing is that these people hope to take control of the Union by traducing the officials of the Union. I make this promise – that at my age of 66 years I will bury them'. The balance sheet was adopted and a resolution congratulating Oliver and his executive on the way they had conducted branch affairs was carried unanimously by Convention. Dougherty then launched a scathing attack against Cameron over his statements in Federal Parliament against Oliver. Dougherty moved a motion expressing 'deep concern' over the FPLP and the ALP Federal Executive's failure to discipline Cameron for his 'recent unwarranted, untruthful and vicious attacks' and vowing, in the face of any further attacks by any member of the FPLP, to call upon all branches of the AWU 'to disaffiliate from the Australian Labor Party, and instructs that if it becomes necessary a meeting of the Executive Council of the AWU be held for the purpose of altering any rules required to ensure the implementation of this decision'. Oliver seconded the motion; Don Cameron was the only speaker against, and the motion was eventually carried 33:3 with one abstention. Convention then went on to declare that the South Coast Representatives Committee had no constitutional authority to speak or act for the union and that it was thus a 'bogus organisation'.[41]

Nevertheless in October 1969 the McKay-led rank-and-file revolt swept the leadership of the NSW Branch from power. Of the twelve Oliver team organisers only four remained; Mawbey was among those defeated. As Oliver had been elected unopposed in the 1967 ballot he remained NSW Branch secretary, but the remainder of the executive were Better Deal officials, including McKay. A *Sydney Morning Herald* report observed that 'Union officials said they could not remember a defeat of such magnitude in a union ballot' – a result which threatened continued right-wing control of the NSW ALP. McKay immediately challenged Oliver to resign, declaring, 'Mr Oliver has aligned himself unhesitatingly and completely with men who have been rejected by the branch membership'.[42]

This was not the end of Oliver or his supporters. Reg Mawbey and several other defeated officials organised an 'Action Committee' to regain control of the NSW Branch. Their first aim was the December 1969 ballot for eight delegates from the NSW Branch to represent the branch at Convention. Oliver led the Action Committee ticket while McKay led the recently victorious 'Better Deal' team. Oliver's team won, completely reversing the October result. This time, with Oliver personally contesting the ballot, he defeated McKay 3258:1912. Mawbey recalls, 'so we won. And ... of course convention intervened and they overruled the NSW Branch Executive decision to sack Charlie. Well, then that started off a mammoth court case'. In January 1970 the Better Deal-dominated NSW executive hurriedly sacked Oliver as secretary, attempting to circumvent the imminent Convention, which simply rein-stated Oliver. The Executive Council was charged with responsibility for implementing the reinstatement, a task which like many other AWU disputes was to prove easier to proclaim than to enforce.[43]

### 'A Great and Welcome Change': Industrial Growth and ACTU Affiliation

By the 1960s, the AWU was still Australia's largest union, boasting a mem-bership of 170 000, with almost 74 000 of this number claimed by the all-powerful Queensland Branch. But the industrial character of that membership had changed in the post-war years. Since its inception, the AWU's base had been firmly anchored in rural industries. Primary industry employment levels continued to decline. In 1944 the average annual employment in rural industry (per thousand) was 462.0; in manufacturing, it was 834.1. Within twenty years, the figures were 457.4 and 1244.1 respectively. Moreover, population in rural areas nationally had fallen from 2 354 248 in 1947 to 1 872 180 by 1961.[44]

Tom Dougherty told the 1961 AWU Annual Convention that 'because of the ever-changing scene in the industrial field it is vitally necessary that this Union is continually alert in regard to the extension of industrial coverage to employees engaged in industries covered by the AWU con-stitution'. Dougherty singled out the fledgeling petro-chemical industry as an example and pointed to the expected competition the AWU would face for coverage in this field. In 1961 Australia's first commercial oilfield was discovered at Moonie, about 300 kilometres west of Brisbane. Production started here in 1964 and at another field at Alton, not far from Moonie, two years later. In the same year oil was discovered in Central Australia 2200 kilometres south-west of Alice Springs and on Barrow Island (about 250 kilometres north-west of Exmouth Gulf), along with a gas field. Oil and gas were also discovered in that same year in Bass Strait in the geological area known as the Gippsland Basin. Further discoveries in this area were made between 1966 and 1971. Production commenced in 1970, and within ten years the Bass Strait fields were providing more than 80 per cent of Australia's crude oil. Between 1965 and the end of the decade, natural gas fields were discovered in the Northern Territory, Queensland, Western Australia and at Moomba in South Australia. By 1970 the AWU was playing a major role in this new industry. In 1964 the AWU obtained a federal award for oil drilling, and most workers employed on the construction of the oil pipeline from Moonie to Brisbane had AWU tickets. Another mineral discovery which would launch a new field of employment for AWU members was bauxite, the chief source of aluminium. As early as 1960, an aluminium plant was operating near Geelong in Victoria and within six years another refinery had been built at Kwinana in Western Australia. The Nabalco company had agreed to spend $100 million on a development at Gove which would include a refinery, a port and a township. In 1966 the Comalco company began mining bauxite at Weipa and had indications within a year that Weipa held nearly a quarter of the world's known potential bauxite deposits. The quantity of bauxite mined in Australia increased from 71 000 tonnes in 1960 to 9 256 000 by 1970. Aluminium production (per thousand tonnes) increased from 11.8 to 205.6 in the same period.[45]

The AWU would achieve majority worker coverage in the petrochemical and aluminium industries during the 1960s, but not without its role being vigorously contested by other unions. These 'intrusions', as the AWU liked to call them, were evident from the beginning of the decade. Dougherty told the 1961 Convention that in the previous year the federal office had to 'intervene before the Conciliation and Arbitration Commission on numerous occasions to preserve its rights against other Unions seeking to encroach Federally on Awards covered by the AWU'. The unions involved on that occasion were the Federated Storemen and Packers Union, the Federated Artificial Fertilizer and Chemical Workers Union, the Federated Ship Painters and Dockers Union, the Merchant Service Guild and the Liquor Trades Union. At the 1963 Convention delegates were told that the AWU's application for an award covering employees in the aluminium industry had attracted the intervention of fourteen other unions at the initial court hearing of the claim. Subsequent logs of claims were lodged on employers by the Federated Ironworkers Association, the Transport Workers Union, the Federated Engine Drivers and Firemen's Association and the Clerks Union. The FIA's claim ignited a demarcation dispute of which there appeared, Dougherty told assembled delegates, 'little possibility of determining . . . by conciliation'.[46]

In 1963 the Commonwealth Conciliation and Arbitration Commission held that the FIA had no rights in the mining section of the aluminium industry nor in the production of alumina, except as trades assistants. In 1966, however, at the hearing of the AWU's claims on a new award, ten other unions, including the FIA, sought and were granted leave to intervene in the dispute. The FIA again sought coverage of 'all persons employed in the treatment of bauxite and the production of alumina'. Again the commission upheld the AWU's objection. By the end of the decade Dougherty was able to announce improvements by way of increases for certain classifications, new classifications and improved conditions by way of direct negotiations with the various aluminium industry companies. New rates of pay and some new classifications had been obtained in the 1968 award, but Dougherty warned of the need 'to ensure as far as possible that we retain our full rights of membership in the mining and alumina production sections of this industry having full regard to the continual efforts of both the FIA and the FEDFA to infiltrate at every opportunity'. The AWU was also facing intrusion by the Transport Workers Union and the FEDFA in the gold and metalliferous mining industry. In a review of 1969 Dougherty warned of the need for 'continual vigilance' about further moves by these unions into work on mining production and into plants generally. The AWU had been forced to defend its territory against moves by the Merchant Cooks Association to cover galley personnel on oil rigs, dredges and punts, an application for registration by a newly formed United Firefighters' Union and an action by the Transport Workers' Union which the AWU perceived as a move 'to take over ... our organised membership in driving and associated occupations in a number of industries in Queensland and Western Australia ... and further ... to extend their field of operations into other industries and callings' in other States. But if its ground in some industries was under threat, the AWU had consolidated its coverage in others. In 1964 the union won a court judgment confirming its coverage under the Construction Award for construction, alteration, repair and maintenance of water and sewerage works. By 1967 the AWU had obtained full coverage in the construction industry, having been granted by the Commonwealth Conciliation and Arbitration Commission in the face of a challenge by the FEDFA 'the constitutional right ... to enrol such employees employed in the construction and maintenance industry in Victoria, South Australia, Western Australia and Tasmania'.[47]

Diversification of its membership had brought the AWU into closer contact with many of the craft unions, and this proximity brought with it, as we have seen, more opportunity for conflict. The more specialised craft unions discovered that AWU coverage in an industry made their wage bargaining and award-making processes more complex. These unions, affiliates of the Australian Council of Trade Unions, saw the obvious advantages in bringing the AWU into the ACTU fold. The AWU had traditionally viewed the ACTU as a nest of communists, particularly after the council's early affiliation with the Pan Pacific Trade Union Secretariat, an organisation closely aligned with the Red International of Labour Unions and which vocally criticised the White Australia Policy and Australia's arbitration system, both articles of faith to the AWU. By the 1960s the AWU recognised that the forces of the industrial Right were strengthening their position on the ACTU executive.[48]

By the late 1950s the initiative to move towards ACTU affiliation was coming from the renegade SA Branch, which probably only delayed Dougherty's agreement to affiliate. At the 1959 Convention, SA Branch delegate Don Cameron moved a resolution to affiliate, arguing that such a step would strengthen the ACTU, which had done little towards initiating a review of the national basic-wage question. Cameron pointed out that, in any case, all branches except Queensland were affiliated with the various Trades and Labour Councils which, in turn, were affiliated with the ACTU. Cameron's arguments fell on barren ground. Dougherty responded by suggesting that what was needed was an alternative to the ACTU and proposed the establishment of an Australian Federation of Trade Unions 'which will be free of communistic influence'. 'Communists today', Dougherty added, 'were the most dangerous persons in the Commonwealth'. Interestingly, Charlie Oliver entered the debate and made it known that he supported neither the motion nor Dougherty's alternative scheme. He could not see how another peak union council could develop greater unity within the labour movement, but thought it would probably become a focus of further conflict. It was not often that Dougherty was opposed on the Convention floor. His proposal, as an amendment to Cameron's motion, was carried.[49]

The anti-affiliation lobby within the AWU grabbed centre-stage at the 1962 and 1963 conventions. This time the motions were framed around a large number of similarly worded shed resolutions, almost all of which emanated from Queensland centres, either commending the stand adopted at previous conventions resisting ACTU affiliation or calling for further pledges against this move. At both conventions the previous policy was endorsed. An attempt by some of the South Australian delegates to have the question decided by a members' plebiscite was defeated. Yet at the 1964 Convention Dougherty gave the first indications that the AWU leadership's attitude towards a closer association with the ACTU was about to change. Dougherty alluded to discussions between AWU and ACTU officials over a co-ordinated approach on the basic-wage claim and associated industrial matters. Dougherty himself had spoken with ACTU secretary Harold Souter and president Albert Monk and reported that 'the AWU was in complete co-operation with the ACTU and other unions in this claim'. Speaking in support of Dougherty, Charlie Oliver noted how pleasing it was to him to know that Dougherty had discussed matters with Monk and Souter 'and that there was an atmosphere of friendliness between these two organisations'.[50]

At Convention in January 1966, Dougherty announced that the question of ACTU affiliation had been referred to the federal Executive Council for consideration. Dougherty declared that 'the communist influence in the ACTU is diminishing' and spoke in glowing terms of the 'very fine trade unionists and trade union leaders' who were 'slowly asserting their authority in their unions against the insidious growth of communism inside the Trade Union Movement'. He saw the AWU's role as being one which obliged the organisation to help and assist them. 'We say, "Welcome brother; you are walking our road, and we are prepared to walk with you"; and invariably we must, because the enemies are building against us, we must say, "Walk a little bit over our way and we will walk a little bit over your way.'[51]

Within six months, the Executive Council took the unanimous decision to seek affiliation with the ACTU. A newpaper report noted that 'the moderate section of the ACTU is already in control over the Communist and extremist groups and will be greatly strengthened by affiliation with the 170,000 strong AWU'. Speculating correctly that the main opposition to affiliation had come from the powerful Queensland Branch, the report observed that the AWU had been careful to stress unity, with Queensland Branch president Gerry Goding seconding Dougherty's motion to affiliate. The step had been taken, Dougherty said, as a result of 'a great and welcome change' which had come about within the ACTU since the last congress which had reduced the influence and strength of the communists to negligible proportions and the 'value of the ACTU to the trade-union movement through the extraordinary ability of ACTU industrial advocate, Mr R. Hawke (Hawke had played an important behind the scenes role in persuading Dougherty to accept affiliation)'. At the 1967 Convention, which confirmed the affiliation decision, Charlie Oliver remarked, 'I feel like it is coming home'.[52]

The affiliation entitled the AWU to send sixty-three delegates to the ACTU Congress, almost double the largest delegation at the last biennial congress. The right-wing *Australian International News Review* saw the move as a means whereby 'the AWU will protect its own future, and at the same time play a valuable anti-communist role within the ACTU'. *Tribune* was far more sceptical about the motives for the reversal of AWU policy. It reported the suspicions of the CMC, which saw the move as an attempt 'to move the Australian trade union movement to the Right'. Conceding that the AWU could be a powerful force if it used its weight to 'back up the pressing demands facing the Australian people', *Tribune* concluded that 'unfortunately the present AWU leaders see the union as a force to try to impose anti-working class policies on the ALP and now the trade union movement'.[53]

The 1967 Convention ratified the Executive Council decision of the previous year. Both Albert Monk and Harold Souter addressed the Convention, with Monk hailing the occasion as 'an outstanding event in the history of the Trade Union Movement' and reassuring delegates that the occasion would mark 'a lasting affiliation with the ACTU'. Within less than two years, the composition of the ACTU executive would shift to the left, heralding an outbreak of internal conflict which would prompt the 1970 AWU Annual Convention to express concern at the lack of ACTU unity and authorise its Executive Council to take whatever action it deemed necessary to protect the interests of the AWU in regard to its affiliation with the peak council.[54]

If the AWU had broken with a long-standing tradition in joining forces with the ACTU it was not about to reverse its commitment to a White Australia. Brahma Davis, in his presidential report to the 1961 Annual Convention, was almost contemptuous of the presumption of a Melbourne-based organisation of mainly university academics and students called the Immigration Reform Group, recently formed to propagate the idea of 'the creation of a multi-racial community in Australia based on some hair-brained [*sic*] scheme under which the Commonwealth Government will negotiate agreements with Asian and African countries, to the number of about 40 or 50, for the admission of their nationals into Australia'. Davis, who identified 'stunt-hungry' newspaper editors, communists and members of the Democratic Labor Party among the group's supporters, thought that if they were successful in their aims, they 'could destroy Australia's living standards and the homogeneity of our people by the introduction of anything up to 50 000 Asians into Australia a year for the next ten years. The fact that such an influx of unassimmilatable [*sic*] people could be most dangerous from the point of view of defence, of industrial peace, of the maintenance of our living standards and of social amity, does not seem to worry the young eggheads one iota'. Davis vowed that the AWU could redouble its efforts over the next year to counter the propaganda of those 'who would introduce into this country the evils of miscegenation that afflict America and South Africa and some other countries; evils from which, up to date, we have been providentially spared'. Convention carried a resolution moved by Dougherty that it affirmed its support for the White Australia Policy and congratulated the leader of the federal Labor Party, Arthur Calwell, on the capable manner in which he had supported the policy. In 1964 Convention carried a further resolution to seek representation on the Federal Government's Immigration Council. Sponsored by the Queensland Branch, the move was designed to counter the growing influence of those who wished to see Australia's strict immigration laws reformed and to shore up support for the White Australia Policy. As in the 1961 debate, supporters of the resolutions took great pains to emphasise that their stand was not on the basis of discrimination against colour but rather 'a discrimination against people exploiting this country and lowering the standards of this country and ... a protection for the working people of this country'. It was too late. In March 1966 the Holt Government relaxed immigration laws to allow non-Europeans to apply for citizenship after five years – the same period which applied to European applicants; previously, non-Europeans had had to wait fifteen

UP  FOR  VAGRANCY

What May Soon Happen in Queensland

Enduring Values. In 1961 the AWU published an 'annual' to mark the seventy-fifty anniversary of the union. Among several old cartoons reprinted was this Monte Scott cartoon from the Brisbane *Worker* of 1899. The 1961 caption noted that the cartoon 'is a striking reminder of the times when so many employers, country and city, preferred coloured labour'. *AWU Collection.*

years. Immigration Minister Hubert Opperman explained that 'the changes are of course not intended to meet general labour shortages or to permit the large scale admission of workers from Asia; but the widening of eligibility will help fill some of Australia's special needs'. Australia still did not have an officially non-racial immigration policy, and bureaucratic obstacles remained for Asian and other non-European immigrants. But the White Australia Policy was being steadily eroded.[55]

As the decade drew to a close, there were ominous signs for the AWU leadership that the challenges to its authority which had emerged during the last ten years would continue into the next decade. A fierce factional war had erupted within the NSW Branch with the appearance of yet another 'bogus' rank-and-file organisation which would test the endurance of the leadership well into the 1970s. Much had changed. The bushworkers' union, characterised by the shearer and rural worker in broad-brimmed felt hats, was being transformed into a new generation of workers in hard hats: workers in the emergent bauxite, uranium-mining and petro-chemical industries. As the traditional areas of coverage for the AWU were diminishing, new industries and attendant opportunities were created. The union required a leadership with the foresight and capacity to identify and exploit the changing situation. Fallon, Bukowski and Davis had passed on (Davis died in 1968) and the formidable Dougherty would only survive until 1972. It would be left to their anointed successors, Edgar Williams, Gerry Goding and Charlie Oliver, to carry the union as it marched towards its centenary.[56]

# CHAPTER 13

# Too Good for the Lot of You

*Charlie Oliver Builds an Empire, 1970–79*

Keep in touch – the AWU will be making news.
*Newly elected AWU general secretary Frank Mitchell
to a reporter, February 1973.*[1]

By the time Frank Mitchell made this prediction in 1973, the AWU of the 1970s had already been making news and would continue to do so throughout the decade. Not that it was entirely the sort of news Mitchell had in mind: most of the headlines the AWU attracted arose from upheavals within the NSW Branch, first over the power struggle between the Oliver and anti-Oliver forces for control of the branch and later over the amalgamation of the NSW Shop Assistants Union with the NSW AWU, temporarily driving the branch's membership past 92 000 – until the marriage turned sour. In a way, the 1970s was for the AWU a continuation of the challenges and struggles which had beset the leadership in the previous decade. A dispute within a single branch had repercussions for the national leadership, and the decline in pastoral employment and the challenges of technological change coincided with the AWU's continued expansion into industries of significant growth potential: oil, minerals and chemicals. But it was Charlie Oliver, at first the darling then the demon of the AWU leadership and the focus of power politics within the union during this period, who held centre-stage in AWU affairs, often to the immense frustration of Frank Mitchell, the former WA Branch secretary who became general secretary after Tom Dougherty's death in October 1972.

## The End of the Dougherty Era

When Tom Dougherty was a young teenager, his first job was as a hand on an isolated dairy property in far north Queensland, 'away out at the back of Lake Cootharaba'. After each long day of work he spent his nights on a corn-husk bunk which had been previously used by the cattledogs. Although grateful for a lifelong immunity to flea bites, he decided after thirteen weeks that he'd had enough. He walked away into the bush, spending two days alone before he came to the town of Kincairn. By night he had been stalked by wild dogs. 'I had this strap around my basket, and I climbed a tree and tied myself around the tree, because otherwise I was a bit concerned about those red dogs trailing behind me. That's a long while ago now.'[2]

Since then, for over fifty years, Tom Dougherty had been looking after himself. As a canecutter: 'Cane cutting was hard work but if you were young you were strong, you were lithe and you had the rhythm of your movement. Well, you can make money at it and I did'. As an AWU official he had taken no prisoners: 'I've been hurt, but I've hurt back'. He was contemptuous of his enemies, as he explained to journalist Robert Moore in an ABC-TV 'Profiles of Power' interview in 1970. 'For instance there's one man today, he's a Federal Member of Parliament, he's as busy as a little bee running around organising inside the AWU against what he calls an oligarchy. But fortunately he's not a good organiser.'[3]

Time is relentless. At 70 years of age Tom Dougherty remained ready to square up to his enemies, but his enthusiasm for the fight was waning. And he knew that what he was fighting for was irrevocably changing. He told Bob Moore that 'the great days as an individual union I would say are over, yes'. The AWU now reached across many industries – mining, construction – but the old union was slipping by. 'Today mechanisation, and to some extent automation, and closer settlement, and the fact that the city and its attractions bring a lot of people from the country – the rural industries are not, today, a big section of this union.' And by the early 1970s two of the characteristic traits of the old bush union, the *Worker* newspapers and the union's fierce commitment to a White Australia, were subjected to immense external pressure. As Dougherty commented to Moore about ACTU affiliation, the AWU was 'part of the whole now'.[4]

By 1973 inflation and rising postal charges meant that the AWU could no longer ignore the losses sustained by the Worker Printery. Don Austin, advertising manager of the *Bulletin* (owned by the Packer family's Consolidated Press), was commissioned by the Executive Council to advise on amalgamating the *Australian Worker* and Brisbane *Worker*. In June 1974 the federal Executive Council resolved that the Queensland *Worker* be absorbed by the *Australian Worker* and that henceforth there would be one AWU newspaper, the *Australian Worker*, which would be a national paper, published monthly instead of fortnightly, with each issue increased from an average eight pages to twenty. The printery at 420–426

Pitt Street, Sydney, and an associated property at 34c Campbell Street
would be sold. Austin was contracted to publish the new newspaper using
commercial printers. The AWU kept a firm hand on the direction of the
newspaper by retaining its traditional watchdog, the Australian Worker
Board of Control. Redundancy arrangements for the printery's workers
were negotiated with the Printing and Kindred Industries Union and the
last edition of the old *Australian Worker* was published on 28 August 1974.
The editorial in the final issue lamented the closing of the printery as
'the sad end of a glorious chapter in the history of the Australian
Workers' Union', paying tribute to the 'immortals' who had graced its
pages since the first issue in 1892, names such as Mary Gilmore, Henry
Boote, George Black and the cartoonist Will Donald. The first editorial
of the new *Australian Worker*, published on 30 September 1974, promised
a 'wider and comprehensive coverage of Union activities and Branch
reports'. The editorial concluded with a rhetorical flourish reminiscent
of the Boote era: 'But there will be no departure from the magnificent
traditions of the Worker in its old form, not letting up in its demands for
a better Australia in which all the nation's workers obtain wage justice, a
greater share of the national wealth and constantly improving social and
welfare benefits'.[5]

In 1972 the AWU Annual Convention ended discrimination against new
members on the basis of race. With this decision the AWU formally
renounced an article of faith which it had defended for over seventy years:
the commitment to a White Australia. It was a renunciation thrust upon it
by external circumstances, given the changes in community and government attitudes to restrictive immigration, particularly since the Holt
Government's 1966 reforms. ALP policy had already been reformed,
putting further pressure on the AWU. The 1971 federal ALP Conference
altered the immigration platform to assert unequivocally that there must
be no discrimination on grounds of race or colour or nationality.[6]

At the AWU Annual Convention held in January 1972, Dougherty
moved to remove all reference to the racial origins of members by the
amendment of the Full Membership rule, Rule 6. Dougherty claimed
that the origin of the rule 'was at the time Chinese and Kanakas were
being brought into this country by very wealthy land-owners, mine-
owners and sugar-owners. We were not biased against coloured peoples;
this rule was not adopted on colour bias, but adopted at a time when
cheap labor was coming into the country and being exploited to the
detriment of the Australian workman and his wife and children'.
Dougherty emphasised that not one person who had made an application to the union had been rejected by the Executive Council (but
without conceding that many may have been deterred from applying by
the mere wording of Rule 6). WA Branch secretary Frank Mitchell

seconded the motion, conceding that 'the current rule was out-dated
and misunderstood in a lot of cases'. The motion was carried unanimously. Dougherty's words represented a quantum leap in attitudinal
change. Barely two years before, he had told ABC interviewer Bob
Moore, in answer to a question as to whether it was fair to distinguish
between migrants on the basis of their colour: 'Well, you know if I were a
praying man, I'd get down on my knees and thank God for our pro-
genitors in this country. That policy they introduced in the latter part of
the last century, and the early part of this century, saved Australia from
the great racial problem that's upsetting America and destroying that
country today ... I think there's a justification for retaining it [White
Australia]'. The Whitlam Government put its policy into effect almost
immediately after being elected to office in December 1972. Immigration Minister Al Grassby introduced the Migration Bill in March 1973,
'the provisions of which will wipe from the national statute book the last
piece of racial discrimination that exists in our national laws'. With
bipartisan support, the Bill quickly became law.[7]

The ending of membership discrimination was only the most obvious
of the changes the AWU leadership apparently wanted to implement.
'What has happened', said the *Sydney Morning Herald* in a report of the
1971 AWU Annual Convention, 'is that the union's national officials and
annual convention delegates have taken a long, hard look at some
features of the union and decided they do not like them'. The AWU had
decided it should 'move with the times, reorganise its structure and not
get left behind'. Some delegates to the Convention had said that they
had 'had enough of Court actions and inter-union brawls', maintaining
that the union should be 'showing the way in modern unionism and
industrial relations'. Dougherty apparently concurred with this new
direction, accepting that 'a move with the times' meant that 'I've got to
improve relations with the press and radio'. The research and industrial
facilities of the State branches would, said Dougherty, be provided with
federal union funds to 'step into the 1970s'. In what must have been a
difficult decision for Big Tom, he had announced the previous day that
Convention would give full support to federal Labor 'irrespective of likes
or dislikes, or of what any person may, or may not have done to this
union'. This was a clear reference to his arch enemy, Clyde Cameron.
When asked whether his offer included the former SA Branch secretary
and executive councillor, Dougherty replied, 'Of course'.[8]

This was uncharacteristic of Dougherty, a fearless fighter. He had
battled Cameron for thirty years and such was their rivalry that on more
than one occasion he had been prepared to place the AWU's relationship with federal Labor on the line rather than give Cameron any respite.
Nor had there been any indication that Cameron was becoming

Federal ALP leader Gough Whitlam calls on AWU general secretary Tom
Dougherty to receive a $10 000 campaign donation from the AWU, prior to the
crucial 1972 federal elections. By this time the AWU was well established as one
of the biggest financial supporters of the ALP. *Noel Butlin Archives, Australian
National University.*

conciliatory; his attacks on the AWU were far from over. So had
Dougherty mellowed? He was 71 years of age and had been the AWU's
senior executive since 1944. 'I'm getting too old to say I enjoy fights',
Dougherty explained to Robert Moore. 'But I put it this way, I will never
run away from it.' In the event, time was running out for Big Tom. The
January 1972 AWU Convention was his last. Speaking after the unanimous defeat of a resolution calling on all union officials to retire at age
65, Dougherty said, 'I think that one was aimed at old Uncle Tom. But
Uncle Tom will still be here when the snipers are gone'. Within ten
months Tom Dougherty was dead, after a sudden heart attack on
14 October 1972.[9]

Fred Wells, the *Sydney Morning Herald*'s long-serving industrial reporter, knew Dougherty well.

> It is hard to think that Tom Nicholson Pearce Dougherty, long-time federal
> secretary of the Australian Workers' Union, is dead. A big man – over 6 feet
> 2 inches, with an 'admitted' age of 72 – lean, well-dressed, handsome, with a
> razor-sharp mind, he seemed indestructible. It has been popular these last few
> years for lesser men to vilify him, but I always found him kindly, tolerant and
> helpful. If he had a fault it lay in his fierce sense of Australia's national identity.

Clyde Cameron recalled his irritation that Dougherty's sudden death had deprived him of the satisfaction of watching CMC supporters defeat Dougherty in a ballot. Wendy Pymont, who had worked with Dougherty since 1961, remembered in later years a lonely man who lived in Macdonell House and travelled every second weekend to the family home at Laurieton, on the New South Wales north coast, where he died. In answer to a question from Bob Moore on how tough the union business was and whether Big Tom was the tough man he had so often been described as, Dougherty replied: 'You can't wrap yourself up in brown paper in this union. There's things you must do if you want to do your job that really hurt you in your own heart, but you must harden yourself and do it'.[10]

### Charlie Oliver and the NSW AWU

For thirty years the NSW AWU had also been dominated by a man who had put his union career ahead of a personal life. Charlie Oliver became NSW Branch secretary in 1951, leaving behind his family in Western Australia. On his elevation to the post Dougherty had described him as a 'fearless and capable union official and Labor man'. He might have been describing himself. Oliver and Dougherty recognised each other's mutual worship of power and career. For Charlie Oliver, this single-mindedness had dramatic consequences for the NSW AWU throughout the 1970s, and well into the next decade.

During his long period of office Oliver had put the NSW Branch in a healthy financial and membership position. The branch owned neither land nor buildings in 1951. Over twenty years, Oliver purchased or built five buildings throughout the State. This decentralisation policy and alternative income source, Oliver maintained, had enabled him to keep membership fees low and build branch real estate assets to around $1 million. The branch serviced 103 industrial agreements, ninety-four State awards, seven federal awards and four Australian Capital Territory awards by 1970, on behalf of 33 000 members.[11]

### The Better Deal Challenge

Despite these successes, Oliver was a secretary under siege. The Better Deal team led by former organiser Lew McKay had captured most branch executive positions in 1969, although, crucially, they had been defeated by Oliver's supporters in a subsequent ballot for Convention delegates. Yet McKay was determined to get rid of Oliver. In January 1970 the branch executive voted to dismiss Oliver as secretary so as to 'overcome the grave difficulties in the proper administration of the Branch

[and] for the general welfare of the membership'. The decision was hastily implemented, as Oliver found when he was unable to enter his office because the locks had been changed. Later that same month Oliver appealed to the AWU Convention, which ruled that he had not been formally charged with neglect of duty or misappropriation, and that he had not been given adequate time to prepare a defence of the allegations against him. His appeal against his dismissal was upheld and he was immediately reinstated. McKay had other ideas. Later at the Convention, Dougherty read to delegates a letter he had received from McKay, emphasising his intention to remain as branch secretary until the court-controlled ballot (arranged for September 1970) was held. He warned Dougherty that 'any attempt to displace me forcibly from office, or to usurp the authority of our Executive on the hollow claim that the Branch is in danger will arouse unrest, hostility and disunity throughout the whole Union.'[12]

The protagonists were in court almost before the Convention delegates had time to return to their respective branches. Both McKay and Oliver sought a ruling from the Commonwealth Industrial Court clarifying which of them was the legitimate branch secretary. On 14 May 1970 the court found that Oliver had been denied natural justice and that he had at all times remained the duly appointed branch secretary. Costs of both applications were awarded against McKay and four other members of the executive, Hogan, Ronald Whitby, Louis Luckins and David Owen (eventually they would face over $90 000 in court costs). When Oliver returned to the AWU office he found the door to his room still locked. Fergus Lake recalls that Oliver overcame this obstacle by putting his shoulder to the door.[13]

Oliver was back, and the McKay executive was still in place. On 19 May 1970 the Executive Council decided, over the sound of a small street protest demanding 'Hands Off McKay, Leen, Barnes and Hogan' and 'Members say Stop the Oliver Twist', that Dougherty should conduct an inquiry into the NSW AWU, following allegations by Oliver of certain administrative and financial malpractices. Dougherty and Oliver should be appointed as a 'management committee' to manage the business of the branch and to carry on business until completion of the inquiry. Oliver set about routing his enemies. By the middle of June he had dismissed five organisers, all members of the McKay group, including Barnes, Hogan and McKay himself for various alleged offences. Neither McKay nor Hogan accepted Oliver's decision and Hogan refused to hand over his car. The McKay group then established a rival branch office at 646 George Street, Sydney. Announcing the branch 'relocation', Barnes told journalists that Oliver would be instructed that the George Street premises was the official office and that he would be required to

work from there. All members would be informed of the changes and
they would be instructed to forward all money and correspondence to
the new address. The group was now printing and selling its own
membership tickets and all money received was to be paid into a union
account under the care of branch trustees. Oliver responded by telling
the McKay group to 'go to Bourke'. At a meeting of the Executive
Council held in Sydney on 27 July 1970, Dougherty presented his report
of the investigation into the affairs of the NSW Branch. McKay and his
supporters were expelled on charges of misconduct and breaches of the
rules. The Executive Council then made pro-Oliver appointments to the
NSW Branch executive to carry out official duties pending the calling of
a fresh election.[14]

Oliver had not escaped unscathed. On 23 October 1970 he announced
that he was relinquishing the position of NSW ALP president, a post he
had held since 1960. ALP general secretary Peter Westerway declared
that ALP members and unionists would regard Oliver's resignation as
'the end of an era'. McKay later said that Oliver resigned because he
(McKay) had exposed Oliver for 'using Union money to "STACK" the
ALP Annual Conference with excess Delegates'. But it was more likely
the result of the disclosures of the Burns Report, an investigation commissioned by the Federal Executive of the ALP into the NSW Branch and
presented shortly after Oliver's resignation. Burns concluded that there
was a 'crisis of confidence' in the branch, noting in particular that the
1970 Conference had been improperly constituted by Oliver's disregard
of Rule 26 in allowing AWU delegations to vote on their own admission.
There were also other instances of his partiality: gagging, the bias of the
timekeeper, and other devices used to harass speakers.[15]

NSW Branch members did not have to wait long into the new year for
fresh episodes in the McKay–Oliver saga. On 19 January the Commonwealth Industrial Court ruled that the resolutions passed by the Federal
Executive expelling Barnes, McKay, Hogan and four others were invalid
(the Queensland Branch was over-represented on the executive when
the resolutions were passed). A further hearing of McKay group summonses on 4 February saw the court order the reinstatement of ten
McKay group members to positions in the State branch. Among these
were six branch executive officers, giving the Better Deal group a
majority on the nine-man executive. Within a week the group had dismissed nine AWU staff: six organisers and three office staff, including
Oliver's trusted head clerk, Necia Holloway. Several appealed the
decisions to the Commonwealth Industrial Court without success. The
Executive Council responded on 8 February, ordering the reinstatement
of the nine dismissed AWU employees and 'to refrain from giving effect
to the purported resolutions' which upheld the appeals and reinstated

the McKay group members as organisers and branch committeemen. This ruling brought the dispute to an impasse, as neither side had really succeeded in ultimately prevailing over the other. McKay had again angrily rejected the Executive Council's ruling, and Dougherty and Oliver probably knew that they could not enforce it – at least not without another tortuous and expensive round of legal clashes. When the Executive Council resumed the following day, however, Jack Wright, a South Australian delegate who with colleague Jim Dunford had been consistently sympathetic to McKay and his group (Cameron's South Australian-based CMC had supported the Better Deal team), moved an amendment that the Executive Council initiate a conference with the NSW Branch executive to attempt to overcome existing problems and to seek legal advice on the validity of Convention and the Executive Council to interfere in branch decisions. Both sides agreed to this compromise.[16]

For the time being the battle was over, although the decision posed a critical problem for the controlling right-wing faction of the NSW ALP. The Better Deal group was now back to six members on the nine-member executive, controlling the largest union in the State. While not avowedly left-wing, the group was thought more likely to vote with the Left than with the Right. At State ALP conferences, the previous AWU delegation of forty-one had consistently voted with the controlling right-wing officers' group. But the Better Deal group was insisting that the AWU could only justify a delegation of twenty-five, which would deprive the Right of 18 votes and, on some issues, increase the vote of the Left by 25.[17]

Oliver and his supporters did not give up the fight. Reg Mawbey says that shortly after the reinstatement of the Better Deal team Oliver's supporters formed the Members' Action Committee. With contributions from their superannuation pay-outs and long service leave entitlements, Mawbey was able to devote himself to full-time organising in readiness for an opportunity to regain control of the branch. Circulars were distributed each month critical of the branch administration. In December 1971 Oliver's team again made a clean sweep of the ballot for Convention delegates. This was the beginning of the end for the Better Deal team. Within a year the Oliver–Mawbey team won a decisive victory in the 1972 NSW Branch elections against the McKay group and a CMC ticket of Leen and Cunningham (former McKay supporters who had fallen out with him), taking all twenty-seven official positions. Oliver defeated McKay for branch secretary and Ernie Ecob was successful against Sid Barnes for the branch presidency. By February 1973 both McKay and Hogan, who were still branch executive councillors, had been charged by Oliver with a contravention of the rules relating to the back-dating of membership tickets, found guilty by the branch executive and removed from office. McKay was eventually appointed a federal arbitration inspector by Clyde Cameron, who by this time held the portfolio of Labour and Immigration in the Whitlam Government.[18]

## The SAU and BWIU Amalgamations

Charlie Oliver had always had big plans for the NSW AWU, and, as he advanced into his mid-seventies, was apparently a man in a hurry. He had hardly dusted off after the struggle with McKay when in April 1974 he announced plans to amalgamate the NSW AWU with the NSW Shop Assistants Union – an amalgamation of State-registered unions, uniting the AWU membership in an unlikely partnership with the States' shop assistants in the retail industry. The federal AWU and the federally registered Shop, Distributive and Allied Employees Association were not officially involved, although it would be an understatement to say that the federal officials of the two unions were keenly interested in the outcome of this unusual proposal. Discussions between Oliver and Barry Egan, the secretary of the NSW SAU, had been going on for several months. There appears to have been little or no consultation with other AWU officials, some of whom were said to have learnt of the proposal in the daily press.[19]

As a result of the amalgamation, there were now two registered unions of the AWU in New South Wales. One was federally registered as the 'Australian Workers Union' and controlled all assets and payment of wages and other outgoings; Oliver remained as branch secretary of this union. The other, also called the 'Australian Workers Union' was the State-registered union which embraced the amalgamation, with a General Branch covering the existing AWU membership. Shop assistants became members of the Shop Distributive Branch. Members of the State AWU also held tickets in their respective federal unions. Oliver became the general president and Egan the general secretary of the State union, which had an executive of ten members drawn equally from the two former unions and a total membership of about 75 000. Oliver hailed the amalgamation as a 'milestone in the magnificent history of the unions', while Egan saw it as 'an excellent opportunity to blaze a trail for democratic membership participation in the union'. The amalgamation failed to draw a public response of any kind from general secretary Frank Mitchell or other federal officials. Mitchell made no mention of the amalgamation in his report to the 1975 AWU Convention, nor was the matter discussed or debated in that forum. The Executive Council meeting of 21 June 1974 noted the amalgamation and agreed that the general secretary 'should enter into negotiations with the General Secretary of the Shop Distributive Allied Employees' Association with the object of merging ... [that union] into The Australian Workers' Union'. An Executive Council meeting of

31 July 1974 discussed plans for a similar amalgamation proposal in Queensland and, in the long term, federally.[20]

For a while, Oliver's gamble to build his own union in New South Wales seemed to have paid off, despite forebodings that there was 'little affinity' between shop assistants and the existing AWU membership. In June 1974 Oliver was able to announce that a settlement had been reached with retail traders to pay New South Wales shop assistants a minimum equal pay rate of $100 a week and grant four weeks' annual leave. The *Worker* reported that during a 24-hour stoppage by members, more than 3000 male and female shop assistants 'overflowed' Sydney Town Hall to hear the branch recommendation and accept the settlement. Oliver thought the outcome 'would have very significant repercussions throughout a wide range of industries'. Employers seemed a little spooked by the union's success, as there was evidence of employer-inspired mass resignations from the union of supervisory staff from the major Sydney stores. This seems to have been balanced by the 'steady stream of enquiries from non-Union members seeking to join the Union'. A year later the *Sydney Morning Herald* reported that the AWU had almost 92 000 members in New South Wales including about 40 000 shop assistants. The union had apparently even resumed recruiting supervisory staff.[21]

By 1977 things had started to go wrong for Oliver, and like many complicated union disputes, the trouble started over money. At the AWU Convention in February, Oliver moved an increase in the annual price of membership tickets for the NSW and WA branches, from $30 for those on adult male rates and $20 and $15 for those on female and junior rates respectively, to $40, with a $20 junior rate. Both branches had registered a deficit in the preceding year. Despite the arguments of Oliver, Mawbey and Gil Barr, the WA Branch secretary, Convention defeated the proposal. Oliver did not believe that this definitely meant 'no'. In early August the Executive Council met to consider its response to Oliver's increase in the annual price of membership tickets for the *State-registered* New South Wales union to $40, and then issuing these tickets for membership of the State union to federally registered AWU NSW Branch members. Under AWU rules, AWU members could have membership in both the State and federal unions for the price of one ticket, and it also meant that Oliver had circumvented the Convention ruling vetoing the dues increase. Oliver was interrogated by his fellow executive councillors in August 1977 over his flagrant disregard of the decision on membership tickets taken at the Convention in January. Oliver gave as good as he got. Victoria–Riverina Branch secretary Don McIntosh, exasperated by Oliver's response to a question, told him, 'You are too good for me'. Oliver replied, 'I think I'm too good for the lot of you'. A little later

McIntosh threw his arms above his head and announced despairingly: 'I have been coming here 25 years. I am stunned. I am buggered. I don't know what it is all about'. Councillor Bradford (Queensland Branch Southern District secretary) then moved that Oliver be called formally before the Executive Council to show cause why he should not be expelled from the AWU. Seconding the motion, McIntosh, somewhat optimistically, observed, 'We will get a cheap legal opinion and it will get Oliver out of my hair'. The vote was tied 6:6, but was carried on the casting vote of the president and Queensland Branch secretary, Edgar Williams. Oliver was unfazed, vowing to 'present his defence at the [next] Executive Council meeting' and pledging 'to invoke every process

Still in front. Having survived the turmoil of the AWU in the 1970s (to which he was a key contributor), the 79-year-old NSW AWU president Charlie Oliver leads NSW branch secretary Ernie Ecob and organiser 'Bluey' Rodwell to a 1981 pastoral industry members meeting at Dubbo. *Oliver Strewe.*

of the law in defence of his membership of the Union'. He told the *Sydney Morning Herald*, 'Whatever they do to me, I'll still be at this desk tomorrow'. No doubt his spirits were lifted by pledges of support such as the following:

> Congratulations. You have joined a select band of militants at last. But don't worry, Charles. Conviction is assured. However you will do them over in the courts. [signed] Wright, Dunford, Groth. [These were some of the SA Branch officials temporarily expelled by the Executive Council in 1965; Oliver was one of those who voted for their expulsion.]
>
> Good luck to you Charlie my friend. We are with you all the way. Best wishes victory from your old mate. [signed] Rex Connor. [Connor was the former Whitlam Government Minister for Minerals and Energy.][22]

At the Federal Executive Council meeting on 26 October 1977, Oliver was expelled from the AWU, once again on the casting vote of the president. Oliver's response was brief: 'Well, another experience. Thank you, gentlemen'. The council appointed an administrator, Ian Ferrier, a Sydney chartered accountant, to take over the affairs of the NSW Branch of the federal union. It had no powers over the State-registered union and Oliver remained president of this organisation and Secretary of its General Branch. Oliver immediately instituted court action to challenge the decision of the Executive Council, and Reg Mawbey, secretary-elect of the NSW Branch, announced he would seek an interim order against the appointment of the administrator. Oliver's expulsion lasted a single day. The Executive Council vote had included a proxy Queensland member who had been appointed by a postal ballot, when the rules called for appointment by a properly constituted meeting of the branch executive. Hence the meeting which had expelled Oliver had been improperly constituted (general secretary Mitchell later maintained that the meeting was aware of the illegitimacy of the proxy but went ahead with the expulsion anyway). Confronted with these facts at a hearing of the Federal Court of Australia, the Executive Council was forced to rescind its resolution of expulsion. Oliver gave an undertaking that he would not, without approval, interfere in matters where the Executive Council had authority.[23]

That was round one in Oliver's clashes with the Executive Council. On 2 August 1977 the *Sydney Morning Herald* unintentionally set off the next round with an 'exclusive report' of a proposed merger between the NSW State-registered AWU and one of its traditional construction industry rivals, the Building Workers Industrial Union (BWIU). This would increase the NSW AWU's estimated membership of 87 000 members to 104 000. The announcement came as a complete surprise. Reg Mawbey, Oliver's close ally, recalled that Oliver had kept discussions with the

BWIU 'under his belt' and had not consulted with anyone. Two weeks later the merger was approved by the AWU State executive. BWIU State secretary Stan Sharkey said he was 'heartened and strengthened' by the unanimous support for the merger within his union, and New South Wales Premier Neville Wran described it as 'thoroughly commendable'. The AWU's federal officials did not share this enthusiasm for Oliver's empire-building. General president and Queensland Branch secretary Edgar Williams published an open letter to the membership in the *Worker*, reviving the communist 'bogey (the BWIU was a left-wing union)' and calling on them to 'beware of strange bedfellows': 'Developments in the past and present show that there is always a valid need to be aware and alert to the activities – the poisonous proddings and cloaked communism of those determined to take the "Australian" out of the Australian Workers' Union'. Equally disenchanted with the idea was Brian O'Neill, New South Wales secretary of the federal branch of the Shop Distributive and Allied Employees Association, who said he opposed the merger on 'ideological and industrial grounds'. O'Neill's concern was shared by SDA president Jim Maher, a union official known for his fierce anti-communism. O'Neill and Maher called a mass meeting of shop assistants to protest vigorously about the plan. They also sought a court injunction to terminate the SAU–AWU amalgamation.[24]

The amalgamation rapidly unravelled. Over 1000 shop assistants voted unanimously to resign from the AWU in protest against the BWIU amalgamation at the mass meeting called by O'Neill and Maher, and called on employers to stop deducting union fees. The 'big six' major New South Wales retailers were quick to oblige, actively encouraging employees to resign from the AWU and join the SDA. The extent to which the major retailers were involved in the struggle between the AWU and the SDA is demonstrated by the fact that the management of one unnamed retailer issued written guidelines to branch managers on introducing SDA delegates at organised meetings of employees:

> The Manager should address staff ... to introduce the [SDA] delegate/spokesperson:
> 'We are aware of the concern of many staff regarding current industrial problems. Accordingly I have pleasure in introducing Mr ... the store Union Delegate, to talk to you. I should add the Company will deduct from your pay, union dues on behalf of the SDA.'
> Delegate/Spokesperson should then take over the meeting and sign up all staff in a group, prior to them commencing work. Cards, registration and Enrolment should be collected and taken immediately to Accounts.

Interference from employers was met by stern action from the AWU and BWIU. By 5 September 1977, eight building industry unions imposed an indefinite ban on all concrete deliveries to four major building sites in Sydney at which retail centres were under construction. The AWU warned that other sites would be included unless the NSW Retail Traders Association discouraged opposition to the merger. Oliver announced: 'If the bosses want to fight over this one they can be sure that the unions are ready to fight them'. Tom McDonald, BWIU president, echoed these sentiments, warning that it was 'now war against the big six and anyone else that wants to take their side'. By early November, however, Maher was able to claim that 32 000 shop assistants had resigned from the State-registered AWU. While the AWU had award coverage, Maher pointed out that the SDA had the membership and the union fee deduction agreement with the major retailers. The three-year-old amalgamation was effectively over, and the NSW Supreme Court put the final nail in the coffin in February 1978, when it ruled that the amalgamation was always invalid because certain provisions of the NSW Trade Union Act had not been observed. With the demise of the 1974 amalgamation came the end of any suggestion of a similar arrangement with the BWIU. Oliver's State-registered AWU underwent formal re-registration as a legitimate legal entity with the NSW Industrial Commission and its existence continued, but as a poor imitation of the colossus envisaged by Oliver four years before. There was to be no reconciliation between Oliver and his federal counterparts. In the midst of the BWIU amalgamation proposal, Oliver had nominated against the incumbent Frank Mitchell for the position of AWU general secretary in the 1977 ballot for federal positions. According to Mawbey the move was motivated more by mischief than anything else, and Mitchell won comfortably. Many years later Mitchell still saw the challenge by Oliver as a 'last desperate attempt to gather momentum in respect of his plans to control the AWU', the success of which would have been 'a disaster for the union'.[25]

Barry Egan's fortunes fell further than Oliver's. From joint control of the largest union in New South Wales (and one of the largest in Australia), he became an increasingly marginalised official of the NSW AWU. He had no chance of returning to a position within the SDA. Mike Forshaw, who became an industrial officer in the federal AWU office in 1976, recalls that with the collapse of the SAU amalgamation 'Egan's opponents in the NSW Labor Party [had] a chance to get back at him ... Egan had been a strong supporter of the [ALP] Right in NSW ... however with the creation of this huge state union, he tried to exercise power and influence ... and tried to create a third force [between the Right and the Left] in the NSW ALP'. Egan became the focus of the enmity which resulted from the unwelcome factional instability created by the SAU–AWU amalgamation, and intensified by the proposed amalgamation with the BWIU. In his diaries Clyde Cameron recalls an October

1977 conversation with federal Labor MP Lionel Bowen, who had talked with fellow MP and NSW ALP president Paul Keating a few days previously. Keating had told Bowen triumphantly, 'Egan is gone!' Keating said the SDA had almost all the shop assistants signed up. Cameron reported this conversation to Egan, who optimistically declared that although the SDA had 'captured practically the whole membership of the six biggest stores', he still expected that the AWU would cling to the shop assistants' membership. Egan was wrong. Mike Forshaw recalls, 'I think they maintained a few hundred members in some local company warehouses in New South Wales, but effectively they were destroyed. I used to see him [Egan] around the [NSW AWU] office, but I've got to say in those days people had a lot of trouble trying to figure out precisely what the issues were and what hats they were wearing'. The ageing Oliver presided over a much-diminished empire. Barry Egan remained with the AWU until 1984, when he took up a position with the Federal Government's Veterans' Review Board.[26]

## The Pastoral Industry

Industrially, the AWU was challenged in two major directions during the 1970s: consolidation of AWU coverage in both new and traditional workplaces, and the battle to achieve wage justice for members in the rural sector. By 1970 the AWU was becoming increasingly concerned with the low level of wage rates in the pastoral industry, particularly those of station-hands, who were receiving a minimum wage of $42 for a 44-hour week. In that year the Arbitration Commission had declined the union's application for a standard 40-hour week for station-hands and other improved conditions. The AWU nevertheless resolved that station-hands should work only a 40-hour week, Monday to Friday, with overtime at the rate of time and a half for the first three hours and double thereafter; after a series of stoppages and work bans on properties which refused to accept these conditions, the commission agreed to rehear the matter. The commission again refused to award a 40-hour week but did increase wage rates by $4 to $46.60 a week. Dougherty told delegates at the 1972 Convention that the decision 'did nothing to enhance the use of the Arbitration Commission by this Union or to resolve our declining confidence in its discriminating approach to the working conditions of station hands'.[27]

The 1970s saw an end to the years of post-war abundance. International economic developments had a major impact on the Australian economy with the result that in the early years of the decade economic activity had slowed, wage–price inflation had taken off and unemployment had risen. Growth in gross domestic product, which had shown a rise of 8.6 per cent in 1968, could only manage a rate of 3.2 per cent in

1970–71. In the rural sector, wool prices collapsed in the eighteen months to the beginning of 1970, when the lowest prices for twenty years were recorded, a situation compounded by spiralling production costs. In the late 1950s wool added 50 per cent of the aggregate value of Australia's exports; this had fallen to 20 per cent by the early 1970s. This decline had industrial consequences. Charlie Oliver told the 1972 AWU Convention that workers in the industry had received fewer wage increases than workers in other industries. Frank Mitchell thought most of the trouble in the industry could be sheeted home to the growers. He accused them of having been idle since the Great Depression about technological research in the industry: they 'had sat back and grown fat and reaped rewards in the last 30 years'. Wool was rapidly losing ground to synthetic fibres, with a consequent reduction in demand for fleece.[28]

Nevertheless the AWU was able to make some progress with increases in the Pastoral Industry Award. During 1973–74 shearing rates were increased from $26.05 to $42 per 100. Weekly wages for shed-hands increased from $104.40 to $120.45 a week. Station-hands now received up to $84.80 a week, depending on experience, an increase from $71.83. Mitchell hailed this as 'the biggest single increase ever gained in the Federal Pastoral Award'. By the end of the decade, the Federal Pastoral Industry Award provided for a shearing rate of $68.13 per 100 for flock sheep, station-hands were granted a wage of $149.90 a week without keep, adult shed-hands earned $198.30 a week, and station cooks were guaranteed a weekly wage of $265.60. The federal rates were substantially in parity with the rates under the Queensland State Award, where the shearing rate was $68.29 per 100 and shed-hands were paid between $207 and $211 a week. But there were problems on the horizon. AWU officials were increasingly concerned about the steady increase in the numbers of New Zealand shearers working in Australia using wide combs – combs wider than the 64 mm defined in the Pastoral Industry Award. The 1975 AWU Convention resolved that the Commonwealth Government require all pastoral workers seeking employment in Australia to have a work permit and to provide a legislative guarantee that overseas workers would not breach Australian trade union work and wage conditions. The ACTU was urged to take 'positive action'. In 1978 the AWU Convention asked the New Zealand shearers' union to inform its members that wide-gauge gear was illegal in Australia. Five years later, these simmering concerns would erupt into the bitter wide-comb dispute.[29]

## Resources and Construction

Throughout the decade the AWU was challenged by other unions over its right to cover workers in a range of industries. The resource and construction industries saw the most significant confrontation. Dougherty informed delegates at the 1971 AWU Annual Convention of 'intrusions' by other unions in the oil-drilling industry, citing the Federated Iron-workers Association, and moves by the Transport Workers Union in the oil refineries. Dougherty said the ironworkers were attempting to poach AWU members covered by the Oil Drilling Rig Workers Award, particularly in Victoria. The Transport Workers Union had been warded off, 'more or less successfully' after having made a 'strange' application to absorb the area the AWU had been servicing in Queensland, parts of Western Australia and areas in some of the other States. The AWU lost some members to the Professional Divers Association in 1974 when the latter obtained an award to cover oilfield diving. But the AWU recorded a number of successes in the oil industry during the 1970s. In 1974 the industry obtained a 35-hour working week which, in particular, meant more leisure for shiftworkers, most of whom were AWU members. Within a year the combined oil unions had also won wage increases of around $34 a week throughout the industry. In July 1977 the Commonwealth Conciliation and Arbitration Court awarded further increases of between $15 and $26 a week to oil industry workers. At Convention the following year, Frank Mitchell announced to delegates that the AWU was now the 'pace-setter' in the oil industry, and said that any improvements achieved by other unions in the industry 'have been a mere flow on from AWU benefits'. Throughout the 1970s and the early 1980s the oil industry remained a key sector for union efforts to win wage increases which could then be spread to other industries.[30]

While the AWU has experienced various confrontations with other unions over demarcation issues during the course of its history, none rivals the intense industrial war fought between the Builders Labourers Federation and the AWU during the period 1976–86. The AWU, and several other major unions in the construction industry, were faced by a fiercely militant BLF, determined to increase its membership coverage in an industry where technological change was increasingly displacing un-skilled labourers, and where several unions had the expertise and constitutional coverage to be able to enrol BLF members.

In 1974 the federal BLF was deregistered, mainly because of the militant industrial and environmental activities (the Green Bans) of the Jack Mundey-led NSW BLF. The AWU opposed BLF re-registration in 1976, although Mitchell conceded that the application would succeed because the ACTU had ruled that unions should not enrol members of a deregistered organisation. The AWU's antipathy towards the BLF had been aggravated by a demarcation dispute between the two unions early in 1976, over coverage of workers building railway stations on the new underground rail loop project in Melbourne. The picket line at

Parliament Station was described by one former BLF official as a 'drawn
out, bitter affair'. Mitchell attacked the BLF's 'disgraceful and violent
attacks on our members'. The BLF was re-registered in October 1976 and
in 1977 served a log of claims throughout Australia, seeking to intrude
on AWU coverage in North Queensland, in batching plants, concrete
product yards and construction work in all States. The AWU negotiated
with its persistent competitor, and at the 1978 Convention Mitchell
optimistically announced that it had been agreed that the status quo
would prevail between the two unions. Mitchell later announced that the
AWU was developing its own ambitious plans for a new Civil Engineering,
Construction and Maintenance Award to cover 20 000 workers constructing aluminium smelters, mines, roads, bridges, power stations and
water and sewerage works – any of the private and public sector civil
construction projects which employed AWU members. The AWU wanted
a 35-hour week for workers covered by the award, $800 a week for
general work (they already earned up to $500 a week), and $1000 a week
for workers handling mechanical equipment. By the beginning of the
decade Mitchell, metaphorically rubbing his hands together, hoped that
the AWU might cover 80 000 workers under this award – 'once the
resources boom gets going'. But while the AWU hoped for a peaceful
development of its plans, the BLF had other ideas.[31]

The decade 1976–86 was one of barely restrained industrial warfare
between the two unions, as the BLF persistently sought to poach AWU
work. During this period the AWU fought hand-to-hand demarcation
disputes with the BLF over the construction of Alcoa's aluminium
smelter at Portland in Victoria, over bridge construction in Tasmania,
Victoria and South Australia, the concrete products industry in Canberra
and the construction of the Loy Yang (Victoria) and Tomago power
stations (New South Wales). During 1984–85 this workplace struggle
intensified, with highly publicised disputes on projects as diverse as the
Melbourne Cricket Ground light towers, the Portland smelter, the
Federal Parliament House building, and the F9 freeway. In New South
Wales, the BLF targeted AWU and FIA members working at Alcan's
Granville factory in April 1984, related to the BLF's efforts to cover
workers on aluminium smelter construction. After several violent inci-
dents the AWU and the FIA sought the BLF's suspension from the
ACTU. This move was unsuccessful; the BLF was still able to muster
support from left-wing ACTU affiliates, whose members it had not yet
targeted with the same aggression with which it had pursued members of
the right-wing AWU and FIA during the 1970s and 1980s. But time was
running out for the BLF. In January 1985 the NSW Government
deregistered the State-registered BLF, after prolonged industrial conflict,
particularly on the site of the new Sydney Police Centre, a dispute which

united left- and right-wing New South Wales unions against the BLF. In June 1985 BLF national secretary Norm Gallagher was convicted of corruptly receiving twenty secret commissions from building companies, leading to virtual anarchy in the building industry, particularly in Victoria, as the BLF defied the verdicts of the courts, governments and the ACTU in a frenzied effort to maintain its influence in the workplace. In March 1986 the ACTU finally abandoned the rebel union, citing its failure to adhere to ACTU wage policies (the BLF tried to win the support of building workers with disputes over big wage claims), and in April 1986 the Federal and Victorian Governments enacted legislation to deregister the union in their industrial jurisdictions. The BLF was also deregistered in the Australian Capital Territory and the Northern Territory. The AWU celebrated the BLF's demise. General secretary Gil Barr declared that 'the AWU has borne the brunt of the BLF's attacks on the membership of other unions, and we now intend to take back everything that rightfully belongs to the union'. The AWU negotiated agreements with the BWIU, the FEDFA and the remnants of the BLF (the BLF remained registered in Queensland, Tasmania, Western Australia and South Australia, covering a few hundred members. These branches merged with the BWIU in 1991), to absorb the BLF's membership in Victoria and New South Wales and define the blurred lines of demarcation in the civil construction industry.[32]

As the AWU approached its centenary, it was being drawn further away from its pastoral roots. Frank Mitchell estimated that in the early 1980s shearers comprised a mere 5 per cent of AWU membership. Between 1969 and 1979 average annual employment in the rural sector fell from 427 000 to 370 000. In mining, employment increased from 63 600 to 81 100 and in building and construction, from 479 900 to almost 534 000. There had been two minor amalgamations during the 1970s; with the Sugar Workers Union in 1975 and with the Basil and Wool Workers Union the following year. Yet AWU membership had fallen over the decade, from around 150 000 at its beginning to 120 000 by the end.[33]

The focus of Frank Mitchell's report to the 1979 AWU Annual Convention was a gradually worsening problem, 'the social disaster commonly termed unemployment'. Registered unemployed in Australia had risen steeply from 51 000 in 1970 to 417 000 by 1979. Mitchell saw automation as one of the principal causes of the nation's malady. He urged the government to establish 'an immense development programme to utilise more fully the Nation's resources' and thus restore employment to a reasonable level or face the question 'of socially maintaining the victims who have been cast from employment through industries' desire to change from manual labour to machines'. Unemployment seemed to be an intractable problem, resisting easy cure.[34]

The problems the AWU faced in the 1980s were, if not intractable, certainly difficult. The AWU of 1980 was a very different body from that which had emerged from the turmoils of the 1960s. The long Dougherty era had ended; Charlie Oliver's ambitions had been unceremoniously deflated by the amalgamation disasters of 1977. What remained to be seen was how successful the AWU would be in surviving the economic roller-coaster in the decade ahead, and the aggressive challenges of New Right employers in the mining and pastoral industries.

CHAPTER 14

# Out of the Past
*Wide Combs, Robe River and Renewal, 1980–94*

Origins are never once and for all, but in the way of imagination re-arise
intuitively, by demand, at various points in time and at different places
*Roger McDonald*[1]

The 1980s were apparently an era of success for the labour movement.
From March 1983 unions shared unprecedented industrial relations
power with the national Labor Government led by Prime Minister Bob
Hawke. The instrument of this power-sharing was the Prices and Incomes
Accord, through which wage restraint was traded by unions for a say in
the national political agenda. Yet this success bred an employer reaction
from two important sectors of AWU coverage. While employers in the
manufacturing industries continued to adopt a cautious approach to
industrial relations, mining and rural employers emerged as the
champions of the New Right and the heroes of the H. R. Nicholls Society,
challenging the union movement in a way not seen since the pastoral
and maritime battles of the 1890s. The New Right wanted to decentralise
arbitration and unravel the intricate web of comparative wage justice, the
principle which linked wage increases across industries. In the rural
sector, the National Farmers Federation, the peak industry employer
council established in July 1979, became the most strident – and often
successful – advocate of fighting union power. Victory in the wide-comb
dispute in 1983 encouraged the NFF to a decade of aggression against
the AWU. In the mining sector, the 1986 dispute at Robe River
symbolised the zeal with which the New Right wanted to remove unions
from the relationship between worker and management: freedom of
contract, freedom to manage. It was the fear of these aggressive
employers, acting in concert with future anti-union Liberal–National
Party governments in Canberra and the States, which gave a sense of

urgency to the union amalgamation program encouraged by the ACTU, and the Keating Government's embrace of a 'controlled' form of enterprise bargaining in the 1994 Industrial Relations Reform Act. The Labor era 1983–94 had been troubled by an urge to anticipate hostile employers, and to restrain the persistent demand for deregulation of the labour market. Yet the deregulatory logic of Labor's national reform agenda since 1983 had pushed industrial relations law and practice in this very direction – a difficult environment for organising unions.[2]

The Queensland Branch remained the key to the AWU's complex politics. In 1981 the branch had 50 000 members, nearly half the total membership of 115 000. Its ten-strong delegation to Annual Convention was twice the size of those of the next largest branches, New South Wales and Victoria. But in the early 1980s its potential power both within the union and the Queensland labour movement was not fully realised. Between 1982 and 1988 neither general secretaries Frank Mitchell (1972–84) and Gil Barr (1984–88) nor general president Allan Begg (1982–89) were Queenslanders, and Barr and Begg were politically left-wing in outlook. Edgar Williams retired as federal AWU president in 1982, after having served since 1965. He also retired as Queensland Branch secretary after twenty-two years, during which time the Queensland AWU had been unable to recover the political influence it had enjoyed before the Labor split of 1957. During the 1980s the AWU was able to restore its political power in Queensland. Within the AWU, the attitude of the Queensland Branch was crucial to the success of the planned amalgamation with the Federated Ironworkers Association, a proposal temporarily destabilised when Queensland Branch secretary Bill Ludwig fell out with his predecessor Errol Hodder (1982–88), who became the AWU's general secretary in August 1988.[3]

The industrial nature of the AWU's membership changed greatly in the twenty years before the 1993 amalgamation. Rural sector employment continued a steady decline; unskilled work in manufacturing and mining processes and in the sugar industry felt the increasing impact of technological change. Tourism lured young job-seekers away from timber-getting. AWU members, scattered across the nation, worked in local government, brickyards, horse-racing; they were greenkeepers; they picked grapevines and fruit trees. Yet despite this diversity, or because of it, the image of the AWU as the shearers' union remained constant. It was a reassuring point of reference amid the blizzard of disparate callings, a touchstone of past greatness to which the *Worker* regularly paid homage. Ex-shearers dominated official positions, far exceeding their proportion of the overall membership, which was down to around 5 per cent by the late 1980s.

It was a robustly, doggedly male identity, which NSW AWU secretary Ernie Ecob was determined to defend in the face of the relentless

One of the few: NSW woman shearer Trudi Anesbury, *c.* 1980. *National Library of Australia.*

Packing 'Ovalteenies', Hobart, 1985. Women AWU members have traditionally worked on production lines in the fruit and food industries. *Oliver Strewe.*

changes separating image from reality. In 1989 he warned that young women were introducing sex and drugs into the shearing industry, and were undermining male employment by taking shed-hands' jobs. 'They live among the men. When the two get together, they play.' He shouldn't have worried; it was a very slow form of moral decay. In 1994 there were only an estimated six women shearers in Australia, and only two in New South Wales. Of an estimated 1500 shed-hands, about 400 were women, some of whom were long tired of this discrimination. In 1974 the 'disgusted' daughter of a female shed-hand gave Frank Mitchell a piece of her mind, complaining that her mother and a friend had been denied shed work because they were of the 'weaker sex'.

> This is not so. I will have you know that my mum packs the best punch in the Riverina, and her mate has the reputation of being one of the best crack shots from here to Booligal ... You should be ashamed of yourselves. I reckon that they could shear the pants off you and any of your so-called 'workmen'. In fact, I strongly suspect that you're just scared to let them be rouseabouts because you sense their inward superiority of brain and brawn. Give them a go, you horrible little men, and pretty soon you'll see the power and skill of these famous ladies (Cassius Kate and Lightning).[4]

Yet as hairdressers (the NSW Branch amalgamated with the State-registered Hairdressers and Wigmakers Association in 1982), cannery workers, grape-pickers, Queensland hospital workers and in various manufacturing industry jobs, women were accepted as AWU members. But perhaps they were because they worked in jobs where women 'belonged'. The same Ernie Ecob who complained about women in the shearing sheds observed in 1985 that the wage indexation principles under the Accord increased discrimination against women:

> Since equal pay arrived in 1972 there are many women, members of ours employed particularly in the manufacturing industry who whilst doing work comparable to men in the same industry have been paid lesser rates because they have been pushed into particular classifications or areas of work which have been downgraded. In a sense these have become women only jobs and they are not receiving equal pay for equal work value.

In 1986 the first female Convention delegate, Queensland Branch industrial officer Deirdre Swan, attended the union's centenary Convention in Ballarat. She was one of the few female industrial staff employed by the AWU, a reflection of the broader labour movement. While the workforce changed, in 1986 only 11 per cent of Australian union officials were women. It was just one of the changes the AWU was slowly accepting. But as the union moved in new directions, the past followed in step.[5]

### 'Bringing Back the Raddle': the Pastoral Industry, 1980–93

In August 1982 shearers across Australia walked out of the woolsheds during the spring shearing season, frustrated by the refusal of graziers to grant a $36.69 a week wage increase. A newspaper correspondent recorded that 'these men, who were once the aristocrats of rural labour, have seen their relativities dwindle drastically in the past 25 years. In 1956 a man who could shear 100 sheep a day earned $73 a week' – almost double the average weekly wage, then the equivalent of $36 a week. The strike was also an expression of the shearers' anger at both their declining wage status and the difficult conditions they had long had to endure to follow their calling. 'The shearers and their pastoral workmates say there's not a metalworker in the country who would put up with the conditions that they have to endure – on some stations living quarters are still primitive, there is only a lavatory out the back instead of a septic system; at night they read by the light of kerosene lamps.' As one shearer sardonically observed, 'for entertainment there's only the cook to chase when the food is crook'. In 1982 it was estimated that there were 13–14 000 shearers across Australia, but Ernie Ecob said there were few

gun shearers left. 'They'd got out because the pay's no good', an assessment apparently borne out by a 1986 study by rural training experts
which showed that Australia's then estimated 12 000 shearers were aging.
One-third of shearers were over 40 years old; only 8 per cent were under
20. Of these, as few as 5–7000 were permanent full-time shearers. In 1982
the shearing rate was $82.88 per 100, which over a weekly period
amounted to a little more than national average weekly earnings, which
were $316.50. Shed-hands earned $203 a week after paying $41 for board
and lodgings. On this occasion, the strike seemed to fulfil its aims. The
Commonwealth Arbitration Commission granted a two-stage $36 a week
increase under the Pastoral Industry Award, a flow-on (following the
principle of comparative wage justice) of increases granted under the
Metal Industry Award. In September 1982 the commission handed down
an immediate increase of $22 a week, with the additional $14 to be
deferred and relisted for hearing in February 1983. At this hearing the
National Farmers Federation based its renewed opposition to the
increase on an 'incapacity to pay', a chant the NFF would repeat throughout the decade. In 1982–83 life was tough on the land. Many commodities like wheat, wool and sugar had been hit by low prices, and drought
had also taken a toll, exacerbating the debts many farmers accumulated
– and continued to accumulate – in the 1980s. Further hearings of the
$14 claim were deferred in June 1983 and February 1984. On 2 July 1984
a full bench of the Arbitration Commission finally awarded an $11 a week
increase, the judgment referring to 'a noticeable recovery in the rural
sector since the earlier proceedings'.[6]

For many pastoral workers, grievances over wages and conditions were
part of a pattern of change and decline. Old AWU loyalists regretted the
advent of the weekend shearer, the 'sugar bag' shearer, driving out to
shear Monday to Friday, returning home of an evening and on the
weekends, unravelling the bonds of traditional mateship – and union
membership – forged in the shearing shed, or by sharing experiences
around a hut fire. As SA Branch organiser and former shearer Rocky
Gehan recalls, older shearers once had the time to correct any tendency
among younger members who might be tempted to cut corners or erode
long-established conditions. 'You went to a shed and you stayed there
until it was finished. Whether it was a fortnight or six weeks or two
months. You could talk to each other, and educate one another.' For
many shearers, the erosion of this unity seemed to be symbolised by a
New Zealander brandishing wide-comb shears.[7]

Keith Plunkett was a shearer and organiser with the SA Branch, reared
to abide by the traditions of the AWU. 'It was my life, the shearing
industry, the first thing in my life used to be the union ... I suppose if I
had any other religion it was Labor. I come from a union family, my dad

Keith Plunkett (right) as a young shearer in 1961, with fellow shearer John
Nestor at Cuthero Station, New South Wales. The pastoral industry standards
of Keith's youth had irrevocably changed by the 1980s. *Betty Plunkett.*

was a union man – a shearer – [and] the first thing he told me was to
make sure you've got your union ticket.' As far back as the 1960s, he had
challenged shearers, often New Zealanders, who worked Australian sheds
with a crude form of the wide-comb shear – the 'pulled' comb shears and
'merry widows'. As he explained, 'the pulled comb was a [standard
64 mm] comb that the blokes used to put in a rifle barrel or a piece of
iron or something and they just pull the edges out, pull two teeth out and
make it a bit wider'. The 'merry widow' was a comb which was wider
again than the pulled comb (as shearer and NSW Branch secretary
[1993–] Mick O'Shea explained, the merry widow was so named because
'we reckoned we could get a bit more out of them'). These wide combs
were preferred by New Zealand shearers because of the kind of sheep
they were used to shear – what Plunkett calls 'open cutting' sheep.
'There's not many Merinos over in New Zealand, they are mainly all
Corriedales or the big sheep – plain sheep, there is no wrinkles ... [they]
cut a lot easier than Merinos do.' Seventy-five per cent of Australia's
sheep were Merinos, bred specifically for their rich fleece of fine-quality
wool. The AWU believed that wide-comb shears – up to 86 mm wide –
could damage the dense fleece and heavily wrinkled skin of Merino
sheep. And given the competitive nature of shearing, the use of a

standard-size 64 mm comb meant that all shearers were competing on even terms. As the number of New Zealand shearers working Australian sheds steadily increased in the 1960s and 1970s, so too did their non-conformist shearing techniques. Plunkett believed the New Zealanders were less committed unionists than the Australians, and were more willing to ignore traditional union rules. During 1982–93 the AWU repeatedly lobbied the Federal Government to restrict the employment of New Zealanders in the Australian shearing industry, but the government would only offer to ensure that New Zealand shearers conformed with local tax laws.[8]

Running parallel with the NFF applications to restrict wage rises through the 'incapacity to pay' application, several State graziers' associations had applied for the approval of the Commonwealth Arbitration Commission to officially allow the use of wide-comb shears in the Australian shearing industry. In May 1982 the *Worker* saw the threatened introduction of wide combs as the thin end of the wedge: 'Not long ago the woolgrowers supplied us with a bed and a cook, but now that is generally a thing of the past. Now they want the wide comb. Next they'll want us shearing seven days a week. Then they'll want to bring back the raddle. If they don't like the way you shear a sheep they'll mark it as a reject and you won't be paid for it. In no time we'll be back to the conditions the industry had before 1900.'[9] As Keith Plunkett observes, 'wide combs were only one part of it. Because the hours – we had unique hours for workers, all my life I never did overtime ... now they can shear any bloody hours. If I caught a bloke shearing weekends – once I caught a bloke one Friday night shearing about seven or eight o'clock at night and geez I put the wood right on him. But now that's nothing because they shear bloody seven days a week in some cases. But virtually, the shearing industry – all their conditions went backwards – all the things that we fought for all those years – all of a sudden went backwards.'[10]

On 10 December 1982 Arbitration Commissioner McKenzie agreed to remove the clause of the Pastoral Industry Award which effectively forbade shearers to use a comb more than 64 mm wide, commenting that 'stripped of its emotionalism, the shearers' case has little merit in it'. He was unimpressed by AWU invocations of the 'spirit of the forefathers of the 1890s' to justify opposition to the 'immoral and repulsive' wide comb; this emotive language, 'to the objective observer, appears to be hedged in by conservatism and tinged with hysteria'. McKenzie was apparently swayed by a University of New England study which concluded that 'wide combs result in a reduction in time required to shear in the order of 17 per cent, cause no significant reduction in the quality of the shearing job, and cause no increase in the proportion of skin cuts'.[11]

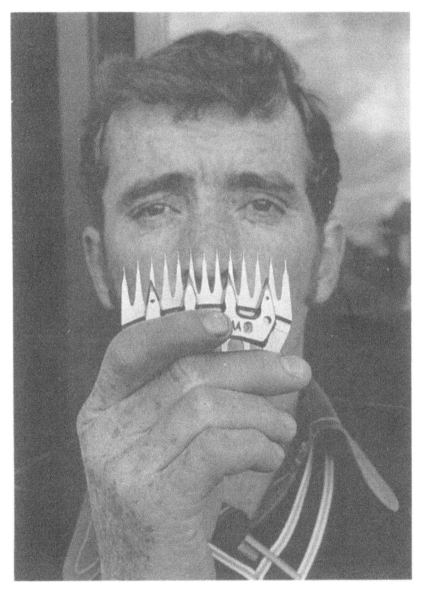

An AWU shearer brandishes an offending wide comb, Dubbo 1981. The simmering resentment of wide-comb shearers – often from New Zealand – erupted into industrial conflict and sporadic violence in 1983–84. *Oliver Strewe.*

On 23 March 1983 the AWU lost an appeal against McKenzie's decision, and the next day shearers in New South Wales, Victoria and South Australia voted to strike. At a mass meeting in Dubbo (NSW), members voted 531:1 to strike. Ernie Ecob told the meeting that Western Australia had been the weak link in the AWU's opposition to wide combs. He said that most of the commission's evidence came from Western Australia, a State where local and New Zealand shearers using wide combs had been prevalent for some years, and where the AWU's presence in the pastoral industry was weakest. He claimed that AWU membership among WA shearers had dropped from 900 to less than 100. The AWU's Executive Council endorsed strike action on 30 March and urged the Federal Government to place restrictions on the entry of New Zealand shearers into Australia during the course of the strike.[12]

Some shearers did not support the strike. On 6 April, a meeting of shearers in Wagga voted 166:1 to return to work. A spokesman for the meeting claimed that shearers had to pay bills and had families to feed. 'Unions are good if they are controlled, but it's starting to get out of hand when a bloke tells you you can't get to work.' Two days later, a meeting of 250 AWU loyalists in Dubbo declared the Wagga dissidents 'insignificant ratbags', and claimed that union members were solid in support of the strike. Across south-eastern Australia there were sporadic outbursts of anger and violence between strikers and non-strikers. On 14 April fifteen men attacked twelve working shearers at Mutooroo Station in north-east South Australia. The intruders arrived in four cars and demanded that the men stop work. The manager agreed, after he and the overseer were assaulted. Reports of violence also came from Victoria and New South Wales; at a station near Heywood in the Western District of Victoria twenty men armed with guns and sticks invaded a property where shearing was under way. The station owner commented that 'our five shearers ran off as soon as the men arrived and they haven't been back'. A shearing shed near Parkes was burnt to the ground on 10 May, as the strike entered its sixth week. By April the NSW Livestock and Grain Producers Association claimed that the dispute was costing the industry $10 million a week and could result in the destruction of hundreds of thousands of sheep unless they were shorn immediately.[13]

There were signs that shearing might be soon back to normal. On 9 May shearers in South Australia voted to return to work, and shearers in Victoria and Tasmania followed this lead a few days later. The strike had never really taken off in Western Australia, where, as Ecob indicated, AWU support was low; and there had been no industrial action taken in Queensland (the prohibition on wide-comb shearing remained undisturbed in the Queensland Pastoral Award). Finally, on 16 May, New South Wales shearers also voted to return to work, after an assurance that a 'full ranging medical inquiry' would be launched by Commissioner McKenzie into the occupational health and safety implications of using wide-comb shears. The NSW LGPA estimated that 300 000 ewes and lambs collapsed and died under the weight of excess wool during the eight-week strike; each striking shearer had lost around $2000 in wages.[14]

It was an uneasy peace. In many country towns, particularly in New South Wales, brawls frequently broke out over the use of wide combs. In June 1983 forty men entered a property at Moree and broke shearing gear; fights were also reported at Walgett, Coonamble, Warren, Bourke, Hay and Deniliquin. According to Ernie Ecob, New Zealanders provoked many of the fights sensationally reported by the media. All of this played into the hands of the NFF, with many graziers, in defiance of the award, refusing AWU organisers entry to their properties to inspect sheds. Ecob added, 'This is why the Employers are so adamant that the wide comb decision should remain, as it has put the workers of Australia back to 1890 when the Army was called in to give support to the Graziers of this country to down the workers'. On 5 June 1984 Commissioner McKenzie confirmed his 1982 decision to allow the use of wide-comb shears. It was another five months before shearers in New South Wales voted at a meeting at Dubbo on 24 November to accept the decision to use combs up to 86 mm wide. Rocky Gehan later listened to some South Australian shearers acknowledging that they could quickly tote up bigger tallies – and bigger cheques – with the wide combs. But he didn't see much benefit for the shed-hands, weekly wage employees who needed a long shearing season to earn reasonable money. 'They [the graziers] didn't employ any more shedhands. They cut the sheds out a lot quicker. They used to shear up until Christmas, now they are home a month before Christmas.'[15]

In November 1984 the AWU held a National Pastoral Industry Conference in Sydney to prepare claims for two new awards to supersede the old award structure, one covering the shearing industry and the other covering farmworkers. By 1984, there were 70 000 farmworkers employed around Australia, working for $220–223.60, well below the average weekly wage of $316.50. The 77-year-old Station Hands Award which regulated their conditions covered working with animals, but not motor vehicles, tractors or bulldozers. General secretary Gil Barr said that the new award would provide for higher wages and allowances for operating farm machinery. Barr noted that AWU plant operators in other industries could earn up to $500 for skilled work, with free board and lodgings, which rural workers usually had to pay for. The NFF responded that any wage increases would cost jobs; farmers were themselves struggling on low pay.[16]

The NFF's fierce resistance to even modest National Wage Case increases during 1985–86 forced the AWU to set aside its applications for new pastoral and station-hands' awards. As Barr explained to the 1987 Convention, 'until the various incapacity to pay cases had been completed we were unable to serve a detailed log of claims throughout the industry to renew the Award'. The NFF's opposition to NWC increases persisted despite an upturn in commodity prices (wool prices reached a record level in 1986–87) and despite the industry's ability to fund an anti-union Fighting Fund, established by the NFF in 1985. The *Worker* observed that the NFF apparently 'CAN'T SPEND $5 per week on workers – CAN SPEND $15 million fighting unions' (The NFF claimed that fund only contained $10 million). Despite these difficulties, in November 1989 the AWU proceeded with an application for a 3 per cent increase in the Pastoral Industry Award and presented the new Federal Industrial Relations Commission (a new Industrial Relations Act superseded the 1904 legislation in 1988) with a detailed award-restructuring submission. The NFF again opposed this application on the grounds of 'incapacity to pay'. Finally in February 1991 Commissioner Merriman created a new Pastoral Industry Award. The award provided some significant wage increases for shed-hands and cooks, and increased various allowances, but the increases provided for shearers and wool-pressers were low. And in two important respects, the AWU believed the decision was 'disastrous', as it introduced provision for weekend shearing and changed the way shed-hands and cooks were to be paid: from a weekly

NSW AWU Organiser Mick O'Shea confers with shearers, 1981. The meeting offers a brief respite from the punishing routine of shearing. *Oliver Strewe.*

basis to payment by the run, which could lead to lower wages for these workers if work was disrupted or if shed-hands were engaged on a short-week basis. The AWU unsuccessfully appealed against these changes, although the full bench decision of April 1992 did restrict weekend work to offsetting time lost to wet weather during the ordinary working week. The commission also ruled that workers could not be compelled to work weekends. The shearing rate set by the award was $146.90 per 100 for a shearer using his own handpiece ($144.20 if not), and shed-hands would receive $524.20 for a full week of twenty runs (the old full-week rate was $424.70). Rates for station-hands were also increased to $325.40–$375.40, depending on length of experience. A new pastoral industry super-annuation scheme was also introduced in 1992, the Rural Employees Award Plan, administered by Mercantile Mutual Insurance with both employer and employee representatives. REAP's birth had also been difficult, with the NFF initially preferring to support two existing funds managed by insurance companies with which farmers' associations had maintained commercial links.[17]

The AWU's decade-long difficulties with the rural sector did not ease with the April 1992 decision. In Victoria, the recently elected Kennett Liberal Government quickly set about deregulating the Victorian indus-trial relations system to provide for individual employment contracts between workers and employers, with unions barred from 'interference' in the contract negotiation process. These moves were welcomed by the Victorian Farmers Federation, which in July 1993 encouraged members to embrace individual employment contracts, in part by resigning membership from another NFF-related employer organisation which was registered under the Federal Industrial Relations Act. An NFF spokesman claimed that Victorian farmers had signed 7000 individual employment contracts with farm and pastoral workers since the deregulation of the Victorian industrial relations system. In protest at this deregulation, the Victorian Branch of the AWU staged a one-day strike on 15 October 1993. This action did not prevent the formation in Ballarat, Victoria, in April 1994 of the breakaway Shearers and Rural Workers Union (S&RWU), led by former Victorian Branch organiser Steve Roach. Roach claimed that pastoral workers were unhappy with the November 1993 amalgamation of the AWU with the Federation of Industrial, Manufacturing and Engineering Employees (see below), and wanted their own separate union to press their industrial claims. AWU-FIME joint national secretary Ian Cambridge (1994–) argued that the S&RWU, which was not an industrially registered organisation, simply played into the hands of the NFF, and could not effectively bargain on behalf of pastoral workers. By mid-1994 the S&RWU had attracted the support of less than 200 pastoral workers.[18]

By 1994 it seemed that the NFF and the AWU had exhausted their capacity for conflict. In February the two organisations announced that they were negotiating to create a long-term shearing industry agreement, 'which will incorporate further major restructuring of the pastoral industry award and a framework for determining future wage rises'. As a first step, the AWU agreed to delay until October 1994 an $8 a week pay rise for shed-hands and cooks on minimum award rates (the 'safety net' increase approved by the Australian Industrial Relations Commission for low-paid workers awarded in October 1993). In return, the NFF withdrew the 'incapacity to pay' case which had been delaying the payment of the 2.5 per cent increase originally granted by the commission in April 1991. An NFF spokesman said that these changes were not necessarily the end of disputes with the AWU, but an attempt to resolve 'particular issues'. AWU general secretary Mike Forshaw (1991–94) said the union would 'wait and see' how this more co-operative approach developed. In November 1994 the AWU-FIME and the NFF agreed to an average $24 a week increase for shearers, shed-hands and cooks to be implemented over three years. The first $8 increase, delayed since February, lifted the shearing rate from $144.60 to $146.70 per 100.[19]

Perhaps the improved economic conditions and higher wool prices of 1994 encouraged NFF moderation. Perhaps it was a belief that they had won the industrial war. In 1993 the journal of the Australian Farmers Fighting Fund, the *Farmers' Voice*, boasted that 'the very existence of the AFFF acts as a deterrent against industrial action'. Established in 1988, the *Farmers' Voice* strongly reflected the rhetoric of the *Pastoralists' Review* of the 1890s. Rural and waterfront unions, and their political friends in Canberra, were the enemy. They did not understand the dynamics of the export-oriented rural sector competing in an unsentimental world – an ignorance shared by manufacturing industry employers, coddled by protectionism. As the NSW LGPA's industrial officer, Ian Manning, said in 1982, comparative wage indexation 'had been led by employers in tariff protected areas'. These employers, as much as the unions, were the spoilt children of Henry Bournes Higgins, the architect of arbitration and comparative wage justice, concepts which enraged and frustrated the NFF's leaders. The incapacity-to-pay cases had been their weapon against the Higgins legacy. By the late 1980s they believed that they had won that ideological battle. 'Both the Federal Government and the ACTU now accept that wage increases have to be related to increases in productivity'. The Fighting Fund was the instrument of victory, used to pay the legal bills generated in the incapacity-to-pay court cases, and against the striking meatworkers at Mudginberri Abattoir (the AMIEU was forced to pay $1.5 million damages to the abattoir's owner, Jay Pendarvis), against the waterfront unions, to defeat the Hawke Government's proposed

1987 Industrial Relations Act (withdrawn before the 1987 election after an NFF publicity campaign), and to aid Troubleshooters Available (a labour hire firm which sidestepped unions and awards) in its legal actions against the BWIU. By the mid-1980s it seemed that this 'New Right' aggression would sweep all enemies before it, particularly when battle was joined on another front, in the mining industry. The exporters had led the fight against the unions in the 1890s. It seemed that they would again succeed, ninety years later.[20]

## The Resource and Construction Industries

On North Rankin A AWU members are working for Australia.[21]

Scattered through the *Worker* in the 1980s are various awe-struck accounts of the extent of Australia's natural resources. In 1982 the *Worker* reported that 'the not so dead heart yields buried riches to fuel capitals and cars.' Beneath the harsh red desert of 'the corner', the region of north-eastern South Australia which bordered the Northern Territory, Queensland and New South Wales, lay the vast natural gas and oil fields of the Cooper Basin. From a network of wells emerged up to 80 000 barrels of oil and gas a day – one-fifth the production from the Bass Strait rigs. New roads were cut through the scrub; five airfields were built. There were over thirty-five oil wells and up to 168 gas wells. Long gleaming silver pipelines vaulted across the dunes, linking the fields with Stony Point, near Whyalla in South Australia, and Adelaide and Sydney. The statistics for both pipeline capacity of the fuel (380 000 barrels) and storage at Moomba (400 000 barrels) are also both meaninglessly large. The *Worker* clarified them with this sobering description of conspicuous consumption: 'While these volumes appear huge, it should be remembered that the total tank-plus-pipeline capacity is little more than one day's petroleum consumption for Australia'. Over 500 AWU members were employed on Cooper Basin projects. When the Moomba–Stony Point pipeline was completed ahead of schedule in 1983 the AWU members working the project received an early-finish bonus of between $6000 and $8000.[22]

In some ways the AWU seemed surprised that its members had been invited to share in the riches reaped from the earth, and marvelled at the sophistication of the work. In 1989 general secretary Errol Hodder and assistant general secretary Mike Forshaw visited Woodside Petroleum's North Rankin A liquefied gas platform, the world's largest. Located 135 kilometres off the Western Australian coast, the North-West Shelf oil and gas fields provided 15 per cent of Japan's liquefied natural gas requirements. Hodder commented that 'our members are amongst those in this country who are working at the cutting edge of space age technology. The onshore facility at Karratha is like something out of Star Wars'.[23]

There were always big sums of money involved in Australian resource development. It cost the joint venture partners $12 billion to develop the North-West Shelf operations. And there were big rewards: in 1981 Australian mineral exports reached over $7 billion, the nation's largest primary sector contributor to gross domestic product and the leading source of Australia's export income, with production shipped to over a hundred countries. AWU members expected their share of this largesse, and were not averse to struggle to obtain it: during the 1970s and 1980s, Mount Isa miners, refinery workers and the Bass Strait oil riggers, and AWU members at many other sites, all took strike action over pay issues. Mike Forshaw estimated that oil industry workers could earn as much as $50–60 000 a year by the late 1980s.

> For refinery operators, their wage rate went from an award rate of about $600 up to $750 per week – that would give them $35–40,000 a year, but they could earn probably another 50% or even another 100% on top of that with shift penalties and overtime. In the major mining centres, underground miners at Mount Isa or other places have been known to earn $80–90,000 a year, with bonuses and their contract mining rates. Off shore oil workers, these days, are offered staff packages by the employers – often $100,000–$110,000 in packages.

Despite the large sums, it was not easy money, with hazardous conditions and long hours and, given technological changes, a need for highly skilled workers. And the money came with a measure of uncertainty: the fate of many of these massive developments could rise and fall on the whim of international market forces and, increasingly, environmental concerns. In the 1980s these complications affected planned resource and construction projects, changing the development agenda in Australia, and sometimes leaving AWU members out in the cold. The most dramatic of these changes unfolded in Tasmania, in the bitter 1979–83 struggle over the proposed construction by the Tasmanian Hydro-Electric Commission of the Gordon-below-Franklin dam.[24]

The Tasmanian AWU leadership were unequivocal dam supporters, an enthusiasm fuelled in 1981–82 by the economic recession affecting local jobs. In September 1981 all branch organisers reported retrenchments and shift cutbacks in the mining, building and pulp and paper industries, the Forestry Commission and the Department of Main Roads. In another time, the HEC might have been relied on to stimulate the local job scene with a big project – a duty the HEC took seriously, as it claimed that 'competitively priced electricity is the main reason Australia's major producers of newsprint, carbide and ferro-manganese are located in Tasmania and why it is a big producer of zinc, aluminium, fine papers,

Constructing the lower Pieman River dam, Tasmania 1985. The AWU were firm supporters of the Tasmanian HEC's ambitions for hydro-electric development. *Oliver Strewe.*

copper, tin, pelletised iron ore and woodchips'. All these industries
employed AWU members. But in 1981 organiser L. K. Evans lamented
that 'the question of just where and when the next HEC scheme will be
is another classic case of bungling and lack of common sense leadership
by the present State Government' – a Labor government which in AWU
eyes had failed its supporters with its inability to approve the Gordon-
Below-Franklin project. 'Yet again people's futures are being toyed with
while a bunch of so-called political leaders and a gang of half-baked
canoeists and conservationists slug it out.' It was all too much for Tasmanian Labor; the government split and collapsed over the issue in May
1982. The new Liberal Government of Robin Gray was determined to go
ahead. By early 1983 the HEC had begun preliminary road construction
into the south-west wilderness, amid the highly publicised protests of the
green movement. The Federal Government, led by Liberal Prime
Minister Malcolm Fraser, refused to intervene to stop the dam's construction. The Federal Labor Party was promising, if elected, to use the Commonwealth's external affairs power to legislate to stop the project. The
AWU Annual Convention, meeting on 18 January 1983, resolved on the
motion of Tasmanian Branch secretary John Butler to support the construction of the Gordon-below-Franklin dam and advise the ALP of
its decision. It was too late. The new Labor Government of Bob Hawke,
elected in March 1983, honoured its promise to veto the dam's
construction.[25]

In Tasmania, environmental concerns prevailed over economic development and jobs. Uranium mining, which excited opposition on environmental and anti-nuclear weapons grounds, was another matter. In South
Australia, AWU members benefited from the mining of vast deposits of
uranium, copper and gold at the Olympic Dam mine, at Roxby Downs, 500
miles north of Adelaide. The giant Mount Isa mine had copper deposits
totalling 5.5 million tonnes; the deposits discovered at Roxby in 1975 had
7.5 million tonnes. The Roxby mineralised zone also contained 500 000
tonnes of uranium oxide – all other Australian deposits totalled no more
than 299 000 tonnes. In 1982 the joint venture partners Western Mining
Corporation and BP Australia conservatively valued the deposits at $140
billion. Their preparations to mine the site ran parallel with a prolonged
debate within the labour movement on the uranium-mining issue. The
1977 ALP National Conference declared that a Labor government would
place a moratorium on the mining of uranium and repudiate existing
contracts for the recently opened Ranger and Nabarlek uranium mines in
the Northern Territory. The 1977 ACTU Congress adopted a similar
stance, although the ACTU leadership realised that several of the twenty-
two unions with members in the uranium industry would defy the ban.
Prominent among these unions was the AWU. In June 1975 the Executive

Council decided to support continued uranium mining; its members had previously mined uranium at Radium Hill (SA) and Mary Kathleen (Queensland). Characteristically, the Executive Council declared that 'the Australian Workers Union is not accustomed to putting "black bans" on industry merely because it has been called upon to do so by some outside body'. The 1977 Convention reaffirmed this decision. Because of this inability to unite all affiliates against a comprehensive ban, the ACTU softened its policy at the 1979 Congress. In 1984 the ALP National Conference adopted the three mines resolution to accommodate uranium mining at Ranger, Nabarlek and Roxby Downs, where mining operations commenced in 1988. By 1994 400 members of the new AWU-FIME Amalgamated Union worked at the Olympic Dam mine, including 120 underground miners. In that same year an opportunity emerged for the AWU-FIME to expand its coverage to new mines in Western Australia, provided that the Keating Labor Government could change Labor's three mines policy at the 1994 ALP National Conference, and allow new uranium mines to open in Western Australia and the Northern Territory. But it was the AWU-FIME, combined with the Left, which blocked the uranium policy change. AWU-FIME national president and Queensland Branch secretary Bill Ludwig was determined to punish the mining company CRA, which owned one of the Western Australian uranium deposits at Kintyre, where CRA was keen to press ahead with open-cut operations. But CRA had, since 1991, also been attempting to 'deunionise' many of its workplaces, particularly in Western Australia, pursuing a union-busting strategy which was proving increasingly difficult for the AWU-FIME (for details, see below). Ludwig declared that 'while ever CRA maintains their current belligerent attitude to the accepted industrial relations process they cannot expect the labour movement to take their position on uranium mining seriously'. Despite immense pressure from the Keating Government ministers and the party machine, the 1994 National Conference ended without a change to the policy.[26]

During the 1980s the Queensland AWU was troubled by the threat to resource-based jobs posed by the fierce opposition of environmentalists to work long performed by union members. The AWU maintained a determined defence of logging operations on Fraser Island, arguing in 1983 that logging was 'stringently controlled so as not to upset the ecology of these areas'. At stake were 500 jobs in logging and sawmilling and $3 million income for the local Wide Bay community on the mainland. Branch secretary Errol Hodder commented that 'the jobs created by tourism after sand mining on Fraser Island [in 1976] ceased completely failed to replace the jobs lost'. The battle continued into the 1990s, with the Fitzgerald inquiry into logging operations on the island recommending the ending of logging in September 1991, although a

generous compensation package for the displaced workers eased the
blow. Far Northern District secretary Ted Brischke seemed to concur
with Hodder's gloomy assessment in 1988, which he foresaw as a crisis
year for logging around Cairns, when 'the full force of the detrimental
effects of World Heritage listing will be evident in widespread mill
closures and the inevitable redundancy of the industry's workforce'. The
AWU supported the Hawke Government's decision to seek World
Heritage listing for the northern Queensland rainforests, although as
Hodder conceded, it had been 'a difficult issue for the union'. In June
1988, fifty workers were retrenched when Hancock Brothers closed their
sawmill in Cairns, which had been providing employment for fifty years.
Brischke noted, however, that 'unlike previous retrenchments in the
North Queensland timber industry retrenched workers ... have not been
thrown on the unemployment scrap heap'. Short-term work, training
and a special package of assistance from the Commonwealth Employment Service had been negotiated. And perhaps tourism offered some
long-term job alternatives after all. In March 1989 Brischke told *Worker*
readers that more than 2000 jobs could soon be created by tourist
developments in Cairns, as that once isolated fishing port was transformed by the construction of twenty high-rise hotels, resorts and an
international airport to cater for the needs of American and Japanese
tourists. 'AWU members are employed in all aspects of this growth
industry', Brischke enthusiastically recorded. In May 1989 Errol Hodder,
by then AWU general secretary, made it clear that the AWU had
recognised the link between tourism employment and 'our fabulous
beaches, rainforests, mountains, deserts, wildlife and sophisticated urban
centres [which] provide leisure opportunities that cater to all manner of
tourists with all manner of tastes and expectations'. The Queensland
AWU's extensive State rules gave the union almost exclusive coverage of
hotel and resort workers in the tourism industry, from Cairns to the
Whitsunday Islands to Sea World and Movie World on the Gold Coast.
For the Queensland AWU, the exploitation of natural resources was
being transformed from felling to ogling.[27]

For some Australians, a contemplation of their environment brought a
more sober reflection. In August 1984 a solicitor with the NSW Aboriginal
Legal Service told a federal parliamentary inquiry that James Hardie
Industries had shown a 'reckless and callous disregard' for Aboriginal
workers who had mined white asbestos at the company's open-cut mine at
Baryugil, 80 kilometres north-west of Grafton. The mine was adjacent to
an Aboriginal settlement where the workers and their families lived.
Between 1942 and 1979, when the mine closed, mine operations regularly
sent dust clouds over the town; the men walked home in dust-laden
clothes. Asbestos tailings had been used to build local roads, and a

children's playground; some homes had been built on asbestos waste. Although the health risks associated with asbestos had been known since the late 1930s, the company had never informed the workers of the risk to themselves and their families. The Legal Service solicitor also criticised the AWU, which had enrolled the miners in the 1960s. He said the union had displayed little interest in the workers' needs. 'The AWU not only had no teeth and no eyes but it also had no bark.' An unknown number of miners had died from asbestos-related disease; others were ill. In October 1984 the House of Representatives Standing Committee on Aboriginal Affairs recommended a quick hearing of workers' compensation claims, the establishment of an Aboriginal medical service in Grafton and the evacuation of the Baryugil township. In July 1990 race discrimination commissioner Irene Moss said that little had been done to implement the committee's recommendations. 'The history of the failure of responsible authorities to address this significant health risk to the Baryugil community constitutes a gross disregard for the human rights of the residents.' The medical centre had still not been established. The mine site and the tailings dump remained unfenced. The commissioner likened living conditions at Baryugil and nearby Malabugilmah to those prevailing at Toomelah, which had received international criticism. The Banjalong people of the Clarence River Valley had been displaced from their tribal lands by the expansion of the pastoral industry in the nineteenth century. They had been relocated to Baryugil in 1920. As the parliamentary inquiry noted in 1984, the community had welcomed the development of the mine in the 1940s. 'Full employment meant that the community broke away from the chronic poverty which characterised other rural reserves. Individual breadwinners had the satisfaction of providing for their families and of doing hard work well.'[28]

### The New Right Challenge: Robe River and CRA

The Robe River dispute illustrates vividly that what is at stake is – like it or not – essentially political ... there can be no sanitised distinction between industrial relations and the polarised politics we have in Australia.[29]

In August 1986 Charles Copeman, chief executive of mining multi-national Peko Wallsend and one of the founders of the H. R. Nicholls Society, decided that work practices at the company's iron ore mine and port facilities at Robe River, in the remote Pilbara region of Western Australia, provided an opportunity to assert 'management's right to manage'. Copeman's ire was roused by a claimed 284 restrictive work practices at the Robe River operations, and the inability of local management to lift productivity by challenging the entrenched power of local union delegates. On 31 July 1986 Copeman sacked and replaced most of the local managers and issued an ultimatum to the workers: there would be cutbacks to the mine workforce; working hours would be increased, and contract work arrangements introduced; meal times would be restricted; the influence of unions and union delegates on management decisions would be curtailed. The company also exacerbated the situation by arbitrarily transferring workers from one job to another, and by sacking workers who opposed management decisions. Peko ignored WA Industrial Commission orders instructing the company to negotiate with unions. The confrontation reached a climax on 11 August, when Peko closed the Robe River operations and locked out the 1160 workers. The company did not allow operations to resume until 8 September.[30]

The AWU, and other unions with members at the mine, reacted angrily to Peko's 'highly inflammatory and heavy handed approach'. The AWU's WA Branch secretary, Joe Keenan, said the union was aware of the nation's economic troubles and export needs (the Robe River dispute came just a few months after Paul Keating's infamous 'Banana Republic' comment about the possible fate of the Australian economy) and had taken 'a non-aggressive approach in working to fulfil the genuine needs of our Pilbara members'. The unions used the Western Australian arbitration system to force the company to resume operations, and began proceedings to oppose Peko's application to move the prevailing State industrial agreement to a federal award. In the workplace, Peko's uncompromising regime prevailed. During the month-long lock-out, workers were told that as they were no longer employed by the company, they would have to move out of their company-provided housing. As it became likely that Peko would have to reinstate its workforce and resume operations, the company tried to provoke a fresh confrontation by using staff labour to work the mine a few days before the official resumption of work (Peko hoped that the workers would strike in retaliation to this move, allowing the company to sack them again). The workers were determined to protect their jobs, and 'normal' operations resumed. As AWU organiser Charlie Butcher observed, 'each day the workers at Robe River turn up to work to run the gauntlet of blatant employer harassment and provocation, that has engulfed the worksite in razor sharp tension'. Another dispute over work practices flared in January 1987, reflecting the enduring tension at Robe River.[31]

For Charles Copeman, there was a fundamental political aspect to the dispute. Robe River was seen as the culmination of a series of New Right victories against unions – Mudginberri, SEQEB (where the Queensland Government sacked strikers employed by the South-East Queensland Electricity Board in 1985), wide combs – and to many unionists it appeared that these victories were a conspiracy to reduce workers to the master-and-servant relationships, and the wages and conditions, of the nineteenth century. The *Worker* described the New Right as 'secret subversives' flouting the laws of the land. Whether or not the New Right acted as a conspiracy, there is no doubt that Copeman benefited from a network of powerful supporters. As industrial commentator Shaun Carney observed, 'The H. R. Nicholls contacts did come in handy for Copeman: he spoke about his industrial problems with Pendarvis (the owner of Mudginberri abbatoir) one week before he sacked his workers. Houlihan [Paul Houlihan, NFF industrial officer], who had helped Pendarvis win the Mudginberri battle in the courts, provided advice early in the Robe dispute. And Costello [Peter Costello, lawyer and future deputy leader of the federal Liberal Party] acted as Copeman's legal adviser'. Costello had also acted as NFF advocate in the incapacity-to-pay cases and an unsuccessful case opposing pastoral industry super-annuation. This network was also politically encouraged by Federal Opposition leader John Howard, whom the H. R. Nicholls society had praised for shaping the Coalition's May 1986 industrial relations policy, which called for voluntary contracts between workers and businesses, enterprise bargaining and the possibility for the parties to 'opt out' of the centralised arbitration system. In 1992 Charles Copeman became a trustee of the NFF's Fighting Fund. The *Farmers' Voice* said that 'his expertise will be a considerable asset to the farm sector'.[32]

Other Australian mining companies pondered Peko's experience, and although they rejected dramatic confrontation with unions, some remain determined to assert 'management rights' and even to entirely remove unions from their workplaces. In 1991 CRA, the giant mining and aluminium multinational, began a campaign to created an 'all staff' workforce in all its Australian and New Zealand operations. As *Business Review Weekly* observed,

> The company's strategy is as simple as it is potentially devastating for unions. By offering higher base wages and other staff benefits, the company aims to mould a flexible, dedicated and industrious workforce whose first and only loyalty is the corporation. Although union membership remains optional, it will become less relevant because the exclusion of third parties in salary negotiations is a condition of staff employment.

In December 1993, 1400 workers at Hamersley Iron (a subsidiary of Conzinc Rio-Tinto, or CRA) accepted staff positions. Several other CRA sites had previously become 'staff' operations, but the decision by Hamersley Iron workers to accept the deal meant that another of the major Pilbara mines had been 'lost' to the unions. As *BRW* noted, 'No longer could Robe River be painted as the rogue employer, the exception to the rule'. In December 1994, however, CRA suffered a major industrial defeat, when its attempt to deunionise the Bell Bay aluminium smelter (operated by CRA subsidiary Comalco) was rejected by the Australian Industrial Relations Commission. The commission criticised CRA for 'deliberately trying to deunionise the workplace, deceive employees about the purpose of meetings, and tell them wrongly that their award would remain as a safety net if they signed contracts'. At the time of writing, CRA has challenged the Bell Bay decision in the High Court of Australia. AWU-FIME joint national secretary Ian Cambridge argued that CRA workers should be protected by enterprise agreements registered with the Australian Industrial Relations Commission. 'All of CRA's plans to obtain more flexible workplace arrangements can be achieved under the new Act.' The Keating Government's 1994 Industrial Relations Reform Act legislated for a new era of enterprise bargaining, regulated by the AIRC. Conservative State governments in Western Australia and Victoria have provided for non-union enterprise bargaining, clearing the way for employers and workers to choose between union and non-union participation. The onus was now on unions in those States to inform and persuade workers of the benefits of membership, without the assistance of the state.[33]

In 1984 the AWU established a National Mining Committee to co-ordinate award, health and safety, and training issues. In 1990, the union held a National Mining Conference which updated policy on these and other issues, as part of its drive to secure principal union status for the metal-mining industry. As a development of its amalgamation and rationalisation strategy, the ACTU proposed to define industry unions, by 'principal', 'significant' and 'other' categories, with the principal union the dominant organising union for that industry. By the early 1990s, the AWU had coverage of 18 000 mineworkers, 72 per cent of the unionised workforce, in 142 major mine sites around Australia, eighty-six of which were in Western Australia. These sites were governed by forty-two federal awards and a multitude of State-registered agreements. In recognition of this extensive coverage, in December 1991 the ACTU granted principal metal mining status to the AWU, despite the objections of the Construction, Forestry, Mining and Energy Union (see p. 336), a union which rivalled the AWU in several industries. In June 1992 the Industrial Relations Commission, in a test case brought by the AWU, upheld the AWU's rights to exclusive coverage to metal mining workers in South Australia and Tasmania.[34]

### AWU Politics and the AWU–FIME Amalgamation

'Some people play golf or bowls when they retire. I'm playing unions.'

By early 1980, at age 79, 'Big' Charlie Oliver had finally relinquished the secretaryship of the federally registered NSW AWU, only to emerge as President of the State-registered union, with his own office and busy schedule. He confessed to a reporter in November 1980 that he felt some 'withdrawal' symptoms from his retirement from the secretaryship. The reporter asked him when he was going to retire completely from the union. 'In reply, Big Charlie leaned his bulk across the desk and began stamping a pile of papers.' He had been a cunning participant in many union battles down the years, and he had one more big fight left in him.[35]

The consequences of Oliver's continued role in the union soon became obvious in increasing tension between himself and the new branch secretary Ernie Ecob, manifested in the 1985 NSW AWU elections. Oliver, saying that he had 'made a mistake' in supporting Ecob for secretary in 1980, announced in January 1985 that he intended to support former Canberra organiser Bill Preece, who was running against Ecob for the secretary's position in the elections due later in the year. Oliver maintained that Ecob had mishandled the wide-comb dispute and bungled the 1980 sale of Macdonell House (purchased and resold by a developer for a substantial profit). A loss by Ecob and his supporters would mean political problems for both the national AWU and the NSW labour movement. The AWU sent a large delegation (nineteen delegates) to the NSW ALP Conference, which could be relied upon to solidly support the right-wing Centre Unity group which controlled the NSW ALP. The branch also sent nine delegates to the Right-controlled NSW Labor Council. Within the AWU, an actively left-wing NSW Branch – the second largest branch in the union, after Queensland – would have prompted enormous political tensions within the union. Its two most senior officials, general secretary Gil Barr and general president Allan Begg, were left-wingers, and the SA Branch officials were also left-wing, although the union's overall political outlook, given the influence of the Queensland Branch, continued to be to the right of labour movement politics; this was sharply underlined in the 1985 ballots, when federal industrial officer Keith Brown stood unsuccessfully against Barr, on a broad right-wing-Queensland ticket, which also featured a bid by Queensland Branch secretary Errol Hodder to become general president. The supporters of Bill Preece's rank-and-file team were confident of the first left-wing victory in the NSW AWU since 1943. The pre-election atmosphere was tense, with a 'raid' by Preece supporters on the NSW AWU office in January 1985. In November, as the ballots for federal and state positions were about to begin, Preece and Begg placed an advertisement in the Sydney press warning people 'who have been approached to allow their addresses to be used for the receipt of ballot papers' that they risked criminal prosecution. The Commonwealth electoral officer, who was supervising the elections, said that the police had cleared the ballot of any impropriety. Despite these trials, Ecob and his supporters were comfortably returned at the subsequent elections, after a hard campaign which stressed fears of BLF-style militancy if the left-wingers won. Barr and Begg were also returned, with the vote against them split among several rival candidates.[36]

True to a commitment given before the election, Charlie Oliver retired as State president at the end of 1985. Oliver had been a NSW AWU official since 1951, with twenty-nine years as branch secretary. With the retirement of general president and Queensland Branch secretary Edgar Williams and Queensland Branch president Gerry Goding in 1982, the last of the senior leadership generation, who could recall working conditions in the 1920s, had retired. In Charlie Oliver's case, his working life had begun in his native Wales in 1915. At 13 years of age he had joined his first union, the Agricultural Employees Union, and later lost his front teeth in the acid steam of an English steelworks. He emigrated to Western Australia, working in the mining industry and organising for the AWU. After a stint in the WA Parliament (1948–51) Oliver became NSW AWU secretary at Tom Dougherty's request. Cecil Thompson 'Charlie' Oliver died aged 87 on 24 February 1990. Ecob

The close links between the AWU and the Labor Party are emphasised by the regular appearance of Labor leaders at AWU conventions. AWU general secretary Errol Hodder with Prime Minister Bob Hawke, 1989. *AWU Collection.*

remained as NSW AWU secretary until his retirement in May 1993, his tenure periodically marked by controversies which including the sacking of office staff and his robust objections to women and New Zealanders in the shearing industry. Ecob was succeeded by Michael O'Shea, branch president and former shearer.[37]

Another ex-shearer was making his way up the AWU's ranks. Errol Hodder was 49 years old in 1988 and at the peak of his union career. He had made his mark in Queensland Labor politics by supporting Wayne Goss in his bid to become State ALP Leader and, through his position as ALP vice-president, by restoring the AWU's influence within the Queensland ALP. In January 1983 Federal Opposition leader Bill Hayden recognised this when he told the AWU's Convention that in Queensland, 'the AWU could be called both the midwife to the Labor Party and its godmother and with the recent election of Mr. Hodder as Vice-President I suppose it could also be said that you are also providing a political godfather'. Now Hodder planned to extend this influence into the national labour movement. The first challenge was to maintain the AWU's position as a major ACTU affiliate by securing an amalgamation with the Federated Ironworkers Association. His appointment as general secretary to fill the vacancy created by Gil Barr's retirement and the creation of a new elected position, assistant national secretary, for senior industrial officer Mike Forshaw, was seen as preparation for the amalgamation and the internal restructuring which would flow from combining the leadership of both unions.[38]

By 1986, the year the AWU celebrated its Centenary with its Convention and elaborate festivities in Ballarat, it was clear that the union had to face the changes affecting the labour movement. Convention considered the possibility that the AWU might, under restructuring proposals, lose its industry representation on the ACTU executive. When the AWU affiliated with the ACTU in 1967, it was given, in recognition of its size and breadth of coverage, a dedicated position on the ACTU executive. All the other affiliates had to compete for representation on a broad industry basis – the building industry, the metal industry, etc. But by the late 1980s, as unions moved to fulfil the amalgamation agenda proposed in ACTU secretary Bill Kelty's 1987 paper *Future Strategies for the Trade Union Movement*, this executive structure was becoming increasingly irrelevant. And the nature of the workforce was changing. Hodder, the AWU's representative on the ACTU executive, explained to Convention that the AWU had once affiliated with the ACTU on the basis of 150 000 members; now it was down to 121 000. 'What you had now is competing interests in the trade union movement saying that they are almost as large as the AWU – the teachers, the shop assistants, liquor trades, etc., – and they are saying why should the AWU be entitled to this privileged

position.' Despite Convention's decision to obliquely threaten disaffiliation if its representation was diluted, Hodder understood that the only
way to preserve the AWU's prestige was to move with the times.[39]

In December 1988 the front page of the *Worker* declared: 'Amalgamation – Full Speed Ahead'. The article dispelled claims in some union
quarters that an amalgamation of the FIA and the AWU was industrially
inappropriate. To these critics, it appeared that 'the FIA and the AWU have
cut across strict industry lines to form a large right-wing bloc ... a forward
defence by the Right against the Left bloc in the building industry'.
Industrial rivals the BWIU and the FEDFA also planned to amalgamate (by
1992 these two unions, together with the Timberworkers and the United
Mineworkers Federation, had combined to form the Construction,
Forestry, Mining and Energy Union). In the metal industry, the Amalgamated Metalworkers Union and the Association of Drafting, Technical and
Supervisory Employees were also moving towards amalgamation. These
mergers were also 'as much factionally harmonious as they are industrially
suitable'. The AWU and FIA leadership believed that they had the
ingredients for similar harmony. The *Worker* maintained that the two
unions had 'a community of interest in the major key industries of this
country', including chemicals, oil, aluminium, mining and construction.
The Executive Council decided to pursue the amalgamation in November
1987, and the 1988 Convention confirmed the plan. It was hoped that an
amalgamation ballot would be held in 1989. Despite these early indications of unity, problems soon emerged within the AWU.[40]

AWU elections were due in late 1989 for all State and federal executives, and left-wing opponents to the incumbent officials were opposed
to the amalgamation and the restructuring of the AWU's administration.
Hodder had also proposed to centralise the financial structure of the
union, to bring it into line with the FIA's practices. This move aroused
the ire of Queensland Branch secretary Bill Ludwig, who had fallen out
with Hodder (Ludwig had not been Hodder's preferred replacement as
branch Secretary). Ludwig, one of the leaders of Queensland's right-
wing Labor Unity faction within the ALP, had continued the AWU's
dominance of the local labour movement since Hodder's 1988 departure
for Sydney. It was estimated that the AWU controlled the voting of twenty-
one of fifty-four MPs in the Queensland parliamentary Labor Caucus and
6 votes in the federal parliamentary Caucus, an influence which was to
prove crucial to Prime Minister Bob Hawke's ability to withstand Paul
Keating's unsuccessful June 1991 leadership challenge (although insufficient at the second challenge in December). The bedrock of this political
power was the 57 000 members of the Queensland AWU, half the
national total. The idea of transferring branch membership fees to
federal office control was hardly appealing. Ludwig also believed that

Assistant general secretary Mike Forshaw (extreme right) watches as the Queensland delegation votes at the 1990 AWU Convention. Tensions within the AWU over central funding led to a series of heated Convention debates and court challenges. On the extreme left is Deirdre Swan, Queensland Branch industrial officer and the first woman Convention delegate. Queensland Branch secretary Bill Ludwig is seated next to Swan. *AWU Collection.*

signing over the branches' finances to the control of the federal office could imperil its State registration, the source of the AWU's wide industrial coverage in Queensland.[41]

Ludwig had forged an alliance with WA Branch vice-president Bruce Wilson, who had nominated against Hodder for the general secretary's position. Wilson believed that the federal officials were too closely aligned to the agenda of the ACTU and the Hawke Labor Government. A reform group in the Victorian Branch ballot also opposed the amalgamation on factional grounds. In December 1989 Hodder was narrowly re-elected, as was the moderate leadership of the SA and NSW branches. But the Victorian Branch went to the Left, which, taken with the continuing opposition of Queensland, resulted in Hodder losing control of the numbers at the Executive Council and at Convention. Bill Ludwig was also elected as general president, after the retirement of Allan Begg. This shift in numbers effectively stymied moves towards the FIA amalgamation and central funding. It was an impasse unresolved until

May 1991, when Hodder left the union to take up a position as a commissioner with the AIRC. Ludwig and new general secretary Mike Forshaw agreed to go ahead with the amalgamation with the now Federation of Industrial, Manufacturing and Engineering Employees (the FIA had amalgamated with the Australasian Society of Engineers in 1991), with the central funding issue set aside (following the AWU–FIME amalgamation, the Queensland, Victorian and WA branches chose not to participate in centralised financial arrangements; the other States did so). Mike Forshaw said that the AWU must proceed with the amalgamation to 'build a stronger union to face future challenges, and to provide a better range of services for members.'[42]

During the 1980s the ACTU executive watched a steady fall in trade union membership, from a high of 62 per cent in the early 1950s to below 40 per cent by 1992. All affiliates accepted that if they were to be able to offer members the kind of sophisticated services they increasingly demanded – industrial protection enhanced by financial and consumer services – they would need to rationalise operations and boost income. Amalgamation offered a means to this end and a better base for resisting the expected onslaughts of labour market deregulation, proceeding slowly but steadily under Federal Labor, accelerated under Liberal–National Party regimes in the States – an experience vividly dramatised by the industrial relations policies pursued by the Liberal Victorian Government in 1992. In September 1993 86 per cent of AWU and FIMEE members voted to support the amalgamation, which took effect on 1 November 1993 with the creation of the AWU–FIME Amalgamated Union. The first joint national secretaries were Mike Forshaw and Steve Harrison, the former FIMEE national secretary, presiding over a union of 180 000 members in the steel, metalliferous mining, civil construction, chemical, oil, manufacturing, service and rural sectors. Members had been invited to create 'Australia's No. 1 Union'. The ambition to create one big union, the envy of its rivals, endured.[43]

CONCLUSION

# Rocky Gehan's Ledger

We believed that if you were strong enough to be a shearer and represent
shearers you were strong enough to represent anybody.

*Rocky Gehan*

'A lot of things pass your memory, and I've destroyed a lot of my records,
bar this thing here.' Rocky Gehan, retired shearer and organiser, thumbs
his well-worn ledger, its pages creased to a permanent grimy frayed bend,
a wave of work. 'You'd never read that.' He gestures at the tight hand-
written entries which roll down the pages, the members of whom he had
kept account. 'What I've done, where I went ... that's the last thirteen
years ... there's that many jobs, and that many industries. After you've
been out there thirteen years you meet their kids, you meet their wives,
and we were one big happy family'. He runs a long, sun-scarred finger
absently along the spine of the book. 'I was never disappointed that I
never finished up in politics because I'd hate to be branded a politician.'

Rocky Gehan, the tall shearer with an edged, ruddy face, doesn't think
much of politicians, but nor does he have a bad word for anybody. He
worked with officials who clashed and tried to be a bridge between them.
Nor had he any criticism for his mates who went into Parliament. It was
just that for Rocky, 'you look after one house and the house you were
looking after was the union'. Looking after the union as an AWU
organiser wasn't glamorous or easy. In the 1950s and 1960s he travelled
the remote districts of South Australia in a Volkswagen with all the seats
removed, except the driver's. With no travelling or accommodation
allowance, it was office and motel room. 'I'd pull up to the side of the
road, cook yourself a meal ... you always had to sleep there because you
couldn't afford to go anywhere, so you'd be crawling out of the VW
probably at 5.30 in the morning in winter into showers or blizzards and

339

race into town somewhere to get into the toilet to have a wash before the people started.'

Rocky thinks that he owes everything to the people, 'grateful that I am to the members that I had for years for keeping me in office'. Ernest Gehan changed his name to Rocky by deedpoll because the people didn't know who E. Gehan was on the ballot paper. They wanted to vote for Rocky, and eventually they made him the president of the South Australian Branch. He had won the respect of the people in the ledger, the AWU members 'that formed the thing', who had struggled. 'You'd never see a heap of politicians out there going on strike, putting on a great big stoppage and supporting themselves, it's the union members that done this sort of thing as far as I was concerned and they're the ones who I support – still support in preference to politicians.' He stamps his finger into the ledger. Rocky has a gentle nature, but you wouldn't want to be on the wrong side of him in a dispute. He gets this determined look.

Listening to Rocky Gehan is like reading shearers' letters in the *Town and Country Journal* or the *Shearers' Record* a hundred years ago, before they forged the wonderful machine. It was once enough to be a shearer – but never a sugar-bagger. 'They go out Sunday, Saturday, night-time, under lights or any flamin' thing at all. It's ruined the pastoral industry.' Rocky shakes his head. 'A lot of shearers wouldn't know what a copy of the Shearers Accommodation Act looked like.'

The advent of the politicians, the changes to the pastoral industry; none of these things are new. In 1958 historian Russel Ward wrote in *The Australian Legend*: 'Though some shearers are now said to drive to their work in wireless-equipped motor-cars, the influence of the "noble bush-man" on Australian life and literature is still strong'. The image echoes dimly now, partly because Australia has continued to change beyond the ambitions of the bush unions, partly because the bushmen fulfilled their promise to help make that change.

Tom Dougherty saw the changes coming at the end of his life, changes to work and industry which began in the 1920s, but profoundly felt in the years after the Second World War: declining employment in the pastoral industry, the rise of manufacturing, civil construction, mining. For Rocky Gehan, trundling around South Australia in his battered car, these changes happened slowly, expressed in unwelcome renovations of pastoral work practices.

Henry Drucker observed: 'The past can be kept alive as long as it is believed. There is nothing about the movement of clocks which diminishes it'. The AWU clung to its bush identity as change accelerated. As Oliver, Dougherty, Edgar Williams and Gerry Goding passed from the scene in the 1970s and early 1980s, Gil Barr, Allan Begg, Frank Mitchell, Mick O'Shea, Ernie Ecob and Errol Hodder all emerged as senior AWU leaders. They were all shearers. Hodder restored the AWU's political influence in Queensland and revived the branch's authority within the national AWU. When Hodder became general secretary in 1988, he passed that inheritance on to his successor as Queensland branch secretary, ex-shearer Bill Ludwig.

The AWU's attachment to its shearing identity attracted the scorn of critics, no more so than during the 1983 wide-comb dispute, a dispute which seem to stir all the intangible qualities of the bush ethos, and drew a sullen, instinctive hostility from Australian shearers. It was more 'logical' to shear with wide combs. But there was something wrong, something changing; many AWU shearers could not put their finger on the precise disturbance. As Mike Forshaw – a non-shearer who emerged as general secretary in 1991 – tries to explain:

> Well, most other people [outside the AWU] don't give a stuff about that issue. They listened to the union carrying on, and they'd say to us, 'but why don't you like to use wide combs, you can shear more sheep, you can earn more money'. It becomes very difficult to explain to the public ... when you talked about the problems with New Zealand and with the shearing, it was very easy for people to say 'it's just the AWU being racist'. But funnily enough, you can run the same issue in other industries [and] have a different flavour altogether, you can talk about foreign [competition] in the clothing industry, and it's more respectable.

What had the AWU achieved? The AWU entrenched the award system and won better wages and conditions for its members, and for many others, in the face of sustained employer efforts to obliterate the union and all its works. It was the bulwark of those Labor politicians who enacted many of the things Rocky believed in, like the Shearers Accommodation Act, which may have outlived its time, or whose benefit has been forgotten. There was no shortage of employers in the late nineteenth century reassuring workers that there is no need for unions to meddle in the relationship between employer and employee. There doesn't appear to be a shortage now.

More than anything else, the AWU helped to forge an identity for its people. The voice of the bush was not just the voice of the squatter and the landed gentry. Quite often, if you were good enough to organise shearers you were good enough to organise anybody. But it didn't always happen well enough. Ardour cools to common practice, a job to be done. And some, like the people of Baryugil, seem to exist entirely out of sight, and out of conscience. The AWU mirrors the society from which it had been formed, and the gap between our ideals and our actions.

There was a price to be paid in the collision of competing ambitions, the struggle between noble causes and human instincts. In early 1916, William Guthrie Spence sits in pride of place in a photo of Convention

Delegates to the 1916 AWU Annual Convention. This thirtieth convention was
the last attended by Spence, who had presided over the first. (seated front, left
to right) John McNeill (Victoria), Frank Lundie (South Australia); (second row,
left to right) J. M. McKay (official reporter), C. Collins (Queensland), Henry
Boote (editor, *Australian Worker*), Edward Grayndler (general secretary),
William Guthrie Spence (general president), Jack Bailey (NSW), Arthur
Blakeley (NSW), G. Harry Coyne (Qld), Hector Lamond (manager, *Australian
Worker*); (third row, left to right) Bill McCormack (Qld), W. H. Lambert (NSW),
Jas. Mooney (Tasmania), F. Martyn (Qld), M. Kelly (Qld), W. J. Dunstan (Qld),
Senator John Barnes (Vic.), J. H. Black (Vic.), Con Ryan (Qld); (back row, left
to right) A. J. McNaught (Qld), C. A. Ackhurst (minute secretary),
J. M. Cullinan (NSW), W. Harvey (SA), T. P. Holloway (Vic.), C. Last (NSW),
W. Murphy (SA), T. C. Butler (WA), A. J. Watts (WA), Jack White (NSW).
*AWU Collection.*

delegates, gathered around him like a family. A few months later he is a
villain of conscription, an outcast denied homage. Since 1874 he had
helped to nurture the fledgeling union movement. It was his life. But in
1916 a new generation of unionists rejected his idea of duty; it was not
enough. If Australian workers were to be sacrificed in war, they had a
right to do so by choice, by an act of their own determination. They
would have a say in their fate. Spence declared in 1890: working men
must take their place in the nation. And so they did.

APPENDIX
AWU CHRONOLOGY, 1886–1994

| | |
|---|---|
| 1886 | William Guthrie Spence and David Temple begin organising shearers; establishment of Australasian Shearers Union in Creswick. |
| 1887 | Creswick, Bourke and Wagga unions form Amalgamated Shearers Union of Australia; Creswick dominates. Spence, president, Temple secretary. Formation of Queensland Shearers Union. Biggest Queensland union by 1889. |
| 1888 | First ASU Conference Wagga Wagga (February) |
| 1888–90 | ASU grows interstate (NSW Vic. & SA); Membership claimed: 20 000 shearers |
| 1889 | Formation of Queensland Pastoralists Association. |
| 1890 | Establishment of Brisbane *Worker*. |
| 1890 | ASU conference: decision to enforce closed shop/blockade; affiliation with Trades Halls in New South Wales and Victoria. QSU affiliates with Australian Labour Federation. |
| 1890 | July. Inaugural meeting of NSW Pastoralists Union; elected 30-man Governing Council. |
| 1890 | Maritime Strike (August–November). |
| 1891 | ASU organises General Labourers Union February 1891 on behalf of shed-hands; QSU and Queensland Workers Union (shed-hands) form AWUQ. |
| 1891 | Queensland pastoral strike. |
| 1891 | ASU Executive Council concedes freedom of contract July |

|  | 1891; Wagga Branch publishes *Hummer;* becomes Sydney *Worker.* |
|---|---|
| 1894 | Macdonell successfully pushes for ASU/GLU amalgamation in New South Wales to form the Australian Workers Union; Temple walks out of conference; Spence replaces him as general secretary. 1894 pastoral strike. |
| 1895 | Impact of economic depression and drought prompts membership fall from estimated 17 000 to 7000; continues falling throughout 1890s; AWU closes branches; AWU head office shifts to Sydney. |
| 1898–99 | Arthur Rae general secretary. |
| 1899 | AWU first union to gain representation at Political Labor League conferences; PLL asks AWU to organise country New South Wales. |
| 1900 | Donald Macdonell becomes general secretary; Temple resigns as Creswick Branch secretary |
| 1901 | Spence elected as Labor Member for federal seat of Darling; Macdonell becomes NSW Member for Cobar. |
| 1902 | AWU membership estimated at 14 000; 1902 pastoral strike; pressure from Machine Shearers Union. |
| 1904 | AWU and AWUQ amalgamate: total membership 30 000, 'largest and wealthiest union in Australia'. |
| 1907 | MSU collapses; first Federal Pastoral Industry Award. |
| 1911 | Macdonell dies; replaced as general secretary by Tom White |
| 1912 | White dies; Edward Grayndler becomes general secretary |
| 1913 | Amalgamation with the AWA (Qld); Sydney *Worker* becomes *Australian Worker.* |
| 1916–17 | Conscription referendums; 1917 strike in New South Wales. |
| 1917 | Amalgamation with the FMEA. Membership estimated 86 000. |
| 1917–23 | One Big Union movement rises and collapses. |
| 1927 | Formation of the Australian Council of Trade Unions. |
| 1928 | AWU membership estimated at 160 000. |
| 1931–32 | Great Depression. Federal Labor split; the *World* revives and collapses. Pastoral Workers Industrial Union active in New South Wales and Victoria. |
| 1932 | Clarrie Fallon becomes Queensland Branch secretary. Queensland largest AWU branch with estimated 53 000 members. |
| 1941 | Grayndler retires. Fallon general secretary. |
| 1942 | AWU dissents from Curtin Government decision to send conscripts to the South-West Pacific theatre of operations. |
| 1943 | Beecher Hay general secretary |
| 1944 | Hay deposed as general secretary by Tom Dougherty. |

| 1945 | Formation of industrial groups in some ALP State branches |
|------|-----------------------------------------------------------|
| 1949 | Coal strike. Henry Boote, *Australian Worker* editor (1916–43), dies. Snowy Mountains Scheme begins. |
| 1954–55 | AWU denounces groupers; ALP splits. |
| 1956 | Shearers' strike. |
| 1957 | Queensland ALP splits. |
| 1959 | Clyde Cameron forms Council for Membership Control. |
| 1960 | AWU membership estimated at 170 000. |
| 1964–64 | Mount Isa dispute. |
| 1966 | AWU affiliates with the ACTU. |
| 1972 | Tom Dougherty dies; Frank Mitchell becomes general secretary. AWU abandons White Australia policy. |
| 1974 | Merger of Brisbane *Worker* and *Australian Worker;* New South Wales AWU announces amalgamation with Shop Assistants Union. |
| 1977 | Proposed amalgamation between BWIU and AWU in New South Wales revealed; AWU–SAU amalgamation collapses. |
| 1976–86 | Demarcation battles with the BLF. |
| 1983 | Wide comb dispute; first 'incapacity to pay' application by NFF. |
| 1984 | Frank Mitchell retires; Gil Barr general secretary. National ALP conference adopts 'Three Mines' uranium policy. |
| 1985 | Charlie Oliver retires as New South Wales AWU president. |
| 1986 | Centenary AWU Convention, Ballarat. Deirdre Swan, first woman delegate. Robe River dispute. |
| 1988 | Errol Hodder becomes general secretary. |
| 1991 | Mike Forshaw becomes general secretary. |
| 1993 | AWU amalgamates with FIMEE to form the AWU–FIME Amalgamated Union. Combined membership estimated at 160 000. Inaugural joint national secretaries: Mike Forshaw and Steve Harrison. |
| 1994 | NFF–AWU 'peace deal'; CRA attempt to de-unionise Bell Bay aluminium smelter rejected by AIRC; CRA appeals to High Court. Ian Cambridge replaces Mike Forshaw as joint national secretary. |

# NOTES

### A Note on Sources

The main collection of AWU records is held by the Noel Butlin Archives of Business and Labour, Australian National University, Canberra. The Archives staff have prepared a comprehensive guide to these records. Access to the records can only be gained through the permission of the Australian Workers Union. A wide range of other primary and secondary material has also been researched for this book, and this material is cited in the notes below. The following former or current AWU officials, employees and members were interviewed for this book: Lawrie Buckman, Neil Byron, Clyde Cameron, Don Cameron, Mike Forshaw, Rocky Gehan, Gerry Goding, William Hall, Errol Hodder, Alf Kain, Reg Mawbey, Keith Plunkett, George Pont, Wendy Pymont, Bill Spellman and Edgar Williams. Eric Reece and Frank Mitchell were previously interviewed by Russell Finlay.

### Abbreviations

| | |
|---|---|
| ADB | *Australian Dictionary of Biography* |
| AFR | *Australian Financial Review* |
| APR | *Australasian Pastoralists' Review* |
| ANU | Australian National University |
| CAR | *Commonwealth Arbitration Reports* |
| CPD | *Commonwealth Parliamentary Debates* |
| ML | Mitchell Library, Sydney |

NLA      National Library of Australia, Canberra
*SMH*     *Sydney Morning Herald*
*T&CJ*    *Australian Town and Country Journal*
*Worker*  Refers to the *Australian Worker*. Specific reference is made to the Brisbane *Worker*.

### Introduction

1. W. G. Spence, *The Ethics of the New Unionism*, Worker Pamphlet, 1892
2. R. Markey, 'New Unionism in Australia, 1880–1900', *Labour History* no. 48, May 1985, pp. 25–6
3. Spence, *Ethics of the New Unionism*, p. 4; Patricia Cayo Sexton, *The War on Labor and the Left: Understanding America's Unique Conservatism*, Westview Press 1991, pp. 50, 190–2; Barbara Tuchman, *The Proud Tower*, Macmillan 1981, pp. 425–6; Kenneth Morgan, *Labour People*, Oxford University Press 1989, p. 78
4. R. McKibbin, 'Why was there no Marxism in Britain?', in R. McKibbin, *The Ideologies of Class Social Relations in Britain*, 1880–1950, Oxford University Press 1990, pp. 14–15
5. Eric Hobsbawm, 'General Labour Unions in Britain, 1889–1914', in *Labouring Men*, Weidenfeld & Nicolson 1964, p. 179; H. Pelling, *The Origins of the Labour Party*, Oxford University Press 1965, p. 84
6. R. Markey, *The Making of the Labor Party in New South Wales*, NSW University Press 1988, p. 148; R. Markey, 'New Unionism in Australia, 1880–1900', p. 21
7. Russel Ward, *The Australian Legend*, Oxford University Press 1958, pp. 1–2
8. Henry Drucker, *Doctrine and Ethos in the Labour Party*, Allen & Unwin 1979, pp. 30–4
9. Roger McDonald, *Reflecting Labor*, National Library of Australia 1991, pp. 2–4, 44
10. Henry Lawson, *Poems*, John Ferguson, Sydney 1979, pp. 30, 50; J. Barnes (ed.), *The Penguin Henry Lawson Short Stories*, Penguin Books 1986; Barbara Baynton, *Bush Studies*, Angus & Robertson 1972; G. A. Wilkes, *A Treasury of Bush Verse*, Angus & Robertson 1991
11. Mary Vinter, 'Henrietta Greville', *ADB*, vol. 9 1891–1939, p. 104; Marilyn Lake, 'The constitution of political subjectivity and the writing of labour history', in T. H. Irving (ed.), *Challenges To Labour History*, University of NSW Press 1994, p. 79
12. V. G. Childe, *How Labour Governs*, Melbourne University Press 1964, pp. 72–3
13. W. G. Spence, *Anti-Socialism: What It Means*, Worker Pamphlet, 1905, p. 12; Humphrey McQueen, *A New Britannia*, Penguin Books 1970, pp. 42, 51; for Lane's racial views see also Verity Burgmann, 'Racism, Socialism and the labour movement, 1887–1917', *Labour History*, no. 47, November 1984, p. 39
14. Markey, *The Making of the Labor Party*, pp. 6–14, 312–13; P. Kelly, *The End of Certainty*, Allen & Unwin 1992, pp. 1–10
15. Brian Fitzpatrick, *A Short History of the Australian Labor Movement*, Rawson's Bookshop 1940, pp. 100–6
16. McQueen, pp. 220, 233–6; Ian Turner, *Industrial Labour and Politics*, Hale & Iremonger 1965, pp. 10–11, 39; Ken Buckley and Ted Wheelwright, *No Paradise for Workers: Capitalism and the Common People in Australia, 1788–1914*, Oxford University Press 1988, pp. 138–9

17. Eric Hobsbawm, 'The New Unionism in Perspective', in *Worlds of Labour*, Weidenfeld & Nicolson 1984, p. 172; McQueen, p. 236
18. Drucker, pp. 3–4
19. McQueen, p. 7
20. Ross McKibbin, 'Is it still possible to write Labour History?', in Irving, *Challenges To Labour History*, pp. 34–5; John Schacht, 'Labor History in the Academy', *Labor's Heritage*, vol. 5, no. 3, Winter 1994, George Meany Memorial Archives Maryland; Patricia Cayo Sexton, *The War on Labor and the Left*, Ch. 3; H. A. Clegg, A. Fox and A. F. Thompson, *A History of British Trade Unions since 1889*, Oxford University Press 1964; H. Phelps Brown, *The Origins of Trade Union Power*, Oxford University Press 1986
21. McKibbin, pp. 39–41
22. W. G. Spence, *Australia's Awakening*, Worker Trustees 1909; W. G. Spence, *The History of the AWU*, Worker Trustees 1911; Childe, *How Labour Governs*; Ernest Lane *Dawn to Dusk*, Brisbane 1939; Pat Mackie *Mount Isa: The Story of a Dispute*, Hudson Publishing 1989; Edgar Williams *The Isa: Yellow, Green and Red*, Worker Newspaper Ltd 1967; Clyde Cameron, *Confessions*, ABC Enterprises 1990; Turner, *Industrial Labour and Politics* 1965; John Merritt, *The Making of the AWU*, Oxford University Press 1986; Markey, *The Making of the Labor Party in New South Wales*; Robert Murray, *The Split*, Hale & Iremonger 1970
23. R. Frances and B. Scates, 'Is Labour History Dead?', *Australian Historical Studies*, no. 100, April 1993, pp. 472–3, 476
24. Childe, p. 178
25. S. Macintyre and R. Mitchell, *Foundations of Arbitration*, Oxford University Press 1989; Merritt, *Making of the AWU*, p. 363
26. G. Patmore, 'Arbitration and Bureaucracy: The New South Wales Railway Commissioners, 1892–1914', *Journal of Industrial Relations*, vol. 30, no. 4, December 1988, pp. 579–82. One of the few comprehensive industry comparisons of multi-union and employer industrial relations performance is G. Patmore, A History of Industrial Relations in the NSW Railways: 1855–1929, unpublished PhD thesis, University of Sydney 1985
27. Colin Forster, 'The economy, wages and the establishment of arbitration', in Macintyre and Mitchell, *Foundations of Arbitration*, p. 203; P. G. Macarthy, 'Wage Determination in New South Wales – 1890–1921', *Journal of Industrial Relations*, vol. 10, no. 3, 1968, p. 199
28. Forster, pp. 221–2; Macarthy, p. 199
29. W. G. Spence, 'Trade Union Administration and Industrial and Craft Unionism', in M. Atkinson (ed.), *Trade Unionism in Australia*, WEA 1915, pp. 40–5
30. *CPD* IX & X George V vol. 88, 7th Parliament second session 9 July 1919, p. 10 557

## 1 The Knights of the Blade

1. *T&CJ*, 8/5/1886, p. 940; Merritt, p. 92
2. *T&CJ*, 15/5/1886, p. 1011; ASU AGM Sec. Report, April 1887, p. 4; *Shearers' Record*, April 1889, p. 3; 15/4/1890, p. 3
3. *T&CJ*, 24/4/1886, p. 855; 29/5/1886, p. 1097; 19/6/1886; Merritt, pp. 93, 113; Clyde Cameron, 'David Temple', *ADB* 1891–1939, vol. 12, p. 191; Report of ASU AGM, April 1887, p. 3
4. Markey, *The Making of the Labour Party*, p. 36; Merritt, pp. 35, 54–8, 73–6

5. Merritt, pp. 43–4; Geoffrey Blainey, *A Land Half Won*, Sun Books 1983, p. 168; Michael Cannon, *Life in the Country*, Viking O'Neil 1988, p. 177
6. Blainey, p. 263
7. *T&CJ*, 8/5/1886, p. 940; 15/5/1886, p. 1011
8. *Shearers' Record*, April 1889, p. 3; Spence, *History of the AWU*, p. 16
9. *Shearers' Record*, April 1889, p. 3
10. ASU AGM sec. report, April 1887, p. 4; *Shearers' Record*, April 1889, p. 3; 15/4/1890, p. 3
11. Merritt, pp. 98, 138
12. *Shearers' Record*, 15/4/1890, ASU AGM April 1887, p. 5
13. General Rules of the ASU, Ballarat 1887, ML
14. *T&CJ*, 8/5/1886, p. 1010; 29/5/1886, p. 1110
15. Cannon, p. 39
16. *T&CJ*, 1/5/1886, p. 906
17. Merritt, pp. 45–8, 89–91
18. Merritt, pp. 108–17; Spence, *History of the AWU*, pp. 20–2; Cannon, pp. 42–3
19. Spence, *History of the AWU*, pp. 20–2; Cobar Branch ASU report, February 1889, p. 75
20. *Shearers' Record*, February 1888, p. 3; March 1888, p. 7; May 1888, p. 9; June 1888, p. 4; Merritt, p. 117
21. *Shearers' Record*, June 1888, pp. 3, 7; Merritt, p. 62
22. Creswick Branch sec. report, 1888, pp. 49–50; *Shearers' Record*, January 1889, pp. 3, 4–5
23. *Shearers' Record*, January 1889, p. 4
24. Merritt, p. 121; *Shearers' Record*, November 1888, pp. 3–4; Wagga Branch sec. report, 1888, pp. 67–8
25. Merritt, pp. 40–1, 120; *T&CJ*, 5/3/1887, p. 492; 12/3/1887, p. 543; *Shearers' Record*, October 1888, p. 8
26. Sec. report to Conference, February 1889, pp. 50, 53; *Shearers' Record*, June 1889, pp. 4–5; July 1889, p. 1
27. *Shearers' Record*, January 1890, p. 4; Frank Farrell, 'Arthur Rae', *ADB* 1891–1939, vol. 11, p. 323
28. ASU president's address and sec. report, February 1890, pp. 7–11
29. *Shearers' Record*, May 1888, p. 2; May 1890, p. 4; December 1890, p. 7; QSU executive minutes, 12/12/1887, p. 2; 11/1/1890, p. 23; February 1890, ASU Conference report, pp. 20–4, Spence, *History of the AWU*, p. 40; *Worker* (Queensland), March 1890, p. 4
30. R. Gollan, *Radical and Working Class Politics*, Melbourne University Press 1976, p. 107; president's address and sec. report, February 1890, pp. 4, 7–11; *Shearers' Record*, October 1889, p. 1

## 2 Looking for Justice

1. ASU Annual Report, February 1890, p. 4
2. ASU Annual Report, 1889, p. 52
3. R. J. & R. A. Sullivan, 'London Dock/Jondaryan/Bootmakers strikes', in D. Murphy (ed.), *The Big Strikes, Queensland 1889–1965*, University of Queensland Press 1983, p. 55
4. Sullivan, pp. 54–9
5. *Shearers' Record*, May 1890, p. 5; June, p. 1; July, p. 1
6. *Shearers' Record*, July 1890, pp. 1–2, 6–8; *T&CJ*, 12/7/1890, p. 4; Merritt, pp. 154–6

7. Ferguson to Spence 14/7/1890; Spence to Ferguson, 18/7/1890, in *Official Statement of Australian Shearing, Pastoralists Federal Council of Australia*, 1891, pp. 15–16; *T&CJ*, 19/7/1890, p. 19

8. Merritt, pp. 162–3; R. J. Sullivan, 'The Maritime Strike, 1890', in Murphy, *The Big Strikes*, pp. 65, 70–1; *Shearers' Record*, August 1890, p. 4; *T&CJ*, 23/8/1890, p. 13

9. Sullivan, p. 69; *T&CJ*, 20/9/1890, p. 13

10. Spence, *History of the AWU*, pp. 34–5; *Shearers' Record*, 15/9/1890, pp. 1–2, 6; Merritt, p. 165

11. *Official Statement of Australian Shearing*, pp. 5–7; *T&CJ*, 27/9/1890, p. 13; 4/10/1890, p. 12

12. Spence, *History of the AWU*, p. 35; *Shearers' Record*, October 1890, p. 5; November 1890, p. 2; December 1890, p. 2; Rae: *ADB* vol. 11, p. 323

13. Spence, *History of the AWU*, p. 34; Merritt, pp. 164–8

14. *Shearers' Record*, November 1890, p. 1; December 1890, p. 3; Spence, *History of the AWU*, p. 35; *T&CJ*, 11/10/1890, p. 12

15. *Shearers' Record*, December 1890, pp. 4–6; February 1891, p. 1

16. *Shearers' Record*, November 1890, p. 7

17. *Shearers' Record*, November 1890, pp. 1–2; December 1890, p. 2

18. *Shearers' Record*, January 1891, p. 3

19. *Shearers' Record*, April 1890, p. 4–5; July 1890, p. 3; September 1890, pp. 7–8; November 1890, p. 6

20. *Shearers' Record*, February 1891, p. 2; official report of the GLU 1st Annual Conference, February 1891, pp. 5–10; 17

21. *T&CJ*, 12/7/1890, p. 4; 22/11/1890, p. 16

22. *Brisbane Worker*, 10/1/1891, pp. 4–5; Manifesto of the Strike Committee of the Central District Council, Barcaldine, 1/2/1891, reported in *Brisbane Worker*, 7/2/1891, pp. 4–5; *APR*, March 1891, pp. 2–3; Sullivan and Sullivan, p. 80; Merritt, pp. 172, 186

23. *Brisbane Worker*, 24/1/1891, p. 1; 4/4/1891, p. 1

24. Sullivan and Sullivan, pp. 80–3

25. *APR*, March 1891, p. 4; April, p. 32

26. *APR*, April 1891, p. 52

27. *Brisbane Worker*, 21/3/1891, p. 6; 4/4/1891, p. 4

28. *Brisbane Worker*, 4/4/1891, p. 4; 18/4/1891, p. 5; 27/6/1891, p. 3; *APR* May 1891, p. 66; June 1891, p. 126; QSU minutes, 18/5/1891, p. 72

29. *APR*, June 1891, p. 94; *Brisbane Worker*, 4/4/1891, p. 4

30. *Brisbane Worker*, 30/5/1891, p. 5

31. *APR*, March 1891, p. 2

32. *Shearers' Record*, July 1891, p. 1; *Brisbane Worker*, 7/2/1891, pp. 4–5; 16/5/1891, p. 8

33. *Shearers' Record*, April 1891, pp. 2–3; June 1891, pp. 2, 4; July 1891, p. 1; *APR*, April 1891, p. 32

34. *Shearers' Record*, April 1891, p. 3; June 1891, p. 4; *Official Statement of Australian Shearing*, p. 21; Merritt, pp. 195–6

35. Merritt, pp. 197–8; Spence, *History of the AWU*, pp. 37–9; *Shearers' Record*, September 1891, pp. 1–2; 1892 ASU Conference Report, p. 11

36. Conference between the ASU and the Pastoralists Federal Council, 7–8 August 1891, pp. 34–42, 53–4; Spence, *History of the AWU*, p. 38

37. Merritt, p. 201; ASU–Pastoralists Conference report, pp. iv, 43; *Shearers' Record*, September 1891, p. 1

38. C. M. H. Clark, *A History of Australia* vol. 5, Melbourne University Press, 1981, pp. 60–1; Merritt, p. 180; *Shearers' Record*, November 1890, pp. 2, 9
39. *Shearers' Record*, November 1890, pp. 2, 9; June 1891, p. 2; Clark, p. 58; Peter Love, *Labour and the Money Power*, Melbourne University Press 1984, p. 28
40. *Shearers' Record*, June 1891, p. 4, July 1891, p. 1; *Brisbane Worker*, 27/6/1891, p. 1; Ross McMullin, *The Light on the Hill*, Oxford University Press 1991, p. 12; Clark, vol. 5, pp. 78–80
41. *APR*, March 1891, pp. 1–2; June 1891, p. 126
42. *Hummer*, October 1891, p. 1

### 3 The Hustle for Jobs

1. 1892 Conference report, pp. 5, 9, 13, 15
2. Ibid., pp. 3–4, 16, 30–1
3. Ibid., pp. 34–7
4. Ibid., pp. 42–8
5. 1892 Conference report, p. 17; *Shearers' Record*, February 1892, p. 4; May 1892, p. 1; November 1892, p. 2; Merritt, p. 216; *APR*, March 1892, p. 513
6. QSU Minutes AGM, 10/12/1891, pp. 82–3
7. Clark, vol. 5, p. 65
8. *T&CJ*, 2/7/1892, p. 14; 16/7/1892, p. 14
9. *Shearers' Record*, September 1892, p. 3; *T&CJ*, 9/7/1892, p. 17; 27/8/92, p. 17; 3/9/92, p. 16; 22/10/1892, p. 16; 5/11/1892, p. 16
10. *T&CJ*, 2/7/1892, p. 16
11. *APR*, September 1892, p. 807
12. *T&CJ*, 2/7/1892; *APR*, August, p. 756; *Shearers' Record*, June 1892, p. 3; July 1892, p. 2; *Hummer*, 16/4/1892, p. 2
13. *Shearers' Record*, February 1892, p. 4; QSU AGM, 11/12/1891, p. 88
14. *T&CJ*, 2/7/1892, p. 16; 9/7/1892, p. 12
15. *APR*, December 1892, p. 957
16. *Hummer*, 16/1/1892, p. 1; Clark, vol. 5, pp. 87, 100; Gavin Souter, *A Peculiar People*, University of Sydney Press 1981, p. 65
17. Clark, vol. 5, p. 56; QSU AGM, 11/12/1891, p. 84; *Hummer*, 5/12/1891, p. 1
18. ASU 1890 rules, p. 29; AWU 1894 rules, p. 10; 1891, *Shearers' Record*, 16/2/1891, 15/6/1891, pp. 1–2; Andrew Markus, 'Talka Longa Mouth', in A. Markus and A. Curthoys (eds), *Who Are Our Enemies?*, Hale & Iremonger 1978, p. 140; Jack Horner, 'William Ferguson', *ADB* 1891–1939, vol. 8, p. 487
19. ASU sec report, February 1892, p. 13; *APR* January 1892, p. 418
20. *APR*, January 1892, p. 418; NZ Amalgamated Shearers and Labourers Union annual reports, 1894, p. 6, 1895, p. 6.
21. *T&CJ*, 4/3/1893, p. 12; 22/4/1893, p. 14; 29/4/1893, p. 14; 6/5/1893, p. 14
22. *APR*, March 1894, pp. 541–2
23. Ibid., *APR*, August 1892, p. 759
24. 1894 ASU Conference report, pp. 7, 31–2
25. 1894 ASU Conference report, pp. 5, 18–19, 52; *Worker*, 24/9/1892
26. Merritt, p. 229; C. R. Cameron, '"A man is never dead until he is forgotten", David Temple: Founder of the ASU', Commemorative Address published in *Labour History*, no. 60, May 1991, pp. 99–103; 1894 ASU Conference report, p. 4
27. 1894 ASU Conference report, pp. 18, 32, 52; Frank Farrell, 'Donald Macdonell', *ADB* 1891–1939, vol. 10, p. 255. Temple's crucial role in the ASU's

formative years is detailed in Merritt's *Making of the AWU*; Cameron's address was itself part of an AWU recognition of Temple's work with the opening of 'David Temple House', headquarters of the SA Branch of the AWU, in 1990.

28. ASU February 1894 Conference report, pp. 20–2, 34
29. *Worker*, 31/3/1894, p. 3; *APR*, April 1894, p. 102; June 1894, p. 206
30. *APR*, January 1894, p. 526; *Worker*, 17/3/1894, p. 2; Merritt, p. 234
31. *Worker*, 14/4/1894, p. 2; 21/4/1894, p. 2; 28/4/1894, p. 1
32. *Worker*, 5/5/1894, p. 3
33. *Worker*, 23/6/1894, p. 3; 30/6/1894, p. 1; 4/8/1894, p. 3; 25/8/1894, p. 3; 15/9/1894, p. 3; *APR*, May 1894, p. 106; July 1894, pp. 213, 239
34. R. J. and R. A. Sullivan, 'The Pastoral Strikes, 1891 and 1894', in Murphy, *The Big Strikes*, p. 95; *APR*, May 1894, p. 153
35. *T&CJ*, 7/4/1894, p. 18; 25/8/1894, p. 13; 1/9/1894, p. 13
36. *T&CJ*, 8/9/1894, p. 17; 15/9/1894, pp. 13, 35; Sullivan and Sullivan, 'Pastoral Strikes', p. 96
37. *APR*, October 1894, p. 421, November 1894, p. 470, December 1894, p. 480, January 1895, p. 533; 1895 AWU Conference report, p. 24; Merritt, pp. 244–50
38. A. B. Paterson, 'Waltzing Matilda', in G. A. Wilkes (ed.), *A Treasury of Bush Verse*, Angus & Robertson 1991, p. 35. An article in the *Canberra Times*, 27/1/1995 'Banjo's bush tale still waltzing its way into the charts and hearts' – discusses recent research into the origins of 'Waltzing Matilda'.
39. *T&CJ*, 1/9/1894, p. 13; *APR*, October 1894, p. 377

#### 4 Driving in the Iron Heel

1. *Worker*, 16/2/1895, p. 2
2. *APR*, November 1895, p. 492; Markey, *Making of the Labor Party*, pp. 39–41, 164; *Macquarie Book of Events*, p. 223
3. 1895 AWU Conference report, pp. 5–15, 22–3, 30–1; *APR*, March 1895, p. 4
4. *Worker*, 26/1/1895, p. 1; 16/2/1895, p. 2
5. *Worker*, 11/5/1895, pp. 2–3
6. *Worker*, 8/6/1895, p. 4; 15/6/1895, p. 1
7. *APR*, April 1895, p. 100; June 1895, p. 168; July 1895, p. 270; August 1895, pp. 289–90, 342; September 1895, pp. 398–400; October 1895, p. 451; *Worker*, 24/8/1895, p. 3; 14/9/1895, p. 3; 28/9/1895, p. 3; 30/11/1895, p. 3
8. *Worker*, 31/8/1895, p. 4
9. 1896 Conference report, pp. 8, 30; *Worker*, 15/2/1896, p. 3; Merritt, p. 264
10. *APR*, January 1896, p. 659; March 1896, pp. 34, 50; July 1896, p. 266; November 1896, p. 489; October 1897, pp. 393, 431; November 1897, p. 455; January 1898, pp. 558–61; July 1898, p. 268; September 1898, pp. 382–3; Merritt, p. 24.
11. *Worker*, 1/10/1898, p. 8; 15/10/1898, p. 8; 5/11/1898, p. 8; 12/11/1898, p. 8; 3/12/1898, p. 8; 10.12.1898, p. 8
12. AWU 1897 Conference report, pp. 9–14, 18; 1898 Conference report, pp. 9–10; *Worker*, 12/12/1896, p. 2; 26/12/1896, p. 2; Merritt, p. 266
13. McMullin, pp. 17–18, 25, 29, 34; *Worker*, 7/3/1896, p. 3; Bruce Scates, 'William Trenwith', *ADB* 1891–1939, vol. 12, p. 259
14. *Worker*, 2/2/1895, p. 2; 8/6/1895, p. 3; 29/6/1895, p. 1; 6/7/1895, p. 1; 27/7/1895, p. 2; 3/8/1895, p. 1; McMullin, p. 19; Merritt, p. 274
15. *T&CJ*, 11/7/1896, p. 16; *Worker*, 13/4/1895, p. 2; 21/5/1898, p. 8; 1898 AWU Conference report, pp. 9, 16

16. *Worker*, 11/5/1895, pp. 2–3; 30/11/1895, p. 1
17. *Worker*, 15/6/1895, p. 2; 10/8/1895, p. 3; Merritt, pp. 275–6
18. *Worker*, 18/6/1898, p. 2; 30/7/1898, p. 2; 16/9/1899, p. 4; AWU Conference reports: 1899, p. 13; 1900, pp. 17, 19; 1901, p. 11; McMullin, pp. 21, 27–8, 34–7; Jim Hagan and Ken Turner, *A History of the Labor Party in New South Wales, 1891–1991*, Longman Cheshire 191, p. 43
19. 1900 AWU Conference report, pp. 7, 11–13, 18
20. Ibid., pp. 16, 19; Report of Investigating Committee into the Creswick Branch, 7 March 1900. Copy held by the National Library, Canberra, in R. S. Ross papers, MS 3222 folder 8.
21. Cameron, '"A Man is Never Dead Until He Is Forgotten",' pp. 103–5; Merritt, p. 287
22. 1900 AWU Conference report, pp. 13–14, 17; Gavin Souter, 'William Lane', *ADB* 1891–1939, vol. 9, p. 658
23. *APR*, March 1900, p. 42; April 1900, p. 68
24. Clark, vol. 5, p. 170; *Worker*, 7/9/1895, p. 1; 21/9/1895, p. 1
25. *APR*, January 1900, p. 636; September 1900, p. 403; 1901 AWU Conference report, pp. 4–8
26. 1901 AWU Conference report, p. 9
27. 1900 AWU Conference report, p. 7
28. *Worker*, 16/6/1900, p. 7; see also John Rickard, *H. B. Higgins: the Rebel as Judge*, Allen & Unwin 1984, Chs 5, 6.

## 5  The Giant Refreshed

1. 1902 AWU Annual Conference report, pp. 5–6
2. Ibid., p. 43; 1903 AWU Annual Conference report, p. 7
3. *APR*, May 1902, p. 203; February 1903, p. 891; Constitution and Rules of the Machine Shearers and Shed Employees Union, Sydney 1902, pp. 3–4
4. *Worker*, 29/3/02, p. 4; 1902 AWU Annual Conference report, p. 7; *APR*, February 1904, p. 906; Merritt, p. 298
5. AWU manifesto for 1902 shearing season, addendum to 1902 AWU Annual Conference report; 1903 AWU Annual Conference report, pp. 8–9; *Worker*, 30/6/02, p. 6; 5/7/02, p. 7, 9/8/02, p. 4; *APR*, October 1902, p. 587
6. *SMH*, 11/8/02, p. 5; 14/8/02, p. 6; 22/8/02, p. 7; 25/8/02, p. 7
7. *SMH*, 26/8/02, p. 8; 27/8/02, p. 10; 28/8/02, p. 7; 29/8/02, p. 5
8. *SMH*, 30/8/02, p. 7; 4/9/02, p. 7; 6/9/02, p. 7; *Worker*, 13/9/02, pp. 4, 7
9. *APR*, October 1902, p. 541; *SMH*, 12/9/02, p. 6; 1903 AWU Annual Conference report, p. 9; Merritt, p. 314
10. *Worker*, 4/7/03, p. 4; Merritt, p. 318
11. *Worker*, 12/9/03, p. 7; McMullin, p. 44
12. *Worker*, 12/9/03, pp. 4–5; 26/8/05, p. 7; 7/2/07, p. 7; *APR*, March 1904, pp. 70–2; February 1904, p. 906; July 1904, p. 400; 1905 AWU Annual Conference report, pp. 13–14; 1906 AWU Annual Conference report, p. 25
13. 1905 AWU Annual Conference report, p. 25; Certificate of AWU Registration, 16 May 1905, AIRC records; Merritt, pp. 330, 337–8; 1907 AWU Conference report, p. 19; *Worker*, 26/8/05, p. 7; 7/2/07, p. 7
14. Markey, *The Making of the Labor Party*, pp. 312–14; Burgmann, p. 41; *Worker*, 27/2/04, p. 7; 14/1/05, p. 7; AWU 1905 Annual Conference report, p. 13; Brisbane *Worker*, 21/1/05, p. 3; 4/2/05, p. 2; 18/2/05, p. 4; 25/2/05, p. 6

15. See Markey, *Making of the Labor Party*; M. Bray and M. Rimmer, *Delivering The Goods*, Allen & Unwin 1987; M. Hearn, *Working Lives: A History of the Australian Railways Union in New South Wales*, Hale & Iremonger 1990.

16. *Worker*, 1/7/05, p. 5; 2/9/05, p. 1; 1902 AWU Annual Conference report, p. 6

17. W. H. Wilde & I. Moore (eds.), *Letters of Mary Gilmore*, Melbourne University Press 1980, p. 176; AWU Annual Conference reports: 1902, pp. 6, 29–34; 1905, p. 18; 1907, p. 19

18. W. H. Wilde, *Courage A Grace: A biography of Dame Mary Gilmore*, Melbourne University Press 1988, pp. 152–65; *Worker*, 2/1/08, p. 15

19. Wilde, pp. 157, 160–1, 190, 210–11; *Worker*, 7/1/09, p. 9

20. Wilde, pp. 162–3; *Worker*, 9/4/08, p. 9

21. *Worker*, 23/1/08, 30/1/08, 6/2/08, all p. 27

22. 'Labor Papers Limited: A concise history of the struggle for a union-owned and controlled chain of newspapers' The Worker Print, 1925, pp. 10–13; Report by T. Dougherty re Macdonell House and Westland Broadcasting Pty Ltd, undated pamphlet *c.* 1961, p. 3

23. B. J. Guyatt, 'The Publicists – The Labour Press 1880 to 1915' in D. J. Murphy (ed.), *Prelude To Power*, University of Queensland Press, pp. 246–61; AWU Qld Branch Annual 1961, pp. 83–99

24. 1907 AWU Conference report reprinted in *Worker* 7/2/07, p. 19; *APR*, March 1907, pp. 38, 90–2; April 1907, p. 186; July 1907, p. 463; Merritt, pp. 352–5

25. Transcript of evidence, 1907 hearings re Shearing Industry Award, 10 June–8 July 1907, Noel Butlin Archives, ANU, pp. 631–6

26. Diary of Syd Fernandez 1904–24, held by AWU Victorian Branch

27. 1907 Transcript, pp. 135–7, pp. 261–81

28. Ibid., pp. 805–33

29. *APR* supplement, August 1907, pp. 1–3; Merritt, pp. 345–5

30. *APR*, August 15 p. 509; 1908 AWU Conference report reprinted in *Worker* 20/2/08, p. 19; extract from Harvester judgment in F. Crowley, *Modern Australia, 1901–39*, Thomas Nelson 1978, p. 111

31. Turner, *Industrial Labour and Politics*, p. 39

32. 1908 AWU Conference report reprinted in *Worker*, 20/2/08, p. 19; 5/3/08, pp. 30–1; 1909 AWU Conference report, pp. 83–4; 1910 AWU Conference report, p. 4; *APR*, August 1908, p. 542

33. Farrell, *ADB*, vol. 10, p. 255; Mary Gilmore, *Marri'd and other verses*, Geo. Robertson 1910, p. 45; *Complete Stories of Henry Lawson*, Penguin Books, 1986, p. 480; *APR*, October 1911; 1912 AWU Conference report, p. 1. The authors acknowledge the kind assistance of David Fordyce in providing family information about Donald Macdonell.

34. 1912 AWU Conference report, p. 5; *APR*, November 1911, pp. 948–9, 1009

35. 1906 AWU Annual Conference report, pp. 37, 41, 48; *Worker*, 2/10/12, p. 12; 16/10/12, p. 3; 1912 AWU Conference report, pp. 40–2; 1913 AWU Conference report, p. 3

36. 1913 AWU Conference report, p. 11; Frank Farrell, 'Edward Grayndler', *ADB* 1891–1939 vol. 9, pp. 86–7

37. Childe, p. 123; K. H. Kennedy, 'Theodore McCormack and the AWA', *Labour History*, no. 33, 1977, p. 14

38. 1912 AWU Annual Convention report, pp. 50–5; Childe, p. 124; Raj Jadeja, *Parties to the Award: a guide to federally registered industrial organisations 1904–94*, Noel Butlin Archives Centre, Australian National University 1994, p. 3; W. G. Spence, 'Trade Union Administration and Industrial and Craft Unionism',

in M. Atkinson (ed.), *Trade Unionism in Australia*, WEA, Sydney 1915, pp. 42–3.
39. 1913 Annual Report, pp. 4, 31; Childe, p. 126; membership returns as at December 1913 provided to Commonwealth industrial registrar, 3/11/14. Commonwealth Industrial Registry; B. Crouchley and H. J. Gibbney, 'William John Dunstan', *ADB* 1891–1939, vol. 8, p. 382
40. Ross Fitzgerald, *'Red Ted': the life of E. G. Theodore*, Queensland University Press 1994, pp. 41, 57; Crouchley and Gibbney, *ADB*, p. 382
41. 1911 AWU Conference report, p. 46; Turner, *Industrial Labour and Politics*, p. 49fn; 1912 AWU Conference Report, p. 10; H. V. Evatt, *William Holman: Australian Labour Leader*, Angus & Robertson 1979, p. 198

### 6 One Big Union

1. C. E. W. Bean, *The Story of Anzac*, vol. 1, University of Queensland Press 1981, p. 44; Turner, *Industrial Labor and Politics*, p. 69; *Worker*, 14/10/15, p. 19; 20/1/16, p. 5; 5/10/16, p. 23; 30/6/80, p. 7; 1916 Convention report, pp. 6, 65; 1917 Convention report, p. 6.
2. *Worker*, 16/9/15, p. 5
3. 1916 Convention report, p. 101; Turner, p. 102; McMullin, pp. 104–5
4. *Worker*, 14/9/16; 26/10/16, p. 3; Burgmann, p. 41
5. *Worker*, 25/10/16, p. 23; Executive Council minutes, 23/9/16, 13/11/16; Wilde, pp. 194–6
6. Coral Lansbury and Bede Nairn, 'W. G. Spence', *ADB* 1851–1890, vol. 6, p. 168; Coral Lansbury, 'Hector Lamond', *ADB* 1891–1939, vol. 9, p. 654
7. Executive Council minutes, 24/9/19, p. 53; *Worker*, 'No Conscription Special', 7/12/17, p. 1; Crowley, *Modern Australia*, pp. 273, 281–3, 296; McMullin, pp. 108–13; Turner, *Sydney's Burning*, p. 62; Frank Farrell, 'Henry Boote', *ADB* 1891–1939, vol. 7, p. 342; R. Van Den Hoorn, 'Alexander Poynton', *ADB* 1891–1939, vol. 11, p. 272.
8. *Worker*, 28/9/16, p. 19; 2/11/16, p. 5; Turner, *Industrial Labour*, p. 113; Clark, vol. 6, p. 37
9. Hearn, *Working Lives*, pp. 28–32; L. Taksa, '"Defence Not Defiance": Social Protest and the NSW General Strike of 1917', *Labour History*, no. 60, May 1991, p. 16
10. *Worker*, 23/8/17, p. 6; 20/9/17, p. 7; Taksa, p. 22
11. Turner, *Industrial Labour*, p. 159; Hearn, pp. 33–8; Crowley, *Modern Australia*, vol. 4, pp. 288, 335
12. 1915 Amalgamation Report, pp. 4, 6, 15, 19; 1917 Annual Convention report, p. 4; Executive Council minutes, pp. 23/10, 25/10, 27/10, 28/10; Worker, 6/7/16, p. 5; 4/10/17, p. 2; 11/7/18, p. 13; Childe, p. 129
13. Peter Sheldon, 'System and Strategy: The Changing Shape of Unionism among NSW Construction Labourers, 1910–1919', *Labour History*, no. 65, November 1993, pp. 115–35
14. Childe, pp. 129, 250; FMEA Third Annual Conference report, 1914, p. 27; Grayndler to Commonwealth Industrial Registrar, 13/4/18
15. Australian Mines and Metals Association 1918 AGM report, pp. 3–4
16. 1914 Annual Convention report, p. 8; Childe, p. 129; 1917 Annual Convention report, p. 70; 1918 Annual Convention report, pp. 31–3; Executive Council minutes, 11/4/18
17. OBU declarations reprinted in B. McKinlay (ed.) *Australian Labor History in Documents*, vol. 3, pp. 95–8; Turner, *Industrial Labour*, pp. 183–4

18. Lane, p. 208; 1920 Annual Convention report, p. 8
19. Executive Council minutes, 2/5/19, pp. 27–8; 5/5/19, p. 29; 6/5/19, p. 31; *Worker*, 15/5/19, p. 7; Turner, *Industrial Labour*, p. 188
20. Executive Council minutes, 20/9/19, p. 45; 24/9/19, p. 52; *Worker*, 12/6/19, p. 17; Farrell, *ADB*, vol. 11, p. 323
21. 1920 Convention report, p. 8
22. AWU Executive Council minutes, 5/5/19, p. 30; 20/6/20, p. 9; *Worker*, 24/7/19, p. 7
23. 1921 Annual Convention report, p. 30; Turner, *Industrial Labour*, p. 212
24. Turner, *Industrial Labour*, p. 194; Lane, p. 270; Report of Inaugural Convention of the Australian Workers Union: E154/19, AWU Collection, Noel Butlin Archives, ANU; Joan Simpson, 'Radicals and Realists: The AWU Response to the One Big Union Challenge', in *Traditions for Reform In New South Wales*, ALP publication, Pluto Press, p. 48
25. Executive Council minutes, 1/6/23, p. 14; 27/5/24, p. 27; Simpson, p. 49
26. Childe, pp. 65, 72, 79–80; Simpson, p. 49

## 7 Ourselves Alone

1. 'The Old Unionist' in Lawson, *Poems*, p. 236
2. E. L. Barnes, Shirtsleeves to Shirtsleeves, unpublished manuscript; copy in La Trobe Library, Melbourne, pp. 177, 211
3. 1920 AWU Annual Convention minutes, pp. 100–6; Wilde, p. 220; Lawson, *Poems*, pp. 236, 256
4. Lane, pp. 238, 243, 244
5. 1921 AWU Annual Convention report, pp. 13–14; Childe, pp. 171–8
6. Irwin Young, 'Changes Within the NSW Branch of the Australian Workers' Union 1919–1924', *The Journal of Industrial Relations*, March 1964, pp. 51–60
7. M. Rutledge, 'John Bailey', *ADB* 1891–1939, vol. 7, p. 136; Robert Murray, *The Confident Years: Australia in the Twenties*, Allen Lane, 1978, pp. 51–2
8. G. Freudenberg, *Cause for Power*, Pluto Press 1991, pp. 134–7; Hagan and Turner, pp. 118–21
9. Freudenberg, p. 134; Hagan and Turner, p. 76
10. Murray Perks, 'The rise to leadership' in H. Radi and P. Spearritt (eds), *Jack Lang*, Hale & Iremonger 1977, p. 35; Freudenberg, p. 137
11. H. Boote, The Case Of J. Bailey, MLA and Others, in *Bailey, MLA Exonerated. A Frame-Up Exposed*. Report of Inquiry with Comments by H. E. Boote, The Worker Trade Union Print, Sydney, 1923; Irwin Young, *Theodore: His Life and Times*, Alpha Books, 1971, pp. 53–6; 1925 AWU Convention report, p. 56
12. Minutes of the AWU Executive Council, 3/2/33, pp. 7–8; Freudenberg, p. 137; Hagan and Turner, p. 84; Rutledge, *ADB*, vol. 7, p. 136
13. Hagan and Turner, p. 81
14. 1927 AWU Annual Convention report, pp. 98–9, 74, 76; Hagan and Turner, p. 84
15. McMullin, *The Light on the Hill*, pp. 29, 140; Steven Weeks, 'Francis Walter Lundie', *ADB* 1891–1939, vol. 10, p. 169
16. L. Ross, *John Curtin*, Sun Books 1977, p. 63
17. 1925 AWU Annual Convention report, pp. 30–2; Norma Marshall, 'John Barnes', *ADB* 1891–1939, vol. 7, p. 180
18. 1927 AWU Annual Convention report, pp. 85–7; 1930 Annual Convention

report, p. 11; Jim Hagan, *The History of the ACTU*, Longman Cheshire 1981, pp. 22–5, 38–45; Frank Farrell, *International Socialism and Australian Labour*, Hale & Iremonger 1981, p. 138; Frank Farrell, 'International Solidarity', in Markus and Curthoys, pp. 132, 141

19. 1923 AWU Annual Convention report, p. 57; 1928 Annual Convention report, pp. 120–1; Farrell, 'International Solidarity', pp. 135–40; Hagan, p. 94; *Worker*, 5 March 1930, p. 15

20. 1925 AWU Annual Convention report, pp. 36–7; 1925 Central Branch annual report, p. 7

21. Official report, Third Rank and File Conference, 1 and 2 September 1928, Preface; 1927 Queensland Branch Delegates Meeting report; AWU Executive Council Meeting, 22 March 1928, Minute Book, pp. 68, 106–16

22. K. H. Kennedy, 'The South Johnstone Strike', in Murphy, *The Big Strikes*, pp. 176, 181–3

23. 1928 AWU Annual Convention report, pp. 3–4

24. R. Fitzgerald and H. Thornton, *Labor in Queensland: From the 1880s to 1988*, University of Queensland Press 1989, pp. 42–7

25. 1921 AWU Annual Convention report, p. 4

26. Central Branch annual report, 1926; 1929 and 1930 AWU Queensland Branch Delegates Meeting reports: report of branch sec., 1920 Annual Convention report, p. 155; 1925 Annual Convention report, pp. 5, 31; 1925 and 1928 Central Branch report: sec. report and 1920 Vic./Riv. Branch report, p. 1

27. 1929 AWU Convention report, pp. 33–5; *Worker*, 9/4/30, p. 16

28. 1921 AWU Convention report, p. 4; R. W. Ripley, History of the NZ Workers' Union, serialised in the *New Zealand Worker* between July 1974 and June 1977. Copies held in 'NZWU and AWU' folder, Russell Finlay Papers, Box E20, AWU Federal Office, Sydney

29. 1921 AWU Convention report, pp. 21–2; 1922 Convention report, pp. 50–1, 86–94; 1929 Tasmanian Branch sec. report, p. 1

30. 1922 Victoria-Riverina Branch sec. report, p. 1; J. R. Robertson, 'J. J. McNeill', *ADB* 1891–1939, vol. 10, p. 352

31. Chris Wright, 'The formative years of management control at the Newcastle Steelworks, 1913–1924', *Labour History*, no. 55, November 1988, pp. 62–70; R. Murray and K. White, *The Ironworkers: A History of the Federated Ironworkers Association of Australia*, Hale & Iremonger 1982, pp. 52–60

32. *Worker*, 28/10/20, p. 7; 4/11/20; Rickard, p. 253

33. *Worker*, 31/5/17, p. 11

34. *Worker*, 4/11/20, p. 3; N. Windett, *Australia as Producer and Trader 1920–1932*, Oxford University Press, 1933, pp. 48–50

35. 1920 Qld Branch report to AWU Convention, p. 6; *Pastoral Review*, June 1920, p. 340

36. *Pastoralists' Review*, September 1916, p. 899; 16/4/21, p. 256

37. 1922–23 Central Branch report, pp. 3–4; 1923 AWU Annual Convention report, pp. 4–5, 20; *Pastoralists' Review*, 16/10/22, p. 771 and 16/3/23, p. 257; 1923 Adelaide Branch annual report, p. 7

38. 1928 Central Branch annual report, p. 3

39. *Pastoralists' Review*, 15/6/29, p. 509; Kosmas Tsokhas, 'Power, law and conflict in the pastoral industry 1914–1924', *Journal of the Royal Australian Historical Society*, vol. 76, no. 3, 1990, pp. 218–33 and 1925 Annual Convention report, p. 36

40. 1927 Central Branch annual report, p. 7

41. Transcripts of the evidence of James McIntosh, Samuel Turnbull and Hector Bennett in *AWU v. Ashford et al.* 1926) in Box N117/556; Thomas Ryan and Samuel Jamieson and Frank Lysaght in *AWU v. Pastoralists Federal Council of Australia and ors* (1917) in Box N117/552; Roy Cole in *AWU v. Pastoralists Federal Council of Australia and ors* in Box N117/563; Charles O'Brien in 1932 Pastoral Case in Box N117/572. All records held by Noel Butlin Archives, ANU, Canberra. Bill Hall, authors' interview, 10/2/94

42. Geoffrey Blainey, *The Rush That Never Ended*, Melbourne University Press, 1978, pp. 283–8; Windett, pp. 133–5; 1922 Central Branch annual report, p. 4; 1925 Central Branch annual report, p. 10; 1922 Adelaide Branch annual report, p. 7

43. 1921 AWU Annual Convention report, pp. 13–14; 1922 AWU Annual Convention report, pp. 50–1; Blainey, *Rush That Never Ended*, pp. 199, 283–8; Andrew Reeves, '"Yours 'til the war of classes is ended", OBU organisers on Western Australian Eastern Goldfields', and Patrick Bertola, 'Tributers and Gold Mining in Boulder, 1918–1934', both in *Labour History*, no. 65, November 1993, pp. 19, 54

44. AWU Qld Branch 1922 Delegates Meeting report, pp. 6–7; J. Kerr, *Mount Morgan, Gold Copper and Oil*, J. D. & R. S. Kerr, Brisbane, 1982, pp. 165–73; Blainey, *Rush That Never Ended*, pp. 305, 312

45. Marcus James, 'The struggle against silicosis in the Australian mining industry: the role of the Commonwealth Government, 1920–1950', *Labour History*, no. 65, November 1993, pp. 75–91; 1920 Adelaide Branch annual report, p. 8; 1928 Central Branch annual report, p. 14; Blainey, *Rush That Never Ended*, p. 301

46. Transcripts of the evidence of Joseph Cahill, Ernest West, William Bowman, Jack Harigan, Michael Kinsell, Eric Reece, George Stackpoole, Samuel Grieben and Robert Davies in *AWU v. The Arba Tin Mining Company and ors* and *AWU v. The Adelong Gold Estates (NL) and ors. Re Metalliferous Mines – Victoria and Tasmania* (1934/35) in Box N117/623, Noel Butlin Archives, ANU, Canberra

47. James, pp. 86–7

48. Transcript of the evidence of AWU organiser Francis Richardson in *Amalgamated Engineering Union et al. v. J. Alderidge and Company P/L* (1926) in Box N117/627 Noel Butlin Archives, ANU, Canberra

49. Sheldon, 'System and Strategy', p. 118

50. 1923 Central Branch annual report, p. 6; Transcript of the evidence of John Dwyer and John Case in *AWU v. Frank R. Arndt and ors and W. Martin and ors* (1924) in Box N117/606 in Noel Butlin Archives, ANU, Canberra

## 8  A Union that Battles

1. S. MacIntyre, *The Oxford History of Australia*, Oxford University Press 1988, pp. 277–8; 1931 Annual Convention report, p. 5; Qld Branch annual reports, 1930 and 1932; Hagan and Turner, p. 82

2. *Worker*, 11/2/31; Love, p. 100

3. AWU Executive Council minutes, 20/4/31, p. 43; 21/4/31, p. 45; Freudenberg, pp. 163–5

4. *Worker*, 17/6/31, p. 3; Love, pp. 52–3, 104, 125

5. AWU Executive Council minutes, 23/6/31, p. 52

6. Warren Denning, *Caucus Crisis*, Hale & Iremonger 1982, p. 139; McMullin, p. 177

7. Curtin to Boote, 22/12/31, in Boote Papers, National Library of Australia; Ross, pp. 129–36, 142
8. Worker, 23/12/31, p. 1; Executive Council minutes, 21/4/31, pp. 43–4; 'Macdonell House', report by general secretary T. Dougherty, n.d., c. 1961, p. 4
9. J. Hagan, 'Lang and the unions, 1923–32' and F. Farrell, 'Dealing with the Communists, 1923–36', both in H. Radi and P. Spearrit (eds), *Jack Lang*, Hale & Iremonger 1977, pp. 40, 42, 64–5; 'Macdonell House' report, pp. 5–7
10. Fitzgerald, p. 336; Interview with Clyde Cameron, 12/5/94
11. Fitzgerald, pp. 339, 349–50, 364–5; Interview with Clyde Cameron, 12/5/94; Minutes of board of directors of Labor Papers Ltd, 1/11/32, p. 310; 21/11/32; January 1937, p. 343; 13/2/39, p. 356; *Worker*, 8/2/33
12. Ion Idriess, *Lasseter's Last Ride*, Angus & Robertson 1931, pp. 1–4; Blainey, *Rush That Never Ended*, p. 318; Rutledge, *ADB*, vol. 7, p. 136
13. *Worker*, 18/1/33, 8/2/33; Interview with Clyde Cameron, 12/5/94; Rutledge, *ADB*, vol. 7, p. 136
14. Wilde, pp. 258–63; 1928 AWU Annual Convention report; *Worker*, 18/2/31
15. *Worker*, 11/2/31, p. 3; 28/1/31, p. 5; Kosmas Tsokhas, 'Shifting The Burden: Graziers and Pastoral Workers in the 1930s', *Journal of Australian Studies*, vol. 2, November 1990, pp. 40–1; Andrew Moore, 'The Pastoral Workers Industrial Union, 1930–1937', *Labour History*, no. 49, November 1985, p. 61
16. *Worker*, 30/7/38, p. 16; 10/8/38, p. 16
17. *Worker*, 23/6/30, pp. 18–19; 30/7/30, p. 17
18. *Worker*, 20/8/30, p. 19; *Pastoral Review*, August 1930, p. 732; Moore, pp. 62, 65; Farrell, *ADB*, vol. 11, p. 323. In regard to the difficulties unions faced in developing a coherent response to depression-generated wage cuts, see Hearn, p. 47, and Bray and Rimmer, pp. 111, 133–4
19. Moore, pp. 69–70
20. Brian Costar, 'Two Depression Strikes, 1931', in Murphy, *The Big Strikes*, p. 186
21. Ibid., p. 190; Interview with Alf Kain, 25/2/92
22. *Pastoral Review*, 16/2/31, p. 205; Costar, p. 191
23. 1929 AWU Convention report, p. 4; *Worker*, 6/7/38, p. 18; 1/7/36, p. 3; 29/7/36, pp. 18–19 and Pastoral Awards, 1932, 1936, 1938
24. Interview with Clyde Cameron, 12/5/94; A. Davidson, *The Communist Party of Australia: A Short History*, Hoover Institution Press, Stanford, California, 1969, p. 60; *Worker*, 19/8/31, p. 17; 6/1/32, p. 17
25. *Worker*, 9/1/35, p. 18; 16/1/35, p. 18; 13/2/35, p. 18; 1938 AMMA annual report, p. 12; McMullin, pp. 186, 194; Weeks, *ADB*, vol. 10, p. 169; J. Moss, *The Sound of Trumpets: A History of the Labour Movement in South Australia*, Wakefield Press 1985, p. 258
26. 1930 Victoria-Riverina Branch annual reports: 1930, p. 1; 1932, p. 1; 1933, p. 1; 1936, pp. 1–2; 1938, p. 1; 1939, p. 1; 1940, p. 1
27. Tasmanian Branch annual reports: 1930, p. 1; 1933, p. 1; 1936, p. 1; 1938, p. 1; 1939, p. 1; McMullin, p. 192
28. McMullin, pp. 191–2; B. J. Costar, 'William Forgan Smith', *ADB 1891–1939*, vol. 11, p. 665
29. Clyde Cameron, *The Confessions of Clyde Cameron*, ABC Enterprises, 1990, pp. 34, 38
30. Brian Costar, 'Labor and the Depression', in Murphy, *Labor in Power*, p. 420

31. Costar, 'Labor and the Depression', pp. 420–1; R. Fitzgerald and H. Thornton, *Labor in Queensland: From the 1880s to 1988*, University of Queensland Press 1989, pp. 39, 44
32. Costar, 'Labor and the Depression'; 1933 AWU Annual Convention report, p. 3
33. 1936 AWU Annual Convention report, p. 13; 1936 NSW Branch annual report, p. 1; 1946 Annual Convention report, p. 23–4
34. *'Ballot Dodging in Queensland, the Case for a Democratic Ballot in the AWU'*, pamphlet published by the provisional membership rights committee, Innisfail, 14 September 1936
35. *'Ballot Dodging'*, pp. 13–20
36. Minutes of the 24th AWU Qld Branch annual delegates meeting, January 1937, pp. 15, 68
37. 1937 24th Qld Branch annual delegates meeting report, pp. 15–16; 1938 25th Qld Branch annual delegates meeting report, pp. 7, 43
38. Geoff Burrows and Clive Morton, *The Canecutters*, Melbourne University Press 1986, p. 77
39. Diane Menghetti, *The Red North*, History Department, James Cook University, Townsville, c. 1978, pp. 27–8, 52; L. D. Henderson, 'Economic or Racist – Australian Reactions to Italians in North Queensland, 1921–1939', in Henry Reynolds (ed.), *Race Relations in North Queensland*, James Cook University, Townsville 1978, pp. 328–31, 344; Burrows and Morton, p. 75
40. Diane Menghetti, 'The Weil's Disease Strike, 1935', in Murphy, *The Big Strike*, pp. 202–4
41. Burrows and Morton, pp. 80–5; Menghetti, *The Red North*, pp. 40–2
42. Queensland Branch delegates meeting report, January 1936, pp. 19, 21–2; Menghetti, *The Red North*, p. 47; Burrows and Norton, p. 85
43. Queensland Branch delegates meeting reports: 1938 (25th), pp. 37–43; 1941 (28th), pp. 32–3, 57–75, 123; 1942 (29th), p. 177; 1938 AWU Annual Convention report, pp. 42–9; Fallon's reference to 'isms' was reported by J. A. McCallum in 'The Economic Bases of Australian Politics', in W. G. K. Duncan (ed.), *Trends In Australian Politics*, Angus & Robertson 1935, p. 58
44. AWU Annual Convention reports: 1936, pp. 3–4, 72, 77–80; 1938, pp. 3–5; 1944, p. 15; Robertson, *ADB*, vol. 10, p. 352
45. *Worker* supplement, 29/1/36

## 9 A Wonderful Machine

1. P. Hasluck, *The Government and the People, 1942–45*, Australian War Memorial 1970, p. 232; L. F. Crisp, *Ben Chifley*, Longmans, Green & Co. 1963, p. 162; Crowley, *Modern Australia*, p. 76
2. AWU Executive Council minutes, 28/6/39, p. 15; Freudenberg, pp. 186–94; Don Rawson, 'McKell and Labor Unity', in M. Easson (ed.), *McKell*, Allen & Unwin 1988, p. 31
3. Boote diaries, 26/3/40, 27/3/40, 12/4/40; The diaries are held in the National Library of Australia, Canberra. AWU Executive Council minutes, 26/6/40, p. 31; AWU Annual Convention reports: 1943, pp. 68–76; 1946, pp. 40–3; Farrell, *ADB*, vol. 7, pp. 342–3; for Boote's enduring hostility to Lang see H. Boote, Treachery to Labor! an AWU published pamphlet attacking Lang, 1940.
4. Boote Diaries, 4/12/40, 10/12/40

5. Ibid., 7/10/41
6. Ibid., 8/12/40, 20/1/41, 14/2/41; 1941 AWU Convention report, pp. 110, 130–3; Cameron, *Confessions*, pp. 36–7 and interview with C. Cameron, 12/5/94
7. Boote Diaries, 17/11/42, 21/12/42; Executive Council minutes, 23/6/49, p. 8; *Worker*, 19/4/39, p. 7; 9/12/42, pp. 3, 13, 20; 17/1/43, pp. 2, 4; 1943 AWU Convention report, p. 33; McMullin, pp. 221–3; Crowley, *Modern Australia*, p. 76; H. C. Coombs, 'The Economic Aftermath of the War', in D. A. S Campbell (ed.), *Postwar Reconstruction in Australia*, Australasian Publishing Company 1944; M. Saunders and R. Summy, *The Australian Peace Movement: A Short History*, Peace Research Centre, ANU, 1986, p. 29
8. Boote Diaries, 20 and 22/5/42, 1/12/42, 15/1/43, 29/1/43; *SMH*, 24/11/42, p. 6; 8/6/44, p. 4; Hasluck, pp. 234–6; Fitzgerald, pp. 398–9
9. 1942 AWU Annual Convention report, pp. 41–2, 71–4
10. 29th AWU Qld Branch annual delegates meeting minutes, pp. 86–8
11. Boote Diaries, 28/1/41, 30/1/41, 6/5/41; AWU Executive Council minutes, 25/6/40, p. 29; 27/6/40, p. 35; 13/2/41, p. 43; 14/2/41, p. 44; Cameron, *Confessions*, pp. 34–5; Farrell, *ADB*, vol. 9, pp. 86–7
12. Boote Diaries, 21/4/41
13. 27th AWU Qld Branch annual delegates meeting minutes, 1940, p. 75
14. AWU Executive Council minutes, 23/6/41, p. 50; 23/6/42, pp. 64–5; 1942 AWU Annual Convention report, p. 20; 1943 AWU Annual Convention report, pp. 19, 28–30; Cameron, *Confessions*, pp. 41–2
15. 1943 AWU Annual Convention report, pp. 28–32, 56–60; AWU Executive Council minutes, 17/2/43, p. 5; Cameron, *Confessions*, p. 42: Clyde Cameron says that Fallon and Dougherty, realising that Hay would have the numbers at the Executive Council meeting, refused to attend the meeting and flew back to Brisbane directly after the Convention. This is not borne out by the AWU Executive Council minute book for the meeting of 17 February 1943, which shows that both Dougherty and Fallon attended the meeting and were present at the voting.
16. 1944 AWU Annual Convention report, p. 50
17. 1944 AWU Annual Convention minutes, pp. 17, 19; AWU Executive Council minutes, 22–28/6/43, pp. 12–22, 28–8; 26/1/44, p. 32
18. AWU Executive Council minutes, 22/9/44, p. 72; 21/11/44, pp. 83–4; CAR, misc. 119 of 1944, p. 674; *SMH*, 29/1/44, p. 13; 5/7/44, p. 5; 24/11/44, p. 3; Cameron, *Confessions*, p. 43; 1945 AWU Convention report, p. 69; *Tribune*, 30/11/44, p. 6; 15/2/45, p. 4; *AWU Ballot Racketeers Exposed! Facts of Mr Justice O'Mara's Judgement in Hay-Hall v. AWU Executive, and facts of the NSW purge*, Pamphlet, ML
19. AWU Annual Convention reports: 1983, pp. 31–3; 1939, p. 6; 1940, pp. 34–40; 1942, pp. 10–11; 1940–43 NSW Branch sec. reports; *Worker*, 16/6/43, p. 1
20. AWU Executive Council minutes, 21/6/44, p. 40; 22/6/44, p. 42; Cameron, *Confessions*, p. 44
21. *Worker*, 16/8/44, p. 7; Pamphlet, *The Truth ...*, *by Tom Dougherty*, The Worker Print, *c.* 1944, p. 2; Pamphlet, *Fallon's Stooge – Dougherty – Suffers from Red-phobia*, distributed by the NSW Branch executive
22. AWU Executive Council minutes, 5–6/7/44, pp. 47–9; 18–22/9/44, pp. 50–73; 20–23/11/44, pp. 74–87; Dougherty, *The Truth ...*, pp. 24–32; *Worker*, 13/9/44, pp. 1, 7; 27/9/44, p. 1; 1938 AWU Convention report, pp. 5–7

23. 1945 AWU Convention report, p. 15; Executive Council minutes, 19/9/44, pp. 51–2; interview with George Pont, 26/2/92; Cameron, *Confessions*, pp. 43–5
24. *Worker*, 7/3/45, p. 10; 2/5/45, p. 2; 27/6/45, p. 1; 1947 AWU Convention report, p. 7; *SMH*, 8/3/45, p. 4; 10/3/45, p. 3; 26/6/45, p. 4
25. AWU Annual Convention reports: 1946, pp. 6, 60–2; 1947, pp. 14, 46–7, 94–106; 1948, pp. 6–14; *SMH*, 19/2/47, p. 3
26. Cameron, *Confessions*, pp. 30–1; 1940, 1941 and 1949 Adelaide Branch sec. annual reports
27. Victoria-Riverina Branch annual reports: 1941, pp. 2–3; 1942, p. 2; 1944, p. 2; 1943, p. 1; 1946, p. 1; 1948–49, p. 1
28. Tasmanian Branch annual reports: 1943, pp. 1–2; 1946, pp. 1–6
29. AWU Annual Convention reports: 1946, p. 11; 1947, p. 13; 1948, p. 12; *SMH*, 21/2/47, p. 1; *Tribune*, 21/1/50, p. 6; 8/2/50, p. 7; E. Aarons, *What's Left? Memoirs of an Australian Communist*, Penguin Books 1993, p. 48
30. Qld AWU 32nd 1945 annual delegates meeting report, p. 62; D. Blackmur, 'The Railway Strike, 1948', in Murphy, *The Big Strikes*, p. 244; Hagan, p. 122
31. Executive Council minutes: 21/9/48, p. 3; 1/6/49, p. 3; Tom Sheridan, *Division of Labour: Industrial Relations in the Chifley Years 1945–1949*, Oxford University Press 1989, pp. 265–7
32. Sheridan, pp. 304–5; Hearn, pp. 100–2. According to Sheridan, Cameron has denied that Dougherty ever offered or Chifley ever requested AWU labour to work the mines. Sheridan concedes that this may be true in the formal sense but argues that informally it was well known that AWU official-dom was 'willing to marry self-interest with the national determination to defeat the coal strike'. Sheridan, p. 369 fn. 70
33. Annual Convention reports: 1943, pp. 68–76; 1949, p. 35
34. *SMH*, 8/1/50, p. 6; AWU Executive Council minutes, September 1949, pp. 5–6; Cameron, *Confessions*, pp. 42–4
35. Fallon to Boote 10/5/49, in Boote correspondence, NLA; Robertson, *ADB*, vol. 10, p. 352; Cameron, *Confessions*, p. 35
36. Executive Council minutes, January 1950, p. 3; 37th Queensland delegates committee meeting, January 1950, p. 11
37. AWU Executive Council minutes: January 1950, p. 7; 11/5/50, pp. 7–9; 6/2/51, pp. 5, 7, 11; 27/6/51, pp. 9, 12; *Worker*, 18/7/51, p. 7; 1950 AWU Annual Convention report, pp. 29–30, 34, 53–5, 60, 66–7; *SMH*, 28/1/50, p. 5; Cameron, *Confessions*, pp. 47–8
38. *SMH*, 12/1/50, pp. 1–2; *Worker*, 18/1/50, p. 6

### 10 Anxious to See the Light

1. *SMH*, 26/2/90; *Sun-Herald*, 25/2/90; *Worker*, 18/7/51, p. 7; Marilyn Dodkin, Charlie Oliver, A Political Biography, unpublished MA thesis, University of Sydney 1990, pp. 9–12
2. *Worker*, 19/9/51, p. 1; Murray, pp. 79, 84–5
3. *Worker*, 13/9/50, p. 1; *SMH*, 3/3/51, p. 11; 21/7/51, p. 3
4. Cameron, *Confessions*, p. 92; Hearn, pp. 104–5; Crowley, *Modern Australia*, p. 411
5. *Worker*, 2/4/52, p. 1; 30/4/52, p. 4; *SMH*, 27/1/52, p. 4; Murray, p. 41; Hearn, pp. 104–5; Crisp, pp. 401–2
6. *SMH*, 10/6/52, p. 2; Murray, p. 41

7. *Worker*, 11/8/54, p. 7; 25/8/54, p. 7; *SMH*, 16/7/54, p. 5; 23/7/54, p. 3; Cameron, *Confessions*, pp. 87–8; *Labor Nails The "Rebels" Lies!*, pamphlet produced by the NSW ALP Executive, 1955, pp. 19–20
8. *SMH*, 15/1/54, p. 1; 16/1/54, p. 1; 18/1/54, p. 4; 23/1/54, p. 4; 15/6/54, p. 1; Murray, p. 134
9. Murray, pp. 133–5; *Labor Nails The "Rebels" Lies!*, pp. 7–8
10. 1954 AWU Convention report, p. 76; Executive Council minutes: 30/6/54, p. 65; 1/7/54, p. 72; *Worker*, 1/12/54, p. 1; *SMH*, 15/6/54, p. 5; *News-Weekly*, 28/7/54, p. 12; Murray, p. 140
11. Peter Crockett, *Evatt: A Life*, Oxford University Press 1993, pp. 279–83; Murray, pp. 169–74, 179–81; interview with Clyde Cameron, 12/5/94
12. *Worker*, 20/10/54, p. 1; B. A. Santamaria, 'The Movement of Ideas in Australia', 1953. Copy in ML; Murray, pp. 177–8, 190–3; M. Hearn, 'A Movement of Ideas? Lloyd Ross and his contemporaries in the 1950s', paper delivered to 'the Old Left and Australian Historiography' Conference, Macquarie University, 3 December 1993, pp. 2–12
13. *Worker*, 3/11/54, p. 1; 17/11/54, p. 1; 15/12/54, p. 1; *SMH*, 10/11/54, p. 1; 17/11/54, p. 3; 15/12/54, pp. 1, 3; Cameron, *Confessions*, p. 136
14. 1955 AWU Annual Convention minutes, pp. 83–95, 127, 145, 163–4, 180; Cameron, *Confessions*, pp. 106–7, 136; *News-Weekly*, 2/2/55, p. 1; interview with Edgar Williams, 25/2/92; Murray, pp. 135, 309–10
15. Executive Council minutes: 9/2/55, p. 85; 20/6/55, p. 87; *News-Weekly*, 26/1/55, p. 1; *Tribune*, 2/2/55, p. 10; *SMH*, 28/1/55, p. 1; 29/1/55, pp. 1, 4; 1/2/55, p. 6; 2/2/55, p. 6
16. 1956 AWU Annual Convention minutes, p. 127
17. *Worker*, 15/2/50, p. 1; 12/1/55, pp. 4, 6; 9/2/55, p. 12; *News-Weekly*, 12/1/55, p. 3; 26/1/55, p. 1; Crockett, pp. 150–3
18. *SMH*, 8/2/55, p. 2; 18/3/55, p. 1; Murray, pp. 198–230
19. *Labor Nails The "Rebels" Lies!*, pp. 2, 17–21; *SMH*, 8/8/55, p. 1; Murray, pp. 288–9
20. *SMH*, 14/8/55, p. 1; 15/8/55, p. 1; 16/8/55, p. 2; 17/8/55, p. 1
21. *SMH*, 24/1/57, p. 1; 25/1/57, pp. 2, 3; 1957 AWU Annual Convention minutes, pp. 141–51
22. *SMH*, 7/4/58, p. 10; Murray, pp. 301–5
23. Victorian Branch sec. report, 1955, p. 2
24. *SMH*, 2/2/51, p. 12; 20/3/51, p. 3; Commonwealth of Australia *Official Year Book* No. 46, 1960, pp. 451–3; *Note:* The AWU had approximately 142 000 financial members in the early 1950s, with most branches, in this era of negligible unemployment, recording membership increases. The figures listed below err on the side of caution, as the branches were sometimes inclined to include both unfinancial and financial members in their estimates. In 1951, for example, the AWU claimed to have over 174 000 members. Charlie Oliver once acknowledged in the late 1950s that the NSW Branch membership could vary anywhere between 30 000 and 40 000 members, depending on the effort organisers put into selling tickets, prevailing economic conditions and the state of the labour market, etc. As far as possible, these figures, sourced from branch secretary's reports, are for financial members only, and represent average branch membership for the period 1953–55. Queensland: 58 000; NSW: 37 415; SA: 12 700; WA: 10 000; Tas. 7800; Vic.: 17 000
25. 1950 AWU Convention minutes, p. 91; B. Collis, *Snowy: The Making of Modern Australia*, Hodder & Stoughton 1990, p. 135; S. McHugh, *The Snowy: The*

*People Behind The Power*, William Heinemann Australia 1989, pp. 166–7; *Worker*, 11/1/56, p. 11; 25/1/56, p. 11; 7/3/56, p. 2
26. Dodkin, pp. 104–8
27. 1956 Convention report, p. 71; *News-Weekly*, 20/4/55, p. 3; E. G. Whitlam, *The Whitlam Government 1972–1975*, Viking Press 1985, p. 496
28. 1956 Convention minutes, pp. 61–9, 86–90
29. Brisbane *Worker*, 26/11/56, p. 1
30. 1916 AWU Annual Convention minutes, pp. 14–15; Convention reports: 1941, p. 137; 1942, pp. 64, 137; Executive Council minutes, 5/7/60, p. 4; 1968 Convention report, pp. 9–10; *Worker*, 28/12/55, p. 6; 16/12/64, p. 1; CAR, Nos 90, 91 and 245 of 1944, pp. 2–6; *CAR*, Nos 70 and 702 of 1955, 26/1/56, p. 5; Crowley, p. 515; *SMH*, 27/11/64, p. 7; Andrew Markus, 'Talka Longa Mouth', in Curthoys and Markus, *Who Are Our Enemies?*, p. 144
31. *Worker*, 25/1/50, p. 12
32. *The Power of Water: The Making of the Snowy Scheme*, Snowy Mountains Hydro-Electric Authority 1989, p. 9; Collis, pp. 134, 163; M. Unger, *Voices From The Snowy*, NSW University Press 1989, p. 223; *Worker*, 25/1/50, p. 12; Crowley, p. 336
33. *Worker*, 16/5/56, p. 8; Unger, p. 212; Collis, pp. 140, 144, 163; McHugh, p. 164
34. Jim Marwood, *Ways Of Working*, Kangaroo Press 1986, pp. 9–11, 43–7, 67; Blainey, *Rush That Never Ended*, pp. 279–80; AWU Tasmanian Branch sec. 1956 annual report, p. 4; *Worker*, 28/5/58, p. 1; 11/6/58, pp. 1, 6–7, 12; 25/6/58, p. 6; 9/7/58, p. 5; 20/8/58, p. 1
35. Commonwealth of Australia *Official Year Book* No. 46 1960, pp. 1042–4 (mining employment figures quoted do not include the Northern Territory, where the AWU did not have industry coverage); AMMA 1952 annual report, p. 2
36. 1953 Convention minutes, p. 8; *Worker*, 14/2/52, p. 4
37. Crowley, p. 419; *Worker*, 28/5/58, p. 10; 30/9/59, p. 11; 14/10/59, p. 11; 28/10/59, p. 11; 11/11/59, p. 10
38. Crowley, pp. 258, 279, 297, 420, 470; Blainey, *Rush That Never Ended*, pp. 339–41; 1954 AWU Convention minutes, pp. 11–12
39. AWU SA Branch sec. annual reports: 1953–54, p. 3; 1955–56, p. 3; 1956–57, pp. 7–8
40. The AWU maintained financial support for the Nuclear Research Foundation until July 1960, when funding ceased. The Executive Council minutes do not record the reasons for discontinuing support. Executive Council minutes, 6/2/57, p. 153; 6/7/60, p. 15; AWU SA Branch sec. annual reports, 1955–56, p. 5; 1959–60, p. 5; AWU Annual Convention minutes: 1956, pp. 82, 169; 1957, pp. 45–6

## 11  The Meaning of Mateship

1. Minutes of the AWU Queensland Branch 1941 annual delegates meeting, pp. 102–6; Murphy, *The Big Strike*, p. 39
2. Crowley, *Modern Australia*, p. 240; *Worker*, 4/4/51, p. 1
3. *SMH*, 3/9/55, p. 17; 13/12/55, p. 6; 15/12/55, p. 6; *Worker*, 23/4/52, p. 1; 7/9/55, p. 4; 19/10/55, p. 6; 14/12/55, pp. 6–7; 28/12/55, p. 1; 1954 AWU Convention report, pp. 6–11

4. Minutes of a Special Meeting of the AWU Executive Council, 23/2/56, pp. 113–14; *SMH*, 26/11/55, p. 10; 22/12/55, p. 1; 4/1/56, p. 1; 17/2/56, p. 3; 24/2/56, p. 1; *Worker*, 14/12/55, pp. 6–7; 8/2/56, p. 1

5. *Pastoral Review & Graziers Record*, January 1956, p. 13; February 1956, p. 186; March 1956, p. 273; *SMH*, 4/1/56, p. 1

6. *SMH*, 18/3/56, p. 1; AWU Queensland Western District office correspondence and organisers' reports: A. Kain to Watson (n.d., *c.* 11/4/56); Watson to Boland, 28/3/56; McKitrick to Watson, 25/4/56, 25/5/56; Kain to Watson, 4/5/56; Statement from Reg Readon provided to Western District office; Grazcos brochure, 'Your Living, Your Future' 1956. Correspondence and pamphlet in Noel Butlin Archives, ANU

7. Statement provided by William Rayner to AWU Queensland Western District office; Watson to Bukowski, 26/9/56; Bukowski to Watson, 4/10/56, correspondence in Noel Butlin Archives, ANU; *SMH*, 8/10/56, p. 1

8. Interview with Neil Byron, 22/7/93

9. Interview with Reg Mawbey, 7/7/93

10. Interview with Errol Hodder, 24/9/91

11. AWU Casterton Branch 1956 Shearers' Strike Committee minutes; Vandenberg to Gill, 25/7/56; Davis to J. A. Gill, 9/8/56; telegram from Austral Shearing Contractors to J. Tuffnell, 15/5/56. Minutes and correspondence in Melbourne University Archives

12. *Pastoral Review*, June 1956, p. 734; July 1956, p. 869; *SMH*, 10/3/56, p. 6; 17/3/56, p. 1; D. W. Rawson, *Unions and Unionists in Australia*, Allen & Unwin 1986, p. 101

13. *SMH*, 27/1/56, p. 11; 29/6/56, p. 4; *Worker*, 22/2/56, p. 8; 27/6/56, pp. 1, 6

14. *Worker*, 11/7/56, p. 1; *SMH*, 2/6/56, p. 3; 7/6/56, p. 7; 29/6/56, p. 4

15. *Tribune*, 4/4/56, p. 3; 4/7/56, p. 10; *News-Weekly*, 18/7/56, p. 1; *SMH*, 28/2/56, p. 4; Murray, p. 308

16. *SMH*, 28/2/56, p. 4; *Worker*, 14/3/56, p. 6; 21/3/56, p. 1; *Pastoralists' Review*, June 1956, p. 734

17. *SMH*, 7/4/56, p. 5; 17/4/56, p. 3; 4/7/56, p. 8; 22/5/56, p. 4; C. L. Lack (ed.), *Three Decades of Queensland Political History, 1929–1960*, Qld Govt Printer 1962, pp. 443–4

18. Lack, p. 444; Minutes of a conference in Premier's office, Brisbane, 28/9/56, in relation to the Queensland shearing dispute, p. 13; *SMH*, 8/9/56, p. 1; 24/9/56, p. 3; 25/9/56, p. 3; 29/9/56, p. 1; 3/10/56, p. 3; 4/10/56, p. 1; 5/10/56, p. 1

19. *Worker*, 17/10/56, p. 4; *Pastoralists' Review*, November 1956, p. 1404; *SMH*, 10/10/56, p. 1; 12/10/56, p. 2; 13/10/56, p. 1

20. Brisbane *Worker*, 30/7/56, p. 1; Harold Thornton 'Rochins Joseph John Bukowski', *ADB* 1940–1980, vol. 13, p. 291

21. Brisbane *Worker*, 30/7/56, p. 4; authors' interviews with Edgar Williams, 25/2/92; George Pont, 26/2/92; Gerry Goding 27/2/92

22. *SMH*, 28/2/56, p. 6; 29/2/56, p. 3; 1/3/56, p. 1; 2/3/56, p. 5

23. Interview with George Pont, 26/2/92; interview with Gerry Goding, 27/2/92; Lack, pp. 445–6; Brisbane *Worker*, 29/4/57, p. 4. This Brisbane *Worker* article asserts that Gair promised to introduce three weeks' leave and sought a face-saving compromise, but differs from Pont's account inasmuch as there is no reference to Duggan's anger at Gair's concession of the leave entitlement, presumably because such a reference would have contradicted Duggan's strong post-split support for three weeks' leave.

24. Brisbane *Worker*, 1/10/56, p. 1; 31/12/56, p. 1; Thornton, 'Rochus Joseph Bukowski', *ADB*, vol. 13, p. 291
25. Minutes of a conference in Premier's office, Brisbane, 28/9/56, in relation to the Queensland shearing dispute, p. 6; Murray, p. 315; Lack, p. 448
26. *Brisbane Worker*, 21/1/57, p. 4; 15/4/57, p. 1; Murray, pp. 317–21
27. *Brisbane Worker*, 15/4/57, p. 1; 29/4/57, p. 1; interview with George Pont, 26/2/92
28. *Brisbane Worker*, 29/4/57, p. 1; interviews with Edgar Williams, 25/2/92; George Pont, 26/2/92
29. Lack, p. 448; Murray, pp. 325–7
30. *SMH*, 19/12/58, p. 1; 20/12/58, p. 5; Cameron, *Confessions*, pp. 169–70; Thornton, *ADB*, vol. 13, p. 291
31. Interview with Gerry Goding, 27/2/92; Edgar Williams, 25/2/92; Qld Branch annual delegates meeting minutes, no. 45, 1958, p. 61; no. 46, 1959, pp. 14–15; no. 47, 1960, p. 5
32. Murray, p. 310; *SMH*, 29/8/59, p. 2; Brisbane *Worker*, 22/10/56, p. 4; *Australian Worker*, 22/1/58, p. 1; 4/2/59, p. 1

## 12 Making the Truth Hurt

1. Alan Reid, 'The AWU is Rolling Again', *Observer*, 24/12/60, pp. 6–7; AWU Annual (Qld Branch) 1961, no. 1, p. 13; John Howe, Jr, 'Big Tom's 17th Summer', *Nation*, 7/5/60, pp. 10–12; *Bulletin*, 16/7/66, p. 14; *SMH*, 6/7/66, p. 1; 16/8/67, p. 4
2. Interview with Wendy Pymont, 9/5/94
3. *The Voice of the Rank & File*, August 1961, p. 6
4. Cameron, *Confessions*, pp. 1–7
5. Ibid., pp. 43–7; 1950 AWU Convention report, p. 25; *SMH*, 27/1/50, p. 4
6. Minutes of Labor Papers Ltd Board of Directors meetings, 3/7/52, 2/2/53, 2/7/53
7. Ibid., 2/2/53, 4/3/66; Labor Papers Ltd Directors Report for years ending 31/12/58, 31/12/59
8. Executive Council minutes, 11/2/53, p. 34; 26/6/57, p. 167; Howe, pp. 10–12; *CPD, House of Representatives*, 14/5/58, pp. 1786–7
9. Dougherty to Cameron, 29/7/59, Dougherty to Cameron, 24/11/58, Cameron File folder, Box H20, AWU Federal Office; Cameron and Connell: pp. 167–8, 171–2; Executive Council minutes, 8/2/51, p. 14; 24/6/58, p. 188; 20/1/59, pp. 192–3; 28/7/59, pp. 4–7
10. Howe, p. 12
11. *SMH*, 27/4/60, p. 13; Howe, p. 10
12. Cameron, *Confessions*, p. 175; *Adelaide Advertiser*, 7/8/59, p. 6
13. *Barrier Truth*, 17 August 1959, pp. 1–2; CMC Circular to AWU Members (n.d.) in Cameron File folder, Box H20 AWU Federal Office; CMC Pamphlet, 'Great Victory For Rank And File' in Cameron File folder
14. Cameron, *Confessions*, pp. 177–9; *Voice*, April 1961, p. 2; December 1961, p. 1; September 1962, pp. 4–5; June 1963, p. 1; 1965 AWU Convention report, p. 35
15. *Voice*, March 1962, pp. 1–4; March 1963, p. 1; June 1963, p. 1; Cameron, *Confessions*, pp. 177–8
16. 1961 AWU Annual Convention report, p. 42; Executive Council minutes, 22/6/61, p. 15; Freudenberg, p. 237
17 AWU Annual Convention reports: 1961, pp. 49–56, 171–4; 1962, pp. 132–42; Executive Council minutes: 13/2/61, p. 20; 8/2/62, p. 5; *Worker*, 8/4/64, p. 1

18. *The Transcontinental* (Port Augusta), 26/3/64, p. 1; 9/4/64, p. 4; Cameron, *Confessions*, p. 177; 1965 AWU Annual Convention report, p. 101; Pamphlet 'The Facts About the AWU Dispute' in folder 'T. Dougherty – Personal', Box G21 'South Australian Branch Dispute 1965', AWU Federal Office; Executive Council minutes, 24/3/64, p. 2
19. Executive Council minutes: 29/1/65, p. 8; 6/5/65, p. 9; 3/12/65, pp. 1–3; 1965 AWU Annual Convention report, pp. 90–4; *Tribune*, 21/4/65; 'The Facts About the AWU Dispute'; *Advertiser*, 29/4/65, p. 11; copy of letter notifying Executive Council decision to suspended SA Branch officials from Dougherty dated 10/5/65 in 'Alfred Silverston Brice and AWU re: South Australian Branch' folder, Box G22, AWU Federal Office; *Bulletin*, 15/5/65, pp. 19–20; AWU SA Branch sec. annual report, 1966, p. 1; Clyde Cameron, *The Cameron Diaries*, Allen & Unwin 1990, pp. 458–9, 810–11
20. AWU Annual (Qld Branch), No. 1 1961, p. 44
21. Margaret Bridson Cribb, 'Mt Isa Strikes, 1961, 1964', in Murphy, *The Big Strikes*, p. 276; AWU Annual (Qld Branch) 1961, p. 41
22. Williams, pp. 175–6, 202–4, 214; *Nation*, 20/2/65, p. 6; Blainey, *Rush That Never Ended*, p. 308; Cribb, pp. 276–8
23. Williams, pp. 249–54; Cribb, pp. 285–6
24. Mackie with Vassilieff, p. 1; Cribb, p. 283
25. Mackie, pp. 1–14
26. Mackie, pp. 21–2
27. Mackie, pp. 43, 71; Williams, p. 273
28. Mackie, pp. 71, 88–92; Cribb, p. 290
29. *Worker* (Brisbane), February 1965; Mackie, p. 70
30. Mackie, p. 93; Cameron, *Confessions*, p. 178
31. Cribb, pp. 292–3; Mackie, p. 199
32. *SMH*, 21/4/65, p. 4; 6/8/65, pp. 4, 9; Williams, pp. 373–5; Mackie, pp. 277–40
33. Executive Council minutes, 28/7/65, p. 13; Dodkin, pp. 139–40; *Tribune*, 20/1/65, p. 3; *SMH*, 25/1/65, p. 11; 5/2/65, p. 1; 28/5/65, p. 4; 21/10/66, p. 11; Williams, p. 327
34. Williams, p. 359; E. I. Sykes, 'The Mount Isa Affair', *Journal of Industrial Relations*, vol. 7, no. 3, 1965, pp. 278–9; G. H. Sorrell, 'The Dispute At Mount Isa', *Australian Quarterly*, vol. 37, no. 2, June 1965, pp. 32–3; Mackie, p. 6; Buckman interview, 25/2/92; Cameron, *Confessions*, p. 178; Cribb, p. 294
35. Williams, pp. 280, 282, 285
36. Dodkin, pp. 139, 158
37. Reg Mawbey interview, 7/7/93
38. Mawbey interview; *Tribune*, 26/9–2/10/72, p. 8; Dodkin, p. 159
39. *Tribune*, 26/9–2/10/72, p. 8
40. *Worker*, 20/9/67, p. 7; 18/10/67, p. 11; Dodkin, pp. 165–6
41. 1969 AWU Annual Convention report, pp. 80–6, 123–31, 136; *Worker*, 13/11/68, p. 10; *SMH*, 29/7/68, p. 4; 31/7/68, p. 16; 17/9/68; Dodkin, pp. 169, 174–5; *CPD*, 27/11/68
42. *SMH*, 1/10/69, pp. 1, 6; 2/10/69, p. 8
43. Mawbey interview; Dodkin, pp. 182–5; *SMH*, 16/12/69, p. 5
44. R. Maddock and F. Stillwell, 'Boom and Recession', *Australians from 1939*, Fairfax, Syme & Weldon 1987, p. 260; G. Withers, A. Endres and L. Perry, 'Labour' and J. C. Caldwell, 'Population', *Australians, Historical Statistics*, Fairfax, Syme & Weldon 1987, pp. 41 and 149

45. AWU Convention reports: 1961, p. 6; 1969, p. 6; *Worker*, 29/7/64, p. 8; *The Macquarie Book of Events*, Macquarie Library Pty Ltd 1983, pp. 194–7
46. AWU Convention reports: 1961, pp. 6–9; 1963, pp. 6–7
47. AWU Convention reports: 1963, p. 6; 1966, pp. 13–17; 1969, pp. 8–11; 1970, pp. 8–14, 20–2; *Worker*, 25/1/67, p. 9
48. Hagan, pp. 200, 255–7
49. 1959 AWU Convention report, pp. 103–17
50. AWU Convention reports: 1962, pp. 42–4; 1963, pp. 32–9; 1964, pp. 29–31
51. 1966 AWU Convention report, pp. 58–74
52. Executive Council minutes, 5/7/66, p. 3; 1967 AWU Convention minutes, pp. 62–79; *SMH*, 6/7/66, p. 1
53. Hagan, p. 256; *Australian International News Review*, 3/8/66, p. 10; *Tribune*, 20/7/66, p. 10
54. AWU Convention reports: 1967, pp. 62–79; 1970, pp. 104–9; Hagan, p. 270
55. AWU Convention reports: 1961, pp. 22–3, 180–4; 1964, pp. 74–83; Crowley, *Modern Australia*, p. 507; Whitlam, pp. 494–5
56. *Worker*, 2/10/68, p. 1

### 13 Too Good for the Lot of You

1. *SMH*, 14/2/73, p. 8
2. *Profiles of Power*, interview between Robert Moore and Tom Dougherty, screened on ABC-TV 6/9/70. Transcript, pp. 1–2
3. Moore interview transcript, pp. 3, 5
4. Moore interview transcript, pp. 4–5
5. 1975 AWU Annual Convention report, pp. 46–53; AWU Federal Executive Council minutes, 6/2/74, p. 24; 18–19/6/74, pp. 4–7; *Worker*, 28/8/74, p. 2; 30/9/74, p. 2
6. Whitlam, p. 494
7. Ibid., p. 499; *CPD, House of Representatives*, 13/3/73, p. 516; 1972 AWU Annual Convention report, pp. 66–8; Moore interview transcript, pp. 8–9
8. *SMH*, 21/1/71, p. 2; 28/1/71, p. 11
9. 1972 Annual Convention report; *SMH*, 28/1/72, p. 1; Moore interview transcript, p. 6
10. *Sun Herald*, 15/10/72, p. 66; Cameron, *Confessions*, pp. 179–80; Moore interview transcript, p. 14; Interview with Wendy Pymont, 9/5/94
11. *Worker*, 24/7/68, p. 8
12. 1970 AWU Convention report, pp. 40–4, 128; *SMH*, 19/1/70, p. 5; 20/1/70, p. 5
13. *SMH*, 13/5/70, p. 21; Dodkin, p. 186
14. *SMH*, 20/5/70, p. 1; 25/5/70, p. 5; 27/5/70, p. 5; 29/5/70, p. 7; 5/6/70, p. 4; 10/6/70, p. 14; 17/6/70, p. 12; Executive Council minutes, 19/5/70, pp. 2–8; 27–31/7/70
15. *SMH*, 24/10/70, p. 1; 12/12/70, p. 11; Pamphlet, *A Personal Message From Lew McKay*, n.d., Box E21 AWU Federal Office; Hagan and Turner, pp. 211–12
16. *SMH*, 4/2/71, p. 8; 8/2/71, p. 2; 23/3/71, p. 8; 29/5/72, p. 8; 16/12/71, p. 12; *Tribune*, 27/1/71, p. 10; Pamphlet, *Power Against Principle: McKay v. Leen Sellout*, Box E21 AWU Federal Office; Minutes of the AWU Executive Council, 8, 9, 10 and 11 February 1971, Box B10 AWU Federal Office.
17. *SMH*, 11/2/71, p. 2

18. Mawbey interview, 7/7/93; *SMH*, 16/12/71, p. 8; 3/1/73, p. 2; 4/1/73, p. 2; *Tribune*, 26/9–2/10/72, p. 8; NSW Branch Executive Council minutes, 7 and 8/2/73; Cameron, *Cameron Diaries*, pp. 171, 524

19. *SMH*, 16/1/74, p. 2; 27/4/74, p. 2; *Tribune*, 29/1–4/2/74, p. 8

20. *Worker*, 8/5/74, pp. 1–2; *Tribune*, 29/1–4/2/74, p. 8; AWU Federal Executive Council minutes, 21/6/74 and 31/7/74, Box B10 held in AWU Federal Office, Sydney

21. *Tribune*, 29/1–4/2/74, p. 8; *Worker*, 19/6/74, p. 1; *SMH*, 7/11/75, p. 9

22. 1977 AWU Annual Convention report, pp. 31–49; AWU Federal Executive Council minutes, 1–4/8/77, held in AWU Federal Office, Sydney; Notes on the Federal Executive Council meeting, 2/8/77 in 'Papers re Court Cases Involving Oliver – Papers re dispute' Box 202, NSW Branch Office, Sydney; *SMH*, 24/8/77, p. 2; Telegrams: Wright, Dunford Groth to Oliver, 3/8/77, and Rex Connor to Oliver, 10/8/77 in 'Papers re court cases ...'

23. Executive Council minutes, 26/10/77; Report of Federal Executive Council meeting, 26/10/77 in Papers re Court Cases involving Oliver; *SMH*, 29/10/77, p. 21; 1/11/77, p. 3; Mawbey interview, 7/7/93; Russell Findlay interview with Frank Mitchell, n.d.

24. *SMH*, 2/8/77, p. 3; 3/2/77, p. 18, 17/8/77, p. 12; 31/8/77, p. 12; Mawbey interview, *Worker*, 30/9/77, p. 4

25. *SMH*, 1/9/77, p. 3; 2/11/77, p. 2; 6/12/77, p. 3; 23/2/78, p. 2; *Australian*, 5/9/77, p. 2; 'Notes and industrial procedures from the NSW Retail Traders Association to affiliated members re AWU/BWIU merger', folder in Box 127, 'SDA dispute', NSW AWU office, Sydney; Mawbey interview; Findlay interview with Frank Mitchell

26. Interview with Mike Forshaw, 20/7/94; Cameron, *Cameron Diaries*, pp. 681–2; *SMH*, 13/11/84, p. 5

27. 1972 AWU Convention report, pp. 9–12

28. Frank Crowley, *Tough Times, Australia in the Seventies*, William Heinemann Australia 1986, pp. 15–23; 1972 AWU Annual Convention report, pp. 156–7, 169–87

29. *Worker*, 14/3/73, pp. 1–2; 29/8/73, pp. 1, 12; 8/5/74, pp. 1, 7; 31/7/74, p. 1; 31/7/79, pp. 10–11, 18–19; 1975 AWU Annual Convention report, pp. 28–32; 1978 AWU Annual Convention report, pp. 55–6

30. AWU Annual Convention reports: 1971, pp. 77–9; 1974, pp. 16–17; gen. sec. report; 1975 AWU Annual Convention report (unnumbered); gen. sec. report; 1978 AWU Annual Convention report (unnumbered)

31. Table LAB 56–58 in 'Labour', *Australians, Historical Statistics*, Fairfax, Syme & Weldon 1988; 1974 AWU Annual Convention report (Victoria-Riverina Branch Report), p. 36; gen. sec. report to the 1976 AWU Annual Convention (unnumbered); gen. sec. report to the 1978 AWU Annual Convention (unnumbered); *Worker*, 30/9/80, p. 1; *SMH*, 8/12/80, p. 9; Brian Boyd, *Inside the BLF*, Ocean Books 1991, pp. 11–14

32. Gen. sec. reports to 1981 AWU Convention, p. iii; 1985 AWU Convention, p. vi; 1987 Convention, pp. xi–xv; *Worker*, 30/6/80, p. 2; 31/7/80, p. 1; 29/8/80, p. 1; 31/7/81, p. 3; 31/3/82, p. 1; 31/1/85, p. 15; 30/4/86, pp. 1, 3; 29/1/88, p. 18; *SMH*, 6/4/84, p. 1; 7/4/84, p. 1; 16/10/84, p. 1; *AFR*, 15/10/84, p. 13, Boyd, pp. 187, 289, 295, 300, 309

33. Mitchell interview; Annual Average Employment by Industry, Table LAB 50–58, *Australian Historical Statistics*, p. 149; gen. sec. report to the 1975 AWU Annual Convention; gen. sec. report to the 1977 AWU Annual Convention

34. Gen. sec. report to the 1979 AWU Annual Convention; Table LAB 76–85, Registered Unemployed Seeking Full-time Work, *Australian Historical Statistics,* p. 151; 1978 AWU Annual Convention report, pp. 28–31; Mitchell interview

## 14 Out of the Past

1. R. McDonald, *Reflecting Labor,* NLA 1991, p. 2
2. Paul Kelly, *The End Of Certainty,* Allen & Unwin 1992, pp. 112–13, 260
3. *Worker,* 30/1/81, p. 4; 31/8/82, p. 5
4. Eleanor Leleu to Frank Mitchell, 5/12/74, gen. secretary's correspondence, Noel Butlin Archives, ANU
5. 1986 AWU Annual Convention minutes, pp. 6, 25, 63; AWU NSW Branch annual reports: 1982, p. 3; 1985, p. 3; *SMH,* 18/8/89, p. 3; 14/6/94, p. 3; *AFR,* 28/11/86, p. 1
6. Gen. sec. reports to the AWU Convention: 1983, p. ii; 1984, p. iii; 1985, p. vii; *SMH,* 12/8/82, p. 1; *AFR,* 23/7/82, p. 16; 22/9/82, p. 30; 31/10/86, p. 33; S. Carney, *Australia in Accord,* Sun Books 1988, p. 173; *Year Book Australia* 1988, pp. 533–4
7. Rocky Gehan interview, 11/5/94
8. Keith Plunkett interview, 11/5/94; *SMH,* 19/11/82, p. 3; 14/9/92
9. *Worker,* 31/5/82, p. 6; *SMH,* 25/3/83, p. 6
10. Keith Plunkett interview, 11/5/94
11. *SMH,* 25/3/83; *Worker,* 21/12/82, p. 1; J. E. Gibson, 'Some economic aspects of the use of wide combs in the Australian Wool Industry', *Farm Management Report No. 16,* Department of Agricultural Economics and Business Management, University of New England, 1982, pp. ii–iii
12. Minutes of meeting of pastoral workers held at Dubbo, 24/3/83, in AWU Head Office records on wide-comb dispute; *Worker,* 31/3/83, p. 1; *SMH,* 25/3/83, p. 9
13. *SMH,* 25/3/83, p. 9; 7/4/83, p. 1; 8/4/83, p. 3; 15/4/83, p. 2; 22/4/83, p. 2
14. *SMH,* 10/5/83, p. 3; 12/5/83, p. 2; 17/5/83, p. 9; press statement issued by Federal Industrial Relations Minister Willis, 16/5/83 and 20/6/83, AWU papers; *AFR,* 19/5/83, p. 3
15. *Worker,* 30/6/83, p. 13; *AFR,* 6/6/84, p. 2; *SMH,* 7/6/83, p. 5; 27/11/84, p. 7
16. Gen. sec. report to 1985 AWU Convention, p. viii; *Worker,* 30/11/84, p. 1; *SMH,* 27/11/84, p. 7
17. Gen. sec. report to 1986 AWU Convention, p. vi; gen. sec. report to 1987 AWU Convention, p. iv–v; *Worker,* 31/7/86, p. 1; 2/8/88, p. 1; 5/2/90, pp. 43–4; 17/2/92, p. 20; June 1992, p. 5; *Pastoral Worker,* no. 1, November 1992, p. 1; *Farmers' Voice,* no. 6, 1990, p. 2; December 1992, p. 3; *Year Book Australia* 1988, p. 536
18. *AFR,* 14/7/93, p. 8; *Australian,* 31/8/93, p. 8; *Worker,* Spring 1994, p. 9; *SMH,* 30/4/94, p. 13
19. *AFR,* 15/12/94, p. 14; 17/11/94
20. *Farmers' Voice,* November–December 1988, p. 2; September 1991, p. 1; December 1992, pp. 3–4; November 1993, p. 2; *AFR,* 3/6/82, p. 12; *SMH,* 2/6/94, p. 1; 16/6/94
21. *Worker,* 31/3/89, p. 13
22. *Worker,* 21/12/82, p. 9; AWU SA Branch 1984 Year Book, pp. 23, 57
23. *Worker,* 31/3/89, p. 13
24. Ibid., *Year Book Australia* 1983, pp. 433–4; Forshaw interview, 20/7/94

25. *SMH*, 23/2/82, p. 7; *Worker*, 30/9/81, p. 8; Minutes of the AWU 1983 Convention, p. 19; Kelly, p. 528
26. 1977 AWU Convention minutes, pp. 54–63; Hagan, p. 387; *SMH*, 18/6/82, p. 1; 19/6/82, p. 2; *AFR*, 28/9/94, p. 5; 30/9/94, p. 5; McMullin, pp. 405–6, 425
27. *Worker*, 30/11/83, p. 1; 29/1/88, p. 29; 31/3/88, p. 13; 1/6/88, p. 22; 31/3/89, p. 4; 12/5/89, p. 20; 6/8/90, p. 7; 10/10/91, p. 16
28. *SMH*, 14/8/84, p. 4; 'The Effects of Asbestos Mining on the Baryugil Community', Report of the House of Representatives Standing Committee on Aboriginal Affairs, October 1984, pp. 2–14, 43; 'Report by the Race Discrimination Commissioner Irene Moss on a Visit to Baryugil and Malabugilmah, NSW', Human Rights and Equal Opportunity Commission, July 1990, pp. 4–12, 28
29. Speech by Charles Copeman, September 1986, reprinted in Carney, p. 96
30. Carney, p. 95; *Worker*, 29/8/86, pp. 1–4; 30/9/86, p. 6
31. *Worker*, 29/8/86, p. 2; 30/9/86, p. 6
32. *Worker*, 29/8/86, p. 4; Carney, p. 96; Kelly, p. 267; *Farmers' Voice*, December 1992, p. 2
33. *SMH*, 9/12/94, p. 1; 23/12/94, p. 1; *BRW*, 3/12/93, p. 30; 31/1/94, p. 34; *AFR*, 17/2/94; 9/12/94, p. 1; *Worker*, Winter 1994, p. 5
34. 1984 AWU Convention minutes, p. 69; *Worker*, 5/10/90, pp. 1, 48; 13/12/91, p. 1; 24/8/92, p. 1; *AWU Mining Industry Newsletter*, May–June 1992, p. 1
35. *SMH*, 4/11/80, p. 13
36. *Worker*, 31/7/81, p. 1; 31/1/85, p. 1; 31/12/85, pp. 1–2; *SMH*, 2/8/84, p. 11; 22/6/85, p. 8; 13/11/85, p. 20; *Australian*, 24/1/85, p. 1; *Daily Telegraph*, 22/4/85, 23/4/85; *Tribune*, 27/2/85, p. 4; 18/12/85, p. 5
37. *SMH*, 26/2/90; NSW AWU 1990 Branch report, p. 3; *Worker*, July 1993, p. 14
38. 1981 AWU Convention minutes, p. 7; *Worker*, 30/9/88, p. 1; *AFR*, 14/6/88, p. 6
39. 1986 AWU Convention minutes, pp. 61–2
40. *Worker*, 31/3/88, p. 20; 2/12/88, p. 1; *AFR*, 10/7/89, p. 16
41. *Worker*, 5/2/90, p. 19; 2/4/90, pp. 15–20, 28–35; *Australian*, 26–27/10/91, p. 31
42. Interview with Mike Forshaw, 20/7/94; *SMH*, 3/12/91; *AFR*, 21/11/89, p. 6; 20/12/89, p. 7; 23/1/90, p. 5
43. *Worker*, July 1993, p. 2; *AFR*, 14/9/93; 4/7/94, p. 4; M. Costa and M. Duffy, *Labor, Prosperity and the Nineties*, Federation Press 1991, pp. 105, 110–11; D. Rawson, 'Has Unionism A Future?' in M. Crosby and M. Easson (eds), *What Should Unions Do?*, Pluto Press 1992, p. 2

**Conclusion**

Interviews with Rocky Gehan, 11/5/94; Mike Forshaw, 20/7/94; Ward, p. 13; Drucker, p. 32

# INDEX

For EU product safety concerns, contact us at Calle de José Abascal, 56–1°,
28003 Madrid, Spain or eugpsr@cambridge.org.

www.ingramcontent.com/pod-product-compliance
Ingram Content Group UK Ltd.
Pitfield, Milton Keynes, MK11 3LW, UK
UKHW042211180425
457623UK00011B/149